Human Rights
and Adolescence

PENNSYLVANIA STUDIES IN HUMAN RIGHTS

Bert B. Lockwood, Jr., Series Editor

A complete list of books in the series
is available from the publisher.

Human Rights
and Adolescence

Edited by
Jacqueline Bhabha

UNIVERSITY OF PENNSYLVANIA PRESS

PHILADELPHIA

Copyright © 2014 University of Pennsylvania Press

All rights reserved. Except for brief quotations used for purposes of review or scholarly citation, none of this book may be reproduced in any form by any means without written permission from the publisher.

Published by
University of Pennsylvania Press
Philadelphia, Pennsylvania 19104-4112
www.upenn.edu/pennpress

Printed in the United States of America on acid-free paper
10 9 8 7 6 5 4 3 2 1

Library of Congress Cataloging-in-Publication Data

Human rights and adolescence / edited by Jacqueline Bhabha. — 1st ed.
  p. cm. — (Pennsylvania studies in human rights)
  Includes bibliographical references and index.
  ISBN 978-0-8122-4631-5 (hardcover : alk. paper)
  1. Teenagers—Civil rights. 2. Teenagers—Legal status, laws, etc.
3. Teenagers—Social conditions. I. Bhabha, Jacqueline. II. Series:
Pennsylvania studies in human rights.
  HQ796.C657 2014
  305.2350973—dc23

2014007119

In memory of Shanu, whose adolescence was snatched from her, and for the millions like her who survive and thrive despite all the odds

CONTENTS

Introduction. The Importance of a Rights-Based Approach
to Adolescence
    Jacqueline Bhabha   1

PART I. UNDERSTANDING ADOLESCENCE:
DISCIPLINARY PERSPECTIVES

1. Protecting and Promoting Adolescent Rights: The Contribution
of International Law and Policy
    Jean Zermatten   23

2. Transitions to Adulthood in Contemporary Italy: Balancing
Sociocultural Differences and Universal Rights
    Elena Rozzi   39

3. The Science of Adolescent Brain Development and Its
Implications for Adolescent Rights and Responsibilities
    Laurence Steinberg   59

4. Building Capability and Functioning: Reframing the Rights
Agenda for Adolescents Through the Lens of Disability Rights
    Victor Pineda   77

5. Adolescent Social and Emotional Development: A Developmental
Science Perspective on Adolescent Human Rights
    Clea McNeely and Krishna Bose   102

PART II. GROWING UP WITH VIOLENCE: ADOLESCENT TRAUMA, STIGMA, AND RESILIENCE

6. Poverty, Armed Conflict, and Organized Crime: The Impact of Violence on Young People in Colombia
   Christian Salazar Volkmann   127

7. Coming of Age in the Context of War: Reframing the Approach to Adolescent Rights
   Theresa S. Betancourt, Katrina Hann, and Moses Zombo   134

8. Wings of the Phoenix: The Legacy of Violence for Adolescents in Postconflict Reconstruction
   Elizabeth Gibbons   149

9. Adolescents in the Colombian Armed Conflict: Recruitment Realities and Important Lessons for Their Successful Reintegration
   Katie Naeve   170

PART III. SOCIAL INTERVENTIONS: STRATEGIC APPROACHES TO ADOLESCENT RIGHTS

10. Young Arabs and Evolving Realities: Linking Social and Economic Rights
    Jocelyn DeJong and Mary Kawar   187

11. The Challenges Facing India in Advancing Secondary Education Attainment Among Adolescent Girls
    Orla Kelly and Elizabeth A. Newnham   217

12. Rights and Realities for Vulnerable Youth in Urban Brazil: Challenges in the Transition to Adulthood
    Irene Rizzini and Malcolm Bush   236

13. Youth Unemployment: Facing and Overcoming Obstacles in Partnership
    Glaudine Mtshali   251

14. Confined by Narrow Choices: The Stories of Roma Adolescents
    Margareta Matache and David Mark — 270

15. Beginning in the Middle: Ending the Exploitation of Adolescents in India
    Shantha Sinha — 293

16. Indian Adolescence and Its Discontents: Transformational Solutions Through Education, Skill Development, and Employment
    Neera Burra — 309

17. Emerging from the Shadows: Adolescents with Disabilities Claim Their Rights Under International Law
    Kerry Thompson — 326

List of Contributors — 335

Index — 349

Acknowledgments — 369

INTRODUCTION

The Importance of a Rights-Based Approach to Adolescence

Jacqueline Bhabha

This book presses the claim for special attention to adolescence and to the urgency of developing an adolescent rights agenda. *Human Rights and Adolescence* argues that the time has come to utilize knowledge strides made over the past half century and apply principles honed in other fields to advance policy and practice for adolescents. It claims that the cost of inaction on these issues is likely to be dramatic in terms of human suffering, lost social and economic opportunities, and threats to global peace and security. Further, the book argues that a rights-based approach to adolescence is necessary to achieve what has so far eluded policy makers and practitioners—real progress on protecting and enabling the realization of adolescent potential across the globe. Across the range of disciplines that make up contemporary human rights, from law and social advocacy, to global health, to history, economics, sociology, politics, and psychology, it is time for adolescent rights to occupy a coherent place of their own.

Definitions have constituted an important element in human rights work. Building an interventionist agenda with global reach requires deft footwork to overcome the divisive potential of political, cultural, religious, and social difference. To establish a common framework for action, a common language has to be agreed upon. At present, no such consensus about adolescence exists. But as several chapters in this book note, the framework for such a common language exists and much is to be gained from its formal adoption. The international community defines adolescence as the period between ten and nineteen, the second decade of life.[1] A concerted decision to adopt this definition would facilitate comparable data collection, measurable policy implementation, and international (including South-South) collaboration to share innovative practices and approaches. We hope that the publication of this volume contributes to that process.

So far, however, contemporary notions of adolescence show no uniformity. That this should be the case, in the absence of a conscious movement toward and demands for international coherence, is not surprising given the huge variability that exists, not only in lifestyle and cultural contexts but even in the physical onset of puberty (Zermatten; please note that references such as this one [that is, with author names and without dates] are to chapters within this book). As a result there is an enormous range in approaches to adolescence. In Iran, the age of maturity for girls is nine (UNICEF 2011a, 8); by contrast, in Tunisia the average age of marriage for men is thirty-two (DeJong and Kawar). The scope of adolescence itself is contested: in India, "there is no real concept of adolescence at all—there is not even an equivalent term in Indian languages" (Burra).

But variability in lifestyles and cultural norms is compatible with an agreed definition of adolescence, just as such global variation in the approach to childhood has not impeded the universal adoption of a consensus definition of the child as a human being under the age of eighteen (Zermatten, Rozzi). For one thing, it is clear that "drawing legal or social distinctions between adolescents and adults is a universal phenomenon, found in every culture ever studied by social scientists" (Steinberg). Moreover, throughout the world, the biological fact of puberty maps onto the social fact of transition from childhood to adulthood, tracing a continuous evolution from dependence to autonomy, from vulnerability to maturity (McNeely and Bose). To be sure, this evolution is multifaceted, even within states. In contemporary Italy, for example, middle-class Italian children expect to live at home supported by their families well into their late twenties and beyond while in the same country immigrants in their early teens brave the dangers of international migration alone and take on breadwinner roles to support their families (Rozzi). But the reality of the transition from childhood to adulthood is inescapable. So is the legacy that the specifics of this process of evolution, whether positive or negative, leave on the maturing individual (McNeely and Bose, Sinha, Naeve). Attending to the process, and to the needs, desires, and challenges it generates, is an important yet neglected social responsibility.

Human Rights and Adolescence argues that adolescent rights issues constitute a cohesive field that impinges on many key social and political challenges of our time. A rights-based approach to adolescence has so far been largely absent—there is not even a coherent global data bank of statistical information to draw on—and as a result many opportunities to address their needs have been missed, as this book demonstrates. But the circumstances of adolescents today must be a vital concern because they are central to many critical contemporary social and political projects.

A rights-based approach to adolescence has much to offer. It does not replace or displace other approaches to enhancing social justice for adolescents, including the mass youth mobilization movements currently ongoing in the wake of the Arab Spring, or the enduring contribution of development economics to social progress for some of the world's most deprived young populations. Rather it complements such approaches, by strengthening their focus and supplying powerful methodologies for implementation and accountability. Most critically, central human rights principles of non-discrimination and equity uniquely provide a rationale and a strategy for attending to the most marginalized and deprived adolescent populations (Mark and Matache, Thompson). A rights-based approach to adolescence can justify placing the focus of government attention on specific challenges that arise within the broad scope of enabling secondary school access—the challenges facing low-caste rural girls (Kelly and Newnham), or stigmatized European Roma populations (Mark and Matache) or adolescents with disabilities (Pineda, Thompson) or street children (Rizzini and Bush). Unlike broadly based social movements or narrowly technical economic plans, a rights-based approach offers a mechanism for anchoring key policies in binding obligations that are set out in international conventions ratified by the state—conventions such as the UN Convention on the Rights of the Child, the International Covenant on Civil and Political Rights, and the Convention on the Rights of Persons with Disabilities (CRPD). These instruments are consensus documents that contain already agreed upon principles. The principles provide important road maps that facilitate the translation along the arduous path from principle to budget line item to institutional realization (Kelly and Newnham, Rizzini and Bush). What is more, rights-based approaches bring with them well-honed toolkits—interpretative guides and easy to apply precedents that facilitate policy development, and enable capacity building on the ground. Many chapters in this book make reference to such tools and demonstrate their efficacy as instruments of change (Rizzini and Bush, Burra, Naeve). Policy makers thus have an arsenal of applied techniques to draw on rather than the daunting challenge of inventing de novo strategies for getting from problem to solution.

The chapters in this book cover salient examples of challenging adolescent situations, some of them amenable to tried and tested rights-based solutions. They discuss the stubborn persistence of high rates of child marriage despite legislative prohibition (Kelly and Newnham, Sinha), and the devastating extent of teen maternal mortality despite global advances in public health (DeJong and Kawar). Also covered are pressing contemporary concerns about pervasive youth participation in and subjection to violence (Volkmann), disproportionate rates of female illiteracy and educational exclusion (Burra), and adolescent anger and despair over lack of jobs (Mtshali).

Like many successful human rights projects of the past, the issue of adolescent rights requires an organized advocacy constituency to bring entrenched conceptual and protection lacunae to the forefront of global attention. Recent history is instructive: the international community decided, shortly after World War II, that refugee protection was a priority given the millions of stateless and displaced persons in Europe; the project included defining the term refugee (1951 Convention on the Status of Refugees, art. 1 A). In the following years, advocates of children (1989 UN CRC, art. 1), migrants, the disabled, trafficked people, smuggled people, and indigenous people's rights[2] have pressed their claims for special attention and protection; their campaigns too have included work crafting consensus definitions of their respective constituencies and detailing nonnegotiable rights claims as a basis for international engagement with the issues.

What then are this project's chances of success in enhancing public attention to adolescent rights? The chapters in this book are motivated by a common perspective—a rights-based approach to adolescence. Cumulatively they suggest that the justification for a more vigorous, international focus on adolescents—their rights, the challenges they face, and the opportunities they deserve—arises from the importance and increasing difficulty of a successful transition from childhood to adulthood. There are several reasons why this transition is increasingly challenging. First, we are in the process of developing ever more specialized and technologically sophisticated social structures that require vigorous, confident, and educated individuals capable of autonomous decision making and effective productive engagement. An increasingly globalized world, and one in which children and adolescents constitute a growing proportion of the population, has the potential to reap a sizable demographic dividend: the benefit of an increasingly healthy, educated, and young workforce. But to harness this dividend requires a focus on adolescents and their rights. Adolescents who are impoverished, uneducated, traumatized by violence or stigma, or unused to the discipline of employment or the social intercourse of work will have difficulties making valuable contributions and securing rewards that generate a basis for the enjoyment of human rights, a sense of inclusion, and investment in their society. Second, our societies, armed with ever more lethal self-destructive tools, require well-adjusted members able to control their violent or predatory instincts in favor of group harmony and social cohesion. Adolescents, not yet fully equipped to control intense and potentially aggressive emotions and desires (Steinberg; McNeely and Bose), if schooled in the bitterness of exclusion and deprivation, in gang warfare, gender-based violence, or ethnic hatred, will find peacetime integration challenging (Naeve; Gibbons; Betancourt, Hann, and Zombo). They are likely to be serious liabilities to their neighbors and beyond. Third, a growing proportion of the world lives in nations and regions exposed to increasingly heterogeneous populations, along vectors of ability/disability, race/ethnicity/religion, and socioeconomic status. In a globally networked universe, young people at different points on those spectra have an ever growing capacity to see how others live, to emulate, fear, or resent, to coexist or attack the "other." The smooth transition from home to the wider domestic community, until recently a relatively homogenous grouping of conationals and coreligionists, is no longer automatic. As they mature into adulthood, adolescents need the capacity to negotiate difference, to build public spheres conducive to mutual respect, empowerment, and dialogue. Teenagers accustomed to participating actively in their communities, to exercising collaborative authority in the institutions they inhabit, and to navigating social differences as respected players rather than infantilized pawns or invisible bystanders, along the lines described in the chapters by Mark and Matache, Mtshali, Burra, and Thompson, will be invaluable assets. Adolescents forced into the margins, on the other hand, are likely to face unfulfilling, harsh lives and may, at worst, become dangerous liabilities. Finally, and perhaps most critically of all, rapid globalization and exposure to the social and cultural change that it produces, unsettles established gender norms, exacerbating the already pervasive scope for physical and mental abuse of children, for extreme gender-based brutality, and for heightened human rights violations inflicted on many adolescents, but particularly on girls and young women, on sexual minorities, on adolescents with disabilities. Several chapters in *Human Rights and Adolescence*, including those by Thompson, Sinha, McNeely and Bose, Kelly and Newnham, and Burra, highlight the gender-specific complexities associated with adolescence. During the production period of this writing, two horrific incidents shocked a global public—the brutal assault (resulting in skull and jawbone fractures) on a teenage Pakistani girl shot at close range by the Taliban for advocating education for girls (Flynn 2012), and the throat slitting of a fifteen-year-old Afghan girl after her father refused a marriage proposal (Graham-Harrison 2012). They were followed, with a short time lag, by the horrific gang rape of the twenty-three-year-old Indian student on a bus in a public road in New Delhi. Incidents of comparable brutality and depravity across the globe continue to be reported on a daily basis.

Adolescent health and resilience have always been crucial building blocks of human thriving and well-being for society—the vitality of the next generation affects us all. Securing these foundations depends on realizing a broad spectrum of rights encoded in international and domestic laws for decades. Why then do we need to reframe the approach to adolescence, to contribute to stimulating new and sustained attention to the issue? There are several answers. One is that these rights are challenging to realize in the absence of electoral pressure (most adolescents do not have a vote) and a powerful constituency demanding them. So far this has not existed. Another reason is that strengthening adolescents' access to critical rights-enhancing attributes is expensive, politically and economically, particularly at a time when social spending is under increasing public attack, so a strong and explicit case must be made for it. As Volkmann and Rizzini and Bush argue, youth are an unpopular, even feared constituency. Third, adolescent human rights do not flow automatically from the implementation of more general social and economic rights. As several chapters in this book demonstrate, social implementation of generic rights must specifically target the needs and wishes of adolescents to have an impact on them. Kelly and Newnham demonstrate that Indian government investments in primary schooling have not automatically produced success in secondary education enrollment. It is not simply a question of building more secondary schools (or even female toilets) or hiring more secondary school teachers. Burra in India and Mtshali in South Africa show that an increasing *quantity* of higher education alone does not necessarily generate an employable work force. DeJong and Kawar note that attention to primary health care in many Arab countries has not adequately translated into serving the needs of populations going through puberty or early pregnancy. Menstrual hygiene management and maternal health are particular challenges for adolescents, and burying them in a more general focus on women's rights may not be an adequate strategy for successful engagement with the issues. And in the context of Colombia, Guatemala, and Sierra Leone, respectively, Naeve, Gibbons, and Betancourt, Hann, and Zombo illustrate the inadequacies of one-dimensional postconflict demobilization and reintegration programs that ignore the multifaceted needs essential to healing, learning, and thriving for adolescents swept up in devastating violence. What is more, as demographic predictions suggest an inverse pyramid of carers to dependents in the coming decades (You and Anthony 2012)—fewer babies born and more elderly surviving longer—the cost of inaction on adolescent issues becomes more dramatic. A growing cohort of frail dependents will suffer if the carers they have to rely on lack the attributes of empathy, critical thinking, and creative problem solving, attributes that depend on peaceful childhoods, sustained nurturing, and educational opportunity.

As they come of age, adolescents face a series of challenges—physical, psychological, economic, social, and legal—that require societal engagement and attention with some contemporary urgency. This book argues that, across a broad spectrum of concerns, adolescent issues have emerged in this, the second decade of the twenty-first century, as massive in scale and importance. Conceptual obstacles to addressing adolescent needs and demands—what weight should be attached to their opinions, what equilibrium between protection and autonomy is appropriate, what measures should be specially tailored to their aspirations, what sanctions should apply to their lawbreaking—have not adequately featured in mainstream policy discussions. For example, as Rozzi notes, legal complexities relating to the importance of family in an assessment of the "best interests" of adolescents have not been consistently examined by states charged with decision making in this area. Many social challenges arising out of adolescent sexuality and reproductive freedom have not been met, such as the consequences of deferral of marriage age beyond thirty in societies where extramarital sex is proscribed, to cite one example discussed by DeJong and Kawar. And what should we make of the growing evidence, reviewed in different geographical settings, in chapters by Mtshali, Mark and Matache, and Sinha, that growing cohorts of young people are ill-prepared for the employment opportunities offered in their societies, even where the economies in their societies are growing and jobs are plentiful?

Human Rights and Adolescence does not just argue that the time is ripe, strategically, for greater attention to adolescence. It also claims, more substantively, that work is necessary to improve the content of our current framework for adolescent rights and to take note of relevant scientific and social scientific advances. One argument is based on equity. By comparison with other vulnerable young demographic constituencies, vulnerable adolescents as a whole, and some constituencies in particular (including the disabled, rural girls, and ethnic minorities), have been neglected. Progress in protecting the economic and social rights of children in their first decade of life, particularly in the 0–5 age group, fuelled in part by the obligations set out in the widely ratified 1989 UN CRC, and the priorities articulated in the Millennium Development Goals, contrasts sharply with the failure to understand and address the needs of their second-decade peers. Consider the case of Brazil. Over a ten-year period ending in 2008, nearly 81,000 Brazilian adolescents between fifteen and nineteen were murdered—nearly three times the number of under-fives' lives saved over the same period as a result of more effective Brazilian vaccination policies.[3] The chapter by Rizzini and Bush probes this dramatic statistic, setting it within the context of a society torn apart by steep inequalities and acute violence directed at highly vulnerable groups such as street children. Globally, the increased life expectancy of the very young compounds the demographic and social pressure to address the needs of those reaching the next decade of life.

Another argument in the book highlights the costs of inaction, suggesting that benefits foregone by policy failures regarding adolescence are more costly, in both human and financial terms, than timely action to address them would have been and more consequential, too, than policy makers have realized. Increasing political will directed at adolescent rights issues could reverse these serious costs but this requires sustained attention to issues that can be more contentious and unpopular to air in public fora than protection dilemmas concerning preteen children. As McNeely and Bose demonstrate in their chapter with respect to the Arab world (but their point applies more generally), attention to basic supports necessary for healthy adolescent development, such as parental mentoring, more general adult guidance and education on sex and sexual development, and the encouragement of individuality and exploration, is fraught and has, as a result, been severely lacking. And yet without a range of environmental inputs that include both preventative protections from neglect, violence, and exploitation as well as proactive (and expensive) provision of confidential medical care and sustained support for education and uncensored information, adolescents cannot thrive or take their place as productive members of a society. The following case study illustrates this point. According to a comprehensive and carefully structured economic analysis of the situation in Rwanda, failure to expand secondary education in line with the progress on primary education will result not only in a decline in the proportion of primary school graduates who continue their education (a direct consequence) but also in decreased future earning capacity of a growing proportion of the population, with consequential (known) impacts on maternal mortality, under-five survival rates, and total fertility rates (Anand et al. 2012). A similar argument can be made for access to appropriate opportunities for adolescents to develop their problem-solving skills in a safe environment or for provision of expert medical and psychological supports for healthy sexual development. In their absence, as Zermatten points out in his chapter in this volume, the teenage discovery of sexuality, and the attendant curiosity it generates, can rapidly lead to exploitation by predatory adults.

A third argument advanced in this book originates in the public health and biomedical spheres. The chapter by Steinberg provides a compelling account of the dramatic physical changes now known to be associated with adolescent brain development. Steinberg argues that these changes—general tendencies rather than predictable specific facts in individual cases—produce an asynchrony during the teen years between cognitive and emotional capacity (the former increasingly mature, the latter much slower to advance) that has significant but complex implications for policy development. These scientific findings have considerable relevance for policy makers. Most fundamental for human rights lawyers, they challenge the association implicit, in the CRC, between increased physical maturity and increased "voice" or autonomy. What if the need for protection does not progressively decrease as children grow up but spikes unpredictably at different stages, even as intellectual capacity is expanding? Steinberg argues that it is not enough to simply accept the fact that adolescence is a time of dramatic change for adolescents in several key physical and psychological dimensions. A more nuanced, disaggregated understanding of the different vectors of change is required for effective and sensible progress. An interesting application of this approach is suggested by Zermatten: adolescents should be given opportunities to exercise rights before they are burdened by responsibilities that require the exercise of discretion, emotional judgment, and often the weighing of incommensurables. The chapter by McNeely and Bose takes this insight one step further, applying it to the psychological and psychosocial literature and the complex challenges generated by global cultural diversity. *Human Rights and Adolescence* engages the debate on the appropriate policy correlates of these multifaceted changes. The book argues that adolescent rights, unlike infants' rights for example, vary with social and economic context but also with the decisions taken by adolescents themselves, in anything but a linear progression. From his vantage point as a senior international children's rights lawyer, Zermatten probes the import of the CRC for the advancement of adolescent rights, arguing that a central factor governing public policy making in this field must be acknowledgement of the paradoxical and often contradictory states and behaviors that characterize the adolescent phase. He suggests that the scope for exploitation caused by the characteristic emotional oscillations between desire and fear, between elation and desire, requires careful and consistent social planning of a kind that is as yet unavailable. For Zermatten, as well as for Sinha, Mtshali, and Pineda, wise harnessing of adolescent agency, and carefully crafted mechanisms for eliciting and empowering it, emerge as a central factor driving the articulation of a new framework of adolescent rights. As Zermatten puts it, we need to separate "age" from "maturity."

Some contributors to the book challenge universalist assumptions about the importance of postpuberty as a time of exploration, independence, and freedom, and point out that the luxury of adolescence in this sense eludes many communities struggling with the daily battle for survival. These situations place quite different demands on the adolescent human rights framework. Mark and Matache, Rozzi, and Gibbons, in particular, stress the extreme pressures affecting teenagers from economically and socially deprived backgrounds, drawn into adult responsibilities and roles as soon as they pass puberty. Other authors, including Sinha, Burra, and Mtshali, question what they see as the undertheorized acceptance of adolescent labor in place of secondary education, arguing instead that the fundamental right to education must not be compromised by inappropriate adoption of relativist arguments prioritizing teen work over learning. They suggest instead that encouraging respect, if necessary outside a confining family context,[4] for the development of individuality, particularly for girls and disabled adolescents, is critical for the stimulation of higher academic achievement. Secondary education should, like primary education, be a nonnegotiable right. Without it, opportunities for self-realization and secure employment in the twenty-first century are radically curtailed. Yet others, including Rizzini and Bush, Kelly and Newnham, and Naeve, explore coercive responses to expressions of adolescent independence and rebellion[5] and suggest alternative strategies for enhancing a rights-based approach to coming of age. These different approaches deconstruct notions of "security," "threat," "family," and "violence" to stimulate discussion about a metric for assessing the proportionality of punishment and repression in the context of juvenile deprivation.

With one in five (or 1.2 billion) of the world's current population between the age of ten and 19, the argument for reversing the neglect or mismanagement of this population's distinctive needs and desires is significant. As the following chapters demonstrate, advances in information technology and the mobility of persons, goods, and ideas have contributed to dramatic transformations in low- and middle-income countries, but adolescents and youth have been largely excluded from the benefits. Global connectivity has made glaring inequalities instantaneously apparent, provoking outbursts of violence, riots, social disruption—from the suburbs of French cities, to the downtown areas of the United Kingdom and the United States, to Brazil, Turkey, and the metropoles of the Arab world. Moreover, policy lacunae related to the transition to adulthood—the integration of education with skill training and employment generation, the development and encouragement of youth political representation, social and cultural agency—have exacerbated the consequences of economic recession and postconflict trauma, to generate a widespread sense of hopelessness and social obsolescence. In some areas, youth unemployment has reached epidemic proportions—23.4 percent in the Arab world in 2011, according to the International Labour Organization; at or exceeding 30 percent for female Arab youth (International Finance Corporation 2011), and 36.5 percent in Italy at the end of 2012 (Donadio 2012). In others, adolescents lacking marketable skills are either thrown back on informal and marginal activities or driven into illegal pursuits as sole sources of income. Many of these "jobs"—engagement in armed conflict, sex work, drug dealing, begging, stealing—present acute dangers to the adolescents themselves, particularly when they are, as is often the case, coupled with irregular migration and its attendant lack of legal status.

Strategies for addressing these dangers, whether in the sphere of migration opportunities, reproductive rights and health protections, or enterprise development and support, are particularly sparse for the adolescent age group where they are most needed. Data on reproductive rights and protections illustrate this point: one in seven girls in developing countries are married before the age of fifteen (International Center for Research on Women 2012).

One can cite other troubling statistics: childbirth-related complications are the number-one killer of girls aged fifteen to nineteen worldwide (UNAIDS 2010); 15–24-year-old girls in sub-Saharan Africa are eight times more likely to be HIV positive than their male counterparts (UNAIDS 2010).

These examples of adolescent difficulties illustrate some of the unresolved challenges. Most central among them, and extensively covered in the following pages, is the absence of an institutionally grounded conception of needs and rights as adolescents move away from home—circumstances that distinguish them from young children usually closely anchored within the family. These circumstances include the tension between adolescents' need for relative independence and qualified dependence, in all its local variations; and the difficulty of empowering adolescent exploration, originality, and idealism without compromising the rule of law. Coherent and consistent solutions are not easy to come by. In some parts of the world, there is concern that adolescence drags on well into what should be independent adulthood because the opportunity for independent living—for earning, for getting accommodation, for establishing oneself independently—is so elusive: young people who would otherwise be homeless are forced to live at home with their parents when they should be out on their own. In other contexts, adolescence is an elusive luxury—children become providers, earners, parents without any transitional period: reclaiming adolescence rather than shortening adolescence is the goal here. In yet other contexts, adolescence is a peculiarly dangerous phase—for HIV infection (one-third of all new HIV cases occur among people aged fifteen to twenty-four); for mental illness (at least 20 percent of adolescents suffer from a form of mental illness, mostly depression or anxiety, in any given year); for recruitment in armed conflict (at least 300,000 adolescents are directly involved).

When the UN CRC first came into force in September 1990, its arrival was heralded with great enthusiasm because no other international human rights instrument had been as quickly or as widely ratified. Child rights scholars and advocates took this felicitous start as a sign that, despite previous neglect or indifference, policy makers were now resolved to attend to the (undefined) "best interests" of children and adolescents under eighteen, regardless of this constituency's lack of political clout. In a decisive break with tradition, the opinions of children themselves, as they matured, would now be taken into account in decisions affecting them. The results of this new child-centered approach would be visible as children moved into adulthood "fully prepared to live an individual life in society . . . in the spirit of peace, dignity, tolerance, freedom, equality and solidarity" (UN General Assembly 1989, Preamble). As the CRC itself has come of age, a balance between the nonnegotiability of human rights principles and the negotiability of adolescent values and priorities needs to be crafted to protect the transition to adulthood. Young people themselves are voicing their impatience, as an eighteen year old pleads in a recent report: "As adolescents, we cannot in any way enforce our agenda without those in power standing behind us.... All we can do is ask, beg, write letters and organize events, trying to pressure those who have power to decide—but at the end of the day, most of us will have the feeling that their commitment has fallen on deaf ears" (UNICEF 2011b, 9). To transition safely and ably to adulthood, adolescents need a voice, a clear framework of rights and responsibilities, a human rights agenda that addresses their particular circumstances. They need an ambitious agenda.

Human Rights and Adolescence hopes to provide strong arguments in favor of, and pointers toward, a new road map for thinking about adolescent rights. The book discusses how adolescent rights differ from children's and adults' rights in general, how they apply in different contexts, and what mechanisms are best suited to their enforcement. The book has an ambitious policy agenda: to build on the disparate efforts to address adolescent rights issues that have emerged over the past months and years. These include the following: the decision by the Committee on the Rights of the Child to develop a General Comment on adolescence; the organization of several special UN sessions dedicated to the topic of youth mobility and migration; the creation of an international network of groups working on issues of disabled adolescents' rights; the growing attention to "the girl effect" and acknowledgement that secondary and tertiary education for girls needs much greater support; the choice of adolescence as a key focus area from 2013 to 2016 for nations in the Asia and Asia Pacific region; and the search for participatory models that move beyond the tokenism of occasional teenage spokespersons at international events.

This book builds on the extensive empirical and normative work already done over the past decades on human rights violations facing children. The first section of *Human Rights and Adolescence* provides a set of framing concepts for thinking about adolescent rights from different disciplinary perspectives. By exploring the lacunae in current approaches to adolescence, and developing alternative theories for moving toward solutions, these chapters unpack the relevance of "the best interests of the child," a key concept central to the CRC, but one that has received little attention in relation to older children. Given that adolescents' views of their own interests are often at odds with the views of adult experts or guardians, whose responsibility is it to structure the resolution process where families and adolescents disagree? How do the different axes of transition—family/marriage, school/work (to use Rozzi's felicitous schema)—map onto rights' entitlements and responsibility challenges? And how can preconceptions that limit access to rights be dislodged for the benefit of marginalized populations such as Middle Eastern adolescents with disabilities, or poor Roma migrant teenagers living in unauthorized camps in northern Italy? In different ways, drawing on their varied disciplinary competences (law, sociology, neuroscience, political science, and psychology), the book's opening chapters engage these questions. In doing so, they unsettle some well-established truisms and challenge us to think along new lines, emphasizing the benefits of a rights-based approach to adolescence.

The second section tackles one of the most egregious and intractable of adolescent rights issues, their massive exposure to and participation in violence, its devastating consequences, and the complexities of delivering protection and institutionalizing effective preventative policies. This section spans a wide range of situations, from contexts where children are born into societies devastated by poverty and armed conflict and grow up never having known anything else, to situations where they participate voluntarily in combat as an act of self-definition. Country case studies and comparative analyses are at once windows on particular situations as well as instantiations of more general challenges related to adolescent trauma, resilience, and family reconstruction. Chapters in this section describe a range of responses—legal, psychological, and socioeconomic—designed to strengthen adolescents' abilities to overcome the legacies of conflict and engage with peacetime activities that generate future opportunities. In some cases the challenges seem quite overwhelming. In Colombia, by contrast, developments in postconflict reintegration described by Naeve seem somewhat more successful. Her careful study of Colombia's approach to postconflict reintegration and rehabilitation of youth involved in the decades-long civil war leads her to challenge the government's restrictive approach to child soldiers. She argues that it should be refocused on the age of recruitment (to include all those who were recruited as children) rather than limited by the age of demobilization (covering only those who demobilized before eighteen) given the common history of trauma within this whole cohort. Her analysis illustrates the benefits to policy making that can flow from meticulous and grounded empirical research, and suggests why enhanced resources in this area are urgently needed. Other chapters tackle the postconflict situation across a range of countries in Latin America and Africa—in Sierra Leone and Guatemala, for example—probing the reintegration and development problems affecting adolescents exposed to prolonged conflict, and the inescapable sequels of trauma, stigma, and educational deficit. They advance creative strategies for addressing the challenges. Instead of the rolling bandwagon of short-term humanitarian projects, all the authors explore long-term, holistic, and integrative engagements. Rich in local detail, they avoid sweeping generalizations while deploying syncretic theoretical perspectives. They showcase a range of intervention methodologies, from the sophisticated public-health-inspired quantitative surveys and longitudinal studies of former child soldiers presented by Betancourt, Hann, and Zombo, which track the impact of violence over the trajectory of the adolescent's life cycle, to the textured legal analysis proposed by Volkmann, a senior child rights expert working within an international organization, to the multifaceted and insightful probing of psychosocial resilience and its drivers covered by Gibbons, also an experienced international child rights advocate. All these authors ask themselves common questions: What variables are central to the breakdown of protective prevention? What mechanisms and partnerships are essential to reconstructing adolescents' lives and securing their human rights? What are the roles of different stakeholders in the adolescent empowerment process—parents, educators, peers, law enforcement agencies, civil society organizations, trade unions, employers? The authors explore a rich set of alternatives, from legal accountability to psychological strengthening, from socioeconomic accompaniment to instructional mentorship. In the process they suggest innovative practices with multiple possible applications.

The final section of *Human Rights and Adolescence* moves the discussion toward a focus on strategic interventions. Taking as their starting point a minimum platform of nonnegotiable fundamental rights owed adolescents, the authors explore different facets of their incomplete realization. They probe the relationship between the state, as *parens patriae* charged with obligations to protect the rights of minors within its jurisdiction, and other nonstate actors, influentially engaged in complementing or supplementing state provision. Ranging from the United States to South Africa, from Tunisia to Oman, and from Gujarat to Andhra Pradesh (in the west and south of India, respectively), these chapters explore the complexities of reconciling the tensions inherent in the axes of adolescent transition noted above—family to marriage, school to work—in relation to key social structures: independence, education, health care, and employment. Noting the complex intersections between these domains, the authors highlight how laudable public policy goals are defeated or compromised by entrenched social and cultural prejudices. Predictably, gender emerges as a central battleground, whether in the case of adolescent rural girls seeking secondary education in India in the face of irreconcilable familial expectations centered around domestic obligations, or male and female adolescents in the Arab world confronting the clash between traditional values and contemporary aspirations.

Just as it investigates the tension between family and marriage or independent living, so this section is also rich in reflections on the fraught but critical adolescent transition from school to work. Each chapter, in different ways, explores the obstacles currently facing adolescents. But the third section also canvasses a range of positive precedents and experimental solutions that have contributed to overcoming hurdles and driving successful change. Across a spectrum of situations, the chapters describe innovative partnerships, collaborations that link public and private sector actors, entrepreneurial transformations and grassroots mobilizations that have succeeded in pushing the adolescent rights agenda forward. DeJong and Kawar survey the extensive and varied landscape of Arab adolescence. They argue that, despite the enormous diversity of economic and social circumstances in the region, an absence of opportunity for self-expression, for autonomy, and for self-realization characterizes the circumstances of young people across the region. They suggest that an enduring legacy of exclusion, across multiple interconnected socioeconomic layers, generates an urgent imperative for attention to adolescent rights issues, highlighted by recent political events. Mark and Matache's discussion of metropolitan Europe examines the circumstances of severely stigmatized Roma adolescents trapped in hazardous employment and living conditions at the heart of one of the most prosperous regions on earth, and the ambitious work of Roma nonprofit organizations engaged with this community. Rizzini and Bush, basing their far-reaching analysis of the reality of street children in Brazil on that country's enthusiastic adoption of the CRC and a rights framework, usefully document creative public-private partnerships designed to instantiate participation and provide learning opportunities for adolescent governance, a novel and imaginative approach capable of replication in a wide range of settings. Sinha, a prominent Indian child rights policy maker, makes a powerful argument in favor of a rights-based approach to quality education, at both primary and secondary level. She explores how such rights would help impoverished, often exploited, Indian adolescents negotiate the barriers of power and authority that continue to oppress them. Starting from the current situation, where millions of young Indians are consigned to a life of drudgery, she argues that uncompromising insistence on the right to education is fundamental as a launchpad for agency and equality. Burra, a seasoned development specialist and expert on issues related to gender, children, and youth, presents a series of fascinating transformative initiatives in India, each rich in detail and powerful as potentially replicable examples. The case study of a program targeting disabled youth for skill training and employment poignantly illustrates the revolutionary impact on individuals' lives, social prejudices, and access to economic and social rights that relatively economical program innovations can generate. From being depressed and isolated "victims," left at home when the rest of the family went out to work, girls in the program Burra describes became respected breadwinners, a radical role reversal. To quote one of her informants, commenting on the impact of the training and employment program: "We are no longer dependents. We are providers. We are supporting our parents in their old age." This is a particularly remarkable turnaround for girls living with severe disabilities in a rural setting in India. As Thompson, a disability rights activist, notes in the final chapter of the volume, violence against children and adolescents with disabilities is at epidemic proportions, double the already pervasive level of violence inflicted on young people as a whole. She argues that this is not a function of socioeconomic scarcity but of discriminatory targeting, since violence against children and adolescents with disabilities is nearly equal in high- and low-income countries while this is not true for their nondisabled counterparts. She makes her point with a compelling example: in Norway, a top-ranked country according to the United Nations' Human Development Index, a startling "80% of deaf adults reported being abused in their childhood." This final chapter combines several useful reframing devices that, mutatis mutandis, apply to the volume as a whole. It relates the approach and impact of the CRC (a radically powerful instrument in its own right) to the much more recent and less widely ratified CRPD. Thompson charts the new lens brought by the CRPD to questions of disability, recasting it as an issue of nondiscrimination rather than of special needs, and thus changing the paradigm of normalcy. She argues that it is the persistence of disabling social norms—the lack of signing for those with hearing impairment, the absence of mobility aids for those unable to walk without them, the paucity of support for the visually or mentally impaired, and above all the pervasive stigma against all these groups—that isolates and cripples them, not the impairments per se. A second radical reframing is also critical. With particular reference to disabled adolescents and in connection with an account of nonprofit organizations led by disabled adolescent activists, "Nothing about us without us," she notes affirmatively, citing the not sufficiently widely heard rallying cry of the disability rights movement. Another powerful reframing capable of being scaled across a wide range of adolescent issues and sites! It is the collective hope of all the contributors to this volume that the issues raised and arguments advanced contribute to a revitalized focus on a rights-based approach to adolescence worldwide.

Notes

1. UNICEF, *Adolescence: An Age of Opportunity, the State of the World's Children 2011*.

2. Respectively, migrants: 1990 UN Convention on the Protection of the Rights of Migrant Workers and Their Families; those with disabilities: 2006 UN Convention on the Rights of Persons with Disabilities; those trafficked: 2000 Protocol to Prevent, Suppress and Punish Trafficking in Persons, Especially Women and Children, supplementing the United Nations Convention against Transnational Organized Crime; those smuggled: 2000 Protocol against the Smuggling of Migrants by Land, Sea and Air, supplementing the United Nations Convention against Transnational Organized Crime; and indigenous people: 2007 UN Declaration on the Rights of Indigenous Peoples.

3. *Adolescence: An Age of Opportunity, the State of the World's Children 2011*.

4. The transformative work of the MV Foundation and the Youth 4 Work organization, both in Andhra Pradesh, India, discussed in chapters by Sinha and Burra, are powerful examples of the benefits of this strategy.

5. Young Egyptian women played a central role in Egypt's revolution, though they are now struggling to maintain the momentum for women's rights. See UN Women, "Egypt's Youth Revolution: Building a New Future": http://www.unwomen.org/2011/08/egypts-youth-revolution-building-a-new-future/.

References

Anand, Sudhir, Chris Desmond, Habtamu Fuje, and Nadejda Marques. 2012. *The Cost of Inaction*. Cambridge, Mass.: Harvard University Press.

Donadio, Rachel. 2012. "As a Premier Prepares to Depart, the Talk Is of Lost Opportunities." *New York Times*, December 13. http://www.nytimes.com/2012/12/14/world/europe/as-mario-monti-prepares-to-step-down-italians-express-disappointment.html?ref=world&_r=0.

Flynn, Joel. 2012. "Pakistan's Zardari in UK, Meets Girl Shot by Taliban." *Reuters*, December 8. http://www.reuters.com/article/2012/12/08/us-britain-pakistan-malala-idUSBRE8B70D220121208.

Graham-Harrison, Emma. 2012. "Afghan Man Slit Throat of Teenager He Had Wanted to Marry, Say Police." *Guardian*, November 29. http://www.guardian.co.uk/world/2012/nov/29/afghan-man-slit-throat-teenager.

International Center for Research on Women. 2012. "Out of the Shadows: Facts and Figures." Accessed December 31. http://www.icrw.org/out-shadows-facts-and-figures.

International Finance Corporation and Islamic Development Bank. 2011. "Education for Employment: Realizing Arab Youth Potential." http://www.e4earabyouth.com.

UNAIDS. 2010. *Report on the Global AIDS Epidemic*. Geneva: UNAIDS. http://www.unaids.org/globalreport/default.htm.

UN General Assembly. 1989. "Convention on the Rights of the Child." United Nations, Treaty Series, vol. 1577, 3. http://www.unhcr.org/refworld/docid/3ae6b38f0.html.

UNICEF. 2011a. *Adolescence: An Age of Opportunity, the State of the World's Children 2011*. New York: UNICEF. http://www.unicef.org/sowc2011/pdfs/SOWC-2011-Main-Report_EN_02092011.pdf.

———. 2011b. *State of Our World: Adolescence–Beyond the Stereotypes*. New York: UNICEF, Adolescent Development and Participation Unit. http://www.voicesofyouth.org/posts/adolescence-beyond-the-stereotypes.

UN Women. "Egypt's Youth Revolution: Building a New Future." http://www.unwomen.org/2011/08/egypts-youth-revolution-building-a-new-future/.

You, Danzen, and David Anthony. 2012. "Generation 2025 and Beyond: The Critical Importance of Understanding Demographic Trends for Children in the 21st Century." Occasional Papers no. 1, November. New York: UNICEF, Division of Policy and Strategy. http://www.unicef.org/media/files/Generation_2015_and_beyond_15_Nov2012_e_version.pdf.

PART I

Understanding Adolescence: Disciplinary Perspectives

CHAPTER 1

Protecting and Promoting Adolescent Rights: The Contribution of International Law and Policy

Jean Zermatten

In Article 1 of the UN Convention on the Rights of the Child, a child is defined as "every human being below the age of eighteen years unless under the law applicable to the child, majority is attained earlier" (UN 1989). Consequently, adolescents up to eighteen years old are holders of all the rights enshrined in the Convention. In particular, their best interests must be considered in policies affecting them, just as they must for much younger children for whom this mentorship role might seem more obvious. Adolescents up to eighteen years old are not only entitled to a range of special protective measures applicable to all children. They are also, according to their evolving capacities, entitled to progressively exercise their rights (Article 5). As a child's capacities grow, according to the CRC, so does the child's agency, his or her ability to have a voice, to participate, to be listened to. The difficult question is: What is an adolescent? There is no definition of this group or category in the CRC. Yet in some regions of the world, such as Latin America, policy makers frequently use the expression "children and adolescents," thus marking a difference between a child and an adolescent.

Is such a distinction necessary? It could be argued that adolescents should simply be considered children, to whom the same recognized rights and rules apply. This is precisely what the Convention does, by *not* explicitly addressing this group. But many international organizations, such as the World Bank, are anxious to engage with adolescents. The absence of a clear target may complicate the engagement process.

It is hard to define adolescence, partly because it does not correspond to clearly stipulated age limits, and partly because this state varies for every individual and is linked to the individual's evolving maturity, cognitive skills, and emotional aspirations. The onset of adolescence is often associated with the physical phenomenon of puberty. The difficulty of definition remains, however, since puberty occurs at different times for different individuals, varying according to gender, lifestyle, diet, pollution, and other factors.

Physical change is an important factor to consider. Psychological change is, in my view, even more important. Unique individual factors can trigger such change at diverse times of life. Moreover, addressing age limits in national legislation (that is, in relation to education, labor, military enrollment, or age of marriage) cannot provide a precise definition of adolescence, since those limits necessarily fluctuate. These limits instead mark a line for the child between dependence and independence when the exercise of a role or right is concerned.

I will therefore not attempt to define adolescence here, but will take the United Nations Children's Fund's definition of an adolescent as "a person between the ages of ten and nineteen" (UNICEF 2011, 12), and adapt it slightly to "a person between the ages of ten and eighteen." Some scholars distinguish between preadolescence (10–14) and proper adolescence (15–19) or make even finer distinctions. For example, Peter Blos (1962) discusses early adolescence, adolescence proper, late adolescence, and postadolescence.

There is value in acknowledging that adolescents (within the global category of children) require specific attention to be able to exert their rights. In addition, adolescents may experience multiple forms of discrimination, for instance, if they are living with a disability, in street situations, or are part of indigenous or migrant communities. Above all, they are at a stage where children leave their lives as children and move into a period of limbo before reaching adulthood. This transitional stage, where the authority and presence of parents may decrease but the supports essential to independent adult living may not yet be in place, may complicate the task of determining the young person's best interests; it may highlight tensions between the rights of the adolescent and the rights of others within his or her sphere, including parents, siblings, and other social group members. The challenges of this time can bring hardship and tears, but they may also bring happiness and achievement.

Issues Raised by Adolescence

Adults frequently view adolescence as little more than a bumpy and transitional period of life: a stage full of uncertainty, tensions, and contradictions. We often underestimate the idealism and enthusiasm of this phase of life.

The transition to adulthood cannot be achieved in a singular, rapid, definitive way. Adolescents must move through various steps, progressions, and regressions along a path strewn with fear and recklessness. They go through multiple trials, failures, and successes. The child must pass through these phases to become an autonomous adult. No one else can do that for her or him. However, many civilizations and cultures have invented and practiced rites of passage to help the child initiate, pass through, or celebrate the completion of these steps. Some cultures pay no particular attention to this transition, some celebrate it, while others have a mistrust and fear of adolescents. If the child does not move along this path to autonomy, she or he will remain a child or an adolescent in many ways and will only take on the appearance of an adult. Many of the challenging situations discussed later in this volume illustrate the impact of obstacles to a rights-respecting transition to adulthood on young people's future behavior.

The issues raised by adolescence can be outlined as follows:

- The adolescent becomes aware of significant physical, psychological, and emotional modifications of her or his being that may be perturbing physically, psychologically, and emotionally;
- Among the main changes experienced during adolescence is the discovery of sexuality. This frequently leads the teenager into situations of heightened curiosity that can require decisions about difficult choices and risks without the experience or wisdom necessary to make them;
- Forms of disruption may provoke extreme behavior (such as violence, substance use, and crime) that is linked to the socialization process and conflict over limits or norms (family, social, and legal).

Such behavior is characteristic of this period of life, without necessarily being an automatic or systematic symptom of profound or long-term problems;
- The adolescent attempts to sever dependency (material, educational, and affective) on parents or guardians and strives to acquire independence (material, educational, and affective) that the adolescent is not yet able to assume;
- The transition from education to employment also has an important significance, since there is a change of environment, social values, and economic independence that may not be immediately or fully realized. This transition is also associated with issues related to unemployment, difficulties finding a good job, and the uncertainty of economic crises, which can leave the adolescent in an extended phase of transition. This situation might require renegotiation of the adolescent's role or place in the family, the imposition of new responsibilities, or the need for independent housing. These issues represent the uneasy balance between the opportunity for freedom versus a long period of transition, a balance that also strains the relationship to parents and to the home;
- Adolescence is also the age of high idealism and illusions, cruel disappointment, and tremendous hope and despair. Such paradoxical emotional states can lead to eccentric behavior toward others, or in some instances, self-aggressive behavior that culminates in suicide.

The many contradictions just outlined that characterize adolescents' transition out of childhood have an impact on parents, families, and other adults. This impact may be fractured and inconsistent, it may oscillate between different extremes, or be restricted to one set of problematic approaches. Adult reactions toward adolescents may include understanding, special attention, valorization, or even glorification of this special period. At the same time, adults may fear adolescents, depict them as dangerous and violent delinquents, view them as a threat to public security, exclude them from social interaction, and sometimes deprive them of their liberty. Yet others take advantage of the vulnerability and contradictions of this age and exploit adolescents through forced labor, sex, armed conflict, and often indoctrination.

Accordingly, in my view, it is particularly important to pay specific attention to this group of children—adolescents. They face objective difficulties as they transition from the status of childhood, of persons in need of nurturing and protection, to the status of would-be adulthood that has not been fully attained but which may be close at hand and already realized in some respects.

The International Legal Framework Applicable to the Rights of Adolescents

Even though the CRC does not explicitly define adolescence, it cannot avoid the issue of adolescence. Indeed the Convention is quite usefully equipped—perhaps with underestimated tools—to tackle this age span in the life of a child. Since the CRC has been ratified by over 98 percent of the member states of the UN, and since many of its provisions are incorporated into the domestic laws of states, understanding the framework it establishes and the tools it provides for enforcing that framework is critical for engaging with adolescent rights issues.

Two important points must be mentioned here: "the evolving capacities" of the child and the four general principles of the Convention. Within the Committee on the Rights of the Child (the treaty body that oversees implementation of the Convention and that I currently chair), we are convinced that these tools have the capacity to essentially answer the questions posed by adolescence.

The CRC is not only a list of recognized rights of the child—or, in this case, of the adolescent. It is based on the idea that children are able to take part in and influence decisions affecting their existence. This requires accommodating the relationship between adults and children in an innovative mode over the long term, just as it was necessary for female-male relationships in the past century.

This new concept of the status of the child is often referred to as "participative status." The broad meaning of this technical phrase is that the child is not merely an object of protection—someone who is being protected and provided with the necessities of life, someone whose best interests must be considered by adult decision makers. The child is also an agent, a subject—someone entitled to have her or his views heard and taken into account. Adolescents may be asked to participate in, and even influence, decisions concerning their future in accordance with their individual age and maturity. The CRC provides a broad context for such participative status; it includes not only participation in personal decisions affecting the adolescent as an individual but also a right to participate politically, including to voice political opinions and enter into political associations. Several subsequent chapters discuss the implications of these participatory rights in the context of ongoing contemporary social movements with a substantial adolescent presence.

Though adolescents may not yet enjoy all political rights, they do possess personal, inalienable, and equality-based rights related to their personhood and dignity. They are, in other words, subjects or holders of rights. The implications of this rights-bearing status transcend the narrow legal arena. They affect policy priorities of service providers such as educational and medical facilities (including reproductive rights agencies), the conduct of public institutions that interact with adolescents such as law enforcement and juvenile justice entities (including juvenile detention facilities and child welfare agencies), as well as the obligations of private individuals and corporations that interact with adolescents (including employers, trainers, and teachers).

Article 5: Evolving Capacities

The child is by definition a being in development, evolving from birth until the age of eighteen, the legal landmark that signifies the end of being a child. During this time, individual capacities evolve, as does the autonomy that accompanies the exercise of rights, growing gradually as the child progresses in age and maturity. These two notions of *age* and *maturity* are repeatedly addressed in the Convention (particularly in Article 12 on the right of the child to be heard). The notion of age depends on the civil register, and by implication on an efficient system of birth registration. Maturity is more complex and has to be assessed taking into account the physical, emotional, cognitive, and social development of the child. Age and maturity serve as criteria to single out the successive steps from the moment the child is completely under the responsibility and influence of the parents, through the stages where the child is more emancipated and has achieved progressive autonomy, until the child is able to fully exercise his or her rights (independence).

This notion of gradual and progressive evolution is very important with regard to adolescence, since it allows for a realistic, individualized, and nuanced approach. It also avoids an arbitrary cut-off point between childhood and adulthood. This approach further provides for a basis of respect for adolescents by allowing them the progressive exercise of their rights without burdening them with the premature requirement of carrying out responsibilities before they have developed all the capacities to do so. The Innocenti Research Centre Research Report on *The Evolving Capacities of the Child* (Lansdown 2005) explores the strategic choices facing policy makers engaging with this tension between adolescents' best interests and their agency.

The principle of evolving capacities provides an answer to the dependence/independence question, offering a way to balance the tension between the rights and responsibilities of parents and the right of children to exercise their rights. Because children are vulnerable, they must be protected. However, the balance between measures of protection (often limiting the exercise of personal rights) and measures of empowerment (meaning the full exercise of those rights) often poses problems, especially in adolescence. Areas that often bring up these tensions include the right to freedom of movement, the right to privacy, the right to expression, or the right to have access to information; the need for renegotiation of the place of the adolescent in the family; the exercise of sexual activities and reproductive rights; or demonstrated extreme behavior, including risky situations. Very often the need to protect the physical or mental integrity of adolescents motivates restrictive decisions. Any decision taken by parents, teachers, or judges requires a case-by-case examination, linked to determination of the best interests of the child (see below).

Here the question of age and maturity, expressed and integrated in the concept of evolving capacities, is crucial. In a rights-based approach, as maturity increases the balance should tend to privilege empowerment rather than the protection emphasized for younger children. In the period of adolescence, the exercise of individual rights becomes concrete and real, notably the rights of the child to participate, express views, choose a mode of thought and religion, associate with others, and possibly enter into a sexual relationship. The contribution of a rights-based approach to navigating this complex and often fraught terrain is significant: it provides international guideposts that public players can adapt to their specific circumstances, it provides a framework within which stakeholders can exercise the complex balancing acts and exercise of discretion that are required. To operationalize this approach effectively, legislation must remain flexible. It should include the concepts of age and maturity so that there are tools to recognize the stage of autonomy that a particular adolescent has reached. Juvenile procedures in many jurisdictions lack these tools, to the detriment of the rights of the young people processed by them.

The CRC's General Principles

The Convention on the Rights of the Child lays down a number of articles that constitute umbrella provisions, provisions that shelter all the others, in contrast to articles containing substantive rights granted to every child. For example, Article 1 defines the notion of the child, indicating who is a child from the point of view of the CRC and therefore who are the subjects of the Convention. On the other hand, Article 7 (the right to be registered after birth, the right to a name, a nationality, the right to know one's parents and not to be separated from them) outlines substantive rights that should be available to every child from birth. These rights entail immediate and clear obligations for states. They are designed to prevent irregular fostering arrangements, child abandonment, and child-parent separations (as a case in point, consider the Latin American experience during the period of the dictatorships. The remedy envisaged is establishing birth and civil status registers, providing nationality and identification documents, registering parents' identity, and providing family care services. As subsequent chapters in this volume note, many of these rights still elude significant populations of adolescents (the Roma are an example), who struggle to establish a legal identity for themselves.

There are four articles that constitute the working tools of the CRC, the mechanism that makes the wheels of the system turn. They are Article 2 on nondiscrimination (Lansdown 2005); Article 3 on the best interests of the child; Article 6 on the right to life, survival, and development; and Article 12 on the right of the child to be heard. The following discussion outlines the application of these articles to adolescence.

The imperative of nondiscriminatory conduct is a building block of the human rights approach. In the context of the CRC, applying the principle of *nondiscrimination* requires duty bearers—teachers, doctors, police officers, social workers, for example—to analyze whether children in the same circumstances are treated in the same manner. It is difficult to recognize rights for every child without undertaking this examination. Since the CRC is a universal instrument (ratified by all member states of the UN except for the United States, Somalia, and South Sudan) its provisions are applicable under all latitudes and in all circumstances. (Of course what nondiscrimination means and what the critical variables needing examination are will vary with context).

The fact of being an adolescent in itself can be a source of discrimination. In daily life, numerous situations arise in which adolescents experience discrimination due to their status. Adolescents may be treated as dangerous and be deprived of their liberty or their right to education. As chapters in this volume demonstrate, they may be sold or exploited for labor, prostitution, or pornography; or they may be betrothed into early marriage. These discriminatory behaviors are pervasive. Adolescent girls often experience double discrimination. The principle of nondiscrimination can be an effective tool in the hands of a decision maker.

The principle of the *best interests of the child* compels the decision maker to ensure that every decision taken about a child respects that child's best interests. Equally, when decisions are taken concerning a collective group of children, the decision maker must also ensure that these decisions promote the well-being of the children concerned, and perhaps favor their participation and their access to the benefits of mainstream society.

The best interests of the child principle may be a vague legal concept, but it is not an arbitrary one. Decisions should be based on objective criteria that allow those responsible for the decision to arrive at similar solutions to similar cases and different ones to different situations. The decision on best interests has to be reached case by case, taking into account numerous perspectives, and the specificities of the case analyzed. When making decisions about children (here adolescents), the personal circumstances of the person should determine which are the individual's best interests.

It is essential that this individualized examination of the impact of a decision be carried out systematically. It is a crucial step in the decision-making process, necessary to ensure that decision makers respect the interests of this human being (or group of human beings) going through the difficult phase of adolescence. This systematic individualized examination demonstrates that we consider adolescents as beings with particular needs that must be taken into account and cannot be dealt with in an automatic or cavalier way.

Conflicts of interests, especially between adolescents and parents, arise in a range of different contexts. They may manifest themselves in the interface between adolescents and the law, or adolescents and school, or adolescents and their peers, to name but three. Adolescents may feel compelled to support their families by working in circumstances where the broader society expects them to attend school. Or they may be eager to enter into emotional and sexual relationships that their parents disapprove of. From a rights-based perspective, the following criteria are relevant in resolving such conflicts:

(i) the rights of the child should not to be limited if this is not necessary
(ii) consideration must be paid to the age and maturity of the adolescent (as explained above)
(iii) an adolescent's personal circumstances (identity, personality, privacy, family relationships, vulnerability) must be taken into account; generic rulings and rigid policies are not appropriate
(iv) an assessment of the degree of risk should be carried out
(v) the views and opinions of the adolescent should be heard

In the case of a conflict of interests, a holistic determination of the situation has to be made to reconcile, where possible, the different interests and to find the solution that least restricts or limits the rights in conflict.

The *life and survival of the child* is of course essential for the enjoyment of her or his rights, while the ability to enjoy progressive development is needed to reasonably make use of those rights. The measures taken by states, the mechanisms implemented, and the services provided should foster full and harmonious development of the adolescent. This is a stage of life when young people are often filled with doubt and sometimes with fear or despair. The services provided (health care, education, protection, juvenile justice) must therefore aim to facilitate individual development in difficult circumstances.

Focusing on life and survival for adolescents requires the prioritization of attention to at-risk behavior engendered by recklessness (including drugs, sexuality, violence, and accidents). This context could also raise the issue of economic exploitation of adolescents versus their right to develop.

The *right of the child to be heard* is an obligation that must be met by administrative, judicial, and even legislative authorities. No decision may be undertaken about a child without first having heard from her or him. The child's opinion must be seriously taken into account "in accordance with the age and the maturity of the child." Adolescents are agents of their own development and possess the capacity to influence decisions taken toward them. As other contributors to this volume note, adolescents should not be stereotyped as dangers to society, but rather must be recognized as providers of solutions for themselves and their peer group. Adolescents are more able to influence decisions related to their lives than younger children, since their autonomy to exercise their rights is complete or almost complete.

Applying these four provisions of the CRC leads to the conclusion that it is impossible to talk about any substantive right of the adolescent without first examining the question of fair treatment; soliciting the adolescent's opinion to determine her or his best interests; and finally, aiming for a harmonious outcome, by recognizing the rights of the individual beneficiary, namely, a person in the difficult transition between childhood and adulthood. These four provisions make the mechanisms of the CRC work. They also provide answers to the contradictions of adolescence.

Engagement of the UN Committee on the Rights of the Child with Adolescent Rights

The UN Committee on the Rights of the Child is the treaty body that monitors the implementation of children's rights in the 193 countries that have ratified the Convention and its two Optional Protocols. Following its regular country analysis in Geneva, the Committee issues a list of practical, actionable recommendations to be taken by states to ensure effective national-level implementation of the Convention.

Moreover, the Committee drafts and publishes general comments dealing with various issues, or with the rights that the Committee considers are in need of further elaboration and clarification. Its specific comments provide guidance to states (and other interested partners, such as professionals and civil society) on ways and means to interpret and implement the Convention and its ensuing obligations.

What interest does the Committee on the Rights of the Child take in the issue of adolescence? First, the Committee issued a general comment on the issue of adolescent health and development (CRC 2003). This twelve-page comment, though focused on the issue of health, also addresses other issues relating to adolescence. The comment considers the dynamics of adolescence; the fundamental principles in the CRC most helpful in considering the issues of adolescents; the need to create a safe and supportive environment; the need in this stage of life for information, skills development, counseling, and health services; the particular issues of vulnerability and risk for adolescents; and the nature of states' obligations to adolescents. The comment is therefore a prominent feature in the attention paid by the Committee to this period of life, and asserts that adolescents need a more subtle and nuanced approach than simply being grouped with all children.

In addition, an analysis of the concluding observations of the Committee (the response of the Committee to the regular official reports from countries) reveals that the Committee makes many recommendations and voices many concerns relating specifically to adolescents.

Here are a few highlights from comments the Committee has made regarding adolescents in its responses to country reports (emphasis added in italics).

Adolescent Health

To New Zealand (CRC 2011, para. 42): "The Committee recommends that . . . [New Zealand]: a) Strengthen its efforts to *provide adolescents with appropriate reproductive health services, including reproductive health education*, in school and to promote a healthy lifestyle for adolescents; (b) Continue to address the *issue of suicidal behaviour among adolescents*, . . . including by studying the root causes of this problem in order to provide targeted preventive measures.

To Spain (CRC 2010c, para. 51): "The Committee recommends that . . . [Spain]: continue and strengthen efforts to *combat substance abuse among adolescents, manage obesity* among children, and pay close attention to child and *adolescent* health, taking into account the Committee's general comment No. 4 (2003) on *adolescent* health and development in the context of the Convention. . . . [and] take all necessary measures to prevent substance abuse."

To Qatar (CRC 2009b, para. 52): "The Committee welcomes efforts made by . . . [Qatar] to protect *the health of adolescents and promote healthy lifestyles*. However, it is concerned at the emerging *trends in obesity, psychological and mental health problems*. The Committee takes note of the very low HIV/AIDS prevalence in the State party and welcomes the State party's efforts to raise general awareness of HIV/AIDS among adolescents. However, it notes with concern that adolescents know little about other *sexually transmitted infections* (STIs)."

To the Democratic Republic of Congo (DRC) (CRC 2009a, para. 58):

> The Committee recommends that . . . [the DRC], taking into account the Committee's general comment No. 4 (2003) on *adolescent* health and development in the context of the Convention . . . , continue and strengthen activities and services under the framework of its national *adolescent health programme and services,* and that it prioritize gathering coherent, systematic and valid data on *adolescent* health concerns through, inter alia, studies on this issue and a more effective monitoring mechanism. The Committee also recommends that the [DRC] elaborate clear policies and, when applicable, legislation, addressing the prevention of *adolescent* health-related issues, *in particular early pregnancies and drug and alcohol abuse.*

Education

To Sweden (CRC 2009c, para. 57): "The Committee recommends that . . . [Sweden] expand and strengthen *measures supporting adolescents to acquire the vocational competencies and qualifications* required to find an occupation. Schools and institutions, which train and further *qualify adolescents with difficulties accessing the labour market,* should receive adequate financial and personnel resources to effectively assist such adolescents in *the transition from school to the labour market.*"

To Argentina (CRC 2010a, para. 72): "The Committee further remains concerned at the high percentage *of adolescents who are the object of economic exploitation*, in particular in rural areas, with associated problems such as high repetition rates, frequent absences and late arrivals."

Adolescents in Street Situations

To Peru (CRC 2006b, para. 65): "The Committee, while appreciating the programme "Educadores de Calle" (PEC), is concerned about the high number of street children mostly *due to socio-economic factors as well as abuse and violence in the family.* The Committee is also concerned about the spreading *of adolescent violence and street-gangs (pandillas),* especially in Lima."

To Guatemala (CRC 2007, para. 10): "The Committee commends [Guatemala] for reducing budget allocations for the military and for transferring resources to the social sector, however it is concerned that significant resources are dedicated to interventions resulting *in the repression of adolescents living or working on the street.*"

Children in Armed Conflicts

To Mozambique (CRC 2002, para. 62): "The Committee joins . . . [Mozambique] in expressing concern that: (a) As noted in . . . [Mozambique's] report, "the needs of children formerly affected by the war continue to warrant special concern"; b) There are still large number of adolescents and young people, in both urban and rural areas, affected by the conflict who lack appropriate education and/or employment opportunities."

Human Trafficking

To Benin (CRC 2006a, para. 71): "the Committee is concerned at the information that a *high number of children under 18, especially* adolescent *girls,* are still being trafficked for purpose of sexual exploitation and domestic labour in other countries."

Discrimination

To Guatemala (CRC 2010b, para. 40): "The Committee is . . . concerned that indigenous *and Garifuna adolescents are more likely to be victims of sexual and economic exploitation* due to the lack of relevant information about their rights as well as to the absence of mechanisms guaranteeing these rights. The Committee is also concerned at *discriminatory attitudes* affecting some sections of the child population, in *particular adolescents, children with disabilities, girls,* . . ."

* * *

We could continue to quote recommendations or annotations from the Committee on the Rights of the Child, but the above excerpts demonstrate how often and across how many varied situations the Committee reminds states of their obligations towards adolescents.

Conclusion

The difficulty of tackling the objective notion of adolescence is serious. It has become even more important in Western countries due to the extended length of this period of life: it starts earlier, and it lasts longer than in many other countries. Puberty frequently occurs earlier and, as Elena Rozzi discusses in this volume, the difficulty of finding employment and becoming independent means that adolescents are living longer and longer with their families. This situation is also occurring because adolescents are remaining for longer periods in higher education and employment training.

Adolescence must also be contextualized in relation to the major changes occurring in families, where half of marriages end in separation or divorce in Western countries. The result is that adolescents live in single-parent families or reconstituted families where the boundaries with adults may have shifted or disappeared and where fathers are absent in many instances. These changes in the basic family structure have obvious repercussions for all children; sometimes they are even greater for adolescents at their sensitive stage. On the other hand, these same adolescents become their parents' teachers when it comes to using new technologies and choosing clothing, movies, and music in accordance with the evolving "adolescent culture." The complexity of their role, oscillating between insecurity and independence, between self-doubt and competence, only compounds the challenge of appropriately protecting their human rights.

Even if the CRC does not provide a strict definition of adolescence or answer every question, it does represent a useful tool for understanding and approaching the issues that render adolescents vulnerable (both individually and as a group) in a world in transformation. It is imperative to recognize the adolescent as a person with dignity and evolving capacities, who has rights and whom we have to accompany on the often tortuous journey toward autonomy and responsibility.

References

Blos, Peter. 1962. *On Adolescence, A Psychoanalytic Interpretation*. New York: Free Press.

Committee on the Rights of the Child (CRC). 2002. "Concluding Comments: Mozambique." CRC/C/15/ADD.172.

CRC. 2003. "Adolescent Health and Development in the Context of the Convention on the Rights of the Child." General Comment No. 4. CRC/GC/2003/4.

CRC. 2006a. "Concluding Comments: Benin." CRC/C/BEN/CO/2.

CRC. 2006b. "Concluding Comments: Peru." CRC/C/PER/CO/3.

CRC. 2007. "Concluding Comments: Guatemala." CRC/C/OPAC/GTM/CO/1.

CRC. 2009a. "Concluding Comments: Democratic Republic of Congo." CRC/C/COD/CO/2.

CRC. 2009b. "Concluding Comments: Qatar." CRC/C/QAT/CO/2.

CRC. 2009c. "Concluding Comments: Sweden." CRC/C/SWE/CO/4.

CRC. 2010a. "Concluding Comments: Argentina." CRC/C/ARG/CO/3-4.

CRC. 2010b. "Concluding Comments: Guatemala." CRC/C/GTM/CO/3-4.

CRC. 2010c. "Concluding Comments: Spain." CRC/C/ESP/CO/3-4.

CRC. 2011. "Concluding Comments: New Zealand." CRC/C/NZL/CO/3-4.

Lansdown, Gerison. 2005. *The Evolving Capacities of the Child*. Florence, Italy: UNICEF Innocenti Research Centre.

UN General Assembly. 1989. "Convention on the Rights of the Child." United Nations, Treaty Series, vol. 1577, 3. http://www.unhcr.org/refworld/docid/3ae6b38f0.html.

UNICEF. 2011. *Adolescence: An Age of Opportunity, the State of the World's Children 2011*. New York: UNICEF. http://www.unicef.org/sowc2011/pdfs/SOWC-2011-Main-Report_EN_02092011.pdf.

CHAPTER 2

Transitions to Adulthood in Contemporary Italy: Balancing Sociocultural Differences and Universal Rights

Elena Rozzi

Adolescence: A Universal Notion?

The adolescent was invented at the same time as the steam-engine. The principal architect of the latter was Watt in 1765, of the former Rousseau in 1762. (Musgrove 1965, 33)

Age is not only a biological fact, it is also a social fact. Of course, the process of biological development sets some limits to what society can expect from an individual at a certain stage of his or her life, as the following chapter by Steinberg clearly explains. But much room is left for social definition.[1] The human rights approach recognizes this. As the previous chapter established, context is a critical factor in evaluating the appropriate application of universal rights norms to particular individual or group needs and rights across the life cycle.

Specific norms define the behaviors and attitudes expected or acceptable at a certain age, which I will call "age statuses." Norms also regulate what I will call "life course calendars," those transitions in individual biographies that play an important role in shaping individuals' self-identity and life strategies. Some norms are legal provisions, such as those concerning compulsory education and the minimum age for admission to employment, but most are social norms not formalized by law.

Norms defining age statuses and life course calendars vary significantly according to historical periods, different societies, and social groups. At certain historical moments, life stages appear that were not previously perceived as separate stages. Today, significant differences can be noted both between industrialized and rural societies, and among industrialized countries. Even in the same society, different social groups may define age statuses and life course calendars in quite different ways. Subsequent chapters in this volume illustrate the broad spectrum of approaches—protective, punitive, economic—that define intergenerational relationships across and within societies.

Particularly variable and socially defined is the transition from childhood to adulthood. We can consider two axes of this transition: one concerning education and work, the other relating to family and marriage.[2] Four thresholds are crossed along these axes: completing education, starting work, leaving the family of origin, and establishing a new family.

From a sociological point of view, adolescence can be defined as that transitional stage between childhood and adulthood, when individuals have reached puberty but have not yet acquired, by crossing these thresholds, the responsibilities and rights that are peculiar to the adult status (Mitterauer 1991, 27).[3]

The biological age at which the four thresholds are crossed, as well as the length of the transition and the presence or lack of midstages between childhood and adulthood, are highly variable, both historically and socially. Just as variable are the responsibilities and rights that are assigned by the family and society to teenagers.

As historians of childhood starting with the works of Philippe Ariès (1960) have demonstrated, up until the nineteenth century European populations had no notion of the life stage that we now call adolescence: individuals passed directly from childhood to adulthood around the age of puberty, usually through public, culturally prescribed rites of passage.

In rural societies, children used to start working as soon as they were physically able, their involvement increasing as they grew up. From the age of twelve to thirteen, they had full working responsibilities, much like adults. In poor families, those children that could not be used as a workforce within the family economy often left to earn their living elsewhere, sometimes even abroad. Between the nineteenth and twentieth century, for example, thousands of Italian children migrated to France, to the United Kingdom, Germany, and the United States, to work as street vendors or in factories (Di Bello and Nuti 2001). On the other hand, girls were usually married off while very young. These patterns are still evident in many developing societies, where adolescents, particularly boys, embark on international migration for primarily economic reasons.

Adolescence only appeared as a separate life stage in the nineteenth century, starting in the bourgeois and aristocratic classes, and only much later, in the twentieth century, in the working class. The appearance of adolescence is strictly connected to social processes related to industrialization, especially the increasing requirements of specialization for the job market and the related extension of the period of life dedicated to education.

It then comes as no surprise that in social groups that have been kept at the margins of these processes, such as rural populations in poor countries but also some very marginalized groups living in rich countries, adolescence does not exist or is very limited.

In Europe in recent decades, the transition to adulthood has been further extended for a number of reasons, especially the constant extension of education and the difficulty of finding a job. While until the 1970s the four thresholds concerning education, work, family, and marriage were usually crossed in a limited range of time and adolescence ended at the time of the acquisition of the adult status, now a new life stage appears: individuals stay for a long period in an ambiguous social status, where they have to some extent acquired the autonomy and responsibilities of adults, but not yet fully.

This tendency is common to all European countries, but with some significant differences that allow us to distinguish between two models of transition to adulthood: a North European model and a Mediterranean one. In the former, the period of job insecurity is shorter; moreover, individuals usually leave their family of origin earlier and do not immediately establish a new family. In the Mediterranean model, on the other hand, youth live with their parents for a longer time, even after finding a stable job, and they tend to get married immediately after leaving their family of origin (Cavalli and Galland 1996, 31–44).

Italian "Bamboccioni": An Extremely Prolonged Transition

> Let's stimulate youth that stay with parents, don't marry and don't become autonomous, to leave their parents' home . . . Let's send the "bamboccioni" away from home!
> Tommaso Padoa Schioppa, the Italian minister of economy, *Corriere della Sera* (2007)

Italy is the most accentuated expression of the "Mediterranean model" and one of the countries in the world where the transition to adulthood is most prolonged with regard to all four of the thresholds mentioned above: completing education, starting work, leaving the family of origin, and establishing a new family. It is also a country with a recently arrived but growing minority population, characterized by different norms and opportunities. It is therefore a particularly useful context in which to develop an extended case study of twenty-first century adolescence. Many of the observations that follow apply, in some way, to other societies discussed in later chapters of this volume.

Under Italian law, twelve years of education, starting from the age of six, are compulsory. After ten years of schooling, adolescents can choose whether to continue secondary school or attend vocational training up to the age of eighteen. Minors can work from the age of sixteen, after finishing their ten years of compulsory schooling[4] and provided that employment does not prevent them from receiving secondary school education or training.

Particularly since the 1960s, there has been an enormous increase in the proportion of the Italian population attending school as well as a significant extension of the period of education. During the academic year starting in the fall of 2009, almost 100 percent of the children in the age group six to thirteen and 92.3 percent of the adolescents aged fourteen to eighteen were enrolled in school, while 63.3 percent of the students who finished secondary school enrolled in university (Istat 2011).[5] By contrast, as regards child labor, only 3.1 percent of the children aged seven to fourteen were officially estimated to be involved in work in 2000.[6]

In Italy, a relatively small proportion of young people above the minimum age for admission to employment actually work. According to official data, in 2009 only 21.7 percent of fifteen to twenty-four year olds were employed, while their unemployment rate was 25.3 percent.[7] The percentage of those who were neither employed nor looking for a job (the economically inactive) was 90.8 percent in the age group fifteen to nineteen and 24.7 percent in the group twenty to twenty-four (Ministero del Lavoro e delle Politiche Sociali 2010, 6–15). Family plays a crucial role in supporting youth while inactive or unemployed.

We thus arrive at the third threshold: leaving the family of origin. The extension of the period in which youth keep living with their parents, even after completing education and finding a job—the so-called long family—is particularly marked in Italy.[8] In 2009, 86 percent of the youth aged twenty to

Table 2.1. Percentage of youth living with at least one parent in Italy, 2009

Age group	Males	Females	Tot.
18–19	97.0	96.9	96.9
20–24	90.6	81.4	86.1
25–29	68.8	48.8	59.2

Source: Ministero del Lavoro e delle Politiche Sociali (2010).

twenty-four and 59 percent of those aged twenty-five to twenty-nine lived with at least one of their parents, with a significantly higher proportion among males.

The last threshold, establishing a new family, is crossed very late: in 2009, the average age at first marriage was thirty-three years for men and thirty-two for women (Istat 2010), while the average age of the women who gave birth in 2011 was 31.4 (Istat 2011). A range of different causes explain the "long family": difficulties in finding a stable job, the lack of policies to support students and unemployed youth, the lack of opportunities to rent a house at low cost (both on the private market and in social housing), and the traditional protective role of the family in Italian society (Cavalli and Galland 1996, 35–38). Finally, it is interesting to note that most of the youth who are employed and live with their parents do not contribute to the running costs of the household but keep their salary for themselves (Cavalli and Galland 1996, 36).

The Clash with Different Models of Transition to Adulthood: Between Ethnocentrism and Cultural Relativism

When I get my salary, at the end of the month, I send money home. This money is important for my family! If it had not been important, I would have studied. We support our parents, it is not like you Italians do.

(Seventeen-year-old Albanian unaccompanied
boy living in Italy, 2000)

I don't want to go to school. We are not so used to it because we marry early. Some girls get married at twelve to thirteen years, but I don't like that, what do they know about what a husband is? When you are sixteen to seventeen, you know it, a little bit . . .

(Sixteen-year-old Romanian Roma girl living in an unauthorized camp in Italy, 2009)[9]

For some minority groups living in Italy, adolescence does not exist as a separate life stage or, if it does, it is very limited: individuals in these communities usually cross the thresholds concerning education, work, family, and marriage, and acquire adult responsibilities, before the age of eighteen. When Italian authorities have to make decisions concerning teenagers[10] who belong to these groups, the clash between different models of transition to adulthood becomes apparent.

Administrative and judicial authorities often deal with these differences in opposite ways: they either simply impose their own model of the transition to adulthood based on the mores of the social majority (the ethnocentric approach)[11] or else they accept the different model as "culturally legitimated" and unquestionable, even in cases where fundamental child rights are at stake (extreme cultural relativism).[12]

I will analyze two case studies—first, the return of unaccompanied migrant children to their country of origin, and second, institutional inaction regarding Roma teenage school dropouts—to illustrate the clash between different models of transition to adulthood, opposing approaches to dealing with these differences, and their implications for a rights-based approach to adolescence.

Returns of Unaccompanied Children: An Example of Ethnocentrism

Every year several thousand minors migrate irregularly (without legal documents) to Italy, unaccompanied by parents or other caregivers (Giovannetti 2008; Bichi 2008). Italian law provides that these children must not be expelled (except for reasons related to public order and state security). An unaccompanied child may only be returned to his or her family in the country of origin through "assisted repatriation," (removal paid for by the Italian government which is not technically expulsion because the child "consents") if the Committee for Foreign Minors (an Italian governmental authority), after tracing the child's family and conducting an investigation in the country of origin, decides that return is in the best interests of that child. Assisted repatriation is therefore not considered a sanction for violating immigration law (like expulsion of undocumented adult migrants), but a measure aimed at protecting the unaccompanied child's right to family unity. But how does the Committee for Foreign Minors assess the best interests of the child?

Consider the approach of the Committee at the beginning of the first decade of the twenty-first century. In those years, more than nine thousand Albanian unaccompanied children were registered in Italy. Most of them were boys aged fifteen to seventeen. They usually came from very poor families living in rural areas. Edison's story is paradigmatic:

> Edison[13] is a sixteen-year-old boy who was born in a village in the area of Diber in the mountains of northern Albania. Edison's parents and five younger brothers still live in the village. They possess one hectare of land, which they cultivate by traditional techniques, and two cows. Edison's father works on their small plot of land, and occasionally finds jobs as a bricklayer; his mother is a housewife.
>
> Edison started to help his father in his work in the fields and as an assistant bricklayer at the age of eleven. He went to school until the age of fourteen, then he stopped because the secondary school was a two-hour walk from his village. Edison wished to work, in order to make a contribution to the family's income, as is normal for a boy of his age. But there were no employment opportunities in Diber.
>
> Many of his friends had left for Italy and succeeded in sending some money home. Edison could not see any future for himself in Albania, so he decided to leave for Italy. His parents gave their consent, although they were afraid of the risks of the journey. They sold one of their two cows, and took out a loan to pay for the journey. Edison paid seven hundred euros for crossing the Adriatic Sea in a dinghy, and landed on the Italian coast.
>
> In Italy, he was accommodated in a reception center, and attended school and a vocational training course as a mechanic. When asked about the opportunity of assisted repatriation, Edison answered that
>
> *(continued)*

> he was completely against it: he wanted to stay in Italy, to study, and
> to find a job, in order to help his family. At the end of the training, he
> was taken on by an artisan as an apprentice mechanic: he started to
> earn eight hundred euros a month, and succeeded in sending half of
> this to his parents.
>
> In the meantime, the Committee for Foreign Minors carried out
> a social investigation in Albania. Edison's parents opposed their child's
> return, because they wanted him to get an education, to find a job, and
> to have a better future for himself in Italy. Nonetheless, since they
> were considered able to take care of their child (there were no problems related to mistreatment, abuse, alcoholism, and so forth in his
> family), the Committee ordered Edison to be returned to Albania, in
> order to protect his right to family unity.
>
> Edison felt that he was a loser. One month later, he left again for
> Italy.

When authorities have to decide whether to return an unaccompanied minor, against his or her will, to a poor context of origin where there is much less opportunity for education,[14] employment, or social assistance than in Italy, a contradiction is apparent between different rights provided by the UN CRC: the right to family unity, on the one hand, and the rights to participation,[15] to education, and to a standard of living adequate to the child's development, on the other.[16]

Around 2000, the Committee for Foreign Minors dealt with this contradiction by giving the child's right to family unity priority over all the other rights recognized by the CRC. Therefore, when the family was traced and no risks were evident, assisted repatriation was deemed to be in the best interests of the child, even though the unaccompanied minor and the parents were against it. According to the Committee, the living conditions and the opportunities available in the context of origin did not have to be taken into account at all in assessing the best interests of the child.

Why did the Committee for Foreign Minors take this position? As previously mentioned, in Italy youth are economically supported by their parents well after adolescence and leave the family of origin very late. The point of view of the Committee members was restricted to a model of transition to adulthood where adolescents are fully maintained by their parents and do not have economic responsibilities; they just go to school and have leisure, and—most important—they live with their parents. In fact, the Committee did not make any distinction between unaccompanied preadolescent children and adolescents: for both, the right to family unity had to prevail over other rights, including the rights to development and to participation. That adolescents should live separated from their parents, work, and send money home was simply considered unacceptable.

But Albanian teenagers coming from poor families held a quite different model of the transition to adulthood and did not identify themselves with this idea of adolescence. In Albanian rural areas at that time, children usually started helping their parents, at home or in grazing cattle, when they were six to seven years old. In 2000, 57 percent of the male children between seven and fourteen years living in rural areas were estimated to be involved in economic activities (UNICEF 2000).

Secondary school enrollment was very low: in 2000 only 37 percent of Albanian adolescents (including those living in urban areas) enrolled in secondary school (UNICEF 2001). In rural areas, boys aged fourteen to fifteen were usually expected to contribute to the family's economy as adults, even by migrating abroad, if there were no employment opportunities at home. This is the same pattern of early work that prevailed for Italian boys of this age in the late nineteenth and early twentieth centuries.

Besides the social norms acquired in the context of origin, migration further accelerates the transition to adulthood. Unaccompanied minors leave their parents' home and their country to enter European Union countries when they are fifteen to sixteen years old, sometimes even earlier. They experience dangerous journeys, which they describe as an initiation ritual. These adolescents find themselves alone, in a strange country, often living for long periods unprotected on the streets. Moreover, families usually urge

Table 2.2. Activity of children aged 7–14 living in rural areas in Albania, 2000 (percentage of children in the relevant age group)

Activity	Males	Females
Economic activity only	24.2	20.7
Combining school and economic activity	33.0	25.8
School only	22.2	25.0
Neither in school nor in economic activity	20.7	28.6

Source: UNICEF (2000).

the emigrated member to send money home, especially if they incurred debts to pay for the journey.

As a consequence of all these factors, most Albanian unaccompanied minors arriving in Italy at that time said that their deepest wish was to find a job and earn money as soon as possible, even though this required living abroad, far from their parents.[17] They could not understand the notion of "assisted repatriation in the best interests of the child," decided upon by the Italian authorities in order to protect the child's right to family unity. It just did not make sense to them. Both unaccompanied minors and their parents perceived the return as a punishment. And many of those who were returned, even when supported back home through reintegration projects, left again: out of a sample of 256 Albanian minors repatriated by Italian authorities between 1998 and 2000, 155 had emigrated again by 2001 (Servizio Sociale 2001, 35–51).

In these cases, not taking into consideration the different models of transition to adulthood prevented the authorities from effectively assessing the best interests of the child.[18]

Accepting Roma Teenagers' Dropping Out of School as "Culturally Legitimated": An Example of Extreme Cultural Relativism

An opposite example of how differences in models of transition to adulthood are dealt with concerns Roma adolescents. Very few Roma teenagers living in "nomad camps"[19] in Italy enroll in secondary school or vocational training. A high proportion of them even fail to complete primary education.

An estimated twenty thousand Roma children in Italy below the age of twelve do not attend compulsory school (Commissione straordinaria 2011, 61). No data are available at the national level on the proportion of Roma minors outside the education system, but the number of Roma students registered by the Ministry of Education is very low, especially in secondary school, when compared to a total estimated population of 140,000 to 170,000 Roma in Italy.[20]

While only estimates are available at the national level, some data are collected locally. For example, in the school years 2006–07 and 2008–09, an average of 57 percent of Roma children living in authorized camps in the city of Turin regularly attended elementary school, while the average of stu-

Table 2.3. Roma children enrolled in Italian schools registered by the Ministry of Education, for the 2008–09 school year

School level	Number of children
Kindergarten	2,171
Elementary school	7,005
Middle school	3,467
Secondary school	195
Total	12,838

Source: Ministero dell'Istruzione, dell'Università e della Ricerca (2009, 31).

dents in regular attendance at middle school was only 8 percent.[21] Almost all adolescents in the fifteen to seventeen age group were outside the school system. No significant differences between boys and girls emerged from these data.

A complex and interlinking range of reasons explains the extremely high level of school dropouts among Roma teenagers:[22] high unemployment and destitution in many Roma families, so that all the members need to contribute to scrape together a living; poor living conditions and evictions in "nomad camps"; discrimination, racism, and harassment affecting Roma students; and a lack of support for non-Italian speaking students, especially in middle and secondary schools. But a significant role is also played by the model of transition to adulthood prevailing in Roma communities living segregated in "nomad camps."

In these communities, boys and girls aged eleven and twelve are usually involved in income-generating activities such as begging or helping their parents by collecting scrap iron or garbage. Girls help their mothers by looking after younger siblings or performing housework. As a consequence, many of these boys and girls are exhausted when they are in school, have little time to do homework, and may even be discouraged or prevented from attending school at all.

Many Roma teenagers do not continue secondary school or vocational training because they get married and have children very early, usually before the age of eighteen and in some groups even at thirteen to fourteen years.[23] Having a child prevents not only the mothers but also the young fathers from going to school, because they must immediately earn money to feed the child. Even before marriage, in some very traditional Roma families, unmarried girls after puberty are prevented from finishing primary school because they are considered adult women who must be protected from any contact with unrelated boys and men.[24]

How do the authorities react to this serious violation of the fundamental right to education? All too often teachers and school directors do not report the Roma students' prolonged absence to the competent authorities, even though the law imposes on them the duty to do so. Social services officials and judges, too, often fail to act. The widespread idea is that not attending school, early marriage, and child labor are all part of the "Gypsies' culture": therefore any intervention to promote the right to education of Roma teenagers is considered useless, or, worse still, disrespectful of their culture.

This kind of approach is clearly illustrated by a letter sent by a nongovernmental organization (NGO) working in a "nomad camp" in Turin to a school director, aimed at justifying a Roma girl's failure to attend the last year of elementary school: "Due to cultural reasons, Jadranka's parents won't be able to send their child to school next year, because it is not 'proper,' according to the cultural codes of the group, that a child of her age still goes to school, since it would embarrass the whole family."

Although in the last decades Italian authorities have carried out a number of projects to promote Roma children's right to education in precompulsory (or preschool) and primary school, almost no attention has been devoted to teenagers belonging to this ethnic minority. Initiatives aimed at supporting Roma boys and girls aged sixteen and seventeen in completing compulsory schooling or attending vocational training are very rare. Roma teenagers are treated as if they were adults, not entitled to the same rights as their non-Roma peers. They are "trapped" in their culture by the majority society: if you are Roma, the prevailing attitude seems to be, you are not allowed to claim your adolescence.

> I met Romina and Cosmin when they were sixteen years old. They lived with their families in a shack and a caravan (trailer) in an unauthorized settlement on a riverbank. Both had stopped attending school before finishing middle school. Cosmin barely knew how to read and write. He helped his father collect and sell objects thrown in garbage cans, while Romina helped her mother look after her four younger sisters. Both earned some money begging and washing car

windscreens (windshields) at crossroads. Neither social services nor any other authority even noticed that: for them, apparently, it was just two Roma youth doing what are considered "Romani activities." Like an ineluctable destiny.

At the beginning of the 2010–11 school year, an NGO proposed that Cosmin and Romina attend an adult school and a vocational training course: if they attended regularly, they would receive a small scholarship each month. With great effort and commitment, they managed to finish compulsory schooling and the vocational training course, Cosmin as a mechanic, Romina as a barmaid. They were the first adolescents in their unauthorized camp to accomplish that result.

In autumn 2011, when they were seventeen, the young couple asked me to be a witness at their wedding. At first I thought, "No, they are just children! It is even illegal. I cannot support and encourage them in that!" Then I had the opposite reaction: "Getting married and having babies before the age of eighteen is part of their culture, who am I to question that?" Finally, I just thought that Romina and Cosmin were in love, they could not have sexual relations before marriage, and they really wanted to marry: so I decided to be their witness. But we talked at length about the importance of their finishing the apprenticeship and finding a job, before having a baby.

One year and a half after the wedding, Cosmin has resumed selling secondhand objects, while Romina is finishing her apprenticeship in a bar and is very appreciated by the employer. They will have a baby in a few months. Romina hopes to be hired by the bar, as soon as she finishes breast-feeding.

Perhaps their child will be able to enjoy the rights that Romina and Cosmin were deprived of, those rights that must be ensured to every child and adolescent.

Toward an Intercultural and Participatory Approach

Both ethnocentrism and extreme cultural relativism prevent the authorities from effectively protecting the rights of teenagers belonging to minority groups.

As the case of unaccompanied minors coming from rural Albania demonstrates, the different model of transition to adulthood that many of these teenagers and their families hold needs to be taken into account in order to understand their needs and wishes. This is particularly important when authorities have to balance different rights in the assessment of the best interests of the child (such as the right to family unity, on the one hand, and the rights to development and to participation, on the other, in the case of return decisions).

Not all values and norms are acceptable, however, just because they are part of a different culture. There is a set of fundamental human rights that are universal and must be guaranteed for every human being. When sociocultural norms produce a violation of these rights, they must be questioned. Although the precise definition of this set of universal rights is highly controversial, some should undoubtedly be included, such as the right to protection from violence, mistreatment, and abuse, as well as the rights to health and to primary education. For example, parental expectations that their children contribute to the family's income cannot justify the fact that very young children, even below the age of ten, are involved in work and, in the case of immigrant children, that they are separated from their families, nor that children and adolescents are denied the right to complete compulsory schooling.[25] Similarly, it cannot be accepted as "culturally legitimated" that Roma girls are married off by their families and have babies at the age of thirteen or fourteen, since such early pregnancies put at risk both the mother's and the baby's health. As regards the minimum age for admission to employment, compulsory education, and the marriageable age, there are also specific legal provisions that cannot be violated in order to respect someone's culture or private life.

Taking into consideration the different models of transition to adulthood existing in minority groups does not mean that teenagers belonging to these groups can be treated as adults. Up to the age of eighteen every individual must be entitled to the rights provided by the UN CRC. The question, here, is not *whether* to apply the Convention, but *how* to apply it most effectively, particularly in cases where different rights provided by the CRC cannot be equally protected at the same time and authorities have to make difficult choices, balancing different rights.

As the previous chapter clearly notes, this approach requires a lot of flexibility on the part of institutions and the ability to find innovative solutions, so as to protect as much as possible the rights of the concerned minors. For instance, when authorities decide that an unaccompanied minor should stay in the host country, they should at the same time provide support to ensure that he or she can keep in contact with their family of origin. Similarly, schools should ensure the right to education to those adolescents who work or have parental responsibilities, providing evening classes, ensuring that young mothers have the opportunity to breast-feed the baby at school, and so on.[26]

It is important to stress that models of transition to adulthood should not be simplistically identified just on the basis of nationality or ethnicity: quite different social norms, in fact, can be found in various groups within a country or ethnic group. The socioeconomic conditions, as well as the level of integration with the majority group, are critical. Thus, for example, Albanian unaccompanied children coming from well-off urban families, as well as Roma teenagers living in nonsegregated neighborhoods in Italian cities, are treated by their families and communities and perceive themselves as "adolescents," quite similarly to Italian non-Roma adolescents.

Moreover, norms related to age statuses and life course calendars, like any other social norm, are not immutable and rigid. They can change when individuals come into contact with different models (either directly or through the media) or, even more, when socioeconomic conditions vary at the macro or micro level. In fact, effective policies aimed at fighting poverty and discrimination and at promoting adult employment are key to ensuring, in the mid- and long-term, that no teenager is prevented from fully enjoying adolescent rights. When parents get an adequately paid job, for instance, the pressure on children to work decreases. Similarly, the marriage age tends to increase when Roma people are less discriminated against in the job market: the investment in education becomes more attractive if they have prospects that it will produce better employment opportunities and that they will not be thwarted by pervasive discrimination against their ethnic group.

Finally, individuals should never be mechanically assigned to a cultural model. Every child and adolescent must be considered and listened to as an individual; his or her opinions should be seriously taken into account. Individuals' and particularly teenagers' wishes and points of view are often different from those of their families and other community members. These differences may produce conflicts with the parents as well as self-identity problems, since the child may feel he or she is falling short of family and social expectations. For instance, unaccompanied migrant children and Roma adolescents who wish to attend secondary school are often discouraged by their families and peers. The parents do not want to lose the income provided by their children and blame them for their ingratitude and lack of support. Friends who earn money or already have babies deride and despise their wish to study, saying that attending secondary school is useless, selfish, or "non-Roma-like." It is crucial that authorities assist these adolescents, providing material support such as scholarships, but also supporting them in negotiating—with their families and communities, as well as within themselves—the burden of responsibilities placed upon their shoulders. This is the only way to ensure that they are at least partially relieved from these responsibilities and finally given an opportunity to live their adolescence.

It is not easy to find a balance between universalism and relativism, to build an intercultural approach, where sociocultural differences are respected (unlike in ethnocentrism) but do not lead to violations of fundamental human and child rights (unlike in extreme cultural relativism). Applying this approach, with careful attention to individual wishes and a constant commitment to ensuring equal opportunities to every minor, is even more difficult. But this effort is needed if we really want to protect and promote the rights of teenagers belonging to minority groups where adolescence does not exist.

Notes

1. On the social definition of age and the transition to adulthood, see Saraceno (2001); Cavalli and Galland (1996).

2. I refer to a broad notion of "marriage," including any form of establishing a new family, even though not legally recognized.

3. Adolescence is very difficult to define, for several reasons, including the transitional nature of this life stage and its high variability according to historical periods and societies. UNICEF defines adolescents as individuals aged ten to nineteen. I refer here to a sociological definition of adolescence, not just based on the biological age, but on the behaviors and attitudes that are socially expected, and in particular the responsibilities and rights assigned to individuals of that age.

4. An exception to this general rule is provided for "apprenticeship," which is a special kind of contract aimed at training and employment of youth: adolescents can be employed through "apprenticeship" from the age of fifteen.

5. It must be stressed, however, that a high percentage of the enrolled students drop out before the end of secondary education (in 2009, the percentage of early school leavers in Italy was 19.2 percent) or before finishing university.

6. Estimates on child labor in Italy significantly vary: from 140,000 children aged seven to fourteen (Istat 2002) compared with 465,000 to 500,000 children aged ten to fourteen (IRES-CGIL 2005).

7. Since then, the global economic crisis has significantly raised the youth unemployment rate.

8. Italy is the EU country with the highest proportion of young adults (aged twenty-five to twenty-nine) living with at least one parent, after Malta. The lowest proportion is found in France, the Netherlands, and Finland, where not more than 15 percent of young adults live with their parent(s). The EU average is 34 percent (41 percent for men and 26 percent for women) (Eurostat 2011, 73–74).

9. These interview excerpts, as well as the following stories and analysis, are drawn from two field research studies I conducted; one on unaccompanied children in 2000 for my MBA thesis, and the other on Roma children in 2009–10, as part of a research project funded by the Compagnia di San Paolo Foundation and the Social Sciences Department of Turin University.

10. When referring to individuals aged thirteen to eighteen belonging to groups where adolescence is not socially defined as a separate life stage, I will use the term "teenager" or "minor," terms that are based only on biological age and have no social implications, in order to avoid confusion with the sociological meaning of "adolescent." As I will further clarify below, the choice not to use the term "adolescent" does not imply that the individuals in question should be treated as adults: up to the age of eighteen every individual must be entitled to the rights provided by the UN CRC.

11. Ethnocentrism was defined by William Graham Sumner as that "view of things in which one's own group is the center of everything, and all others are scaled and rated with reference to it" (Sumner 1906, 13).

12. Cultural relativism is the principle that an individual's beliefs and activities are understood by others in terms of that individual's own culture. I mean by "extreme cultural relativism" what is also defined as "moral relativism," namely the idea that all value systems are equally valid and there are no universal moral standards.

13. All the names cited in the chapter are fictitious.

14. Secondary school education and vocational training are much more accessible in Italian cities than in poor countries' rural areas. Moreover, even though most unaccompanied minors wish to start work as soon as they arrive in Italy, they are required to finish compulsory education before being regularly employed.

15. Participation is defined by the CRC as the right of the child to express his or her views freely in all matters affecting him or her, those views being given due weight in accordance with the age and maturity of the child (CRC art. 12).

16. Of course this contradiction may be solved by allowing the child's family to enter the host country, but this is usually not considered as an option, since interests in migration control override considerations of the best interests of the child.

17. It does not mean that these minors were just like adults: they had protection needs and they missed their parents; moreover, they also had wishes similar to Italian adolescents, such as buying mobile phones, fashionable sneakers, and so on. But the responsibility toward their families usually prevailed. This was true for the Albanian

unaccompanied children arriving in that period from rural areas, as well as for some other groups of unaccompanied minors, but it cannot be generalized: in other groups, the reasons for migration, attitudes, and wishes can be quite different.

18. Some municipalities and police authorities pressed the Committee for Foreign Minors for a higher number of repatriations, aimed at migration control, but the Committee generally opposed this kind of pressure. I think that the above mentioned returns were mainly based on an inadequate assessment of the best interests of the child, rather than on migration control considerations. The Committee has, for the past few years, stated that no assisted repatriation can be ordered when the unaccompanied child is against it.

19. Large "nomad camps" have been established by Italian municipalities since the end of the 1970s in order to guarantee the right of Roma to a nomadic life style; nowadays, however, people living in these camps are mostly permanently settled. Besides authorized camps, a large number of unauthorized settlements have appeared in the last decades. The Roma living in both authorized and unauthorized camps are partly Italian citizens and partly immigrants from Romania and from the former Yugoslavia.

20. An estimated 47 percent are between the age of six and fourteen; 23 percent are between fifteen and eighteen (Commissione straordinaria 2011, 17-18, 45). The criteria used in both estimating the Roma population in Italy and in collecting data concerning Roma students are unclear.

21. Data collected by the Turin Municipality.

22. Commissione straordinaria 2011, 61-72; UNAR 2012, 51-56; ECRI 2012; Saletti Salza 2003.

23. These marriages are illegal since according to Italian law the marriageable age is eighteen; in exceptional cases, for serious reasons, the court can authorize the marriage of a minor aged sixteen.

24. Of course, besides models of transition to adulthood, norms regulating gender issues are even more relevant here.

25. This is particularly true in a rich country such as Italy, where even unemployed, destitute parents are usually able to secure at least nutrition and clothing to their children, thanks to the support provided by public services, charities, and NGOs or just by begging and collecting secondhand clothes, unsold food in markets, and so forth. Thus parents cannot argue that their children are not able to go to school and need to work in order to survive. In many poor countries, on the contrary, children can satisfy these basic needs only by working: in these situations, balancing the rights to education and to protection from child labor against the right to a minimum standard of living, or even to survival, is much more complex.

26. Although very rare, there are some good examples of these kinds of initiatives.

References

Ariès, Philippe. 1960. *L'Enfant et la vie familiale sous l'Ancien Régime*. Paris: Librairie Plon.

Bichi, Rita, ed. 2008. *Separated Children: I minori stranieri non accompagnati*. Milan: Franco Angeli.
Cavalli, Alessandro, and Olivier Galland, eds. 1996. *Senza fretta di crescere: L'ingresso difficile nella vita adulta*. Napoli: Liguori Editore.
Commissione straordinaria per la tutela e la promozione dei diritti umani del Senato della Repubblica. 2011. *Rapporto conclusivo dell'indagine sulla condizione di Rom, Sinti e Caminanti in Italia*. Rome. http://www.senato.it/documenti/repository/commissioni/dirittiumani16/Rapporto%20conclusivo%20indagine%20rom,%20sinti%20e%20caminanti.pdf.
Di Bello, Giulia, and Vanna Nuti. 2001. *Soli per il mondo: Bambine e bambini emigranti tra Otto e Novecento*. Milan: Edizioni Unicopli.
ECRI. 2012. *Report on Italy*. Strasbourg. http://www.coe.int/t/dghl/monitoring/ecri/Country-by-country/Italy/ITA-CbC-IV-2012-002-ENG.pdf.
Eurostat. 2011. *Demography Report 2010*. http://epp.eurostat.ec.europa.eu/cache/ITY_OFFPUB/KE-ET-10-001/EN/KE-ET-10-001-EN.PDF.
Giovannetti, Monia. 2008. *L'accoglienza incompiuta*. Bologna: Il Mulino.
Istat. 2002. *Bambini, lavori e lavoretti: Verso un sistema informativo sul lavoro minorile*. Rome. http://www3.istat.it/istat/eventi/2002/lavorominorile/minori.pdf.
———. 2010. *Indicatori demografici 2009*. Rome. http://demo.istat.it/altridati/matrimoni/2009/tav1_4.pdf.
———. 2011. *Annuario statistico 2011*. Rome. http://www3.istat.it/dati/catalogo/20111216_00/contenuti.html.
"Mandiamo i bamboccioni fuori di casa." 2007. *Corriere della Sera*, October 4. http://www.corriere.it/politica/07_ottobre_04/padoa_bamboccioni.shtml.
Ministero del Lavoro e delle Politiche Sociali. 2010. *I giovani in Italia*. Rome. http://www.lavoro.gov.it/NR/rdonlyres/23D27DC8-8CAE-4D52-81F1-66811C7EE36C/0/I_GIOVANI_IN_ITALIA.pdf.
Ministero dell'Istruzione, dell'Università e della Ricerca. 2009. "Gli alunni stranieri nel sistema scolastico italiano—a.s. 2008/9." Rome.
Mitterauer, Michael. 1991. *I giovani in Europa dal Medioevo a oggi*. Bari: Laterza.
Musgrove, Frank. 1965. *Youth and the Social Order*. Bloomington: Indiana University Press.
Saletti Salza, Carlotta. 2003. *Bambini del "campo nomadi": Romá Bosniaci a Torino*. Rome: CISU.
Saraceno, Chiara, ed. 2001. *Età e corso della vita*. Bologna: Il Mulino.
Servizio Sociale Internazionale Sezione Italiana and Istituto Psicanalitico per le Ricerche Sociali. 2001. *I minori albanesi non accompagnati: Una ricerca coordinata fra Italia e Albania*. 35–51. Rome: SSISI.
Sumner, William Graham. 1906. *Folkways: A Study of the Sociological Importance of Usages, Manners, Customs, Mores, and Morals*. Boston: Ginn and Co.

UNAR. 2012. *Strategia nazionale d'inclusione dei Rom, dei Sinti e dei Caminanti.* Rome.
UNICEF. 2000. *Albania Multiple Indicator Cluster Survey 2 (MICS 2).* http://www.ucw-project.org/Pages/Tables.aspx?id=167.
———. 2001. *The State of the World's Children 2002: Leadership.* New York.

CHAPTER 3

The Science of Adolescent Brain Development and Its Implications for Adolescent Rights and Responsibilities

Laurence Steinberg

As a transitional period between childhood and adulthood, adolescence is the stage of development that is most affected by age-specific regulations that define the rights and responsibilities reserved for adult members of the community. Drawing legal or social distinctions between adolescents and adults is a universal phenomenon, found in every culture ever studied by social scientists (Schlegel 2009). The law defines adolescents, or some portion of adolescents, either as children, who are viewed as vulnerable, dependent, and lacking the competence to make responsible decisions, or as adults, who are viewed as "autonomous citizens responsible for their own conduct, entitled to legal rights and privileges, and no longer entitled to protections" (Woolard and Scott 2009, 345). But, as the two preceding chapters note, where this chronological dividing line is drawn varies considerably across policy domain, locale, and historical time.

In contemporary American society, the range of ages used to determine when adolescents are children and when they are adults is wide. Individuals can be tried in adult court at fourteen in most states (and in some states, at an even younger age for a serious violent felony) but cannot purchase alcohol until they are twenty-one. Between these two extremes are a variety of different ages used to determine when individuals can make autonomous medical decisions, drive, hold various types of employment, marry, view R-rated movies without an adult chaperone, vote, serve in the military, enter into contracts, and purchase tobacco. Whether, how, to what extent, and to what end neuroscience should inform social policies that distinguish between adolescents and adults under the law is an important question.

Interest in whether adolescents are as mature as adults has been rekindled during the past decade by the rapid expansion of knowledge about adolescent brain development. Articles in the popular press describe the teenage brain as a "work in progress," often leading the public to wonder whether the rights and responsibilities we grant young people are correctly synched with their neurobiological maturity. News-magazine cover stories on the prolonged maturation of the prefrontal cortex (for example, Wallis 2004) have generated considerable interest, and public awareness of this phenomenon is widespread. A cartoon in the *New Yorker* depicts parents disciplining their teenage son, ordering him to go to his room "until his cerebral cortex matures" (Smaller 2006).

Explicit reference to the neuroscience of adolescence is slowly creeping into legal and policy discussions as well as into popular culture, most explicitly in recent cases involving the constitutionality of the juvenile death penalty (*Roper v. Simmons* 2005) and life without parole for juveniles convicted of serious crimes other than homicide (*Graham v. Florida* 2010). In each case, advocates for young people drew on the science of brain development to support the argument that adolescents' developmental immaturity—neurobiological as well as psychological—diminished their criminal responsibility and, accordingly, the appropriateness of punishments reserved for individuals convicted of the most serious of crimes (Scott and Steinberg 2008).

Although the Supreme Court's opinion in *Roper*, which abolished the juvenile death penalty, did not specifically cite any developmental neuroscience, it is likely that the justices were influenced by this evidence, given that several of the amicus curiae briefs submitted in the case, including that of the American Psychological Association, drew the justices' attention to that body of research:

> Why do adolescents show differences from adults with respect to risk-taking, planning, inhibiting impulses, and generating alternatives? Recent research suggests a biological dimension to adolescent behavioral immaturity: the human brain does not settle into its mature, adult form until after the adolescent years have passed and a person has entered young adulthood. . . . Of particular interest with

regard to decision-making and criminal culpability is the development of the frontal lobes of the brain. The frontal lobes, especially the prefrontal cortex, play a critical role in the executive or "CEO" functions of the brain which are considered the higher functions of the brain. . . . They are involved when an individual plans and implements goal-directed behaviors by selecting, coordinating, and applying the cognitive skills necessary to accomplish the goal. Neurodevelopmental MRI studies indicate this executive area of the brain is one of the last parts of the brain to reach maturity.

(American Psychological Association 2004, 9–10)

Five years later, in *Graham*, neuroscience was again highlighted in several amicus briefs and was referenced explicitly by Justice Anthony Kennedy in his majority opinion, prohibiting the use of life without parole as a sentence for juveniles convicted of nonhomicides: "No recent data provide reason to reconsider the Court's observations in Roper about the nature of juveniles. . . . Developments in psychology and brain science continue to show fundamental differences between juvenile and adult minds. For example, parts of the brain involved in behavior control continue to mature through late adolescence" (*Graham v. Florida* 17).

Continuing this trend, the same amici who authored briefs in *Roper* and *Graham* drew the Court's attention to the latest developments in adolescent brain science in briefs submitted in *Miller v. Alabama* and *Jackson v. Hobbs*, two cases that the Court heard in 2012, on the constitutionality of life without parole as a sentence for juveniles convicted of homicide:

Neuroscientists continue to accumulate evidence that the adolescent brain is not yet fully developed in critical respects. By now, "[T]here is incontrovertible evidence of significant changes in brain structure and function during adolescence," and "Although most of this work has appeared just in the last 10 years, there is already strong consensus among developmental neuroscientists about the nature" of these changes. While research continues into the precise meaning and effect of the changes in the brain during adolescence, they are consistent with and suggest the possible physiological basis for adolescents' observed psychosocial immaturity.

(American Psychological Association 2012, 25)

The use of brain science to buttress arguments derived mainly from behavioral research is a growing trend worth exploring in some detail, especially in view of reservations raised by both scientists (Steinberg 2012) and legal scholars (for example, Maroney 2010) about the privileged status that the legal community appears to give neuroscientific accounts of adolescent immaturity. Consider, for instance, the following exchange during oral arguments in *Roper* between Justice Stephen Breyer and Seth Waxman, the attorney arguing in favor of the juvenile death penalty's abolition:

> Justice Breyer: Now, I thought that the—the scientific evidence simply corroborated something that every parent already knows, and if it's more than that, I would like to know what more.
> Mr. Waxman: Well, it's—I think it's—it's more than that in a couple of respects. It—it explains, corroborates, and validates what we sort of intuitively know, not just as parents but in adults that— that—who live in a world filled with adolescents. And—and the very fact that science—*and I'm not just talking about social science here, but the important neurobiological science* that has now shown that these adolescents are—their character is not hard-wired.
> (U.S. Supreme Court 2004, 40, italics added).

The implication in Waxman's response—that social science is "just" social science, but that neurobiological science is "important"—is consistent with recent studies of what has been called "the seductive allure of neuroscience explanations" (Weisberg et al. 2008). Individuals are more likely to view the results of behavioral research as credible when neuroscience evidence is attached to the social science account. In one widely cited study, when presented with sensible accounts of psychological phenomena, subjects were equally satisfied regardless of whether the explanations referred to the brain. But when presented with circular or otherwise logically suspect accounts, subjects were dissatisfied when the explanations did not contain information about the brain, but satisfied when they did (Weisberg et al. 2008).

Most individuals who care about the welfare of young people applauded the Court's decisions in *Roper* and *Graham*. For those in the youth advocacy community, however, the use of neuroscience to support arguments about the relative immaturity of adolescents is a double-edged sword. The same evidence that has been brought to bear on questions concerning the criminal culpability of youth has been used to argue for placing limits on adolescents' rights. Perhaps the most common application of brain science in this regard has been in calls for placing greater limits on adolescents' driving privileges (for example, Committee on Injury, Violence, and Poison Prevention and Committee on Adolescence 2009).

What Science Tells Us about Adolescent Brain Development

There is now incontrovertible evidence that adolescence is a period of significant changes in brain structure and function. Although most of this work has appeared just in the last fifteen years, there is already strong consensus among developmental neuroscientists about the nature of this change. And the most important conclusion to emerge from recent research is that important changes in brain anatomy and activity take place far longer into development than had been previously thought (Casey, Jones, and Somerville 2011). Reasonable people may disagree about what these findings tell us about how we should treat young people, but there is little room for disagreement about the fact that adolescence is a period of substantial brain maturation with respect to both structure and function.

Four specific structural changes in the brain during adolescence are noteworthy. First, there is a decrease in gray matter in prefrontal regions of the brain during adolescence, reflective of synaptic pruning, the process through which unused connections between neurons are eliminated (Gogtay and Thompson 2010). The elimination of these unused synapses occurs mainly during preadolescence and early adolescence, the period during which major improvements in basic cognitive abilities and logical reasoning are seen (Keating 2004), in part due to these very anatomical changes (Luciana et al. 2005; Giedd 2008).

Second, also occurring in early adolescence, especially around puberty, are important changes in activity involving the neurotransmitter dopamine (Spear 2009). There are substantial changes in the density and distribution of dopamine receptors in pathways that connect the limbic system, where emotions are processed and rewards and punishments experienced, and the prefrontal cortex, which is the brain's chief executive officer. There is more dopaminergic activity in these pathways during the first part of adolescence than at any other time in development (Galvan 2010). Because dopamine plays a critical role in our experience of pleasure, these changes have important implications for sensation-seeking, as I will explain later.

A third change in the brain's structure that occurs during adolescence is an increase in white matter in the prefrontal cortex. This is largely the result of myelination, the process through which nerve fibers become sheathed in myelin, a white, fatty substance that improves the efficiency of brain circuits. Unlike the synaptic pruning of the prefrontal areas, which is mainly finished by midadolescence, myelination continues well into late adolescence and early adulthood (Schmithorst and Yuan 2010). More efficient neural connections within the prefrontal cortex are important for higher-order cognitive functions regulated by multiple prefrontal areas working in concert—functions such as planning ahead, weighing risks and rewards, and making complicated decisions.

Finally, there is an increase in the strength of connections between the prefrontal cortex and the limbic system (Eluvathingal et al. 2007). This anatomical change is especially important for emotion regulation, which is facilitated by increased connectivity between regions important in the processing of emotional information and those important in self-control. These connections permit different brain systems to communicate with each other more effectively, gains that also are ongoing well into late adolescence. If you were to compare a young teenager's brain with that of a young adult, you would see a much more extensive network of myelinated cables connecting brain regions.

Adolescence is not just a time of tremendous change in the brain's structure. It is also a time of important changes in how the brain works, as revealed in studies using fMRI, or functional magnetic resonance imaging. What do these imaging studies tell us about the adolescent brain? First, over the course of adolescence and into early adulthood, there is a strengthening of activity in brain systems involving self-regulation (Luna, Padmanabhan, and O'Hearn 2010). During tasks that require self-control, adults employ a wider network of brain regions than do adolescents, which may make self-control easier, by distributing the work across multiple areas of the brain rather than overtaxing a smaller number of regions.

Second, there are important changes during adolescence in the way the brain responds to rewards. When one examines a brain scan acquired during a task in which individuals who are about to play a game are shown rewarding stimuli, like piles of coins or pictures of happy faces, it is usually found that adolescents' reward centers are activated more than are children's or adults' when they expect something pleasurable to happen (Galvan 2010). (Interestingly, these age differences are more consistently observed when individuals are anticipating rewards than when they are receiving them). Heightened sensitivity to anticipated rewards motivates adolescents to engage in acts, even risky acts, when the potential for pleasure is high, such as unprotected sex, fast driving, or experimentation with drugs. Jason Chein and I have shown that this hypersensitivity to reward is particularly pronounced when adolescents are with their friends, which we think helps explain why adolescent risk taking so often occurs in groups (Chein et al. 2011).

A third change in brain function over the course of adolescence involves increases in the simultaneous involvement of multiple brain regions in response to arousing stimuli, such as pictures of angry or terrified faces (Steinberg 2008). Before adulthood, there is less cross talk between the brain systems that regulate rational decision making and those that regulate emotional arousal. During adolescence, very strong feelings are less likely to be modulated by the involvement of brain regions involved in impulse control, planning ahead, and comparing the costs and benefits of alternative courses of action. This is one reason that susceptibility to peer pressure declines as adolescents grow into adulthood; as they mature, individuals become better able to put the brakes on an impulse that is aroused by their friends (Grosbras et al. 2007).

Importantly, these structural and functional changes do not all take place along one uniform timetable, and the differences in their timing raise two important points relevant to the use of neuroscience to guide law and public policy. First, there is no simple answer to the question of when an adolescent brain becomes an adult brain. Brain systems implicated in basic cognitive processes reach adult levels of maturity by midadolescence, whereas those that are active in self-regulation do not fully mature until late adolescence or even early adulthood. In other words, adolescents mature intellectually before they mature socially or emotionally, a fact that helps explain why teenagers who are so smart in some respects sometimes do surprisingly dumb things (Steinberg et al. 2009).

To the extent that we wish to rely on developmental neuroscience to inform where we draw age boundaries between adolescence and adulthood for purposes of public policy, it is therefore important to match the policy question with the right science. In his dissenting opinion in *Roper*, the juvenile death penalty case, Justice Antonin Scalia criticized the American

Psychological Association, which submitted an amicus brief arguing that adolescents are not as mature as adults, and therefore are too immature to be eligible for the juvenile death penalty. As Justice Scalia pointed out, the same organization had previously taken the stance, in *Hodgson v. Minnesota* (1990), that adolescents should be permitted to make decisions about abortion without involving their parents, on the grounds that young people's decision making is just as competent as that of adults.

These two positions may seem inconsistent at first glance, but it is entirely possible that an adolescent might be mature enough for some decisions but not others (Steinberg et al. 2009). After all, the circumstances under which individuals make medical decisions and commit crimes are very different and make different sorts of demands on individuals' brains and abilities. State laws governing adolescent abortion require a waiting period before the procedure can be performed as well as consultation with an adult—a parent, health-care provider, or judge. These policies discourage impetuous and short-sighted acts and create circumstances under which adolescents' decision making has been shown to be just as competent as that demonstrated by adults. In contrast, violent crimes are usually committed by adolescents when they are emotionally aroused and with their friends—two conditions that increase the likelihood of impulsivity and sensation-seeking, and that exacerbate adolescent immaturity. From a neuroscientific standpoint, it therefore makes perfect sense to have a lower age for autonomous medical decision making than for eligibility for capital punishment, because certain brain systems mature earlier than others.

There is another kind of asynchrony in brain development during adolescence that is important for law and public policy. Middle adolescence is a period during which brain systems implicated in our responses to rewards are at their height of arousability but when systems important for self-regulation are still immature. The different timetables followed by these different brain systems create a vulnerability to risky and reckless behavior that is greater in middle adolescence than before or after (Steinberg 2008). It is as if the brain's accelerator is pressed to the floor before a good braking system is in place. Given this, it is no surprise that crime peaks during middle and late adolescence—as do first experimentation with alcohol and marijuana (Substance Abuse and Mental Health Services Administration 2012), automobile crashes (Simons-Morton et al. 2011), accidental drownings (Centers for Disease Control and Prevention 2011), and attempted suicide (Kessler, Borges, and Waters 1999).

In sum, the consensus to emerge from recent research on the adolescent brain is that teenagers are not as mature in either brain structure or function as adults. This does not mean that adolescents' brains are "defective," any more than we would say that newborns' muscular systems are "defective" because they are not capable of walking or that their language systems are "defective" because they can't yet carry on conversations. The fact that the adolescent brain is still developing, and in this regard is less mature than the adult brain, is normative, not pathological. Adolescence is a developmental stage, not a disease, mental illness, or defect. But it is a time when people are, on average, not as mature as they will be when they become adults.

Implications of Brain Science for Our Understanding of Adolescent Behavior

Although there is a good degree of consensus among neuroscientists about many of the ways in which brain structure and function change during adolescence, it is less clear just how informative this work is about adolescent behavior. Because all behavior must have neurobiological underpinnings, it is hardly revelatory to say that adolescents behave the way they do because of "something in their brain." Moreover, we hardly need neuroscience to tell us that, relative to adults, adolescents are more likely to engage in sensation-seeking, less likely to control their impulses, or less likely to plan ahead—observations about young people that were made by Aristotle nearly twenty-five hundred years ago (Aristotle 1954 [350 B.C.]). So how does neuroscience add to our understanding of adolescent behavior? What is the value, other than advances in basic neuroscience, of studies that provide neurobiological evidence that is consistent with what we already know about human behavior? I'd like to consider four such possibilities, two that I think are specious, and two that I think are reasonable.

The first mistake is to interpret age differences in brain structure or function as conclusive evidence that the relevant behaviors must therefore be hard-wired. A correlation between brain and behavioral development is just that: a correlation. It tells us nothing about the causes of the behavior or about the relative contributions of nature and nurture. In some cases, the behavior may indeed follow directly from biologically driven changes in brain structure or function. But in others the reverse is true; that is, the observed brain change is the consequence of experience. Adolescents may develop better impulse control as a result of changes within the prefrontal cortex, and it may be true that these anatomical changes are programmed to unfold along a predetermined timetable. But it is also plausible that the structural changes observed in the prefrontal cortex result from experiences that demand that adolescents exercise self-control, in much the same way that changes in muscle structure and function often follow from exercise (Bengtsson et al. 2005; Crone 2009; Takeuchi et al. 2011).

A second mistake is assuming that the existence of a biological correlate of some behavior demonstrates that the behavior cannot be changed. It is surely the case that some of the changes in brain structure and function that take place during adolescence are relatively impervious to environmental influence. But we also know that the brain is malleable, or plastic, and there is a good deal of evidence that adolescence in fact is a period of especially heightened neuroplasticity, which makes it a period of such vulnerability to many forms of mental illness (Steinberg et al. 2006).

How, then, does neuroscience contribute to a better understanding of adolescent behavior? First, and perhaps most important, neuroscientific evidence can provide added support for behavioral evidence when the neuroscience and the behavioral science are conceptually and theoretically aligned. Because scientific evidence of any sort is always more compelling when it has been shown to be valid, when neuroscientific findings about adolescent brain development are consistent with findings from behavioral research, the neuroscience gives us added confidence in the behavioral findings. But it is incorrect, as is frequently done, to privilege the neuroscientific evidence over the behavioral evidence. In science, familiarity breeds skepticism, and the lack of knowledge that most laypersons have about the workings of the brain, much less the nuances of neuroscientific methods, often leads them to be overly impressed by brain science and underwhelmed by behavioral research, even when the latter may be more relevant to policy decisions.

Second, neuroscience can help us in making attributions about individuals' behavior, an application that is beginning to have an impact on the practice of criminal law. I recently was asked to provide an expert opinion in a Michigan case involving a seventeen-year-old named Anthony who was part of a group of teenagers who robbed a small store. During the robbery, one of the teenagers shot and killed the storekeeper. Although the teenagers had planned the robbery, they did not engage in the act with the intention of shooting, much less murdering, someone. But under the state's criminal law, the crime qualified as felony murder, which in Michigan carries a mandatory sentence of life without the possibility of parole for all members of the group involved in the robbery—including Anthony, who had fled the store before the shooting took place.

At issue now is a challenge by Anthony—who has been in prison for thirty-three years—to vacate the sentence in light of the Supreme Court's ruling in *Graham* that life without parole is cruel and unusual punishment for juveniles convicted of crimes other than homicide. The challenge to Michigan's law is based on the argument that the logic behind the *Graham* decision applies to felony murder as well.

I was asked specifically whether a seventeen-year-old could have anticipated that someone might be killed during the robbery. It is quite clear from the trial transcript that Anthony *didn't* anticipate this consequence, but *didn't* isn't the same as *couldn't*. Studies of adolescent brain development might be helpful in distinguishing between the two.

There was no doubt that Anthony was guilty of the crime with which he was charged. But even when someone is found guilty, many factors can influence the sentence he receives. Generally speaking, individuals who are deemed less than fully responsible are punished less severely than those who are judged to be fully responsible, even if the consequences of the act are identical (Bonnie et al. 1997). The question in Anthony's case, as it was in *Roper* and in *Graham*, is whether seventeen-year-olds are fully responsible for their behavior. If they are not, they should not be punished as severely as individuals whose responsibility is not diminished.

In order for something to diminish criminal responsibility, it has to be something that was outside the individual's control (Morse 2000). If someone has an untreatable tumor on his frontal lobe that is thought to make him unable to control aggressive outbursts, he is less than fully responsible for his aggressive behavior as a result of something that isn't his fault, and the presence of the tumor would be viewed as a mitigating factor if he were being sentenced for a violent crime. On the other hand, if someone with no neurobiological deficit goes into a bar, drinks himself into a state of rage, and commits a violent crime as a result, the fact that he was drunk does not diminish his responsibility for his act. It doesn't matter whether the mitigating factor is biological, psychological, or environmental. The issue is whether the diminished responsibility is the person's fault and whether the individual could have compensated for whatever it is that was uncontrollable.

Judgments about mitigation are often difficult to make because most of the time factors that diminish responsibility fall somewhere between the extremes of factors that are obviously beyond an individual's control, like brain tumors, and those that an individual could have controlled, like self-inflicted inebriation. In many cases, things are not so clear-cut. One must make a judgment call, and one looks for evidence that tips the balance in one direction or the other. Profound mental retardation that compromises foresight is a mitigating condition. A lack of foresight as a result of stupidity that is within the normal range of intelligence is not. Being forced to commit a crime because a gun is pointed at one's head mitigates criminal responsibility. Committing a crime in order to save face in front of friends who have made a dare does not.

As I have discussed, studies of adolescent brain anatomy clearly indicate that regions of the brain that regulate phenomena such as foresight, impulse control, and resistance to peer pressure are still developing at age seventeen. And imaging studies show that immaturity in these regions is linked to adolescents' poorer performance on tasks that require these capabilities. Evidence that the adolescent brain is less mature than the adult brain in ways that impact some of the behaviors that mitigate criminal responsibility suggests that at least some of adolescents' irresponsible behavior is not entirely their fault.

The brain science, in and of itself, does not carry the day, but when we add it to the behavioral science, it tips the balance toward viewing adolescent impulsivity, short-sightedness, and susceptibility to peer pressure as developmentally normative phenomena that teenagers cannot fully control. This is why my colleagues and I have argued that adolescents should be viewed as inherently less responsible than adults, and should be punished less harshly than adults, even when the crimes they are convicted of are identical (Steinberg and Scott 2003). I do not find persuasive the counterargument that some adolescents are able to exercise self-control, or that some adults are just as impulsive and short-sighted as teenagers. Of course there is variability in brain and behavior among adolescents, and of course there is variability among adults. But the average differences between the age groups are significant, and that is what counts if we are drawing age boundaries under the law on the basis of science.

Brain Science and Boundary Drawing

Beyond criminal law, how might social policy involving young people take adolescent brain science into account? Science may be able to help us decide where best to draw the lines between people who are ready for the rights and responsibilities of adulthood and those who are not.

Let us assume that there is an age range during which adult neurobiological maturity is usually reached. (It is useful to frame this as an age range, rather than pinpointing a discrete chronological age, because doing so accommodates the fact that different brain systems mature along different timetables, and different individuals mature at different ages and different rates.) Research on brain development suggests that the lower bound of this age range is probably somewhere around fifteen years. In other words, if we had an agreed-upon measure of adult neurobiological maturity (which we don't yet have, but may at some point in the future), it would be highly unlikely that we would find many individuals who would have attained this mark before turning fifteen (Casey et al. 2005). Science also suggests that the upper bound of the age range is probably somewhere around twenty-two years (Dosenbach et al. 2010). That is, it would be unlikely that we would find many normally developing individuals who have not reached adult neurobiological maturity by the time they have turned twenty-two.

If we were to choose either of these endpoints as the legal age of majority, we would be forced to accept many errors of classification, because granting adult status universally at age fifteen would result in our treating many immature individuals as adults, which is dangerous, whereas drawing the boundary at twenty-two would result in treating many mature individuals as children, which is unjust. So what are we to do? I think there are four possibilities.

The first is that we pick the midpoint of this range. We would end up misclassifying some immature individuals as adults and some mature ones as children, but this is true no matter what chronological age we pick, or on what basis we pick it, and assuming that the age of neurobiological maturity is normally distributed (an untested assumption, but a reasonable one), we would make fewer errors by picking an age near the middle of the range than we would at either of the extremes. Doing so would place the dividing line somewhere around eighteen, which, as it turns out, is the presumptive age of majority pretty much everywhere around the world. In the vast majority of countries, eighteen is the age at which individuals are permitted to vote, drink, drive, and enjoy other adult rights. Thus, the presumptive age of majority in most countries is strikingly consistent with modern developmental neuroscience—despite the fact that this age was arrived at without the benefit of brain imaging.

A second possibility would be to decide, on an issue-by-issue basis, what it takes to be "mature enough" to satisfy society's needs for laws that are practical as well as just. We do this regularly in the United States, and much more so than in most other countries. Although the presumptive age of majority in America is eighteen, we deviate from this age more often than we adhere to it. Consider, for a moment, the different ages we use to draw age boundaries for different purposes. As I noted earlier, the age of majority with respect to various matters ranges from fifteen (driving in several states) to twenty-one (purchasing alcohol); again, the law here is surprisingly consistent with what we know about brain development. The only deviation that falls out of this range is our inexplicable willingness under criminal law to try people younger than fifteen as adults, but, in part because of the influence of brain science, treating young adolescents as adults is a policy that is now being questioned, not only in the Supreme Court, but in many jurisdictions around the country.

A third possibility would be to shift from a binary classification system, in which everyone is legally either a child or an adult, to a regime that uses three legal categories: one for children, one for adolescents, and one for adults (Zimring 1982). We do this for some purposes under the law now, although the age boundaries around the middle category aren't necessarily scientifically derived. For example, many states have graduated drivers' licensing, a system in which adolescents are permitted to drive but not granted full driving privileges until they reach a certain age. We use this model in the construction of child labor laws, where we let adolescents work in the formal labor force once they've reached a certain age, but place limits on the types of jobs they can hold and the numbers of hours they can work until they reach adulthood. In our book, *Rethinking Juvenile Justice*, Elizabeth Scott and I (2008) have argued that this is how we should structure the justice system, treating adolescent offenders as an intermediate category, neither as children, whose crimes we excuse, nor adults, who are held fully responsible for their acts.

A final possibility is acknowledging that there is variability in brain and behavioral development among people of the same chronological age and make individualized decisions rather than drawing categorical age boundaries at all. This was the stance taken by many of the Supreme Court justices who dissented in *Roper* and in *Graham*. They argued that, instead of treating adolescents as a class of individuals who are too immature to be held fully responsible for their behavior, we assess each offender's maturity to determine his criminal culpability. The justices did not specify what tools we would need to do this, however, and reliably assessing psychological maturity is easier said than done. Using neuroscience to guide the formulation of policy and using it to determine how individual cases are adjudicated is not the same thing. Although we may be able to say that, on average, *people who are Johnny's age* are typically less mature than adults, we cannot say whether *Johnny* himself is. We may someday have the tools to image an adolescent's brain and draw conclusions about that individual's neurobiological maturity relative to established age norms for various aspects of brain structure and function, but such norms do not yet exist, and the cost of doing individualized assessments of neurobiological maturity would be prohibitively expensive.

Moreover, there is some evidence that factors that have nothing to do with actual maturity, such as race, influence individuals' judgments; in one study, in which subjects read crime scenarios involving teenagers after half of the subjects had been unconsciously primed to expect that the perpetrator was black, individuals who received the race priming were more likely to rate the adolescent as mature, culpable, and deserving of harsher punishment, a pattern that held regardless of the subject's own race (Graham and Lowery 2004). Thus, it is not clear that we would end up making better decisions using neurobiological assessments than those we make on the basis of chronological age or than those we might make if we used behavioral or psychological measures. Put concretely, it makes far more sense to rely on a driving test than a brain scan to determine whether someone is ready to drive.

Concluding Comments

The study of adolescent brain development has made tremendous progress in a very short period of time—it has only been about fifteen years since scientists have been studying the adolescent brain systematically. Whether the revelation that the adolescent brain may be less mature than scientists had previously thought ultimately is a good thing, a bad thing, or a mixed blessing for young people remains to be seen. Some policy makers will use this evidence to argue in favor of restricting adolescents' rights, and others will use it advocate for policies that protect adolescents from harm. In either case, scientists should welcome the opportunity to inform policy discussions with the best available empirical evidence. It is almost certain that neuroscience will have a growing influence on how the law views young people. As we move ahead, the major challenge facing those who wish to apply this research to legal policy and practice will be understanding the strengths and the limits of this research. Brain science should inform our policy discussions when it is relevant, but we should not make policy decisions on the basis of brain science alone.

References

American Psychological Association (APA). 1989. *Amicus Curiae* brief in *Hodgson v. Minnesota,* 497 U.S. 417 (1990).

APA. 2004. *Amicus Curiae* brief in *Roper v. Simmons,* 543 U.S. 551 (2005).

APA. 2010. *Amicus Curiae* brief in *Graham v. Sullivan,* 130 S. Ct. 2011 (2010).

APA. 2012. *Amicus Curiae* brief in *Miller v. Alabama* and *Jackson v. Hobbs.* 132 S. Ct. 2455 (2012).

Aristotle. 1954 [350 B.C.]. *Rhetoric.* Translated by W. Rhys Roberts. Online at classics.mit.edu/Aristotle/rhetoric.html.

Bengtsson, Sara, Zoltán Nagy, Stefan Skare, Lea Forsman, Hans Forssberg, and Fredrik Ullén. 2005. "Extensive Piano Practicing Has Regionally Specific Effects on White Matter Development." *Nature Neuroscience* 8 (September): 1148–50.

Bonnie, Richard, John Jeffries, Jr., Peter Low, and Anne Coughlin, eds. 1997. *Criminal Law.* New York: Foundation Press.

Casey, B. J., Rebecca Jones, and Leah Somerville. 2011. "Braking and Accelerating of the Adolescent Brain." *Journal of Research on Adolescence* 21, no. 1 (March 1): 21–33.

Casey, B. J., Nim Tottenham, Conor Liston, and Sarah Durston. 2005. "Imaging the Developing Brain: What Have We Learned About Cognitive Development?" *Trends in Cognitive Science* 9 (March): 104–10.

Centers for Disease Control and Prevention. 2011. *Injury Prevention and Control: Data and Statistics.* Washington, D.C.: CDC.

Chein, Jason, Dustin Albert, Lia O'Brien, Kaitlyn Uckert, and Laurence Steinberg. 2011. "Peers Increase Adolescent Risk Taking by Enhancing Activity in the Brain's Reward Circuitry." *Developmental Science* 14, no. 2 (March): F1–F10.

Committee on Injury, Violence, and Poison Prevention and Committee on Adolescence of the American Society of Pediatrics. 2006. "The Teen Driver." *Pediatrics* 118, no. 6 (December 1): 2570–81.

Crone, Eveline. 2009. "Executive Functions in Adolescence: Inferences from Brain and Behavior." *Developmental Science* 12, no. 6 (November): 825–30.

Dosenbach, Nico, et al. 2010. "Prediction of Individual Brain Maturity Using fMRI." *Science* 329, no. 5997 (September 10): 1358–61.

Eluvathingal, Thomas, Khader Hasan, Larry Kramer, Jack Fletcher, and Linda Ewing-Cobbs. 2007. "Quantitative Diffusion Tensor Tractography of Association and

Projection Fibers in Normally Developing Children and Adolescents." *Cerebral Cortex* 17, no. 12 (December): 2760–68.

Galvan, Adriana. 2010. "Adolescent Development of the Reward System." *Frontiers in Neuroscience* 4, no. 6 (February): 1–9.

Giedd, Jay N. 2008. "The Teen Brain: Insights from Neuroimaging." *Journal of Adolescent Health* 42, no. 4 (April): 335–43.

Gogtay, Nitin, and Paul Thompson. 2010. "Mapping Gray Matter Development: Implications for Typical Development and Vulnerability to Psychopathology." *Brain & Cognition* 72, no. 1 (February): 6–15.

Graham, Sandra, and Brian Lowery. 2004. "Priming Unconscious Racial Stereotypes About Adolescent Offenders." *Law and Human Behavior* 28, no. 5 (October): 483–504.

Graham v. Florida. 130 S. Ct. 2011 (2010).

Grosbras, Marie-Helène, et al. 2007. "Neural Mechanisms of Resistance to Peer Influence in Early Adolescence." *Journal of Neuroscience* 27, no. 30 (July): 8040–45.

Keating, Daniel. 2004. "Cognitive and Brain Development." In *Handbook of Adolescent Psychology*, edited by Richard Lerner and Laurence Steinberg, 2nd ed., 159–87. New York: Wiley.

Kessler, Ronald, Guilherme Borges, and Ellen Waters. 1999. "Prevalence of and Risk Factors for Lifetime Suicide Attempts in the National Comorbidity Survey." *Archives of General Psychiatry* 56, no. 7 (July): 617–26.

Luciana, Monica, Heather Conklin, Catalina Hooper, and Rebecca Yarger. 2005. "The Development of Nonverbal Working Memory and Executive Control Processes in Adolescents." *Child Development* 76, no. 3 (May–June): 697–712.

Luna, Beatriz, Aarthi Padmanabhan, and Kristen O'Hearn. 2010. "What Has fMRI Told Us About the Development of Cognitive Control Through Adolescence?" *Brain and Cognition* 72, no. 1 (February): 101–13.

Maroney, Terry. 2010. "The False Promise of Adolescent Brain Science in Juvenile Justice." *Notre Dame Law Review* 85:89–175.

Morse, Stephen. 2000. "Deprivation and Desert." In *From Social Justice to Criminal Justice*, edited by William Heffernan and John Kleinig, 114–60. New York: Oxford University Press.

Roper v. Simmons, 541 U.S. 551 (2005).

Schlegel, Alice. 2009. "Cross-Cultural Issues in the Study of Adolescent Development." In *Handbook of Adolescent Psychology*, edited by Richard Lerner and Laurence Steinberg, 3rd ed., vol. 2, 570–89. New York: Wiley.

Schmithorst, Vincent, and Weihong Yuan. 2010. "White Matter Development During Adolescence as Shown by Diffusion MRI." *Brain & Cognition* 72, no. 1 (February): 16–25.

Scott, Elizabeth, and Laurence Steinberg. 2008. *Rethinking Juvenile Justice*. Cambridge, Mass.: Harvard University Press.

Simons-Morton, Bruce, et al. 2011. "The Effect of Passengers and Risk-Taking Friends on Risky Driving and Crashes/Near Crashes Among Novice Teenagers." *Journal of Adolescent Health* 49, no. 6 (December): 587–93.

Spear, Linda. 2009. *The Behavioral Neuroscience of Adolescence*. New York: Norton.

Smaller, B. 2006. [Cartoon]. *New Yorker*, April 24. Retrieved September 1, 2009, from http://www.cartoonbank.com/product_details.asp?sid_122213.

Steinberg, Laurence. 2008. "A Social Neuroscience Perspective on Adolescent Risk-Taking." *Developmental Review* 28, no. 1 (March): 78–106.

Steinberg, Laurence. 2012. "Should the Science of Adolescent Brain Development Inform Public Policy?" *Issues in Science and Technology*, (Spring), 67–78.

Steinberg, Laurence, Elizabeth Cauffman, Jennifer Woolard, Sandra Graham, and Marie Banich. 2009. "Are Adolescents Less Mature Than Adults? Minors' Access to Abortion, the Juvenile Death Penalty, and the Alleged APA 'Flip-flop'." *American Psychologist* 64, no. 7 (October): 583–94.

Steinberg, Laurence, Ronald Dahl, Daniel Keating, David Kupfer, Ann Masten, and Daniel Pine. 2006. "Psychopathology in Adolescence: Integrating Affective Neuroscience with the Study of Context." In *Developmental Psychopathology, Vol. 2: Developmental Neuroscience*, edited by Dante Cicchetti and Donald Cohen, 710–41. New York: Wiley.

Steinberg, Laurence, and Elizabeth Scott. 2003. "Less Guilty by Reason of Adolescence: Developmental Immaturity, Diminished Responsibility, and the Juvenile Death Penalty." *American Psychologist* 58, no. 12 (December): 1009–18.

Substance Abuse and Mental Health Services Administration. 2012. *Results from the 2010 National Survey on Drug Use and Health: Mental Health Findings*. NSDUH Series H-42, HHS Publication No. (SMA) 11–4667. Rockville, Md.: Substance Abuse and Mental Health Services Administration.

Takeuchi. Hikaru, et al. 2011. "Working Memory Training Using Mental Calculation Impacts Regional Gray Matter of the Frontal and Parietal Regions." *PLoS One* 6, no. 8 (epub August 23): e23175.

U.S. Supreme Court. 2004. Transcript of oral argument in *Roper v. Simmons*, No. 03-633. October 13. Retrieved March 10, 2009, from http://www.supremecourtus.gov/oral_arguments/argument_transcripts/03-633.pdf.

Wallis, Claudia. 2004. "What Makes Teens Tick?" *Time*, May 10, 163.

Weisberg, Deena, et al. 2008. "The Seductive Allure of Neuroscience Explanations." *Journal of Cognitive Neuroscience* 20, no. 3 (March): 470–77.

Woolard, Jennifer, and Elizabeth Scott. 2009. "The Legal Regulation of Adolescence." In *Handbook of Adolescent Psychology*, edited by Richard Lerner and Laurence Steinberg, 3rd ed., vol. 2, 345–71. New York: Wiley.

Zimring, Franklin. 1982. *The Changing Legal World of Adolescence*. New York: Free Press.

CHAPTER 4

Building Capability and Functioning: Reframing the Rights Agenda for Adolescents Through the Lens of Disability Rights

Victor Pineda

I have no legs,
But I still have feelings,
I cannot see,
But I think all the time,
Although I'm deaf,
I still want to communicate,
Why do people see me as useless, thoughtless, talkless,
When I am as capable as any,
For thoughts about our world. (emphasis added)
   —Coralie Severs, fourteen, United Kingdom, in
      It's About Ability (Pineda 2008)

In her poem, Coralie Severs, fourteen, asserts that although she may interact with the world in a unique way, she is "as capable as any for thoughts about our world." This chapter builds on the theme, advanced in the previous three chapters, that commonalities and differences between and within societies characterize the period of adolescence. The chapter explores the tension between commonality and difference from the perspective of disability, a perspective that generates rich insights into our notions of what is "normal," "natural," or nonnegotiable for a rights-respecting adolescence. Though this chapter focuses on issues relating to adolescents with disabilities, its approach to decentering a presumed norm and to placing the enhancement of capability at the center of the adolescent rights agenda provides an analytic framework that is instructive for many adolescent constituencies.

My analysis is inspired by Coralie's assertion that adolescents with disabilities are capable. Her insistence that they can, with adequate supports, play a positive role resonates with Amartya Sen's concepts of agency and capability (Sen 1995, 1997a, 1997b, 1998, 1999, 2000, 2004) and is consistent with the recent body of scholarship that has expanded our understanding of the contributions made by persons with disabilities (Oliver 1996; Shakespeare 1996; Albrecht et al. 2001; Davis 2006).

Like other "victim" constituencies, adolescents with disabilities have traditionally been seen as objects of charity. Due to their particular impairment(s) they are not seen as having the same capabilities and potential as their nondisabled counterparts. This approach inculcates a deformed notion of the inherent dignity and social worth of people with disabilities. Research on high school bullying, sexual violence, social stigma, and isolation (Groce 2004; Brownlee and Cureton 2009; Ellery, Lansdowne, and Csaky 2011) attests to the broad set of factors that impact adolescents with disabilities and that compound the frustrations and insecurities about transitioning into adulthood that affect all adolescents.

Impediments to Adolescent Transition into Adulthood

Globally, about 180 million young people between the ages of ten and twenty-four live with physical, sensory, intellectual, or mental health impairments significant enough to make a difference in their daily lives (Groce 2004). They differ in many respects, but share some similarities. The vast majority of these young people, some 150 million (80 percent) live in the developing world. Routinely excluded from most educational, economic, social, and cultural opportunities, they are among the poorest and most marginalized young people in the world. The literature confirms that adolescents with disabilities confront a multidimensional set of hindrances on their path toward adulthood (Davis et al. 2003; Groce 2004). According to UNICEF (2010) and the World Health Organization (2010), they confront stigma, inequality, and discrimination on a daily basis. Their social isolation makes them more vulnerable to physical and sexual abuse (Gross 2000; Shakespeare, Iezzoni, and Groce 2009). A wide range of factors can increase the risk of adolescents acquiring or sustaining serious impairments. Inadequate nutrition, communicable diseases (such as tuberculosis, malaria, and HIV/AIDS), trauma, abuse, violence, and environmental degradation all play a part.

Defining and quantifying disability is a contested and complex endeavor. Genetic, developmental, congenital, intellectual, behavioral, and psychosocial disabilities complicate the challenge of measuring occurrence, severity and prevalence. So does the growing rejection of an absolute dichotomy between impairment and nonimpairment (Albrecht et al. 2001; Clements and Read 2008). The technical complexity of measuring disability is further complicated by the contentious cultural debate over what constitutes a disability and who qualifies as having one (Shakespeare 1996). Definitions and understandings of disability inevitably shape the range of responses by professionals in research, policy, and practice.[1]

My exploration of this phenomenon arises from my direct involvement in collecting data on the social interactions of adolescents with disabilities in their social environment. Furthermore, I experienced adolescence as a middle-class Hispanic male with several severe physical impairments. Throughout my adolescence, I was the only student in my school who had little or no use of his arms or legs. Other adolescents I met had other impairments. Olivia had difficulty hearing, Mohammed had difficulty seeing, and Joanna had difficulty remembering. Each in our own ways would discover that our impairments influenced our evolving capacities and could impinge on our transition to adulthood. As adolescents with disabilities we grappled with stigma, social isolation, sexual insecurities, as well as perceived and real limitations. Taken together these factors could generate apathy, doubt, dependency, and depression in each of us in our own ways. What was unique was that as adults, we individually came to understand our disabilities as strengths and not as weaknesses. How did we come to this realization?[2]

Constructionists would argue, and disability scholars would agree, that social actors[3] are continually defining the social meanings of "adolescence" and "disability." The meaning of these terms is defined and redefined through social interactions that in turn affect social roles and attribute values to the appropriate execution of specific functionings. Traditionally, parents, teachers, and medical professionals are the key social actors that frame the social interaction of adolescents with disabilities and define the meaning of "adolescence" for girls and boys with disabilities.[4] They exercise power over the adolescent that can expand, nurture, or restrict the adolescent's development, capacity, freedom, and sense of self-worth. The group of social actors that exert power over the disabled adolescent has increased over the years due to educational, professional, medical, and psychological specializations and a demand for such specialized services.

Over the past forty years, new cadres of professionals and paraprofessionals have exercised power over adolescents with disabilities in addition to these traditional supports (that is, support from parents, teachers, and medical professionals), especially in developed countries. Adolescents with disabilities negotiate their identities through disability labels and specialized programs managed by social workers, life-skills coaches, psychologists, vocational rehabilitation counselors, orthopedic and physical therapists, and high-school counselors. Depending on particular circumstances, adolescents with disabilities may also be "cared for" by home-care providers, child protective service workers, child welfare caseworkers, juvenile corrections caseworkers, juvenile mental health counselors, and juvenile probation officers.

These professions form an *octopus of agencies* (figure 4.1) personified by the specialized support professional. The actors charged with mitigating challenges may inadvertently hinder the effective transition of adolescents with disabilities into adulthood. To assess whether and how that might be the case requires an awareness of critical questions. Do such professionals work together as part of a consistent and coordinated professional team, and do they

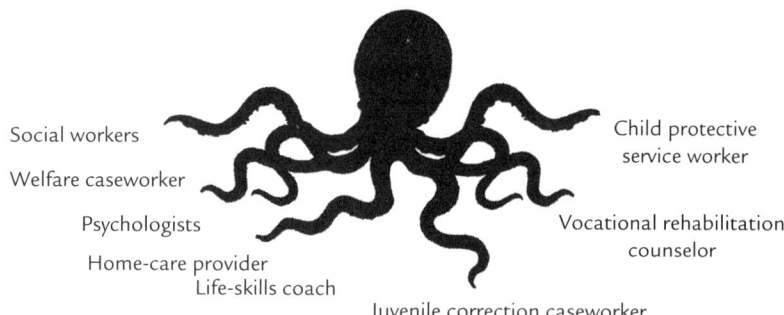

Figure 4.1. Octopus of professionals and support staff that may interact with adolescents with disabilities.
Source: Victor Pineda.

critically assess their assumptions about what the adolescent can and cannot do? What are the underlying treatment philosophies that frame their work?

Dominant Approaches to Disability

The dominant conception of disability is flawed. Mainstream treatment philosophies fail to incorporate contextual factors such as social, environmental, and institutional barriers into the understanding of disability. They reify "disability" as constitutive of the essence of a person rather than as a product of his or her social positioning. Characterizing disability as solely a property of the individual irrespective of his or her social, physical, and institutional environment is one of the main causes of differential outcomes between disabled and nondisabled adolescents. Ignoring the disabling role of the environment places adolescents with disabilities at a structural disadvantage in relation to the performance of certain social functions. This functional disadvantage, otherwise known as "handicap," is created rather than constitutive: it depends on the social environment in which it occurs and the environment's accommodation to the disadvantage. Such a disadvantage is neither necessary nor inevitable.

Disability scholars (Oliver 1996; Mitchell and Snyder 1997; Barnes, Oliver, and Barton 2002; Snyder, Brueggemann, and Thomson 2002; Shakespeare 2006; Chouinard, Hall, and Wilton 2010) have noted that with proper modifications of social, physical, and institutional arrangements, individuals with a wide variety of disabilities including intellectual or developmental disabilities would be able to execute valuable social functionings on an equal basis with their nondisabled peers. By exploring the contested notions of disability we may begin to uncover the value of such arguments in adolescent theory, policy, and practice.

(Re)Imagining Disability

The two main conceptual models of disabilities are the "medical model" and the "social model." The medical model situates disability as an inherent property of the individual (Shakespeare 2006). Under this model, the disabled individual is understood as being medically abnormal and in need of care; not more, not less. The social model situates the disability within social structures and attitudes that fail to accommodate human, biological, or functional diversity, and thus "disable" individuals with impairments. This model places disability outside the individual and puts the burden of disability on social practices and social norms. In so doing, the social model asserts that a disability is simply a failure between an impaired individual and their environment. This model allows for considerations of discriminatory social and institutional arrangements (Oliver 1996). From this perspective, inequity is embedded in neglected physical infrastructure, unrepresentative political processes, unfair institutional practices, and oppressive or controlling administrative procedures.

Notwithstanding this dynamic perspective, practical questions remain. How can such theoretical innovations lead us toward more just and effective policies? How can a new understanding of these models help us redress differential outcomes for adolescents with disabilities? How can we operationalize the social model to provide social supports for adolescents with disabilities in new and effective ways? What specific factors would have to be considered to promote more equitable outcomes?

The Relationship of Individual Agency and Disability

Disability per se is not inherently agency depriving.[5] Discriminatory social arrangements assign value to full human functioning and through purposeful inaction allow agency deprivations to exist among adolescents with disabilities. Such inaction is illustrated through the multitude of external factors that impinge on the basic human agency of adolescents with disabilities.

Amartya Sen provides an explicitly *normative* account of human agency as something we have reason to value, realize in our lives, and exercise jointly in our groups and institutions. Agency plays such an important role in Sen's theory that some have suggested calling it the "agency oriented" capability approach (Crocker 2008). Crocker expands on Sen's notion of agency and notes that a person (or group) is an agent with respect to action X to the extent that the following four conditions hold:

1. *Self-determination*: the person decides for herself rather than someone or something else making the decision to do X;
2. *Reason orientation and deliberation*: the person bases her decisions on reasons, such as the pursuit of goals;

3. *Action*: the person performs or has a role in performing X; and
4. *Impact*: the person thereby brings about (or contributes to bringing about) an impact at any scale.

These conditions constitute decisive factors in assessing the root causes of inequality. Under this analytical framework inequality is the outcome of individual or collective agency deprivations.[6] Redressing inequality would require us refocusing on the individual or collective agency deprivations of adolescents with disabilities. The conditions listed above allow us to (re)conceptualize agency deprivations from an individual or collective lens. Such a conception of agency opens the door for "a group" to exercise agency with/for a person with a disability (for example, when a quadriplegic instructs an assistant to execute a task requiring the use of one's hands and arms that the quadriplegic could not otherwise perform). The concept of "group" agency can also further be extended by this same rationale. Adolescents with disabilities who can conceptualize themselves as belonging to a collective or "community" may also be able to select, weigh, and trade-off capabilities, functionings, and other normative considerations of valued social functionings according to their preferences, experiences, and (dis)abilities. Furthermore, Crocker suggests that both individuals and communities should select, weigh, and trade-off capabilities, functionings, and other normative considerations (Crocker 2008, 4). Developing collective agency through social and political mobilization has been a key rallying cry for many disenfranchised groups including persons with disabilities. Over the past thirty years, politically charged disability advocates have challenged social norms and in the process formed a movement based on human rights, anti-discrimination and equal opportunity. Much like other movements, persons with disabilities organized. Their motto, "Nothing about us without us" serves as a declaration for individual and collective agency.[7] Such is the case of the California Youth Leadership Forum that has brought together fifty adolescents with disabilities each year for over twenty-three years to weigh and trade-off capabilities, functionings, and perspectives on their individual and collective transitions into adulthood. In the process, they come to understand the history of disability rights, the laws that protect them, and their own identity. Through this process they are able to elevate their own understanding of their power to enact change. To date, the California Youth Leadership program has over a thousand alumni, adolescents with disabilities who have taken charge of their lives and have gone on to forge successful careers as community organizers, teachers, accountants, lawyers, policy makers, government leaders, and more. The Youth Leadership program sees adolescence as a time for the exploration of autonomy and experimentation, transitioning into autonomous decision making, planning for college, and obtaining a driver's license.

Disability rights advocates (like children's rights advocates) share a commitment to equity in political and public participation. On the global stage, with the passage of the UN Convention on the Rights of Persons with Disabilities (CRPD), disabled advocates overturned the notion of powerlessness that dominates the conceptions of disability. Supporting equity in individual and community participation furthers a value positive or value neutral notion of disability (as opposed to a value negative notion) by reframing disability from a perceived deficit that is mitigated through exclusion to a perceived asset that is valued and actively engaged. Advocates for persons with disabilities thus challenged unjust norms and in doing so challenged dominant theories of justice, theories that plainly denied justice to individuals with disabilities.

Agency and the Specificity of Adolescence

Agency deprivations to some degree affect all adolescents. As the previous chapter by Steinberg explains, the science of adolescence tells us that during puberty the foremost part of the cortex of the brain develops, allowing adolescents to perform higher-level tasks like those required in executive function. The following chapter by McNeely and Bose describes how executive functioning skills are a set of interconnected competences that support self-assessment and self-regulation. For adolescents to execute agency they need to be able to analyze, organize, decide, and put into practice their will. Individuals with intellectual or developmental disabilities may not be able to perform these functions without support.

Many parents of children with disabilities extend their role as a provider/protector into practices that may limit the child's agency, in essence overprotecting and inhibiting the adolescent's independent decision-making capabilities and coping strategies. The term "spoiling" will be used here with a very particular meaning[8] to elucidate ways in which certain modes of parenting may inadvertently result in parents depriving their child of agency. A child who is insulated from the outside world to such a degree that he or she is never exposed to conditions that stimulate independent action is a child that is spoiled. This is a child with underdeveloped capacity to act independently or through self-determination. As the adolescent ages she becomes incapable of taking action or choosing between competing actions. Spoiling is an extreme form of agency deprivation; it elucidates broader traps in adolescent development. Another trap is deformed preference,[9] which arises when adolescents are not provided with certain opportunity sets. A limited or warped set of opportunities redefines the range of choices for the adolescent. The warped opportunities offset the evaluative and deliberative process of optimal choice. Parenting practices that inhibit individual responsibility, risk taking, goal-setting, and preferences also inhibit agency. Therefore, "spoiling" among children with or without disabilities furthers their dependency; warps their opportunity sets; and increases their real and perceived insecurity, vulnerability, and ability to act upon their preferences and unlock their true potential.

A More Nuanced Approach to Autonomy

There is a bidirectional link between the concepts of agency and autonomy. Enabling agency for adolescents with disabilities requires adjusting or reframing our notions of autonomy. Adolescents with disabilities may lack autonomy because dominant notions of autonomy do not incorporate agency-enhancing localized support. A framework incorporating localized supports can alter dominant notions of autonomy. This framework (figure 4.2) allows for three specific types of agency-enhancing supports[10] to complement and strengthen autonomy, not deny it. The three most common agency-enhancing localized supports for persons with disabilities are: (1) adaptive (or coping) strategies, (2) personal assistance, and (3) assistive technology.

These agency-enhancing supports are localized in and around the impaired individual. They lower the costs of executing valued human functioning and allow individuals with disabilities to direct their lives and act upon their own desires. Localized supports are in line with Sen's capability approach as they unlock agency-enhancing capability sets that allow individuals with disabilities to live the type of life they have reason to value. For instance, we can understand assistive technology (AT) as unlocking potential. This can be illustrated in the following examples. A wheelchair unlocks mobility for an adolescent with cerebral palsy, a hearing aid opens communication

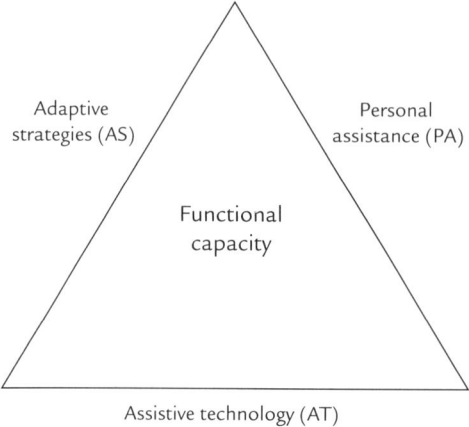

Figure 4.2. Human Accomplishment model of the interface between individuals and environments supports the concept of localized supports for globalized agency. Courtesy of Litvak and Enders.

for an adolescent who is hard of hearing, a braille keyboard opens up work opportunities for an adolescent who is blind. Likewise, adaptive strategies (AS) can unlock new capability sets such as persistence or resilience. These develop through the process of implementing appropriate ways of managing expectations, understanding dietary or nutritional needs, or maintaining a physical or mental health regimen to execute a wider range of valuable social functioning. Finally, personal assistance (PA) is understood in this perspective as enhancing agency, not replacing it. Like AT and AS, an adolescent can exercise an expanded capability set by engaging and using PA. This is exemplified through personal supports provided to the adolescent by trained or untrained siblings, parents, attendants, classroom aides, friends, or other adults. By viewing AT, AS, and PA as agency enhancing, we can alter the notions of what types of local supports (including human supports) are optional and what types of local supports are necessary. Localized supports thus are understood as enhancing the human agency of adolescents with disabilities.

Enhancing the human agency of adolescents with disabilities also raises questions about the nature of autonomy. Can *localized supports* also lead to new notions of assisted autonomy? This question may help further expand disability rights within the broader discourses of what basic rights and basic freedoms should be. More nuanced approaches to agency and autonomy will help enhance targeted approaches toward improving outcomes for adolescents with disabilities.

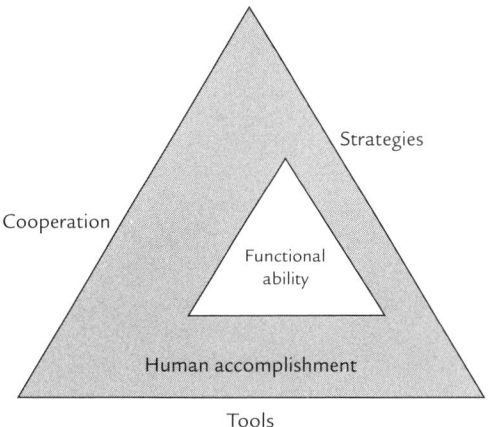

Figure 4.3. Human Accomplishment model of human accomplishments support systems is analogous to the concept of enabling globalized agency through localized supports. Courtesy of Litvak and Enders.

A new agency-enhancing model emerges when we understand localized supports such as AT, AS, and PA as supporting autonomy, not annulling it. In this context it is useful to return to Sen's concept of agency. Sen's approach also explains why agency deprivations are stronger than capability deprivations because they limit individual freedom to act, and thus render inherent capabilities of the individual useless. Understanding localized supports as furthering autonomy and enabling agency helps us transform outdated notions of what adolescents with disabilities can and should be able to do or achieve. The following section illustrates this idea in practice.

Transformative Examples and Empirical Evidence

Three transformative examples illustrate the agency-enabling framework described above. The following cases were developed and implemented with, for, and by youth with disabilities in three cities, Los Angeles, Damascus, and Nairobi.[11] Different sociocultural notions of disability and adolescence impinge on each case but they share similar methods and outcomes. The cases focus on three programs executed by World Enabled, a global nonprofit organization that serves adolescents with disabilities. The programs utilize a human rights-based, cross-disability, educational, and advocacy methodology in line with the agency framework described above. The programs aim to further transformative agency-enhancing outcomes among participants.

Each case showed that providing adolescents with disabilities with the opportunities to develop and exercise their agency was effective. The opportunities minimized the type of agency deprivations that they perceived as furthering differential outcomes relative to their nondisabled peers.

Case Studies on Increasing Adolescent Agency

Breaking Boundaries: The New Media Academy

The New Media Academy was an eight-week after-school course in digital storytelling offered to high school students with and without disabilities in Reseda, California.[12] The course utilized "agency enabling instruction" techniques to engage twenty diverse learners. Participants were recruited from a segregated vocational training school for individuals with intellectual disabilities and a midsized mainstream high school. The "agency enabling instruction" operationalized localized supports and put into practice these supports in the classroom by incorporating principles of Universal Design for Learning (UDL). UDL provides a set of principles to ensure that a curriculum reaches the widest range of learners. UDL challenges instructors to provide multiple means of representation (visual, oral, or written instruction), multiple means of expression (allowing students to communicate their knowledge visually, or through writing, speaking, or performance), multiple means of engagement (tracking progress and supporting executive functions) (CAST 2012). The program was the first to execute a UDL, standards-based digital storytelling and media production curriculum within California schools. It focused on story structure, collecting digital assets, hands-on video production and postproduction, captioning, and showcasing student work.[13] Each student produced a 1–3 minute video based on one of four prompts. The prompts were:

"I feel strong when . . ." "I feel scared when . . ."
"I come from a place . . ." "I keep secrets when . . ."

The prompts were selected to challenge the participants to critically reflect on their individual values and choices. The challenge of teaching in an inclusive environment with different learning levels was met by incorporating substantial localized supports in the form of assistive technologies (such as modified keyboards, computer mice, large screens, and use of personal devices such as camera phones, medical devices such as wheelchairs, white canes for individuals with visual impairments), personal assistance (such as peer mentors, a buddy system, teacher's aides), and coping strategies (such as tips on reasonable accommodations, how to ask for help, how to stay on track).[14]

The New Media Academy program was overwhelmingly successful. Throughout the program students with and without disabilities were engaged and reported a significant increase in level of comfort, understanding of disability, and unexpectedly reported a general increased interest in learning. By implementing UDL principles the course furthered engagement, participation, and choice among all students and in so doing increased agency and mitigated barriers by supporting multiple means of representation, expression, and engagement. Findings showed that these specific agency-enabling practices helped all participants—with or without disabilities—to engage effectively and in different ways through a variety of teaching methods. Such programs improve the performance of disabled and nondisabled adolescents without furthering agency deprivations in either group. In exit interviews both disabled and non disabled participants noted that participating in the course improved their understanding of disability and diversity and that the experience allowed them to learn more about themselves through others. The impact on the disabled adolescent was significant. The availability of localized supports and the frameworks utilized in the implementation of the course allowed for a more authentic form of socialization to develop among and between disabled and nondisabled participants, one that altered perspectives for both groups of adolescents (those with and without disabilities). Their final films showed a common humanity and a dedication and passion to completing the assignment demonstrating authenticity and creativity.

The Silver Scorpion and the Youth Ability Summit

In August of 2010, a few months before hostilities in Syria began, the Youth Ability Summit brought together adolescents with disabilities from Syria and the United States to not only share their experiences, ideas, and culture but to create strategies promoting the rights of youth with disabilities.[15] One strategy that the youth found exciting was developing a comic book that would promote cross-cultural understanding and underline the principles of dignity, equality, and opportunity through the adventures of a disabled superhero. The comic they developed was entitled the *Silver Scorpion* named after their hero who extols the values of both the Syrian and American adolescents with disabilities. When asked, "If you could have any superpower, what would it be?," none of the youth participants (all of whom had disabilities) provided answers that one would normally expect—flying, reading minds, or being super strong. Instead, each of their ideas, in the case of both the Syrian and the American adolescents, was surprisingly original. Perhaps because of their disabilities, the young people think as individuals or outside dominant social conventions. One girl, for example, wanted to have the power to ease frustrations and make people happy. It was noteworthy that none of the young people wanted the hero's power to be something that cured their disability. Both the process of developing the comic book and the disability superhero have had a powerful effect on adolescent agency. Each participant tested their own capacity for understanding diversity and cultural differences, and managed to summon genuine independent and collective creativity during the exercise portion. Participants also benefited from seeing their collective ideas have an impact on the world. The comic has been incredibly successful and has been distributed by the comic book company Liquid Comics in English and Arabic and has since been converted into an Internet comic strip and published on MTV's Voices website as an animated web series.[16] The adolescent participants extended their individual and collective agency by giving birth to a collective alter ego that fights bullying, injustice, neglect, and other forms of agency-depriving factors on their behalf. Through creative approaches such as these, participants strengthened their individual and collective notions of self-determination, reason orientation, and deliberation, action, and impact, thereby contributing to a deeper appreciation of the capabilities of adolescents with disabilities across cultures.

The African Youth with Disabilities Network:
Formation and Findings

The African Youth with Disabilities Network (AYWDN) consists entirely of African youth with disabilities with and without prior experience in disability rights and leadership. Fifty youth advocates with disabilities from twelve African countries convened in Kenya between 2010–2011 to form the AYWDN.[17] They participated in five days of trainings on monitoring disability rights within the African continent. The primary goal in forming the AYWDN and in organizing the trainings was to develop a greater understanding of human rights and further a sense of personal and collective dignity among African youth with disabilities (Aniyamuzaala 2012) and used this training to grow their membership in organized local chapters. The workshop trainings were led by adults with disabilities as well as by young peer leaders. Specific focus was given to the general principles of nondiscrimination, dignity, and gender equality; and the meeting format allowed the participants to frame additional specific measures from a youth perspective. In peer-led sessions, they worked through the barriers and solutions that could help improve outcomes in education, employment, communication, and health for young people with disabilities in each of the participant's countries. Through this process, they took ownership of their individual and collective goals.[18] In addition to this, twenty-six video profiles (three to five minutes long) of AYWDN members were produced and assembled into a playlist on YouTube (Pineda and Mullick 2011). These video profiles form a virtual portfolio of enabled and active youth whose voices and visions increase the visibility and values of the AYDWN. Participants noted that activities such as video testimony, debating policies, and identifying societal barriers have allowed them to improve their communication skills, gain experience talking on camera, and gain exposure by sharing their stories and having an impact beyond their hometown, city, or village. The topics discussed by the participants included their perspectives on and experiences with youth and disability advocacy in Africa; leadership; joining the disability rights movement; the AYDWN; what it is like, and what it should be like to live with a disability; how disability is viewed in the participant's country; the barriers they encountered growing up with a disability; the importance of increasing the participation of youth with disabilities in disability/youth conferences; how youth with disabilities in Africa see the future of Africa; the role of gender-based violence and disability; and their own thoughts on independent and community living. In exit interviews, they each stressed their commitment to stopping violence, exploitation, and abuse in their communities. Furthermore, the participants are now more encouraged to think critically, develop their own plans and goals, and refine and assess where their true interests lie.

The methodology used was agency enhancing in that it allowed participants to express their individual and collective *self-determination* through *reason-oriented deliberation* and *collective and coordinated action*. They developed and approved constitution and governance framework grounded on equity, diversity, and equal representation. Local chapters would decide what issues their local network would tackle, rather than having the network's executive committee make the decision for them. In addition, the network members developed and approved *Robert's Rules of Order* and the practice of structured debate to decide on the network's goals. Finally, the member's individual and collective purpose is to manifest positive societal change through action-oriented campaigns and activities that over time will bring about an impact on Africa. The convening of the AYWDN enhanced individual and collective agency and created an experience that reframed disability from a depravity to a social issue that required their individual commitments and collective action.

Discussion on Transformative Learning

These cases challenged participants to reimagine their worldview and their individual and collective capacities and put into practice an agency-enhancing concept called transformative learning. In doing so, they not only embraced their agency but also engaged in processes that reframed their underlying notions of disability. By engaging disabled facilitators and peer educators, disability was perceived as an asset instead of a deficit. Programs like these that support adolescents with disabilities to critically trace dominant thoughts, beliefs, and ideologies to their particular social situation lead to the the creation of new social understandings.[19] Each of these cases illustrates how authentic and equitable engagement in an inclusive youth-oriented process can also further the critiquing and dissolving of ideological delusions about the limited potential of adolescents with disabilities. The cases also show how a youth-driven inquiry into the agency deprivations that confront adolescents with disabilities can illuminate aspects of hidden coercion embedded in a variety of social practices.

Although the cases mentioned above are impactful, they are rare. In practice, adolescents with disabilities are usually not given the chance to make their own choices but rather experience these outcomes as the result of a lack of agency. As the case studies illustrate, agency deprivations are not inherent to the adolescents' impairment; they are generated by societal attitudes and the lack of adequate agency-enhancing localized supports. By shaping or determining their own lives in a safe and barrier-free environment (low-risk, high-reward scenarios), adolescents who participate in transformative programs can begin to familiarize themselves with their inherent capabilities and further develop their individual agency. These cases show that adolescents with a diverse set of impairments are capable of exercising agency on an equal basis with others. In each case, participants noted that they do not necessarily view their disability as being an inherently unnatural and unwanted human anomaly because they still have the capacity to execute valuable social functionings if given an inclusive, accepting, barrier-free society. As in the case with AYWDN, they are not waiting to be given a welcoming society; they have taken to building it themselves. Strengthening the capacity of adolescents to exercise agency requires us to rethink the ways in which social policies such as education policy, employment policy, health care, and other factors such as public and political participation, awareness raising, accessibility, and social security are either enhancing or depriving the agency of adolescents with disabilities.

Policy-Based Recommendations

The Convention on the Rights of Persons with Disabilities[20] is an international policy instrument intended to stimulate global action toward protecting the rights and dignities of persons with disabilities. Adolescents with disabilities are strongly protected by this treaty. States that are party to the Convention are required to promote, protect, and ensure the full enjoyment of human rights by persons with disabilities. The CRPD set into motion a global policy imperative that greatly benefits adolescents with disabilities.[21] It calls for policies and reforms that are in effect agency enhancing. Such policies nonetheless need to be sensitive to the different cultural, social, and political contexts within which adolescents operate. Such policies also need to recognize the causes and consequences of agency deprivation across specific communities. Policy approaches addressing differential outcomes based on agency deprivations must begin at the local level, with an analysis of the context in which agency deprivations occur. This locally based analysis should inform the design of local interventions while at the same time engaging experienced national or international partners as collaborators who can help identify culturally appropriate strategies for promoting equity.[22]

Policy interventions should ultimately call for state efforts to promote, protect, and ensure the fundamental rights and basic dignities of all persons with disabilities through local and national organizations run by persons with disabilities. Such policies should ultimately foster at the national level an open forum where persons with disabilities (including young persons with disabilities) can identify the barriers and directly participate in the decisions that affect them.

One example would be through the formation of a youth advisory committee for the U.S. National Council on Disability. Such an entity would enable adolescents and young adults to develop agency at the national policy level and provide a vehicle for adolescents and youth with disabilities to engage in *self-determination, reason-oriented deliberation*, and collective or coordinated *action* that has an impact on national policy.

On the personal level, adolescents with disabilities should be given the necessary supports (AT, AS, or PA) to engage in activities on an equal basis with their nondisabled peers. Added attention and specific emphasis on personal, familial, intellectual, and physical resources can ameliorate the adolescent's functional limitations. Supported personal development through extracurricular or recreational training programs could help adolescents to develop and refine important executive functioning skills necessary for achieving a successful transition to adulthood. Such skills include, but are not limited to, setting a goal (understanding what the objective is), planning a course to achieve it (remembering the procedure appropriate to the task and understanding the supports that may be needed), holding the plan in working memory while executing it (knowing that the localized supports are leading toward the achievement of the goal), sequencing the steps in the plan (knowing what needs to happen first, second and so on), and of course initiating and taking those steps and shifting between them (knowing when one step ends and the next one starts). Also important are monitoring progress for both pace and quality (understanding the metrics for success and tracking progress on these indicators), regulating attention and emotional responses to challenges that arise (understanding one's internal temperament and emotional state), making flexible changes in the plan as needed (understanding that sequences may change as challenges or opportunities arise or priorities change), and evaluating the outcome for use of the plan in a subsequent similar activity. In addition to these types of adaptive strategies, individuals with intellectual or cognitive disabilities can also execute these types of executive functioning skills through assisted decision making and other types of supports. After-school programs or community-based centers can provide safe spaces that are inclusive and welcoming. Such supportive spaces can help adolescents with disabilities practice and develop their agency in low-risk and high-reward environments and foster individual responsibility, risk taking, goal setting, and an adequate level of supports. Such inclusive programs must engage with local disabled person's organizations to ensure accessibility and cultural sensitivity. Mentoring and exchange opportunities should be provided so that adolescents with various disabilities can meet adults with similar disabilities who have developed rich professional and personal lives. In addition to personal or localized supports for the individual, the broader immediate environment plays a central role in all of this. Conducting access audits with adolescents with disabilities and promoting accessible environments, mobility, awareness, supports for independent living, and political and public participation through civic programs or activities can further impact adolescent development by decreasing their sense of isolation and increasing their sense of solidarity.

Adolescents with disabilities make up a broad subset of all adolescents who experience attitudinal and environmental barriers. The hindrances that these adolescents encounter form patterns of social failure that in turn generate new landscapes of inequality. Transformative programs such as those discussed above demonstrate that young persons with disabilities want to and can exercise agency, and that participants engaged in transformative programs of this sort can experience deep shifts in thoughts, feelings, and actions related to their disabilities. This altered consciousness can generate newfound agency, dramatically changing the disabled adolescents' perspective on their place in the world and their hunger for knowledge. Consequently, their comfort in speaking up and advocating on behalf of fairness and against injustice and inequity increases. Gradually, participants see themselves as agents of change, not passive victims of circumstances. Enabling agency is, in fact, the way to move forward, and a successful empowerment of adolescents with disabilities is tantamount to an empowerment of all adolescents.

Notes

1. The willingness of parents to identify their children as disabled, for example, may vary according to whether the definition used reflects their own definition of disability, their perception of any difficulties that their child may experience, and the implications (as they understand them) of defining their child as "disabled." Disability labels that highlight and define adolescent deviance are also problematic. In many cultures, adolescents with disabilities are branded as deviants and are seen as embodying social and moral depravity. This is evidenced by the fact that adolescents with disabilities are overrepresented in figures measuring institutionalization and incarceration.

2. This is a question that underlies much of my research.

3. Social actors include parents, teachers, doctors, politicians, nondisabled peers, and adolescents with disabilities themselves.

4. For more information, see literature on the independent living movement and identify formation of adolescents with disabilities.

5. Note that the standard notion of disability does not incorporate agency and fails to incorporate the active disabling role of the individual's environment.

6. In theory, it is possible that an adolescent could exercise agency by dropping out of school, ignoring his or her medical condition, or purposefully rejecting social security or public supports. This form of agency could also be a part of a willed decision.

7. Some members who ascribe to these values describe themselves as belonging to the disability community and view themselves as advocates for social justice.

8. Several questions related to the concept of spoiling arise but will not be discussed in this paper as this topic will be elaborated in subsequent publications by the author: Is it a value assessment without a clear correlate for future outcomes? What is spoiling and who defines it, asserts it, or rectifies it? What evidence do we have that it is overall negative or is spoiling appropriate in a protective role? Or is a protective role always a spoiling role? Who decides? Is there a way to measure or to know a priori and a posteriori or only a posteriori?

9. For more on deformed preferences, see Khader, S. J. (2011). *Adaptive preferences and women's empowerment*. Oxford University Press. Retrieved from http://books.google.com/books?hl=en&lr=&id=J-3T3qb2FfMC&oi=fnd&pg=PP2&dq=Adaptive+Preferences+Preferences+Autonomy+Deficits&ots=Co7V1h0W2p&sig=z9fs9Z5mCxtX95tn-eVqHD5th-w

10. These three concepts were first introduced by Alexandra Enders in Litvak and Enders (2001).

11. The author conceptualized, designed, secured funding, and with a team of colleagues at the Pineda Foundation for Youth, implemented the programs described herein. These programs were carried out using the transformative and agency enhancing framework described herein. These programs were conducted between 2010 and 2011.

12. This course was a pilot program conducted in 2011 in the Los Angeles Unified School District with high school students from Grover Cleveland High School and Joaquin Miller Career and Transition Center that was designed and sponsored by the Pineda Foundation for Youth through a grant from VSA Arts, an affiliate of the John F. Kennedy Center for the Performing Arts. This was the first program to bring together two public schools (one mainstream, and one special education) in an inclusive, standards-based, digital storytelling and media production curriculum under the principles of Universal Design for Learning (UDL).

13. Students with and without disabilities were recruited through calls for auditions among the two schools. Self-selection bias was corrected for by deliberately se-

lecting a broad range of students. Students with various levels of comfort with persons with disabilities, students with nominal understanding of persons with disabilities, and students with experience in an inclusive classroom were recruited. Students with low levels of comfort, low understanding of persons with disabilities, and little experience in an inclusive classroom were selected to participate

14. Supports included (a) a curriculum specifically designed by UDL and digital storytelling experts to meet California education standards to provide multiple means of representation, action and expression, and engagement; (b) two very experienced high school teachers with expertise in audio, video, and media production (but almost no experience teaching developmentally disabled students); (c) one disability expert with extensive experience teaching adolescents with disabilities; (d) college students with disabilities that served as team leaders; and (e) three classroom aides that supported students with severe disabilities.

15. Jay Snyder, founder of the Open Hands Initiative, made this program possible through his generous support. To learn more about the program and participants, visit www.openhandsinitiative.org.

16. The web series can be seen at http://act.mtv.com/posts/silver-scorpion/ and http://voices.mtv.co.uk/category/silver-scorpion/.

17. The Open Society Foundations Disability Rights Initiative and Youth Initiative organized the AYWDN with the participation of the International Disability Alliance and World Enabled/Pineda Foundation for Youth.

18. They drafted and adopted the Nairobi African Youth with Disabilities Declaration on Inclusive Participation and Development and increased their knowledge of the disability rights movement, the CRPD, advocacy skills, identifying barriers and facilitators in society, and identifying the corresponding stakeholders.

19. Mannheim, Wirth, and Shils (1936) stated that social groups form ideologies or premises according to the group's social situation or "life conditions" (1936, 78). Complementary to this, Jürgen Habermas introduced the idea of an "ideal speech situation" as a hypothetical situation of absolutely uncoerced and unlimited discussion between completely free and equal human agents (Habermas 1970; Geuss 1981, 65). Beliefs that agents would agree upon in the ideal speech situation are ipso facto true beliefs (Habermas and Luhmann 1971, 139, 224). Through the proper utilization of social communication new epistemologies can emerge. Engagement in social role definition and redefinition is an expression of youth power. As evidenced in the Arab Spring and the global youth movement, youth power is capable of rupturing pejorative norms or false epistemologies embedded in oppressive power hierarchies.

20. The text of the CRPD was adopted by the UN General Assembly on December 13, 2006 and opened for signature on March 30, 2007. Following ratification by the twentieth party, it came into force on May 3, 2008. As of January 2014, 139 countries have ratified it including the European Union, which "concluded" the treaty (in effect, to the extent that the responsibilities of the member states were transferred to the

European Union, it became ratified) on December 23, 2010. The Convention is monitored by the Committee on the Rights of Persons with Disabilities.

21. The *World Report on Disability* (World Health Organization and World Bank 2011) asserts that out of the 119 countries that ratified the CRPD by that time, fifty have passed disability rights legislation and others are shortly following suit.

22. For example, recent research on stunting has shown that malnutrition impairs an individual's intellectual and physical capacities, thereby placing them at increased risk of agency deprivation. Such forms of agency deprivation should be considered within their sociocultural and economic constructs. Specific contextual factors such as conflict, poverty, or disease can lead to agency deprivation among child soldiers, orphans, or children with physical or sensory disabilities who may experience deep psychological or emotional scarring as a result of trauma or neglect. Such deprivations cannot be untangled from the greater economic and development challenges that these adolescents face. Under these conditions, as is evident from recent poverty research, children with intellectual or cognitive disabilities may internalize external depravity and suffer from externally coerced cognitive underdevelopment.

References

Albrecht, Gary L., Katherine D. Seelman, and Michael Bury. 2001. *Handbook of Disability Studies*. London: Sage Publications.

Aniyamuzaala, James R. 2012. "Raising Our Voices for an Inclusive Society: Challenges and Opportunities for the Disability Rights Movement in Uganda." *Journal of Human Rights Practice* 4, no. 2 (April 18): 280–87.

Barnes, Colin, Mike Oliver, and Len Barton. 2002. *Disability Studies Today*. Malden, Mass.: Blackwell.

Blackburn, Claire M., Nick J. Spencer, and Janet M. Read. 2010. "Prevalence of Childhood Disability and the Characteristics and Circumstances of Disabled Children in the UK: Secondary Analysis of the Family Resources Survey." *BMC Pediatrics* 10, no. 21 (April 16). http://dx.doi.org/10.1186/1471-2431-10-21.

Brownlee, Kimberley, and Adam Steven Cureton. 2009. *Disability and Disadvantage*. New York: Oxford University Press.

Center for Applied Special Technology. 2012. "Universal Design for Learning: Lessons for Differentiated Instruction." http://aim.cast.org/learn/historyarchive/back groundpapers/differentiated_instruction_udl.

Chouinard, Vera, Edward Hall, and Robert Wilton. 2010. *Towards Enabling Geographies: "Disabled" Bodies and Minds in Society and Space*. Burlington, Vt.: Ashgate.

Clements, L., & Read, J. 2008. *Disabled people and the right to life: The protection and violation of disabled people's most basic human rights*. Routledge. Retrieved from http://books.google.com/books?hl=en&lr=&id=tS2Ybl8OlW8C&oi=fnd&pg=PP1&dq=Clements+and+read+2008&ots=s8vpdDSpeV&sig=2Vio6isHB7GO2u34qjpNbkGDtlE.

Crocker, D. 2008. Sens concepts of agency. University of Maryland. Retrieved from http://www.worddocx.com/12053/www.worddocx.com_15775.doc

Davis, J., N. Watson, M. Corker, and T. Shakespeare. 2010. "Reconstructing Disability, Childhood and Social Policy in the UK." In *Hearing the Voices of Children: Social Policy for a New Century*, edited by Christine Hallett and Alan Prout, 192–210. London: Routledge. http://eprints.gla.ac.uk/33829/.

Davis, Lennard J., ed. 2006. *The Disability Studies Reader*. Vol. 2. New York: Routledge.

Dear, M., R. Wilton, S. L. Gaber, and L. Takahashi. 1997. "Seeing People Differently: The Sociospatial Construction of Disability." *Environment and Planning D: Society and Space*, 15, no. 4: 455–80.

Ellery, Frances, Gerison Lansdowne, and Corinna Csaky. 2011. *Out from the Shadows: Sexual Violence Against Children with Disabilities*. London: Save the Children.

Geuss, Raymond. 1981. *The Idea of a Critical Theory: Habermas and the Frankfurt School*. Modern European Philosophy. Cambridge: Cambridge University Press.

Groce, Nora Ellen. 2002. *From Charity to Disability Rights: Global Initiatives of Rehabilitation International, 1922–2002*. New York: Rehabilitation International.

———. 2004. "Adolescents and Youth with Disability: Issues and Challenges." *Asia Pacific Disability Rehabilitation Journal* 15, no. 2: 13–23. http://eprints.ucl.ac.uk/15132/.

Habermas, Jürgen. 1970. "Towards a Theory of Communicative Competence." *Inquiry*, 13(1–4), 360–375.

Habermas, Jürgen, and Niklas Luhmann. 1971. *Theorie Der Gesellschaft Oder Sozialtechnologie. Was Leistet D. Systemforschung? Theorie Theorie-Diskussion*. Frankfurt am Main: Suhrkamp.

Khader, Serene. 2009. Adaptive preferences and procedural autonomy. *Journal of Human Development and Capabilities*, 10(2), 169–187.

Litvak, S., and Enders, A. 2001. "The Interface Between Individuals and Environments." In *Handbook on Disability Studies*, edited by G. L. Albrecht, K. D. Seelman, and M. Burry, 711–33. Thousand Oaks, Calif.: Sage Publications.

Mannheim, Karl, Louis Wirth, and Edward Shils. 1936. *Ideology and Utopia: An Introduction to the Sociology of Knowledge*. International Library of Psychology, Philosophy and Scientific Method. New York: Harcourt, Brace.

Mezirow, Jack, and Edward W. Taylor. 2009. *Transformative Learning in Practice: Insights from Community, Workplace, and Higher Education*. 1st ed. San Francisco: Jossey-Bass.

Mitchell, David T., and Sharon L. Snyder. 1997. *The Body and Physical Difference: Discourses of Disability*. Ann Arbor: University of Michigan Press.

Nagar, Richa, and Saraswati Raju. 2003. "Women, NGOs, and the Paradoxes of Empowerment and Disempowerment." *Antipode* 35, no. 1: 1–13.

Oliver, Michael. 1996. *Understanding Disability: From Theory to Practice*. New York: St. Martin's Press.

Pineda, Victor. 2008. "It's About Ability, An Explanation of the Convention on the Rights of Persons with Disabilities." New York: UNICEF. http://www.unicef.org/publications/files/Its_About_Ability_final_.pdf.

———. 2010. "The Capability Model of Disability: Assessing the Success of the UAE Federal Law No. 29 of 2006." PhD diss., University of California, Los Angeles.

Pineda, Victor, and Nirvan Mullick. 2011. "African Youth with Disability Network: Voices from Africa's Youth." World Enabled. http://youtube.com/pinedafoundation.

Sen, Amartya. 1995. "Rationality and Social Choice." *American Economic Review* 85, no. 1 (March): 1–24.

———. 1997a. "Maximization and the Act of Choice." *Econometrica* 65, no. 4 (July): 745–79.

———. 1997b. "Human Capital and Human Capability." *World Development* 25, no. 12 (December): 1959–61.

———. 1998. "Human Development and Financial Conservatism." *World Development* 26, no. 4 (April): 733–42.

———. 1999. "The Possibility of Social Choice." *American Economic Review* 89, no. 3 (June): 349–78.

———. 2000. *Development as Freedom*. 1st Anchor Books ed. New York: Anchor Books.

———. 2004. "Disability and Justice." Paper presented at the Disability and Development conference, Washington, D.C., December 1, 2004.

Shakespeare, Tom. 1996. "Disability, Identity, and Difference." In *Exploring the Divide*, edited by Colin Barnes and Geof Mercer, 94–113. Leeds: Disability Press. http://disability-studies.leeds.ac.uk/files/library/Shakespeare-Chap6.pdf.

———. 2006. "Critiquing the Social Model." In *Disability Rights and Wrongs*, 29–53. New York: Routledge.

———. 2008. "Disability: Suffering, Social Oppression, or Complex Predicament?" In *The Contingent Nature of Life Bioethics and Limits of Human Existence*, edited by Marcus Düwell, Christoph Rehmann-Sutter, and Dietmar Mieth, 235–46. Springer Netherlands.

Shakespeare, Tom, Lisa I. Iezzoni, and Nora E. Groce. 2009. "Disability and the Training of Health Professionals." *Lancet* 374, no. 9704 (November 28): 1815–16. http://linkinghub.elsevier.com/retrieve/pii/S014067360962050X.

Silvers, Anita, David T. Wasserman, and Mary Briody Mahowald. 1998. *Disability, Difference, Discrimination: Perspectives on Justice in Bioethics and Public Policy*. Point/Counterpoint. Lanham, Md.: Rowman & Littlefield.

Snyder, Sharon L., Brenda Jo Brueggemann, and Rosemarie Garland Thomson. 2002. *Disability Studies: Enabling the Humanities*. New York: Modern Language Association of America.

TenBroek, Jacobus, ed. 1969. *Equal Under Law*. Collier Book. New enlarged ed.. London: Collier-Macmillan.

UN General Assembly. 2007. "Convention on the Rights of Persons with Disabilities and Optional Protocol." New York: UN.

World Health Organization and World Bank. 2011. *World Report on Disability*. Geneva WHO and World Bank.

CHAPTER 5

Adolescent Social and Emotional Development: A Developmental Science Perspective on Adolescent Human Rights

Clea McNeely and Krishna Bose

> Only the proper environmental conditions are required to allow the underlying "seed of compassion" to germinate and grow.
> —The Fourteenth Dalai Lama

Social and Emotional Development

The adolescent years are a quest for social and emotional competence. Humans are social beings, and both their survival and success depend on learning to relate to other people. However, the skills necessary for successful social relationships do not occur unaided or without effort. Social and emotional competence develops from acquired experience derived from both modeled behavior and direct nurturance. For a variety of biological and social reasons, it is during the adolescent years that these skills are most readily acquired. Achieving social and emotional competence are primary developmental tasks of adolescence.

Emotional competence is the ability to perceive, assess, and manage one's own emotions. Social competence is the capacity to be sensitive and effective in relating to other people (Goleman 1994). Social and emotional development work in concert: through relating to others, young people gain insights into themselves and vice versa. The skills necessary for managing emotions and successful relationships include *self-awareness*, *social awareness*, *self-management*, and *the ability to get along with others*. These skills are foundational requirements for success in the adult roles of spouse, parent, family member, employee or employer, and community member.

Self-awareness is the ability to recognize and name one's emotions. Without this awareness, undefined emotions can become uncomfortable enough that adolescents may grow withdrawn or depressed or pursue unhealthy behaviors that distract them from the discomfort of their feelings, behaviors such as oversleeping, drinking alcohol, using drugs, or overeating. Adolescents, as a group, are less skilled at self-awareness than adults, partly because of their still-developing brains, and partly due to lack of practice. As discussed below, brain development and practice with emotional skills may be mutually reinforcing processes.

Social awareness is the capacity to develop empathy and take into account the feelings of others. Social awareness is more difficult for teens than adults, again probably due to both lack of experience and a still-developing brain. Many adolescents have difficulty accurately interpreting others' emotions, particularly negative emotions such as anger or fear (Yurgelun-Todd and Killgore 2006, 194–99). At the same time, due to reasons that are not completely understood, young people appear to have more intense emotional responses—happiness as well as distress—to social interactions, particularly to interactions with their peers (Spear 2010).

Emotional *self-management* is monitoring and regulating one's emotions. Adolescents appear to enjoy intense emotional experiences more than do adults, who, forgetting their own experience as teens, often find the intensity of emotional reactions of young people unsettling or annoying (Steinberg 2001). Nonetheless, adolescents can and do learn to manage their emotions. Self-management in a young person involves using their developing cognitive skills to assess and choose how to react to situations.

As discussed below, adults play a critical role in helping to foster all of these skills.

Healthy Peer Relationships

These three skills in recognizing and managing emotions—self-awareness, social awareness, and self-management—are prerequisites to success in social relationships. Adolescents develop these skills just as social relationships outside the family are becoming highly salient. Indeed, the heightened importance of social relationships provides opportunities to practice these skills. Young people generally prefer to spend increasing amounts of time with fellow adolescents and less time with family. This finding holds true across cultures and, indeed, across mammalian species, suggesting that it is a normal part of adolescent development and not a cultural attribute of individualistic, Western cultures (Spear 2010). The desire to spend more time with other young people and to be affiliated with a group is thought to stem in part from changes in the teen brain. Social acceptance by peers triggers stronger positive emotions during adolescence than during adulthood. Being part of a group offers teens opportunities to learn and practice new skills such as resolving conflict and developing trust and intimacy. Thus spending time with peers appears to support key developmental tasks of adolescence while also providing a shared experience and social support for the many rapid physical, social, and emotional changes that occur during adolescence (Buhrmeister 1998).

The support of peers is not without risk, however. The motivation for belonging influences how readily adolescents will give in to peer pressure and how much influence the group will have in their lives (Chein et al. 2011). In general, the more important it is to a teen to belong, the more susceptible he or she is to peer pressure. Popular teens may be more influential because their social acceptance is more sought after, although this hypothesis has not been thoroughly tested. What is known, however, is that popular teens may be more susceptible to peer influence than previously thought because they work hard to maintain their position at the top of the social pyramid. Part of this work may involve engaging in behaviors they think are expected of them, including smoking, drinking, or sexual activity. For example, in U.S. schools where smoking cigarettes is normative, popular students are more likely to smoke than other students (Alexander et al. 2001). Other researchers have shown that popular students are more likely than other students to drink alcohol and engage in minor deviant behaviors (Allen et al. 2005).

Healthy Sexual Development

During adolescence, teens strive to become comfortable with their changing bodies and rapidly developing sexuality; indeed, this is a central developmental task. Healthy sexual development involves more than sexual behavior. It is the combination of physical sexual maturation known as puberty, age-appropriate sexual behaviors, and the formation of a positive sense of sexual well-being (Monasterio et al. 2010). Healthy sexual development involves a young person's ability to manage intimate and reproductive behavior responsibly and without guilt, fear, or shame.

Sexual development begins well before adolescence. Hormonal changes—an elevation of androgens, estradiol, thyrotropin, and cortisol in the adrenal glands—start to emerge between the ages of six and eight. The visible signs of puberty begin to show up between the ages of nine and twelve for most children. At this age, children become more self-conscious about their emerging sexual feelings and their bodies, and they are often reluctant to undress in front of others, even a parent of the same gender. Boys and girls tend to play with friends of the same gender.

The passage into adolescence typically begins with the onset of menarche (menstruation) in girls and semenarche (ejaculation) in boys, both of which occur, on average, around age twelve or thirteen, although there is wide variety across regions depending on nutritional adequacy. As physical maturation continues, young adolescents may become alternately fascinated with and chagrined by their changing bodies, and often compare themselves to the development they notice in their peers. Sexual fantasy and masturbation, which are normal throughout life, increase between the ages of ten and thirteen (Ponton and Judice 2004). Early adolescents become more interested in interactions with peers of the opposite sex, and in cultures where contact is allowed, some young people may begin experimenting with kissing and touching. The vast majority of young adolescents are not prepared emotionally or physically for oral sex or sexual intercourse. If such adolescents do have sex, they are highly vulnerable to sexual and emotional abuse, sexually transmitted infections, HIV, and early pregnancy (Blum and Mmari 2004).

Middle adolescents, ages 14–16 years, exhibit an increased interest in romantic and sexual relationships. At this age, both genders experience a high level of sexual energy, although boys may have a stronger sex drive due to higher testosterone levels. On an abstract level, adolescents ages 14–16 understand the consequences of unprotected sex, if properly taught, but they may lack the skills to act on this knowledge in situations where they are aroused or coerced (Ponton and Judice 2004). Many young people find themselves in coercive situations in which they do not have power to choose whether or not to have sex or to use protection (Jejeebhoy, Shah, and Thapa 2005).

By the time an adolescent is seventeen years old, physical sexual maturation is typically complete, although late bloomers are not uncommon. Sexual behavior during this time may be more expressive, since cognitive development in older adolescents has progressed to the point where they are capable of intimate and sharing relationships. Intimate and sharing relationships are an essential part of healthy sexual development, and they require the socioemotional skills described above: self-awareness, social awareness, and self-management. Intimate relationships involve love, compassion, and appreciation, and may or may not include sexual acts such as kissing, touching, oral sex, or intercourse (Ponton and Judice 2004).

All humans are sexual beings and develop a sexual identity. Sexual identity is one's identification with a gender and a sexual orientation. Gender identity (masculine/feminine) may differ from a person's biological sex (male/female). Sexual orientation (heterosexual/bisexual/homosexual) is based on an awareness of being attracted to the same or opposite sex. There is considerable diversity in combinations of gender identity and sexual orientation among humans, and this diversity appears in all cultures, regardless of the extent to which the diversity is culturally acceptable (Spear 2010). The manner in which adolescents are educated about and exposed to sexuality influences how they feel about their sexual identity. Some cultural perspectives and religious groups maintain that same-sex attraction, which is biologically normal, is sinful or unnatural. Religious or cultural intolerance can cause deep psychological and emotional anguish for young people (McNeely and Blanchard 2010).

Expressions of sexual behavior differ among adolescents, and whether they engage in sexual activity depends on personal readiness, cultural and family standards, exposure to sexual abuse, peer pressure, religious values, internalized moral guidelines, psychological needs, and opportunity (Michels et al. 2005). The environmental supports that promote socioemotional development also help foster healthy sexual development, in part by providing young people with skills necessary to have successful intimate relationships.

The Neuroscience of Social and Emotional Development: Adolescence as a Time of Opportunity and Vulnerability

Social and emotional development differs from sexual and physical maturation in a profound and important way. Whereas physical growth and the maturation of the reproductive system occur unaided in the presence of adequate nutrition, healthy socioemotional development needs nurturance and socialization. Specifically, socioemotional development must be fostered through positive social interactions with adults and other young people. This socialization requirement for healthy socioemotional development has certain evolutionary advantages. Humans are social beings who must live in cooperative groups to survive. The fact that subsequent generations shape the social and emotional skills of their young allows humans to be more adaptive to changing environmental conditions, including the changing norms of the community (local, regional, or national). However, if adequate socialization does not occur, it leaves young people in a place of particular vulnerability.

In this section we explore the possibility that environmental factors may literally shape the adolescent's brain. In the sections below we describe the key environmental factors shown to promote healthy socioemotional development and explore the extent to which these vary across cultures.

The brain has two major periods of growth, each followed by biological "remodeling" or "sculpting." The first occurs in infancy and early childhood, when billions of brain cells (neurons) and the synapses connecting them are produced, followed by a period of synaptic pruning. The synapses that are retained are those that help the child survive and thrive in his or her surrounding environment. For example, exposure to major stressors in infancy—such as abuse—affects brain development, leading to heightened hormonal and behavioral responses to stressors throughout life (Spear 2010). Such heightened stress reactivity prepares a person to remain vigilant in a threatening environment. However, if the environment becomes less threatening, the now-programmed social and emotional responses of the individual can become counterproductive, leading to stress-related illnesses and to difficult relationships caused by inappropriate perceptions of threat (Heim et al. 2000).

A second period of neuron production followed by synaptic pruning occurs with puberty, and during this period brain development is also sensitive to environmental influences, although less so than during infancy. Up to half of synaptic connections, the junctions between the neurons, are eliminated during adolescence. At the same time, an increasing number of axons—the elongated appendages of the neuron that connect it to the synapses—become insulated with a fatty substance called myelin, also known as white matter. In her exhaustive review of adolescent brain development, Spear summarizes intriguing, albeit preliminary, evidence that the experiences and activities of adolescents influence the way the brain is sculpted—which axons are myelinated and which synapses are pruned (Spear 2010).

Myelination is driven in part by the amount of activity of the axons: the more a neural pathway is used, the more likely it is to become myelinated and, hence, quicker and more efficient at processing information. For example, among a sample of adult pianists, the amount of white matter in certain areas of the brain was associated with the amount of time they spent practicing piano as children and adolescents, whereas there was no association between time spent practicing as an adult and the amount of white matter for those same brain areas (Bengtsson et al. 2005). This pattern seems to hold not just for creative and cognitive functioning but also for the development of social and emotional skills. Choi and colleagues found that parental verbal abuse during childhood and adolescence was associated with less neural connectivity (that is, less myelination and smaller axonal diameters) in brain areas associated with cognitive processing and psychological functioning (Choi et al. 2009).

Synaptic culling during adolescence may be partly experience-dependent as well. For example, social stress during adolescence (studied by housing animals in a new social situation daily) has been found to induce alterations in regions of the amygdala critical for socioemotional control and adaptation to social stressors (McCormick et al. 2007). Although this research requires autopsies and cannot be conducted in humans, it is consistent with decades of behavioral research that shows that severe stressors during adolescence have long-term effects on socioemotional functioning (for example, see Garmezy 1991; Haggerty et al., 1996). The brain systems most affected by environmental influences appear to be those regions that change most during adolescence, that is, the frontal cortical regions and the reward and emotional centers in the brain, as well as the connections between the two. These are precisely the two brain systems involved in socioemotional processing (Spear 2010).

The implications of research on adolescent brain plasticity are intriguing, as they suggest a mechanism that shapes the very health and evolution of societies through time. If the environment can literally shape the way the brain processes social and emotional stimuli, it offers an explanation of why environmental influences during adolescence have a persistent effect on the later life of the individual. The fact that plasticity is heightened during adolescence also suggests that attention to environmental factors during the adolescent years deserves particular attention and investment. This research has potential implications for a human rights perspective. For example, sustained human rights abuses of adolescents, such as verbal, sexual, or physical abuse, might result in detrimental changes in their brain structures (Andersen et al. 2008; Teicher et al. 2004).

Environmental Supports for Emotional, Social, and Healthy Sexual Development

What are the environmental supports critical to healthy social and emotional development? The behavioral research literature in this area is well developed and produces three reliable conclusions across various groups of young people. First, at least five environmental supports are necessary for healthy socioemotional and sexual development; we discuss these at length below. Second, for the most part these five environmental supports are not culturally specific. In other words, basic environmental supports work in a similarly supportive fashion in most cultures. This does not preclude the very likely possibility that additional environmental supports are important in various cultural groups. Third, support may be provided in many contexts: family, school, workplace, and community. Importantly, each context is additive to socioemotional development; personal growth is promoted by all forms of support whatever the context.

The five environmental supports are

1. Physical and psychological safety,
2. Supportive relationships with adults,
3. Respect for individuality,
4. Consistent structure and adult supervision, and
5. Support for efficacy and competence.

PHYSICAL AND PSYCHOLOGICAL SAFETY

Safety is a foundational support for healthy socioemotional and sexual development. In other words, when safety is not present, people tend to focus on getting this need met before any others, consistent with Maslow's hierarchy of needs (Tay and Diener 2011). *Physical safety* is the absence of hunger, inadequate shelter, unsafe working or living conditions, harm from violence, and sexual abuse. *Psychological safety* is the absence of conditions that cause severe psychological harm: emotional abuse and neglect, sexual harassment, and chronic bullying. The exact point at which psychological safety is reached depends on individual perception as well as the objective conditions of abuse and neglect. In general, there is agreement that psychological safety is not present when adolescents experience violence or the serious threat of physical violence, verbal abuse, or sexual harassment (National Research Council and Institute of Medicine 2002). As described above, prolonged stress from the lack of physical or psychological safety in childhood and adolescence results in decreased socioemotional capacities in adulthood and can cause long-term psychological disorders. Correlational data suggests that changes in brain structure—specifically, reduced myelination with white matter in pathways used for psychological and cognitive functioning—might account for the difficulty in recovering from abuse and neglect during adolescence (Choi et al. 2009).

SUPPORTIVE RELATIONSHIPS WITH ADULTS

Supportive relationships with adults have been defined using a plethora of terms: support, warmth, nurturance, connection, good communication, encouragement, and care. In addition to these affective components, supportive relationships provide instrumental supports, such as guidance and help with tasks (Cutrona and Russell 1987; Weiss 1974). The underlying commonality to these varied dimensions of support is an attentiveness and responsiveness to adolescents' subjective worlds (National Research Council and Institute of Medicine 2002).

Supportive relationships with adults occur in multiple settings: family, school, community, place of work, and place of worship. The specific adult actions and behaviors that make young people feel supported varies to some extent across cultures, as described below, but in all cultures support includes the expression of encouragement, affection, care, and the provision of valued resources. Across cultures, support from adults in each of these settings has been linked to healthy socioemotional and sexual development, including better social initiative, higher self-esteem, lower emotional distress, lower substance use, less involvement in minor delinquency and physical fighting, and delayed initiation of sexual intercourse (Barber, Stolz, and Olsen 2005; Peterson and Hann 1999; McNeely, Whitlock, and Libbey 2009; Steinberg 1990; Catalano et al. 2012). Why do supportive relationships matter so much? There are multiple explanations. When parents and other important adults in a young person's life express affection and caring, children develop a feeling of security, trust, and confidence, which in turn allows them to have successful relationships and make prosocial decisions (Bowlby 1969). Similarly, children adopt the behaviors and attitudes of the people they value (Bandura 1997). Adults who model supportive behaviors, which require empathy and self-management of one's own emotions, increase the likelihood that the children they influence will imitate those behaviors. Finally, supportive adults can buffer the toxic effects of stress by increasing children's and adolescents' capacity to cope and reducing their perception of stressful situations as threatening (Cohen and Wills 1985). In sum, the positive consequences of supportive relationships with adults are ubiquitous and robust, perhaps because of the multiple pathways through which they promote healthy social, emotional, and sexual development.

RESPECT FOR INDIVIDUALITY

Respect for a young person's individuality refers to respect for a young person's sense of self and emotional autonomy. In the psychological research literature, which tends to focus on preventing negative outcomes rather than on promoting health, the focus is placed on adult behaviors that convey a lack of respect or *disrespect*. These include behaviors that are psychologically controlling, coercive, manipulative, or intrusive (Barber 1996; Schaefer 1965; Ryan et al. 2006; Baumrind 1991). Barber and colleagues asked adolescents from five cultures in Asia, Africa, and Latin America what their parents did that made them feel disrespected or not worthy of being their own person. The adolescents, ages 14–17, reported they felt disrespected by ridicule ("[They call me] useless"), being embarrassed in public ("Embarrass you in front of friends"), invalidation ("She's like, 'You're not my child'"), violations of privacy ("They look at my stuff without permission"), guilt inducement ("They'll put a guilt trip on me and I'll feel bad"), comparison to others ("When they compare you to a brother or sister"), and being ignored ("They walk away without saying anything"). These behaviors were highly correlated in all five cultures, suggesting that they all serve a similar function—to undermine a young person's sense of self (Barber et al. 2012).

Across cultures, parental respect for adolescents' individuality is universally associated with emotional well-being and with decreased involvement in problem behaviors such as skipping school, drinking alcohol, and early sexual intercourse (Barber, Stolz, and Olsen 2002; Barber et al. 2012; World Health Organization 2002). As with supportive relationships with adults, there are multiple mechanisms through which respect for individuality promotes social, emotional, and sexual well-being: respect for individuality allows the young person opportunities to develop a sense of personal efficacy, self-definition, and to establish a stable identity that is independent of the parent (Barber 1996).

There is little research on adults' respect for the individuality of young people in contexts outside the family, such as schools and communities. In the education literature, respect for individuality is generally conceptualized as choice and participation: the ability to participate in developing rules and choosing activities, as well as being encouraged to be autonomous in problem solving rather than being overly directed (National Research Council 2000). These conditions have been associated with higher academic motivation and self-concept (Eccles, Wigfield, and Schiefele 1998). An important area of future investigation is the extent to which young people perceive that adults in their schools practice the behaviors that undermine their sense of worth as a person (for example, ridicule, public embarrassment, violation of privacy, social comparison) and the extent to which these practices undermine their social and emotional well-being.

CONSISTENT STRUCTURE AND APPROPRIATE ADULT SUPERVISION

A setting with consistent structure has clear, fair rules and expectations, age-appropriate monitoring of youth behavior, and consistently and fairly enforced limits or discipline (National Research Council and the Institute of Medicine 2002). As with all of these contextual conditions, conceptual labels for structure and supervision vary and include behavioral regulation (Barber, Stolz, and Olsen 2005), supervision (McCord 1979), monitoring (Brown, et al. 1993), and enforcement standards (Baumrind 1991).

In all settings—family, school, workplace, and community—young people engage in fewer problem behaviors, including early sexual intercourse, when there are developmentally appropriate expectations for behavior that are consistently and fairly enforced (Connell and Wellborn 1991; Roth and Brooks-Gunn 2000). There are three potential explanations for this relationship. At the most basic level, a stable and predictable reality is necessary to develop trust and confidence (National Research Council and the Institute of Medicine 2002). Second, unsupervised youth spend more time with peers in unstructured activities, which in turn increases their involvement in risk taking, possibly because risk taking in the presence of peers is particularly rewarding to the developing adolescent brain (Osgood et al. 1996; Spear

2010). Third, fair and consistently enforced limits promote self-control over behavior, such that young people who experience age-appropriate expectations and limits imposed by adults are more likely to behave in ways consistent with those expectations when they are by themselves or with peers (Maccoby and Martin 1983).

It is critical that all developmental contexts be age-appropriate, but this is especially the case with structure and supervision. Both too little and too much adult-imposed structure are related to poorer outcomes (National Research Council and the Institute of Medicine 2002). Rules and limit-setting appropriate in early adolescence can be experienced as suffocating by older adolescents, who become increasingly able to create their own structure and self-control (Whitlock 2006). As they grow older, adolescents desire increasing opportunity to have input into the behavioral expectations and how they are enforced. Linda Darling-Hammond (1997) found that in U.S. schools, students were more willing to follow the rules when they had the opportunity to participate in making and enforcing them.

SUPPORT FOR EFFICACY AND COMPETENCE

Young people are agents of their own development. Although their environment influences their brain structure in subtle and profound ways, young people are not passive recipients of those environmental influences. Rather, they choose how to respond to the environmental stimuli and they do so with increasing cognitive and regulatory capacities as their brains mature (see the Steinberg chapter).

Healthy social and emotional development is supported when young people have opportunities to make a difference in their society in ways that are meaningful to them. These experiences give young people a sense of efficacy, that is, a belief in their own competence (Bandura 1997). The types of experiences vary across contexts and culture and can include political activism, community service, missionary work, or participation in the arts. Not all of these opportunities for efficacy are deemed valuable by the adults in power (for example, youth political activism against the Israeli occupation or Arab dictators), but when these activities are meaningful to young people, they can foster healthy social and emotional development (Barber 2008).

Young people also need opportunities to build competence through learning new skills. Cognitive competence is built through schooling and the practice of critical thinking skills. Social and emotional competence is built through the practice of social and emotional skills. Healthy sexual development is supported by the development of socioemotional skills, as well as by accurate education about sexual health and access to reproductive health services (McNeely and Blanchard 2010). There is substantial research evaluating strategies to promote social, emotional, and sexual development, particularly in the United States.[1]

Cultural Differences in Environmental Supports

The section above described environmental supports important to development across cultures and contexts. Given that measures of these environmental supports have been developed primarily by Western researchers, it is reasonable to question whether these environmental supports are applicable in all cultural settings. One study has explicitly addressed this question. Clea McNeely and Brian Barber asked the question: "Do the parenting methods that produce the experience of being loved and supported differ across cultures?" (McNeely and Barber 2010, 602). They analyzed open-ended responses from forty-three hundred adolescents in twelve national or cultural groups to the question: "Tell us four specific things your parents do that make you feel loved" (McNeely and Barber 2010, 602).

This study produced four findings central to the issue at hand. First, adolescents in all settings validated that supportive parenting behaviors were important to making them feel loved. The young people had no difficulty answering the questions. Second, the young people validated existing measures of parental support. This suggests that findings from studies applying Western measures of parent-child relationships in different cultural settings may have utility. Third, adolescents extended the list of supportive parental behaviors to include things not typically measured. For example, adolescents in some cultures said they felt loved when their parents provided moral guidance and advice. This finding affirms the concerns of those who question the completeness of Western measures of social context. Although Western measures may be cross-culturally valid, they may not be measuring the most important attributes of the context for promoting healthy emotional, social, and sexual development.

Finally, McNeely and Barber found that parenting strategies that have been interpreted previously as reinforcing culturally distinct purposes may, in fact, serve a purpose that is common across cultures. For example, the authors found that when parents provide a rare and valued commodity to their adolescent child, it is viewed as a sign of love. However, the specific commodities that are rare and valued vary across cultures. In postapartheid South Africa, black adolescents reported feeling loved when their parents supported their education, to which access had been systematically restricted by the apartheid state. Support for education was not named as a supportive behavior in the U.S. or Australian samples, however, where access to public education is universal. In contrast, many U.S. and Australian adolescents reported feeling loved when their parents provided a different rare and valued commodity: time (that is, spent time with them) (McNeely and Barber 2010). To our knowledge, cross-cultural comparisons from the adolescent perspective of adult behaviors that support emotional, social, and healthy sexual development in other contexts (school, community, and work) have not been conducted.

Contexts of Support

The contexts that influence adolescents most often cited in research are family, school, workplace, and community. Healthy development is enhanced when young people experience appropriate developmental supports in as many of these contexts as possible (Call and Mortimer 2001). The contexts in which young people spend the most time matter the most. This may vary from culture to culture, and also vary according to age.

Implications for a Rights Framework

To a large extent, the five environmental supports described in this chapter neatly map onto the key principles of the human rights agenda (CRC 2003). Psychological and physical safety, for example, is fully consistent with the fundamental human rights principle of protection from all forms of abuse, neglect, violence, and exploitation. Respect for individuality is consistent with the human rights principle of respect for the views of the child. Two environmental supports—support for efficacy and mattering and respect for individuality—are related to the principle of civil rights and freedoms, including free access to information and the right to confidentiality in medical care. Finally, all five environmental supports are relevant to the human rights principle of appropriate guidance in the exercise of rights, which acknowledges the responsibilities, rights, and duties of parents or other legal guardians to provide guidance to the child in the exercise of his or her rights.

Yet these environmental supports have not received much attention from the human rights community; conversely, developmental scientists who study how development unfolds in context have not paid much attention to adolescents as rights holders. The research described above seems to indicate that there are many implications that deserve investigation from both directions.

The efficacy of environmental supports for healthy social and emotional development, and the long-term ill effects of deficient supports, would seem to promote the perspective that these supports are essential for fully realizing one's humanity and, therefore should be considered an essential element in the human rights of adolescents, a right. The developmental science can be drawn on to provide an empirical argument that the protection of human rights is necessary for healthy development, as well as to articulate how to best protect those rights across contexts and cultures.

Conversely, a human rights agenda has implications for the developmental perspective. To the extent that a human rights agenda shifts legal structures and cultural norms through legal action and advocacy, a rights agenda should be identified as a context that provides support for healthy development (which is, after all, its stated aim). This integration of disciplines is illustrated in figure 5.1, in which we incorporate a human rights agenda (defined as legal protocols and the strategies to enforce them) into the traditional ecological model used by developmental scientists and public health practitioners (Bronfenbrenner 1979). The inner ring contains the contexts that are most proximal to the individual and hence have the most direct influence. The outer rings represent more distal influences, which affect young people's development directly (for example, laws about age at first marriage) or indirectly by shaping the more proximal contexts. In this model, a rights agenda is positioned at the distal level because it affects individual social, emotional, and sexual development indirectly through laws, policies, and media, and through advocacy efforts to change social norms. The arrow pointing outwards from the model indicates that these contextual influences change over time as young people develop and the contexts themselves change.

The rights perspective often provides the *moral imperative* to act, whereas developmental science—the study of how people change over time across contexts—can offer guidance as to *when and how* to act. The case of early marriage serves as an example. From the rights perspective, early marriage

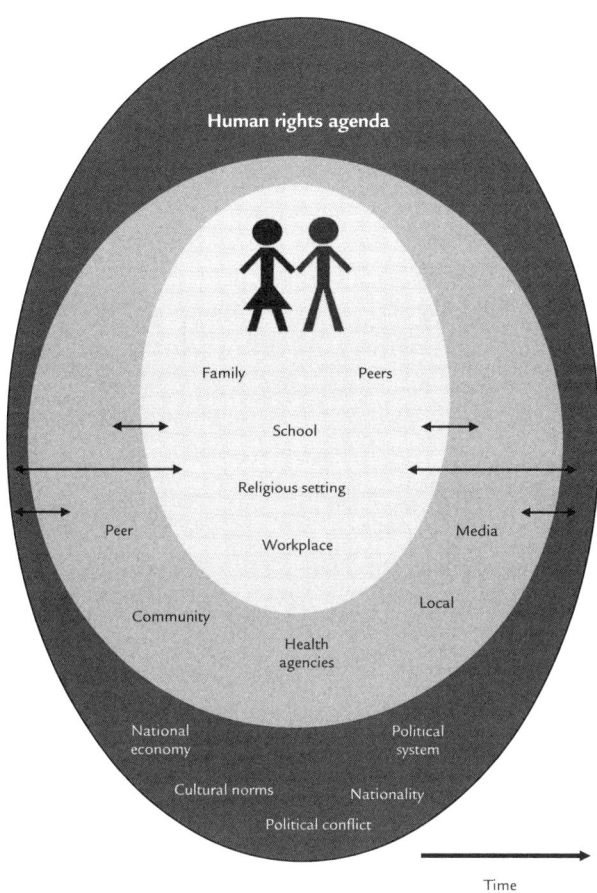

Figure 5.1. Framework incorporating a human rights agenda into an ecological model.

deprives young people of the protections of childhood, such as the right to an education and all of the special protection measures they are entitled to under the CRC (CRC 2003). Since the primary mechanism for enforcing human rights is the legal system, the practical solution from the human rights perspective is to make marriage with or without parental consent illegal before the age of eighteen and to support the capacity of states to enforce such measures.

Relatedly, the developmental perspective considers early marriage a problem because it impedes the social, emotional, and healthy sexual development of young people, particularly girls. Early marriage, from this perspective, harms development when it places young people in a setting that, given their developmental stage, is psychologically or physically unsafe, unsupportive, lacking respect for their autonomy, and does not allow them to develop skills and competencies by attending school or participating in normal activities of youth their age (for example, sports, social organizations). In addition, early marriage can place young people at risk for early childbearing and sexually transmitted infections and HIV/AIDS (World Health Organization 2011). Thus, from a developmental perspective, the *context* of early marriage becomes important in understanding its effects. This context includes the age at which marriage occurs (for example, age twelve vs. age seventeen), the social customs (for example, whether a young bride stays with her own family until age eighteen), the age difference between spouses, and the extent to which the environmental supports are available in the marital home. A developmental perspective would also prioritize the voice of young people themselves, who may desire to marry before age eighteen either for love or to escape a toxic home environment. To translate the developmental science perspective into policy requires considerable research, and the policy recommendations produced tend to be nuanced, which is not always practical for policy makers or advocates.

The value of combining both the human rights perspective and developmental perspectives is illustrated in the recent set of guidelines from the World Health Organization (2011) on preventing early pregnancy and poor reproductive outcomes. The panel strongly recommended that laws and policies to prohibit marriage before age eighteen be enacted and enforced, and agreed that such laws and policies "are important from both rights-based and public health perspectives" (World Health Organization 2011, 25). But the panel also noted potential harms of these interventions: "First, the enforcement of such laws could penalize those who contravene them such as to endanger the livelihoods and wellbeing of adolescent girls and their families. Second, the introduction of these laws and policies may create conflict by disrupting existing social norms" (World Health Organization 2011, 25). The panel also recommended that research be conducted to identify effective ways to formulate and enforce laws and policies to delay age of marriage and the unintended harmful consequences of such laws.

As unprecedented globalization proceeds, we are in an historical time of rapid and dynamic change. The trajectory of civilization is impossible to know, yet every actor, individually and collectively, strives to improve conditions for success. The human rights agenda represents an effort to guide the trajectory by inviting disparate governments to affirm that some rights are common and essential to all.

We suggest that the developmental perspective can guide and support this agenda (and that the human rights perspective can do the same for developmental science). Developmental science has helped to identify the key environmental conditions that promote human development. Because of the plasticity of the adolescent brain, these environmental supports—including safety, supportive relationships with adults, respect for individuality, structure and supervision, and opportunities for building efficacy—have effects on well-being that persist into adulthood and even across generations. Although they manifest in culturally unique ways, these supports appear to operate similarly across cultures. The developmental perspective can also contribute to the human rights agenda by identifying ways that legal frameworks—the tools of the human rights agenda—can support culturally unique expressions of those rights for young people of different ages.

Note

1. For a review of strategies to promote sexual health, see Kirby, Laris, and Rolleri (2007); for a review of strategies for social and emotional development in community programs, see National Research Council and the Institute of Medicine (2002); and for school programs, see Greenberg et al. (2003).

References

Allen, Joseph P., Maryfrances R. Porter, F. Christy McFarland, Penny Marsh, and Kathleen B. McElhaney. 2005. "The Two Faces of Adolescents' Success with Peers: Adolescent Popularity, Social Adaptation, and Deviant Behavior." *Child Development* 76, no. 3 (May): 747–60.

Alexander, Cheryl, Marina Piazza, Debra Mekos, and Thomas Valente. 2001. "Peers, Schools, and Adolescent Cigarette Smoking." *Journal of Adolescent Health* 29, no. 1 (July): 22–30.

Andersen, Susan L., Akemi Tomada, Evelyn S. Vincow, Elizabeth Valente, Ann Polcari, and Martin H. Teicher. 2008. "Preliminary Evidence for Sensitive Periods in the Effect of Childhood Sexual Abuse on Regional Brain Development." *Journal of Neuropsychiatry and Clinical Neurosciences* 20, no. 3 (June): 292–301.

Bandura, Albert. 1977. *Social Learning Theory.* Upper Saddle River, N.J.: Prentice-Hall.

———. 1997. *Self-Efficacy: The Exercise of Control.* New York: W. H. Freeman Publishers.

Barber, Brian K. 1996. "Parental Psychological Control: Revisiting a Neglected Construct." *Child Development* 67, no. 6: 3296–319. doi:10.1111/j.1467-8624.1996.tb01915.x.

———. 2008. "Contrasting Portraits of War: Youths' Varied Experiences with Political Violence in Bosnia and Palestine." *International Journal of Behavioral Development* 32, no. 4 (July): 298–309.

Barber, Brian K., Heidi E. Stolz, and Joseph A. Olsen. 2005. "Parental Support, Psychological Control, and Behavioral Control: Assessing Relevance Across Time, Method, and Culture." *Monographs of the Society for Research in Child Development* 70, no. 4: i, v, 1–147.

Barber, Brian K., Mingzhu Xia, Clea A. McNeely, Joseph A. Olsen, and Krishna Bose. 2012. "Feeling Disrespected by Parents: Refining the Measurement and Understanding of Psychological Control." *Journal of Adolescence* 35, no. 2 (April): 273–87. doi:10.1016/j.adolescence.2011.10.010.

Baumrind, Diana. 1991. "The Influence of Parenting Style on Adolescent Competence and Substance Use." *Journal of Early Adolescence* 11, no. 1 (February): 56–95.

Bengtsson, Sara L., Zoltan Nagy, Stefan Skare, Lea Forsman, Hans Forssberg, and Fredrik Ullen. 2005. "Extensive Piano Practicing Has Regionally Specific Effects on White Matter Development." *Nature Neuroscience* 8, no. 9 (August): 1148–50.

Blum, Robert, and Kristin Mmari. 2004. *Risk and Protective Factors Affecting Adolescent Reproductive Health in Developing Countries: An Analysis of Adolescent Sexual and Reproductive Health Literature from Around the World: Summary.* Geneva: World Health Organization.

Bowlby, John. 1969. *Attachment: Vol. 1: Attachment and Loss.* New York: Basic Books.

Bronfenbrenner, Urie. 1979. *The Ecology of Human Development: Experiments by Nature and Design.* Cambridge, Mass.: Harvard University Press.

Brown, B. Bradford, Nina Mounts, Susie D. Lamborn, and Laurence Steinberg. 1993. "Parenting Practices and Peer Group Affiliation in Adolescence." *Child Development* 64, no. 2 (April): 467–82. doi:10.1111/j.1467-8624.1993.tb02922.x.

Buhrmeister, Duane. 1998. "Need Fulfillment, Interpersonal Competence, and the Developmental Contexts of Early Adolescent Friendship." In *The Company They Keep: Friendship in Childhood and Adolescence,* edited by William M. Bukowski, Andrew F. Newcomb, and Willard W. Hartup, 158–85. New York: Cambridge University Press.

Call, Kathleen T., and Jeylan Mortimer. 2001. *Arenas of Comfort in Adolescence: A Study of Adjustment in Context.* Hillsdale, N.J.: Lawrence Erlbaum Associates.

Catalano, Richard F., Abigail A. Fagan, Loretta E. Gavin, Mark T. Greenberg, Charles E. Irwin, David A. Ross, and Daniel T. L. Shek. 2012. "Worldwide Application of Prevention Science in Adolescent Health." *Lancet* 379, no. 9826 (April): 1653–64.

Chein, Jason, Dustin Albert, Lia O'Brien, Kaitlyn Uckert, and Laurence Steinberg. 2011. "Peers Increase Adolescent Risk Taking by Enhancing Activity in the Brain's Reward Circuitry." *Developmental Science*, 14, no. 2 (March): F1–F10.

Choi, Jeewook, Bumseok Jeong, Michael L. Rohan, Ann M. Polcari, and Martin H. Teicher. 2009. "Preliminary Evidence for White Matter Tract Abnormalities in Young Adults Exposed to Parental Verbal Abuse." *Biological Psychiatry* 65, no. 3 (February): 227–34.

Cohen, Sheldon, and Thomas A. Wills. 1985. "Stress, Social Support, and the Buffering Hypothesis." *Psychological Bulletin,* 98, no. 2 (September): 310–57.

Connell, James P., and James G. Wellborn. 1991. "Competence, Autonomy, and Relatedness: A Motivational Analysis of Self-System Processes." In *The Minnesota Symposia on Child Psychology.* edited by Megan R. Gunnar and L. Alan Sroufe, 43–77. Hillsdale, N.J.: Lawrence Erlbaum Associates.

Committee on the Rights of the Child, *General Comment No. 4 (2003): Adolescent Health and Development in the Context of the Convention on the Rights of the Child.* July 1.

Cutrona, Carolyn E., and Daniel W. Russell. 1987. "The Provisions of Social Relationships and Adaptation to Stress." In *Advances in Personal Relationships*, edited by Warren H. Jones and Daniel Perlman, vol. 1, 37–68. Greenwich, Conn.: JAI.

Darling-Hammond, Linda. 1997. *The Right to Learn: A Blueprint for Creating Schools That Work.* San Francisco: Jossey-Bass.

Eccles, Jacquelynne S., Allen Wigfield, and Ulrich Schiefele. 1998. "Motivation to Succeed." In *Handbook of Child Psychology: Social, Emotional, and Personality Development*, edited by William Damon and Nancy Eisenberg, 5th ed., 1017–95. Hoboken, N.J.: John Wiley & Sons.

Garmezy, Norman. 1991. "Resiliency and Vulnerability to Adverse Developmental Outcomes Associated with Poverty." *American Journal of Behavioral Sciences* 34:416–30.

Goleman, Daniel. 1994. *Emotional Intelligence.* New York: Bantam.

Greenberg, Mark T., Roger P. Weissberg, Mary Utne O'Brien, Joseph E. Zins, Linda Fredericks, Hank Resnik, and Maurice J. Elias. 2003. "Enhancing School-Based Prevention and Youth Development Through Coordinated Social, Emotional, and Academic Learning." *American Psychologist* 58, nos. 6–7: 466–74. doi:10.1037/0003-066X.58.6-7.466.

Haggerty, Robert J., Lonnie R. Sherrod, Norman Garmezy, and Michael Rutter. 1996. *Stress, Risk and Resilience in Children and Adolescents: Process, Mechanisms and Interventions.* New York: Cambridge University Press.

Heim, Christine, D. Jeffrey Newport, Stacey Heit, Yolanda P. Graham, Molly Wilcox, Robert Bonsall, Andrew Miller, and Charles B. Nemeroff. 2000. "Pituitary-Adrenal and Autonomic Responses to Stress in Women After Sexual and Physical Abuse in Childhood." *JAMA* 284, no. 5 (August): 592–97. doi:10.1001/jama.284.5.592.

Jejeebhoy, Shireen J., Iqba Shah, and Shyam Thapa. 2005. *Sex Without Consent: Young People in Developing Countries*. New York: Zed Books.

Kirby, Douglas B., B. A. Laris, and Lori R. Rolleri. 2007. "Sex and HIV Education Programs: Their Impact on Sexual Behaviors of Young People Throughout the World." *Journal of Adolescent Health* 40, no 3. (March): 206–17.

Maccoby, Eleanor E., and J. A. Martin. 1983. "Socialization in the Context of the Family: Parent-Child Interaction." In *Handbook of Child Psychology: Vol. 4. Socialization, Personality, and Social Development*, edited by Edited by E. Mavis Hetherington and P. Henry Mussen, 1–101. New York: Wiley.

McCord, Joan. 1979. "Some Child-Rearing Antecedents of Criminal Behavior in Adult Men." *Journal of Personality and Social Psychology*, 37, no. 9 (September): 1477–86. doi: 10.1037/0022-3514.37.9.1477.

McCormick, Cheryl M., Amber Merrick, John Secen, and Dana L. Helmreich. 2007. "Social Instability in Adolescence Alters the Central and Peripheral Hypothalamic-Pituitary-Adrenal Responses to a Repeated Homotypic Stressor in Male and Female Rats." *Journal of Neuroendocrinology* 19, no. 2 (February): 116–26.

McNeely, Clea A., and Brian K. Barber. 2010. "How Do Parents Make Adolescents Feel Loved? A Cross-Cultural Comparison from the Adolescent Perspective." *Journal of Adolescent Research* 25, no. 4 (July): 601–31.

McNeely, Clea A., and Jayne Blanchard. 2010. *Guide to Healthy Adolescent Development: The Teen Years Explained*. Baltimore, Md.: Johns Hopkins University.

McNeely, Clea A., Janis Whitlock, and Heather Libbey. 2009. "School Connectedness and Adolescent Well Being." In *Handbook on School-Family Partnerships*, edited by Sandra L. Christianson and Amy L. Reschly, 266–86. New York: Lawrence Earlbaum Associates.

Michels, Tricia M., Rhonda Y. Kropp, Stephen L. Eyre, and Bonnie L. Halpern-Felsher. 2005. "Initiating Sexual Experiences: How Do Young Adolescents Make Decisions Regarding Early Sexual Activity?" *Journal of Research on Adolescence* 15, no. 4 (November): 583–607.

Monasterio, Erica, Natalie Combs, Leah Warner, Mara Larsen-Fleming, and Alicia St. Andrews. 2010. *Sexual Health: An Adolescent Provider Toolkit*. San Francisco: Adolescent Health Working Group.

National Research Council. 2000. *How People Learn: Brain, Mind, Experience, and School*. Edited by John D. Bransford, Ann L. Brown, and Rodney R. Cocking. Washington, D.C.: National Academy Press.

National Research Council and Institute of Medicine. 2002. *Community Programs to Promote Youth Development*. Edited by Jacquelynne Eccles and Jennifer A. Gootman. Committee on Community-Level Programs for Youth; Board on Children,

Youth, and Families; Division of Behavioral and Social Sciences and Education. Washington, D.C.: National Academy Press.

Osgood, D. Wayne, Janet K. Wilson, Patrick M. O'Malley, Jerald G. Bachman, and Lloyd D. Johnston. 1996. "Routine Activities and Individual Deviant Behavior." *American Sociological Review* 61, no. 4 (August): 635–55.

Peterson, Gary W., and Della Hann. 1999. "Socializing Parents and Children in Families." In *Handbook of Marriage and the Family (rev. ed.)*, edited by Marvin B. Sussman, Suzanne K. Steinmetz, and Gary W. Peterson, 327–70. New York: Plenum.

Ponton, Lynne E., and Samuel Judice. 2004. "Typical Adolescent Sexual Development." *Child and Adolescent Psychiatric Clinics of North America* 13, no. 3 (July):497–511. doi:10.1016/j.chc.2004.02.003.

Roth, Jodie, and Jean Brooks-Gunn. 2000. "What Do Adolescents Need for Healthy Development? Implications for Youth Policy." *Social Policy Report* 14, no. 1: 1–19.

Ryan, Richard M., Edward L. Deci, Wendy S. Grolnick, and Jennifer G. La Guardia. 2006. "The Significance of Autonomy and Autonomy Support in Psychological Development and Psychopathology." In *Developmental Psychopathology, Vol. 1: Theory and Method*, edited by Dante Cicchetti and Donald J. Cohen, 2nd ed., 795–849. Hoboken, N.J.: John Wiley & Sons.

Schaefer, Earl S. 1965. "Children's Reports of Parental Behavior: An Inventory." *Child Development* 36, no. 2 (June): 413–24.

Spear, Linda Patia. 2010. *The Behavioral Neuroscience of Adolescence*. New York: W. W. Norton.

Steinberg, Laurence. 1990. "Autonomy, Conflict, and Harmony in the Family Relationship." In *At the Threshold: The Developing Adolescent*, edited by S. Shirley Feldman and Glen R. Elliot, 255–76. Cambridge, Mass.: Harvard University Press.

———. 2001. "We Know Some Things: Parent-Adolescent Relationships in Retrospect and Prospect." *Journal of Research on Adolescence* 11, no. 1 (March): 1–19.

Tay, Louis, and Ed Diener. 2011. "Needs and Subjective Well-Being Around the World." *Journal of Personality and Social Psychology* 101, no. 2 (August): 354–65. doi: 10.1037/a0023779.

Teicher, Martin H., Nathalie L. Dumont, Yutaka Ito, Catherine Vaituzis, Jay N. Giedd, Susan L. Andersen. 2004. "Childhood Neglect Is Associated with Reduced Corpus Callosum Area." *Biological Psychiatry* 56, no. 2 (July):80–5.

Weiss, Robert S. 1974. "The Provisions of Social Relationships." In *Doing Unto Others: Joining, Molding, Conforming, Helping, Loving*, edited by Zick Rubin, 17–26. Upper Saddle River, N.J.: Prentice Hall.

Whitlock, Janis. 2006. "Youth Perceptions of Life at School: Contextual Correlates of School Connectedness in Adolescence." *Applied Developmental Science* 10, no. 1: 13–29.

World Health Organization. 2002. *Broadening the Horizon: Balancing Protection and Risk for Adolescents*. Geneva: Department of Child and Adolescent Health and Development, WHO.

———. 2011. *WHO Guidelines on Preventing Early Pregnancy and Poor Reproductive Health Outcomes Among Adolescents in Developing Countries.* Geneva: WHO.

Yurgelun-Todd, Deborah A., and William D. S. Killgore. 2006. "Fear-Related Activity in the Prefrontal Cortex Increases with Age During Adolescence: A Preliminary FMRI Study." *Neuroscience Letters* 406, no. 3 (July).

PART II

Growing Up with Violence: Adolescent Trauma, Stigma, and Resilience

CHAPTER 6

Poverty, Armed Conflict, and Organized Crime: The Impact of Violence on Young People in Colombia

Christian Salazar Volkmann

Young people in Colombia have the same dreams and aspirations as young people everywhere in the world. At the same time, many grow up in a very violent environment where armed conflict, organized crime, and poverty form part of their normal day-to-day experience. Violence is rampant in the shantytowns of the big cities—and it shapes daily life in the countryside, particularly in zones where the armed conflict that has plagued Colombia for decades is still ongoing. Young people are caught in a cycle of violence, whether as victims or as perpetrators.

Although homicide rates in Colombia have fallen over the past decade, the overall level is still very high; young people suffer a heavy portion of this intensive volume of violence. In 2010, the National Forensic Medical Institute of Colombia registered more than 17,400 violent deaths, which equals an average national homicide rate of thirty-eight per one hundred thousand people; the national homicide rate in the United States in 2011 was only 4.7 per one hundred thousand people (Instituto Nacional 2011, 20). Homicide rates in the 18–29 age group are more than twice as high as the national average; for the 18–19 age group the rate is sixty-seven per one hundred thousand (Instituto Nacional 2011). A recent study on the situation in the city of Cali indicated that 37 percent of all homicide victims during the five year period from 2005 to 2009 were young people between fifteen and twenty-four (Alcaldia Municipal de Cali, 2013).

National statistics point at another worrisome trend. While homicide rates of young people over eighteen have remained stable (though high), killings of children are increasing, especially in the 10–14 age group, where homicide rates increased by 24 percent between 2009 and 2010 (Instituto Nacional 2011, 20f).

As discussed in the chapter by Katie Naeve, children and adolescents are at high risk of being recruited by guerrilla groups. As a consequence, recruitment of children and adolescents has become one of the main causes of displacement as parents move their children to prevent their children from being recruited. According to Colombia's National Human Rights Ombudsman office, the average age of recruitment is 12.8 years.

The consequences for children growing up as guerrilla fighters are dire. In an example from 2010, in the department of Nariño bordering Ecuador, the guerrilla group FARC (Fuerzas Armadas Revolucionario de Colombia) sent a twelve-year-old child as "suicide bomber" to a local police station, killing himself, nine civilians, and three policemen. In another case from 2011 in the department of Antioquia, the guerrillas displaced approximately twenty-three hundred children, forcing them and their parents to march in so-called protests against the presence of the army in the nearby town. One member of each family, usually an older person or a very young child, had to stay at home as a "hostage" to ensure the "right" behavior of those who were marching.

In the past, some members of the Colombian armed forces, the government army, have also been a source of violence against children and adolescents, as demonstrated in the infamous "Soacha case," where young men were lured by middlemen far away from their hometown, promising them jobs. They were transported to the north of the country, where soldiers were waiting to kill them and to present them as *guerrilleros* killed in combat. The attorney general is currently investigating more than sixteen hundred cases of this nature; several of the victims are children under the age of eighteen.

The violence of the armed conflict is exacerbated by armed groups that have emerged since the demobilization of paramilitary groups in 2005. These groups—called BACRIM (*bandas criminals*, criminal gangs) by the government—are pursuing criminal activities such as the drug trade and arms trafficking. They are the main source of violence in rural as well as in urban settings, such as the shantytowns of Bogota, Medellin, and Cali. These groups use and recruit adolescents and young people intensively. As Naeve discusses, many youngsters join the gangs because they offer income opportunities and a sense of belonging. There are also many cases of forced recruitment and forced membership.

The challenges for state and society to protect adolescents and young people from violence and to prevent them from committing crimes are huge. Poverty, armed conflict, organized crime, corruption, rampant city growth, and widespread impunity from punishment together form multiple layers of a complex social, economic, and judicial problem.

Colombia was one of the first Latin American states to ratify the CRC on January 28, 1991. The country ratified the two additional protocols to the CRC in 2003 (on the sale of children, child prostitution, and child pornography) and 2005 (on children in armed conflict). Nevertheless, it took a very long time until the country managed to harmonize its national legislation with international standards on children's rights. It was only at the end of 2006 that the new law on children and adolescents was adopted, finally bringing Colombian legislation into conformity with the CRC.

That progress cannot be taken for granted. Currently, we are witnessing attempts to reverse the guarantees for children's rights and citizens' rights, in Colombia as well as in many other Latin American countries. For example, Colombia's minister of interior stated in March of 2011: "We believe there are kids that are really children and should be treated with special care . . . [but] there are dangerous criminals and professional murderers age 16 and 17 that cannot be dealt with softly and that need to be confronted with serious measures" (El Espectador 2011). Hence, Colombia recently passed citizen's security law (law 1453) that substantially increases the punishment for a number of crimes, reduces the age of criminal responsibility, and limits options to avoid imprisonment and alternative forms of punishment.

The Inter-American Commission for Human Rights, in a recent report on public security published jointly by the Commission, UNICEF, and the Office of the High Commissioner for Human Rights, stated: "In a number of countries of the region, the response to the situation has been to reinforce approaches that have proved to be ineffective in solving society's demands for citizen security, based upon harsher penalties, fewer procedural guarantees, and to have adolescents charged as adults when accused of criminal offences" (Report on Citizen Security and Human Rights, 2009).

It is certainly easy to blame young people for security problems and crime rates and to react with repressive measures, which are visible and quickly implementable. In the case of adolescents, these measures are affecting a population group that does not vote. In sum, such measures are attractive for politicians as they demonstrate the state's activism against crime and insecurity.

However, it is doubtful whether reducing civil rights and increasing repressive legal measures against young people will have the desired impact on citizens' security. A strategy focused on stronger and wider punishment of young people is not very likely to succeed in Colombia because the judicial system is already completely overloaded and impunity is widespread. In addition, prisons are overcrowded, so there is not enough space to deal with an influx of young prisoners. Furthermore, worldwide experience demonstrates that putting adolescents and young people into jail has a very negative effect on them as prisons tend to be "schools of crime" rather than centers of reintegration.

Short-sighted repression does not address the underlying structural causes of violence and insecurity. It is not adolescents who run the groups that emerged after the demobilization of the paramilitary organizations. It is not adolescents and young people that foster widespread corruption among public security forces or local authorities and therefore facilitate violence and impunity. (For example, in May 2012, thirty-seven public officials from the department of Choco, among them police officers, members of the judiciary, and local officials, were arrested for collaborating with Los Rastrojos, one of the largest paramilitary groups still operating in Colombia.) The local study of the situation of Cali mentioned above looked at 644 homicides committed by gangs in that city between 2005 and 2009 and indicated that youth gangs accounted for only 13 percent of all homicides in Cali (Alcaldia Municipal de Cali, n.d.). This is surprising, given that public opinion and politicians all over the country tend to blame youth gangs for the safety and security problems in many cities and towns.

This critique of repressive interventions to solve problems related to citizens' security and youth violence is not intended to downplay the need for effective and sometimes tough measures to fight crime and youth violence. But interventions in public security and the judiciary need to be combined with investments in crime prevention and social support for adolescents and young people.

Here lies a huge gap in Colombia, but also in many other countries of the region. Today as well as in the past, state investments in adolescent development and youth policies tend to be minimal. For example, Colombia does not have a national youth policy. A country where more than 26 percent of the population is between fifteen and twenty-nine years of age (Ministerio de la Protección, 2009) has delegated the institutional responsibility for youth policies to a small program called Colombia Joven that is run by the Colombian vice-presidency, has little convening powers, and almost no budget.

Repression may be easy, but prevention is not. It requires significant resources whose impact on citizens' security does not have quick results. Results in prevention are often difficult to demonstrate. Public policies are needed that combine immediate interventions to control the security situation, the daily crime rates, and the homicide rates in certain parts of cities and towns with longer-term strategies that address the structural determinants of violence and insecurity.

In particular, there is a need for an intensive technical and financial push for youth policies in the municipalities. Effective support, protection, and reintegration of adolescents and young people at risk require coordination between local authorities in the barrio (neighborhood): police officers, judges, teachers, street workers (outreach workers), health workers, and NGOs. They all must work together closely for early intervention and referral.

There are successful examples of local roundtables to coordinate preventive efforts of local authorities in the field of youth in the region; there are good examples of adolescent-friendly municipal development plans and budgets; and there are examples of interventions that work, in Colombia as well as in other countries of the region. But the vast majority of municipalities in the region are understaffed, underresourced, and lack technical know-how in the field of youth policies. Hence, progress in the field of local adolescent and youth policies will need special support, attention, and prioritization by national governments.

In my experience, the impact of programs and projects for adolescents and young people is largely connected to the degree to which they encourage young people to participate actively in shaping the programs. As discussed in more detail in the chapter by Naeve in this volume, participation ensures relevance and the buy-in of young people into measures designed to support and protect them. For example, school councils or local youth groups are important means of self-protection and peer support in violent environments and need to be strengthened.

The impact of violence on young people cannot be simply understood as a national phenomenon. The situation in Colombia must be analyzed and addressed as part of a subregional process that draws more and more children and young people systematically into a deadly cycle of criminal violence. Seven of the world's top ten countries with violent deaths of more than thirty per one hundred thousand people are in Latin America and the Caribbean. Colombia occupies the fifth place in this macabre ranking (Geneva Declaration Secretariat 2011). The situation in Colombia is typical of many countries in the region. Many of the state policies of the region neglect adolescents and young people.

Illegal subregional networks that use children and young people as "cannon fodder" for their purposes span a range of Central American societies with a history of violent internal armed conflict, and where the institutional presence of the state has traditionally been weak. The networks are also present in countries such as Colombia, Venezuela, and Mexico and in several Caribbean states that are located in drug trafficking corridors to the United States. These networks have grown steadily over the past twenty years. Their ties have been knit together by illegal actors in the South and in the North. They cannot be untied by one country alone, and these illegal structures will certainly not be disbanded by policies that reduce citizens' rights and repress young people.

Most important, both the governments of the region as well as U.S. agencies that fund security and counternarcotics programs need to pay more attention to prevention, and to coordinate policies and programs that support young people from poor neighborhoods. Currently, the fight against organized crime and violence concentrates on investment in public security forces and neglects investments in social and economic opportunities for adolescents and young people.

More programs for prevention are needed, programs that strengthen the rights of adolescents and young people, that respond to their daily needs and hopes, and that help to protect them from harm and prevent them from inflicting harm on others. Later chapters in this book by Mtshali and by Burra provide examples of relevant and effective initiatives that engage with preventative policies supporting adolescent rights. The dominant recipe of repression against violence and crime needs to change to a paradigm of prevention, a paradigm that strengthens rights in legal frameworks and social practices. States faced with high levels of insecurity and violence should strengthen the rights of adolescents and young people rather than reducing them. Societies that face high levels of violence should support their young generations rather than bashing and blaming them.

In sum, in order to effectively address issues of citizens' security and youth violence, the states in the region will have to increase their efforts to create a supportive and protective environment for adolescents and young people in the years to come.

References

Alcaldía Municipal de Cali, Secretaria de Gobierno, Convivencia y Seguridad, 2009. *Observatorio Social Visión Cali: Homicidios y Pandillas Juveniles en Santiago de Cali 2005–2009.* Cali, Colombia: Alcaldía Municipal de Cali.

El Espectador. 2011. "Gobierno buscara que menores si paguen por sus delitos." March 24.

Geneva Declaration Secretariat. 2011. *Global Burden of Armed Violence 2011: Lethal Encounters.* Cambridge: Cambridge University Press.

Instituto Nacional de Medicina Legal y Ciencias Forenses. 2011. *Población y Principales Indicadores Demográficos de Colombia.* Bogotá: Ministerio de la Protección Social.

Inter-American Commission for Human Rights, UNICEF, Office of the UN High Commissioner for Human Rights. 2009. *Report on Citizen Security and Human Rights.* Costa Rica: OAS (Organization of American States).

CHAPTER 7

Coming of Age in the Context of War: Reframing the Approach to Adolescent Rights

Theresa S. Betancourt, Katrina Hann, and Moses Zombo

War Reshapes Transitions to Young Adulthood

Over one billion children today live in countries affected by armed conflict (UNICEF 2009). According to UNICEF (1996), children in war zones are often as likely as adults to become the victims of rape, torture, and killing. This trend stems, at least in part, from a breakdown in respect for humanitarian law. The majority of contemporary conflicts are civil wars where at least one of the warring parties is a nonstate actor. Nonstate armed forces are much less likely than state armies to know about, or hold themselves accountable to, international humanitarian law. More significantly, civilians have become strategic targets in many of today's wars of destabilization (UNICEF 1996). In fact, actors in many modern conflicts use terrorism against civilians and attempts to undermine the fabric of day-to-day life as key elements of their military strategy. In modern warfare, schools, health clinics, and community structures are targeted along with military forces and facilities. In this manner, modern warfare upsets the entire social ecology that normally supports child health and development, including adolescent transitions to adulthood. In most instances, children and youth in areas affected by war and communal violence face loss; separation from family, friends, and their extended social network; lack of access to critical health and social services; and obstacles to educational and vocational opportunities.

Without protection of their basic rights, children and adolescents in conflict-affected regions have become increasingly vulnerable to a variety of predatory and abusive practices, including abduction or recruitment into armed groups. In this chapter, we will use the example of former child soldiers and other war-affected youth to illustrate the interrelatedness of the core security needs and rights of children, and use the SAFE model of child protection as a lens for analysis (a holistic perspective on child protection that is concerned about the interrelatedness between **S**afety, **A**ccess to basic needs, **F**amily and connection to others and **E**ducational access/**E**conomic security of children).

Acknowledging Youth Agency and Capacity

As previous chapters have discussed, the terms "children" and "childhood" have a range of definitions across cultures and settings. These perspectives also differ by gender, and issues such as class and societal position. Children and youth in adversity cannot be seen simply as members of "vulnerable" groups deserving of humanitarian intervention or protection, but must be considered as individuals with needs, rights and the agency to act and make decisions in accordance with their evolving capacities.

The CRC defines children as "every human being below the age of 18 years unless, under the law applicable to the child, majority is obtained earlier" (United Nations 1989). The idea of the evolving capacities of children is central to the CRC and to its application in improving settings for their development across the lifespan. The capacities of individual children to act on their own behalf, and to participate in decisions that affect them, are constantly evolving as each child matures in his or her social and cultural context.

The importance of considering children's views, and their right to participate in decisions that affect them, is a core theme of the CRC articulated in articles 12–15. To understand children's security, consideration must be given to their experiences and views concerning safety, security, and development, considering both their evolving capacities and the best interests of the child. Attempts to address the child protection issues facing children in adversity and promoting their longer term health and well-being must take into account children's views and developing agency as well as their roles as actors and decision makers in processes that contribute to security or insecurity.

Beyond a Hierarchy of Needs: The SAFE Model as a Rights-Based and Holistic Approach to Child Protection

Maslow's "hierarchy of needs" model is often invoked in debates concerning interventions for war-affected groups and other populations in difficult circumstances. Maslow (1943) argued that there is a hierarchy of human needs beginning with the most important: physiological needs for food, water, and shelter. Basic safety needs then follow, providing sufficient security to permit the satisfaction of the "higher order" needs of love, belonging, and ultimately of esteem and self-actualization.

Such a hierarchical model can be challenged in that it does not capture well the human rights principles of the interdependence and interrelatedness of human rights. Nowhere is this any more critical than in the case of child rights. In particular, attention must be paid to both the linkages between the different rights of the child (which include the rights to meeting physiological needs for food, water, and shelter, as well as needs for safety—and rights to life, survival, and development), and their relationship to the family and community responses to these needs. In thinking of the health and well-being of children in adversity, the ability of states, communities, and families to respect, protect, and fulfill these basic rights is critical.

The SAFE model is a rights-based, holistic model of child protection and basic security. It situates child protection, health, and well-being within the nested social ecologies of families, communities, and their larger political, cultural, and historical context. As opposed to a hierarchy like Maslow's, the SAFE model, shown in figure 7.1, examines the interplay between four core domains of children's rights essential for life, survival and development: Safety/freedom from harm; Access to basic physiological needs and health care; Family and connection to others; and Education/economic security. The model is a framework for analysis rather than an end in and of itself. Like Maslow's model, we recognize the importance of health and fundamental physical conditions (food, water, and shelter) and basic needs for

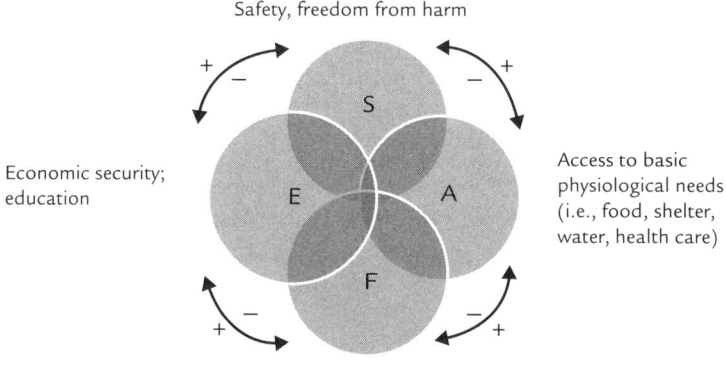

Figure 7.1. The SAFE model of child protection.

personal safety and integrity. While these two conditions are necessary for children's well-being, they alone are not sufficient.

Interdependence and Interrelatedness

Figure 7.1 represents the interdependence and interrelatedness of the security needs of children. Children's survival depends on physiological necessities, safety, communal relationships, and opportunities for personal development. While safety and physiological needs are addressed by food, health care, and physical protection, children's personal development needs are intimately linked to their social environment—their families and communities. The survival of communities in turn relies on the security of the younger generation. In essence, children's security is just as concerned with maintaining attachment relationships as providing for physiological and physical security needs.

When faced with insecurity in any of the SAFE domains, children, youth, and their families may engage in survival strategies. For example, if children are abused and neglected in their family or community, they may seek to protect themselves by joining gangs or armed groups. Joining together for protection and personal advancement can foster a sense of identity and community for young people, even when shaped by war or retribution ideology. Such solidarity may also be a strategy to help children secure their basic needs for food, shelter, and a livelihood. With modern light weapons, children and adolescents are as capable as adults of using deadly force. For these reasons, neglecting the security needs of children can have serious security consequences for the larger society.

The SAFE domains map onto rights delineated in the CRC, such as the rights to life, survival, and development (for example, Art. 6); education (Art. 28); health (Art. 24); family connections (for example, Arts. 9, 20); and protection from violence (Art. 19), as well as various other special protection articles (for example, Arts. 32–40) (UN 1989). Fundamental concepts of the CRC (UN 1989) central to the rights of adolescents, such as evolving capacities (Arts. 5, 14) and participation (Art. 23), are implicit in the model. The model underscores the agency of adolescents by elucidating the survival strategies that are set into motion when any given domain is insecure (Betancourt, Fawzi, et al. 2010). A model such as SAFE is intended to identify and build on adaptive strategies, but to also highlight risky strategies in order to enact preventive interventions, provide alternatives, or end third-party manipulation. In order to secure the protection of adolescents facing insecurity in any SAFE domain, programs and policies must ensure participation of adolescents in the identification or creation of viable, alternative adaptive strategies, if they are to be successfully employed.

The following sections explore the interrelatedness between children's security and rights using examples from a longitudinal study of war-affected children, youth, and families in Sierra Leone. Examples of security threats facing children are identified and strategies to promote their security, using their coping strategies as a guide for intervention, are presented as a means of illustrating the importance of rights-based approaches like SAFE for understanding and responding to the situation of war-affected children and youth.

The Example of War-Affected Youth in Sierra Leone

Sierra Leone's eleven-year civil conflict (1991–2002) involved a number of warring groups, including the Revolutionary United Front, the Sierra Leonean Armed Forces Revolutionary Council, the Sierra Leone Army, and other local groups such as the Civil Defense Forces. During this period, tens of thousands of civilians were killed and roughly 75 percent of the population was displaced (Medeiros 2007; Williamson and Cripe 2002). A wide range of human rights abuses were documented, including mass mutilations and pervasive use of children in armed conflict. Estimates are that as many as twenty-eight thousand children, some as young as seven years old, were conscripted into fighting forces (Coalition to Stop the Use of Child Soldiers 2008; Mazurana and Carlson 2006). While many were abducted into their role as child soldiers, other children assumed a more active role in joining armed groups, in part due to an extremely limited set of opportunities resulting from a breakdown in family and community systems as well as insufficient educational opportunities (Ashby 2002). As a result of their involvement with armed forces and groups, many youths witnessed and even perpetrated acts of intense physical and sexual violence, including executions, death squad killings, torture, rape, detention, bombings, forced displacement, destruction of homes, and massacres. Throughout this time, these children were continually deprived of their rights to the protection of their families, education, and many basic physical needs, such as food, water, clothing, and shelter.

A Longitudinal Mixed-Methods Study

In 2002, a collaboration was launched between the International Rescue Committee (IRC) and the Harvard School of Public Health to conduct a longitudinal study of former child soldiers and other war-affected youth in Sierra Leone. The overall aim of the study was to examine risk and protective factors shaping social reintegration and psychosocial adjustment. This research explored a number of issues that are relevant to the development of children in situations of concentrated adversity. The research questions at the heart of the study pertained to challenges and successes that these youth experience in securing a livelihood, caring for families, completing school, avoiding high-risk behavior, and contributing to civil society. Taking an ecological view, the study examined aspects of child development, such as age of involvement in war, individual experiences of loss, violence exposure, family relationships, social support, and societal stigma in addition to the macro-level opportunities, such as school and work access (Betancourt and Khan 2008).

Methods

The study used a mixed-methods design, integrating both quantitative and qualitative methods over multiple periods of data collection. Qualitative data on local constructs of importance informed the development and selection of core constructs of interest for the quantitative survey, such as community acceptance and family support. Surveys were conducted among war-affected youth, their caregivers, and a comparison group at three time points: 2002, 2004, and 2008. Additionally, a series of in-depth interviews with a subset of youth and their caregivers were completed in 2004 (T2) and 2008 (T3). A number of focus groups were also held in major resettlement communities with community members, caregivers of war-affected youth, and young people themselves, both those involved in armed groups and those not (Betancourt et al. 2008). For an in-depth discussion of the methods employed in this study, see Betancourt et al. 2008.

Findings

Consistent with the SAFE model of security and rights of children, the research highlighted several interrelated processes shaping trajectories of risk and resilience in war-affected youth (Betancourt, Agnew-Blais, et al. 2010; Betancourt et al. 2010; Betancourt, Brennan, et al. 2010; Betancourt, McBain et al, 2012). For instance, in considering the domain of Safety and freedom from harm (S), the study outlined how exposures to war-related violence, particularly experiences of "toxic stress" due to war violence, had an indelible impact on the young people in our sample. Across multiple forms of violence exposure examined, direct victimization of rape or participation in violence perpetration (injuring or killing others) were some of the most enduring experiences for youth in our sample. The effects of rape and participating in injuring or killing others persisted independently of other variables examined. In terms of the domain of Access to basic physiological needs (A), although access to medical care was not directly examined until recent phases of the survey focused on young adulthood, a measure of "daily hardships" (including having sick or impaired family members), assessed in 2004, did contribute to the degree to which the young person showed risk of depression. One of the critical findings of the study is that the long-term mental health of former child soldiers is influenced not only by conflict-related exposures, such as violence exposure (S), but also by postconflict contextual factors, including community stigma, social support (F), and the degree to which the family struggled with food or housing insecurity (A). Being able to pursue one's ambitions for education (E) was also positively associated with prosocial attitudes and behaviors. These findings map onto the four domains of SAFE, highlighting the relevance of these basic security domains and child rights as immediately applicable to the context of maximizing the agency of former child soldiers in Sierra Leone.

The interrelatedness of the rights and human capability of war-affected youth must also be understood. For instance, lower levels of prosocial behavior, such as helpfulness toward others, were associated with having killed or injured others during wartime as well as with experiencing stigma in the postconflict environment. In this way, the effects of the safety domain (S), exposure to violence and forced participation in perpetrating violence, impact an individual's connectedness to others (F), in the form of reducing prosocial behaviors and increasing stigma. In fact, experiencing stigma due to being a child soldier explained a significant portion of the variability in hostility over time (Betancourt, Agnew-Blais, et al. 2010). Hence, the relationship of the safety (S) and connectedness (F) domains is bidirectional; stigma, a threat to connectedness (F), can also negatively impact safety (S) through the use of hostility and even aggression as a survival strategy among traumatized youth in the postconflict setting. Stigma was also inversely associated with prosocial behavior, an example of interdomain effects (F). Increases in anxiety and depression over time were closely related both to younger involvement in fighting forces as well as with social (F) and economic hardships (E) in the postconflict environment. This example shows the profound and lasting effects (in this case, six years) that complex, cross-domain threats to children's well-being can have.

Of importance to programming and policy, the relationships between war-related exposures and poor adjustment were partly mitigated by a range of postconflict factors, including social support (F), family acceptance (F), being in school (E), and increases in community acceptance (F). Overall, community acceptance—both initially and over time—had beneficial effects on all outcomes studied. These protective factors all have important interactions with the individual agency and ambitions of young people affected by war.

It is evident in these findings that psychosocial adjustment and community reintegration for former child soldiers are complex processes involving a range of factors both during and after wartime. The SAFE model can illuminate how the ongoing needs and rights of war-affected children, adolescents, and youth are interrelated and interdependent. Figure 7.2 applies the SAFE model to war-affected children.

Understanding current survival strategies of war-affected youth is particularly compelling for researchers, practitioners, and policy makers, since

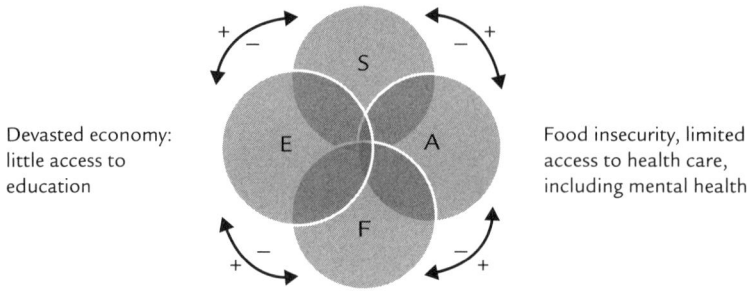

Figure 7.2. The SAFE model of child protection: Survival strategies of war-affected youth.

many of these strategies can be modified, whereas war experiences cannot. Using models like SAFE, program developers can analyze the drivers of risky survival strategies and work to provide alternatives as well as to address third-party exploitation. Similarly, an understanding of what young people themselves and their families are doing to meet these basic needs and rights can be informative for developing programs to support rather than supplant naturally occurring agency. This research and the case studies presented here provide new insights into the long-term well-being of children exposed to some of the most extreme violence imaginable. While both war experiences and postconflict factors contribute significantly to the long-term mental health and social reintegration of former child soldiers, the postconflict environment presents many intervention opportunities that remain untapped. These include the development of policies and interventions that are long-term, sustainable, and focus on supporting adolescent agency and strengthening family and community support, with the active participation of adolescents throughout.

Preventing Adolescent Recruitment into Armed Groups

The recruitment of children into armed groups has remained a global issue, with up to three hundred thousand children estimated to be involved with armed forces and armed at any one time. In fact, Machel's (Machel 1996, 2001) approximation of three hundred thousand "potentially underestimates the gravity of the problem" (Achvarina and Reich 2006). This type of involvement is seldom on a voluntary basis. Joining an armed group is often spurred by lack of any other viable alternative for survival for the child. The child could face immediate death from refusing the orders of a commander, or, as an alternative, living in the bush without access to food or protection. As Betty Bigombe, a lead negotiator in the ongoing conflict in northern Uganda, and Jennings Randolph, senior fellow at the United States Institute of Peace, has noted, "This is not a choice . . . when you have nothing else, it's not a choice" (Dye 2007). Alternatively stated, children and adolescents joining armed groups can be termed a survival strategy. Children who are most vulnerable to recruitment into armed forces are often in or near conflict zones, separated from or without families, socially or economically marginalized, or members of targeted minorities (Boothby 1986). In this manner, the SAFE model can be employed to identify, understand, and analyze the factors that contribute to children's involvement in armed forces, and thus contribute to the examination of prevention strategies using risky and adaptive survival strategies as a guide.

Effective approaches to both programming and preventive interventions to address the issue of child soldiers must work to actualize the spirit of these human rights principles, as well as the Paris Principles and Guidelines on Children Associated with Armed Forces or Armed Groups. Humanitarian responses after the postwar reconstruction period present a particular opportunity to launch the development of sustainable, community-based services and supports to maximize the capacity of war-affected youth long after the end of hostilities.

From the prevention end of the spectrum, there is an array of suggested best practices for the prevention of enrollment of children in armed groups. The Paris Principles and Guidelines on Children Associated with Armed Forces or Armed Groups as the result of a joint UN-NGO and multi-government consultation (UNICEF 2007) include a focus on the prevention of recruitment. These principles target the safety and protection of children (S), including the establishment of reliable birth registration systems and legal requirements for the age limit on participation in armed forces. These provisions create an age criteria and are thus integral to preventing young adolescents' involvement. Reflecting one of the recommendations encapsulated in the Cape Town Principles, Achvarina and Reich (Achvarina and

Reich 2006; UNICEF 1997) highlight the need to adequately protect (S) internally displaced persons (IDP) and refugee camps; they argue that lack of protection itself accounts for an increased use of children in armed groups. A present gap in protection underscores neglect of interrelated issues of safety/freedom from harm (S), access to the satisfaction of basic physiological needs and medical care (A), family and connection to others (F), and educational/economic prospects (E), factors that if secure may reduce risk of recruitment of children into armed forces and armed groups. The SAFE model makes strong theoretical contributions to the development of strategies to prevent recruitment of children into armed forces. It stipulates that a focus solely on one domain undermines the interrelatedness of risks as well as adaptive resources and potential leverage points for protecting children.

Postconflict Sierra Leone has made some great strides forward with the development of the new free health-care plan for children under five years and pregnant/lactating mothers (Donnelly 2011), a new Mental Health Policy and a National Youth Commission; however, the true measure of success will be the degree to which sustainable and high-quality services are implemented to support the ambitions and agency of all war-affected youth. There are innumerable young people who struggle to reach their goals in Sierra Leone, and adequate supports, both formal and informal, are few and far between. As our study has demonstrated, many of the processes important to supporting the agency of war-affected youth occur in families and in the community context. Thus, it is important that social services and psychosocial supports be integrated into other aspects of community life and services. The integration of mental health services into education programs and primary health care is important. Sierra Leone now has this opportunity within the free health-care plan, which is increasing access to care for vulnerable families in many rural parts of the country. The plan presents opportunities to enable families to forge links to child protection and social services. However, the policy's present focus on children under five years and pregnant and lactating mothers will be insufficient to meet the needs of a generation of war-affected and vulnerable youth. Overall, services must also adapt to the evolving needs of individuals and families, as mental health needs of violence-affected youth, particularly those affected by such extreme trauma, change throughout the life course. Through this study and further developmentally informed scholarship, we can enhance our understanding of processes linking war-related traumas to long-term psychological functioning.

It is clear that maintaining resilience and strength in families across the span of child rearing is an important goal and need. We can use models, such as SAFE, to analyze the adequacy of responses to fundamental security dimensions of child health and well-being. Through systematic data collection, a stronger evidence base can encourage local governments and the international community to invest in effective and sustainable responses to support the developmental needs of all war-affected children and maintain resilience and strength in families across the span of child and adolescent development.

Conclusion

It is important to view the phenomenon of the resilience of adolescents and youth affected by violence in context. Holistic, rights-based models, such as the SAFE model, can help us to recognize war-affected young people as individuals with *agency* doing their best to respond to the unnatural circumstances of war. We must understand the interrelated and interdependent nature of the security needs of children and youth. When we do so, we can look to their risky and adaptive survival strategies as a *road map* for preventative and ameliorative interventions. Such interrelatedness also speaks to the need for integrated programs that mirror linkages between the security threats themselves. This does not mean that all services must be all-encompassing, but they must be in communication with one another. For example, while a health-focused NGO may have the resources or expertise to address the injuries to children, effective training of program staff and monitoring of beneficiaries should ensure that children without attachment figures or a reliable caregiver receive appropriate referral and follow-up to organizations that provide enriched foster care. Policy makers must also take into account the interrelated nature of security domains in establishing responses to security threats, by creating cooperative intersectoral policies and programs (such as school-based mental health programs). Civil society and other stakeholders can work with governments to raise awareness and encourage follow-through so that coordination and integration of services become increasingly more of a reality in practice and also become enshrined in policies for war-affected youth. Most important, organizations and stakeholders should preemptively plan links to other organizations, individuals, and community networks that can provide needed services and supports to war-affected youth across the four core SAFE domains; this is especially necessary when they cannot mount an adequate in-house response or when a child protection issue does not explicitly fall under their mandate (for example, when staff at an education program learn that a child is in need of medical attention).

A robust understanding of the interrelated nature of child protection threats can help governments and service organizations to better utilize the limited resources they do have while incurring minimal additional costs. While greater cross-sectoral programming and coordination will likely involve greater start-up costs, early investments may be recouped by prevention of costly negative outcomes or the improved efficiency of existing services in the postconflict setting and the national transition to development. Such approaches are critical for optimizing the limited resources available for supporting violence-affected youth. In taking such steps, we can begin to eliminate the silos that exist in the response to youth affected by violence, bolster adaptive solutions drawing from existing resources, and maximize efforts to protect and fulfill the rights of youth and build on their tremendous agency.

References

Achvarina, V., and Simon Reich. 2006. "No Place to Hide: Refugees, Displaced Persons, and the Recruitment of Child Soldiers." *International Security* 31, no. 1 (Summer): 127–64.

Ashby, P. 2002. "Child Combatants: A Soldier's Perspective." *Lancet* 360, no. 9350 (December 1): s11.

Betancourt, T. S., Jessica Agnew-Blais, Stephen Gilman, David Williams, and B. Heidi Ellis. 2010. "Past Horrors, Present Struggles: The Role of Stigma in the Association Between War Experiences and Psychosocial Adjustment Among Former Child Soldiers in Sierra Leone." *Social Science & Medicine* 70, no. 1 (January): 17–26.

Betancourt, T. S., Ivelina Borisova, Timothy Williams, Robert Brennan, T. Hatch Whitfield, Marie de la Soudiere, John Williamson, and Stephen Gilman. 2010. "Sierra Leone's Former Child Soldiers: A Follow-up Study of Psychosocial Adjustment and Community Reintegration." *Child Development* 81, no. 4 (July–August): 1077–95.

Betancourt, T. S., McBain, R., Newnham, E. A., & Brennan, R. T. (2013). Trajectories of Internalizing Problems in War-Affected Sierra Leonean Youth: Examining Conflict and Postconflict Factors. *Child Development,* 84(2), 455–470.

Betancourt, T. S., Robert Brennan, Julia Rubin-Smith, Garrett Fitzmaurice, and Stephen Gilman. 2010. "Sierra Leone's Former Child Soldiers: A Longitudinal Study of Risk, Protective Factors, and Mental Health." *Journal of the American Academy of Child and Adolescent Psychiatry* 49, no. 6 (June): 606–15.

Betancourt, T. S., Mary Fawzi, Claude Bruderlein, Chris Desmond, and Jim Y. Kim. 2010. "Children Affected by HIV/AIDS: SAFE, a Model for Promoting Their Security, Health, and Development." *Psychology, Health and Medicine* 15, no. 3 (May): 243–65.

Betancourt, T. S., and Kashif Khan. 2008. "The Mental Health of Children Affected by Armed Conflict: Protective Processes and Pathways to Resilience." *International Review of Psychiatry* 20, no. 3 (June): 317–28.

Betancourt, T. S., Stephanie Simmons, Ivelina Borisova, Stephanie Brewer, Uzo Iweala, and Marie de la Soudiere. 2008. "High Hopes, Grim Reality: Reintegration and the Education of Former Child Soldiers in Sierra Leone." *Comparative Education Review* 52, no. 4 (November 1): 565–87.

Betancourt, T. S., Sandra Zaeh, A'Nova Ettien, and Laura Khan. Forthcoming. "Psychosocial Adjustment and Mental Health Services in Post-conflict Sierra Leone: Experiences of CAAFAG and War-Affected Youth, Families and Service Providers." In *New Series on Transitional Justice*, edited by S. Parmentier, J. Sarkin, and E. Weitekamp. Antwerp: Intersentia.

Boothby, N. 1986. *Children in Armed Conflicts: Rights, Reality, and Future Implications*. Washington, D.C.: ERIC Clearinghouse.

Bronfenbrenner, U. 1979. *The Ecology of Human Development: Experiments by Nature and Design*. Cambridge, Mass.: Harvard University Press.

Bruderlein, C. 2000. *The Role of Non-State Actors in Building Human Security: The Case of Armed Groups in Intra-State Wars*. Geneva: Human Security Network.

Coalition to Stop the Use of Child Soldiers. 2008. *Child Soldiers: Global Report 2008*. London: Coalition to Stop the Use of Child Soldiers.

Donnelly, J. 2011. "How Did Sierra Leone Provide Free Health Care?" *Lancet* 377, no. 9775 (April 23): 1393–96.

Dye, S. 2007. "Child Soldiers: New Evidence, New Advocacy Approaches." In *Peace Brief*, edited by U.S. Institute of Peace. Washington, D.C.: United Stated Institute of Peace.

Machel, G. 1996. "Impact of Armed Conflict on Children." Report of the expert of the Secretary-General, submitted pursuant to UN General Assembly Resolution 48/157. New York: United Nations.

———. 2001. *The Impact of War on Children*. London: Hurst & Company.

Maslow, Abraham. 1943. "A Theory of Human Motivation." *Psychological Review* 50:370–96.

Mazurana, D., and K. Carlson. 2006. "The Girl Child and Armed Conflict: Recognizing and Addressing Grave Violations of Girls' Human Rights." 1–20. Florence, Italy: United Nations.

Medeiros, E. 2007. "Integrating Mental Health into Post-conflict Rehabilitation." *Journal of Health Psychology* 12, no. 3 (May): 498–504. doi:10.1177/1359105307076236.

O'Donnell, K., Florence Nyangara, Robert Murphy, and Beverly Nyberg. 2008. "Child Status Index: A Tool for Assessing the Well-being of Orphans and Vulnerable

Children—MANUAL." Washington, D.C.: U.S. Agency for International Development.

Stichick T, Bruderlein C. Children Facing Insecurity: New Strategies for Survival in a Global Era. Policy paper produced for the Canadian Department of Foreign Affairs and International Trade, The Human Security Network, 3rd Ministerial Meeting, Petra, Jordan, 11–12 May, 2001.

United Nations. 1989. *UN Convention on the Rights of the Child*. New York: UN General Assembly.

UNICEF. *The Paris Principles: Principles and guidelines on children associated with armed forces or armed conflict*. Paris: UNICEF; 2007. http://www.unicef.org/emerg/files/ParisPrinciples310107English.pdf

———. *Machel study 10 year strategic review: Children and conflict in a changing world*. New York: Office of the Special Representative of the Secretary-General for Children and Armed Conflict; 2009.

———. 1996. *The State of the World's Children 1996*. New York: UNICEF

———. 1997. "Cape Town Principles and Best Practices." Paper presented at the Symposium on the Prevention of Recruitment of Children into the Armed Forces and on Demobilization and Social Reintegration of Child Soldiers in Africa, Cape Town, South Africa. 27–30 April 1997. http://www.unicef.org/emerg/files/Cape_Town_Principles(1).pdf.

Williamson, J., and Lynne Cripe. 2002. "Assessment of DCOF-Supported Child Demobilization and Reintegration Activities in Sierra Leone." Displaced Children and Orphans Fund and USAID.

CHAPTER 8

Wings of the Phoenix: The Legacy of Violence for Adolescents in Postconflict Reconstruction

Elizabeth Gibbons

The enormity of the horror inflicted upon children and adolescents in recent civil wars, ranging from Central Europe and Central America to East Africa and across to West Africa, lies beyond the capacity of human imagination. In Sierra Leone, it is estimated between fifteen thousand and twenty-two thousand children were forcibly recruited into militia groups (McKay and Mazurana 2004); overall, UNICEF estimated that the civil conflicts of the late 1980s and early 1990s cost the lives of two million children and disabled another 4–5 million boys and girls (UNICEF 1996). In Guatemala alone, the 1999 Report of the Historical Clarification [Truth] Commission documented the deaths of tens of thousands of children during that country's thirty-six-year civil war, noting with "particular concern that a large number of children were among the direct victims of arbitrary execution, forced disappearance, torture, rape and other violations of their fundamental rights.... [and the war] left a large number of children orphaned and abandoned... and the possibility of living a normal childhood within the norms of their culture, lost" (Commission for Historical Clarification 1999, 23).

Yet the horror occurred, time and again, and each society needs to overcome the consequences for itself and for the young generations. But how? Healing the devastating individual and social wounds created by such brutal conflicts seems a challenge whose solution might only lie in divine hands, not in the hands of mere mortals. Yet throughout history, after civil war comes, if not peace, then the absence of war, and the urgent requirement of society to move forward, to break the cycle of violence and learn to tolerate the existence, then the participation, of the erstwhile enemy in communal and national life. Healing these profound wounds takes a generation (World Bank 2011, 10); to accelerate the healing of war-affected societies, the international community and national policy makers need to focus on supporting adolescents and young people, as both agents and survivors, and help them come to terms with their past, construct their identity as citizens in a peaceful, democratic future, and power the wings of the phoenix, rising from the ashes of their childhood and their country's conflict.

Guatemalan Society After 1996: Emblematic of War's Legacy

Guatemala is emblematic of other conflict-affected societies, and there have been many in the last decades: Yugoslavia, Rwanda, Sierra Leone, Liberia, Haiti, Nepal, Afghanistan, Somalia, to name just a few. The legacy of each conflict has its own national specificity, but all share common features with Guatemala. In particular, conflict-affected countries suffer social fragmentation, political division, and distrust resulting from the polarizing effect of war. Indeed, the key finding of the far-reaching War-Torn Societies Project was that: "The central challenge of rebuilding war-torn societies has to do with mending relations and with restoring dignity, trust and faith" (Stiefel 1999, 12), and, that the quality of international assistance needed to improve, not so much in *what* is done, but in *how* it is done (Stiefel 1999, 30). Twelve years later, the World Bank concluded the same: "Confidence-building . . . is a prelude to more permanent institutional change in the face of violence. Why? Because low trust means that stakeholders who need to contribute political, financial or technical support will not collaborate until they believe that a positive outcome is possible" (World Bank 2011, 11–12).

Trust is particularly important to children, adolescents, and young people, if they are to have the confidence to believe in their own future and engage in the life of their community and nation. Guatemala's internationally brokered 1996 Peace Accords had wide-ranging aims of reconciliation, reforming the state, constructing a multicultural nation, and deepening democracy, but fifteen years later the subsequent efforts had not succeeded in winning the trust of young people. In 2010, 62 percent of 15–25-year-old Guatemalans claimed to be "not very" or "not at all" satisfied with democracy (Latinobarometro 2010). A full 80 percent of Guatemalan 15–25 year olds expressed "little" or "no" confidence in government and its institutions, slightly less confidence than the population in general—only 25 percent of which expressed any confidence whatsoever (Latinobarometro 2010). This level of corrosive distrust has increased in a decade of "peace." In a 2000 opinion poll of children and adolescents 9–18 years old, 33 percent stated that "as a place to live, my country is getting worse," while 47 percent stated that they had no confidence in the government (UNICEF 2003).

What has led to these startling levels of distrust among adolescents and young people, whose time of life is normally one of excitement, engagement, and hope? A brief review of the Guatemala experience might shed some light on the distressing perceptions of the young generation.

The armed conflict in Guatemala took place in the international context of the Cold War, and a national context in which the political system was unable and unwilling to address the legitimate aspirations of the vast majority of the population, principally the indigenous peoples, marginalized by abysmal poverty and subject to the racism of the economic elite. The Cold War contributed to the polarization of political dialogue, in which the state increasingly abandoned any role of providing social services to the Guatemalan citizenry, and turned over its apparatus to the military in an anticommunist crusade, which created a state-perpetuated culture of violence. The state apparatus systematically eliminated the leadership of indigenous movements, student movements, union movements, indeed that of any independent organization seeking to participate in the political system or claim their social and economic rights. The authoritarian state was able to co-opt part of the civilian population to engage in a culture of violence, as was the guerrilla movement, creating sharp divisions within communities, often with murderous consequences. Basic trust and confidence broke down between neighbors formerly united by tradition and family ties. With the state as the perpetrator of the worst violence, and its manipulation of laws to facilitate both repression and impunity, the population developed distrust in its institutions, especially the judicial system. The widespread violence, and the total impunity that greeted all acts of torture, terror, rape and murder, inflicted a deep social trauma on society and caused Guatemala to emerge from the war with a legacy of a society wasted in many ways and notoriously abandoned in many others... With the destruction of human lives for more than 35 years, and the accompanying effects of insecurity, suffering and fear, the universal social values and norms governing human behaviour have been eroded ... [and with them] the values of respect for life and human dignity. What takes place in such situations is the weakening of the basic principles of personal trust essential for a healthy growth of social relationships.... Incessant violence undermines respect for the legal and security systems and opens the way to violence on a personal level.

(Torres-Rivas and Arevalo de Leon 1999, 18–20)

The obsessive focus on security during the conflict and the orientation of the state's meager budget to the military also meant that access to and the quality of health, education, and housing actually declined, further aggravating the social exclusion that was a root cause of the war. When the Peace Accords were signed in December 1996, Guatemala faced a serious deficit in all social indicators and services. Without doubt, the war had made things worse for the vast majority, especially the indigenous peoples, whose poverty was further sustained by a racism that the war had greatly exacerbated. Indigenous populations suffered disproportionately from the conflict; after the war, it was estimated that up to 48 percent of indigenous Guatemalans had been directly affected by the hostilities, compared to 7 percent of the nonindigenous population (Adams 2011, 9). In common with other conflict-affected countries, the breakdown in social norms has had a lasting effect, creating a violent society where common crime, lynching, and extrajudicial executions became and remain prevalent. This extends to children, forty-five of whom died violently on average every month between 2007 and 2011 (Morales 2012); worse, roughly 95 percent of these crimes committed against children went unpunished (Alta Comisionada de las Naciones Unidas para los Derechos Humanos 2010). Insecurity affects all ethnic, social, and age groups in Guatemala, and fuels the crisis in confidence in the state's capacity to meet the most minimal expectations, particularly for adolescents who see their path littered with threats to the safety they need to carve out a future in their country.

Manifestations of distrust and apathy have their source in the arbitrary manner in which power was wielded throughout the conflict, and are aggravated by the state's incapacity to meet expectations for providing security and protection from violence and for fulfilling basic political, civil, economic, social, and cultural rights, a point also made, with respect to Colombia, by Volkmann in an earlier chapter in this volume. The generalized despair with government creates a sense of hopelessness, which communicates itself to the young in a very insidious and corrosive manner. A violent, fragmented society, distrust in the state and its institutions, and a lack of role models for democratic participation are the legacy that the armed conflict has left the Guatemalan children, adolescents, and young people of today. In this, the young citizens of Guatemala are not alone: lack of confidence in the state is a striking legacy of most conflict-affected countries today, as revealed through opinion polls. For example, in Liberia, 65 percent of young people 18–29 expressed little or no trust in the local government as did 56 percent of this cohort in South Africa. Trust is higher in countries that have not experienced conflict: for example, only 39 percent of Botswanan and 24 percent of Tanzanian young people express lack of confidence in local government (Africa Barometer 2008).

The lack of trust stems both from disillusionment with the state and from a childhood, which, for many young people, was directly affected by the excesses of war, a childhood where they were either witnesses to atrocities or victims of forced participants in cruel acts. Their parents too are traumatized, a trauma accentuated by a sense of guilt driven by their inability to protect their children from the widespread violence or from being brutally kidnapped from the safety of the family. Beyond repairing the physical damage of these civil conflicts, and investing in social services to enable Guatemala, Haiti, El Salvador, Sierra Leone, Liberia, or any affected country to fulfill the rights and meet the justified expectations of their citizens, the challenge for the postwar transition is that of instigating fundamental cultural and psychological change. Weaving golden threads of tolerance, mutual respect, capacity for dialogue, and consensus from the shreds of the past into a resilient social fabric is a far more complicated endeavor than that of building physical infrastructure, and it cannot be completed in less than a generation. As such, investments to facilitate social change must be made in the children, adolescents, and young people of today. If society does not face the horror produced by the war, create spaces for psychological healing, and create a culture of respect for human rights, then the fabric may never be whole. The cost of a shredded social fabric to children and adolescents is a sense of having nothing to lose, resulting from fragmented families and communities, poor quality education, lack of jobs, and lack of confidence in the state to provide essential security. With nothing to lose, violence and gang participation seem attractive options for cementing identity and increasing status. As Naeve points out in the following chapter, evidence on recruitment into the Colombian rebel militia, the Revolutionary Armed Forces of Colombia or FARC, suggests that many recruits were motivated to join by the status and excitement of rebel life, compared to the indignities and boredom of their former work as agricultural laborers (World Bank 2011, 79). And the violence itself produces more tears in the social fabric, while scaring away investment, costing jobs and hope. The World Bank estimates that criminal violence in 2005 cost Guatemala 7.3 percent of its GDP, cost El Salvador 11.5 percent, and suppressed growth in Haiti and Jamaica by 5.4 percent (World Bank 2011, 65).

Psychosocial Rehabilitation

Preparing truth commission reports is a first step in the process of coming to terms with the rights violations suffered in a conflict, by establishing a historical record that breaks the silence, creating a path to forgiveness and reconciliation, giving some comfort to victims, and helping society purge the past and move on to construct a better future. For truth commission reports to fulfill that function, their contents must be known, understood, and debated if societies are to construct democratic cultures in which such excesses of cruelty become unimaginable. The fora for such dialogue can be national seminars of eminent persons, carefully guided church-sponsored community discussions, and classrooms where trained teachers use child-friendly versions of the truth commission reports. The international community could have an important role as impartial guarantor (provided it is genuinely perceived by all sides as such), able to facilitate a dialogue needed to reach consensus, since the "construction" of history can, itself, be contested and the subject of internal political power struggles, struggles that may persist despite a negotiated peace. Adolescent girls and boys need to be part of that dialogue; with their open, flexible, and forward-looking minds, they are key to sustaining the peace. They are often more able to reach consensus, and go beyond simply knowing the past, to understanding the complex dynamics that caused the conflict, leading to the creation of democratic behaviors: tolerance, respect of differences, dialogue, and peaceful resolution of differences. Needed but not often included in postconflict strategies are programs that empower adolescents and youth groups to communicate with their peers, including through innovative use of theater groups and social media, in order to explain the history of the conflict and the role that they, as a new generation of citizens, have in developing a tolerant and peaceful society.

Open discussion of the past, either through truth commission reports or other mechanisms to facilitate national dialogue, also helps break the silence between generations by revealing a community and national history, the ignorance of which may prevent young people from developing the strong identity essential for constructive participation in society. Studies on human security and conflict caution that "grievances from past conflicts, especially those that have pitted groups within society against each other or have engaged communal identities... can be sustained for decades, even centuries... if not deftly addressed" (Leaning 2008, 137).

While open discussion of the past is an important factor in the rebuilding of war-torn societies, it is insufficient. All the population, but especially children and adolescents whose age and inexperience heightens their vulnerability, need access to psychosocial support. This can come in many forms; very few people will be able to have access to private psychological services, and indeed, given the collective nature of war trauma, community-based services are more effective, especially for children and adolescents who will be looking for a feeling of protection, which a community and its members provide. With the turmoil of loss of parents and home, the witnessing of violence, or living the life of a refugee or displaced person, children most need supportive caregivers and secure communities in which they can regain a sense of normality, recover trust in adults, and thrive. The most sustainable and effective approach to psychosocial recovery is to mobilize what remains of the social care system, and support the rebuilding of social networks. Thus programs that train community leaders, women's groups, health workers, and teachers in how to recognize signs of trauma and how to deal with them in culturally appropriate ways represent a vital resource for reweaving the social fabric. The importance of reestablishing education in conflict-affected countries has long been recognized for its role of providing protection and psychosocial support to traumatized children; today, education programs in Lebanon provide Syrian refugee children with a sense of normalcy and routine that is very healing, while also involving and empowering parents who feel frightened and adrift (Pederson 2012). Education also has an often untapped potential to contribute to long-term peace-building and transformative social change by reestablishing confidence in the state's capacity to provide services, and by sector reforms that address inequality and stereotyping in education, that had been and continue to have the enduring potential to be drivers of conflict (Novelli and Smith 2011, 14). The Complementary Rapid Education for Primary Schools (CREPS) program in Sierra Leone not only provided accelerated learning for children and adolescents who had missed out on their education during the war, but it served a crucial role in reintegrating ex-combatants, enhancing social cohesion, and sustainable peace-building (Novelli and Smith 2011, 29); participating in CREPS changed these adolescents' frame of reference from "fighting" to "future." In Lebanon, after the civil war of the 1970s and 1980s, an informal program, Education for Peace, brought together different segments of the community in a neutral space for reconciliation to envision an alternative future; the initiative successfully spawned other peace education programs that ultimately developed a generation of peace activists who would go on to become leaders of Lebanese NGOs and institutions (Novelli and Smith 2011, 30). However, education is a sensitive sector, which can perpetuate drivers of conflict or fail to fulfill its rehabilitative potential. Where teachers are not trained to recognize and address pupils' trauma, the therapeutic value of school attendance may be less, especially for those forcibly recruited children and adolescents attempting to rebuild their lives after being both perpetrators and witnesses to violence. A longitudinal study of former child soldiers in Sierra Leone found that, although staying in school was associated with improved prosocial attitudes and behaviors, school's impact on reducing anxiety and depression was less than expected, perhaps due to the quality of the schools and the lack of mental health support in the schools (Betancourt, Agnew-Blais, et al. 2010).[1] These severely traumatized children, who participated in atrocities, should not be institutionalized or isolated from the community, as this creates further stigma, distress, and the potential for destructive antisocial behaviors. In the aforementioned longitudinal study of former child soldiers, it was found that when they experienced community acceptance, these young people made an extra effort to be helpful and kind to others (Betancourt, Borisova, et al 2010, 1090).

While war inflicts trauma on all ages, adolescents are particularly vulnerable to suffer long-lasting effects, being at an age crucial for the development of self-esteem and of identity, founded on name, family, and national origin, all elements that might have been lost in the turmoil of conflict. Adolescents, driven from their homes, communities (and, sometimes, even their country), forcibly separated from their families, may have the foundation of their identity kicked out from under them, just at the age when it should be solidifying. When their homes, villages, and towns have been physically destroyed, adolescents' connection to the identity of place is marooned in memory; full reconnection with their past is disrupted forever. As the far-reaching study by Graca Machel, *The Impact of Armed Conflict on Children*, stated: "The extreme and often prolonged circumstances of armed conflict interfere with identity development. As a result, many adolescents—especially those who have had severely distressing experiences . . . cannot conceive of any future. . . . They may view their lives very pessimistically, suffer from serious depression, or . . . commit suicide. . . . Moreover, sudden changes in family circumstances such as death and disappearance of parents, can leave youth without guidance, role models and sustenance" (Machel 1996, 170).

Surprisingly little research has been conducted on adolescent identity formation in postconflict settings, but it can easily be hypothesized that the huge dislocation caused by war interferes with the adolescent's sense of safety in the normal maturation process of solidifying his or her view of self. The psychological difficulty in identity formation is accompanied, we now know, by tremendous physical changes in the brain between the ages of twelve and twenty-five years old. The recent discoveries in adolescent brain development, discussed in more detail in the chapter by Laurence Steinberg in this volume, show that the brain undergoes dramatic (often called "exuberant") spurts of growth during this period, similar to the growth in the fetal brain, accompanied by constant pruning back of this new growth under a "use it or lose it" process. And as McNeely and Bose point out in their chapter, strength is built in the areas of the brain that teens use and where they focus their energy; connections made during this period of life become hard-wired, while unused areas of the brain may permanently lose capacity (Weinberger, Elvevag, and Giedd 2005, 12). This finding raises questions about the extent to which extensive participation in violent acts during the adolescence of war-affected youth may hard-wire aggression in their brains. Might this be one factor behind the legacy of violence left by civil conflicts? In Central America, where criminal networks linked to drug trafficking have become active since the wars' end, the years since 1999 have seen homicides increase 101 percent in El Salvador, 91 percent in Guatemala, and 63 percent in Honduras (World Bank 2011, 58). Clearly, much research is needed before this hypothesis can be confirmed. The Sierra Leone study of former child soldiers suggests that those adolescents with a history of wounding or killing others demonstrate a progressive deterioration over time in their adjustment to family and community life; this is attributed in part to perceived discrimination against the children who had engaged in violent acts (Betancourt, Agnew-Blais, et al. 2010, 17–26), the lack of psychosocial support and of attention given to addressing the mental health consequences of perpetrating atrocities (Betancourt, Borisova, et al. 2010, 1092). But, might it also be due to physical changes in their brains that have been hard-wired? If so, what strategies, if any, might communities, nations, and international actors adopt to reconfigure the neural pathways and facilitate more prosocial behaviors in these survivors of childhood war trauma? Answering this question is a matter of urgency, given the extent of violence that afflicts societies emerging from civil war.

Identity and self-esteem can be particularly distorted if the adolescent belongs to an ethnic group targeted for genocide, such as the Maya in Guatemala (Commission for Historical Clarification 1999, 134) or the Tutsis in Rwanda, or if he or she has been forced to spend childhood displaced from his or her culture and community. As an expert has noted: "In these wars, where communities are split along communal lines . . . individuals and groups targeted on the basis of their communal characteristics are forced to undergo a profound disorientation in their sense of social stability, trust and personal identity" (Leaning 2008, 134). When that identity is under formation, as is true for children and adolescents, the disorientation is particularly profound and long-lasting. In Guatemala, suicide rates among Mayan adolescents from certain targeted areas rose sharply after the end of the war; the reckless violence among youth is a further indication of hopelessness and despair. Guatemalan youth who join gangs stated that they did so "because they were searching for the support, trust and cohesion . . . that they maintained their families did not provide" (Moser 2008 79), or perhaps *could* not provide, due to the immense dislocation and identity disruption of the war. One Mayan leader, interviewed in 2011, rued that "[Guatemalan indigenous] young people are being assimilated very fast—the girls are leaving their *cortes* (traditional dress) behind and fewer and fewer want to speak their language. . . . Some young people have organized themselves and are asking who they really are" (Adams 2011, 34).

Peace brings new opportunities and expectations of access to the wider world, which tempt young people to leave their parents and rural communities behind, straining communication between the generations. War-affected adolescents feel an even stronger sense of alienation from the older generation than is common to all in that age group. In a postwar opinion poll of

Guatemalan children and adolescents 10–18 years old, 44 percent stated that the principal problems they faced were that they felt alone, or that no one would listen to their worries (SOPORTE 2000). In the absence of this intergenerational dialogue, society becomes further fragmented and divided. Hence, participatory programs that foster dialogue between parents and their teenage children, which help to reconstruct the identity and cultural pride of adolescents, can build the self-esteem they need to regain hope in the future, and to become constructively engaged in communal life. As Graca Machel stated in a 2000 follow-up report on children and armed conflict: "Armed with abundant resilience and learning capacity [adolescents] are an invaluable resource, particularly as communicators, information carriers and counsellors for other war-affected youth and the wider community" (Machel 2000).

A program in the Ixil area of Guatemala, where some of the war's worst atrocities occurred, demonstrates the truth of these assertions. Here, teenagers were trained to provide rehabilitative services for younger children and for families, and to reconstruct the local history of the conflict; by reclaiming personal and collective identity, reconstructing history served as a means of healing. School attendance and community engagement shot up, and the self-image of the teenagers improved as community leaders sought their help.

Similarly, in Colombia, which has suffered an internal conflict for almost half a century, displacing and traumatizing millions of children, the "Return to Happiness" program provided urgent mass psychosocial support to children and their families affected by the violence. The crucial component of the program was enabling families and communities to take part in the recovery process. Adolescent boys and girls, supervised by teachers, were key; several hundred were trained in "play therapy" and taught how to cultivate trust and hope in younger children through games, art, puppetry, songs, and storytelling. Through their work as "play therapists," the adolescent volunteers came to serve as role models in their communities. They created a link between families, schools, and communities, forming a network of reconstructive peace-building that reached thousands of children and their families. A 2004 review of the program stated:

> From the start adolescents proved an ideal role model for the younger children. They could understand very well the child's world—the games, songs, stories, riddles and legends. In the towns and villages of Colombia they felt the same impact of terror and

violence. They consoled and supported each other as the volunteers attempted to bring back a sense of normalcy to the lives of younger children. The play sessions not only create open communication and trust in the relationship between adolescents and younger children, but also build self-esteem among the adolescent volunteers. The experience of consoling younger children and helping them overcome their distress teaches the young volunteers how to cope.... In Colombia, one of the key impacts of the Return to Happiness program has been to create a culture of peace in the midst of war, and to prevent the recruitment of children into armed groups. The program offers adolescents a personal, family and community role that builds confidence, self-esteem and a sense of belonging. Many children and adolescents expressed their unwillingness to serve as soldiers after participating and, in one case, an adolescent involved in Return to Happiness moved out of his neighborhood to avoid forced recruitment by the guerrillas. (UNICEF 2004, 30–31, 35–36)

Adolescents remain an underused resource for countries seeking to heal the wounds of war and regain the social capital squandered during years of conflict. Young people are eager to be engaged in their country's reconstruction, as this eighteen-year-old young man stated in Liberia: "We agree that we have destroyed this country. And it is us—the young people—that should be empowered to rebuild our communities.... We need basic training to make the country good again. It can't be the NGOs that do all the work for us. It has to be us" (UN Secretary General for Children and Armed Conflict 2007, 19).

Yet tapping the potential of adolescents to facilitate peace not only among their peers but in their communities and nations is not a mainstream postconflict strategy. For example, one of the major international development policy documents of recent years, the World Bank's *2011 World Development Report: Conflict, Security and Development*, contains not a single mention of adolescents in its analysis of conflict's legacy of distrust nor in its recommendations for overcoming the political, social, and economic consequences of distrust.

Creating a Culture of Rights: Political and Civil Rights

My feelings about the past is I am worried because they've made me lose my dignity, I don't see myself as a complete person like before

and I feel humiliated again, because [of] those people who assaulted me. I did open a case against them, but nothing has happened thus far... That wound is still there because those policemen were just left [unpunished].
 —Potwalo Saboshego, Youth Resistance Fighter, South Africa
  (Truth and Reconciliation Commission of South Africa 1998).

Countries emerging from civil war and other devastating forms of conflict have the dual challenge of dealing with massive human rights violations committed in the past and of establishing democratic institutions that give citizens the confidence and capacity to claim their rights. Such institutions create a new culture to protect rights and bring the impunity of all war crimes to an end, including those committed against children. As the testimony of Potwalo Saboshego eloquently attests, to heal individual and social wounds, a most urgent task is the establishment of a functioning system of justice, which holds wrongdoers to account. Without a robust reform of the judicial system to end impunity, new democratic governments and institutions lose credibility, and vigilante justice increases—in Guatemala in 2009, there were one hundred attempted lynchings, an indicator that the population has become impatient with the slow pace of reforms (Adams 2011, 47).

Building Institutions for the Protection of Political and Civil Rights

The international community, seeking to help a war-torn society recover, has a particular role to play in supporting the International Criminal Court and special war crimes tribunals that set standards of criminal culpability for adults who abduct, recruit, and exploit children as combatants, criteria to establish culpability of juvenile offenders, and special procedures for trying and rehabilitating juveniles. In 2004, the Special Court for Sierra Leone ruled that the recruitment or use of children under age fifteen in hostilities is a war crime under customary international law (contrary to the assertion by one of the accused that he was immune from prosecution, because the recruitment or use of children under fifteen in hostilities was not established as a war crime during the period of the Special Court's authority, preceding the International Criminal Court). This landmark ruling resulted in the indictment of Sam Hinga Norman, the first ever for the recruitment of child soldiers; although he died before he could be convicted, the precedent was established. In April 2012 the Sierra Leone Special Court convicted Charles Taylor, Liberia's former president, of crimes against humanity by abetting murder, rape, and the forced enlistment of child soldiers during Sierra Leone's civil war; this successful prosecution provided some sense of justice for the citizens of Sierra Leone, 95 percent of whom wanted him convicted (Tortora 2008). Encouraging as these global efforts to pursue justice are, the vast majority of cases must be tried in the national courts. A major investment must be made in modernizing national legislation, creating structures and procedures to implement that legislation, training judges and police in how to apply the law, all consistent with international standards of human rights, including the CRC's standard of integral protection. National legislation to implement the CRC is needed to guarantee the rights of juvenile offenders, in all cases where children are in conflict with the law, but especially in those where they were active participants in the war crimes, as was the case in Rwanda. There, almost forty-five hundred young people were imprisoned for alleged participation in the genocide, several hundred of whom were under fourteen at the time of the crime. In dealing with this extreme case of demonstrated need for a juvenile justice system consistent with the CRC, a number of measures to enhance the protection of children's rights were undertaken. These were an information campaign to increase awareness of the relevance of the CRC in addressing crimes committed by juveniles; support for a unit within the Ministry of Justice to deal exclusively with children in conflict with the law; educational and recreational programs for juveniles within prison; training of prison staff, judges, and police; supporting efforts for reintegrating child detainees upon release (extended families, foster families); supporting and organizing defense counsels; organizing and supporting efforts to set up dossiers in each criminal case involving children; preparing and disseminating a manual on justice for under-eighteen offenders.

In addition to creating a functioning judicial system able to prosecute both political and common criminals in a fair and predictable manner, the children and adolescents, like the citizenry as a whole, need responsive mechanisms for making accusations. In Guatemala, the Office of the Human Rights Ombudsman was created to monitor the state's performance in justice matters, and to channel complaints and denunciations of rights violations. One innovation was the creation of municipal boards for child protection; made up entirely of volunteers—teachers, priests, clinic workers, youth leaders, scouts. These boards empowered adolescents with knowledge both of their rights and how to claim them, intervened in cases of child abuse (counseling the parents or channeling the case to the justice system), and generally sought to promote dialogue around, and awareness of, issues affecting the fulfillment of child rights. Such volunteer boards had the potential to contribute to changing Guatemala's culture from one of authoritarianism, citizen fear, and apathy to one of dialogue, participation, and respect for civil and political rights. Unfortunately, due to lack of funding, this promising initiative has been but weakly sustained, dependent as it is on volunteer support.

Building institutions to protect civil and political rights may strengthen the acceptance by young people like Potwalo Saboshego of the importance of mutual respect for fellow citizens, and may generate hope in the nation's future. In the absence of such institutions, a child who has been tortured by state agents, or who, after witnessing his parents' murder, finds that the crime goes unpunished, or who is an adolescent incarcerated for years without any due process, may experience little but anger, resentment, and cynicism toward the law and society in general. Personal experience, combined with a lack of knowledge or understanding of civil and political rights, may lead young people to feel they have no stake in such an unjust society. The probability that they will grow up to rely on old authoritarian patterns of behavior and on the use of force to resolve disputes is high, compromising a sustainable peace.

Mechanisms for Participating in Political Decisions

In a postwar context, ordinary citizens, lacking any experience of influencing events or the political process, may be reluctant to raise their voices, with their disinclination to participate accentuated by the considerable distrust and fear generated by the conflict. Into the vacuum of public participation within countries in transition to democracy step political parties, often based around individuals whose platform grows out of the leader's personal vision, not out of the collective vision, one that would emerge from a general assembly in which all interested citizens could participate. In other words, authoritarian patterns pervade emerging democratic institutions. An Organization of American States analysis of the results of the Guatemalan Peace Accords after ten years noted "an alarming disconnect between political parties and the general public, [with the] political parties unable to transcend clientelistic practices" (Adams 2011, 26) or to develop programs that people could become enthusiastic about. Thus, elections held in the immediate aftermath of war, while very high on the agenda of the international community, often deepen divisions (World Bank 2011, 101 and 146). The winning party either fragments under the pressure of dividing the spoils, or does everything possible to ensure that vanquished parties are thoroughly marginalized from political participation, and thus embittered—with all that implies for a continuation of the conflict in other forms, and for disillusioning adolescents and youth. In Haiti, a country whose parties and democratic institutions are highly fragmented, focus groups of adolescents and youth conducted in 2010 viewed all politics as "dirty," and politicians as thieves or: "'grands mangeurs' or big eaters . . . preying on public resources for personal gain . . . it was clear that regardless of socio-economic background young participants perceived politics as practiced in Haiti as essentially immoral. . . . [they] could not conceive of the possibility that Haitian politicians might commit to real power sharing, stating 'when they are in power they even arrest their opponents!' . . . They were also aware that politics as played out in Haiti do[es] not comply with democratic principles (Lunde and Luzincourt 2010, 2).

International actors can contribute substantially to countries making the painful transition from war to democracy by facilitating mechanisms for consultation, and for constructing consensus between political elites and society, including by opening spaces in which the voices of adolescents and youth can be heard and heeded by politicians; they can also urge that the means for doing so be structured into nascent democratic institutions. Several conflict-affected countries—Rwanda, Nepal, Liberia, and Zimbabwe among them—have established national Children's Parliaments as a means for empowering children and adolescents to participate as citizens in policy decisions that affect them. In 2006, when the civil war ended in Nepal, the society embarked on the development of its first democratic constitution. Consistent with Nepal's ratification of the CRC in 1990, children were actively engaged in the constituent assemblies across the country and prepared a list of priorities for the constitution to consider: these included protection of children against sexual harassment and abuse, against child marriage, discrimination, bonded labor, and protection for the rights of disabled children. Recognition of children's rights led, among other advances, to a National Framework for Child-friendly Local Governance, which mandates that 10 percent of the budget be allocated to programs that benefit the most disadvantaged children, and that 15 percent of total capital investment be dedicated to the children's sector (UNICEF, OECD, and Save the Children 2011, 9).

Realizing their right to participation gives adolescents the experience of practicing democracy and contributing constructively to postconflict society. As such, not only is their tremendous energy channeled in a positive instead of a destructive direction but their stake in the country is increased by having participated in the design of its future.

Widespread Peace and Civic Education Programs

Participatory institutions and mechanisms are essential for promoting consensus and confidence in any emerging democracy. However, they will not function in the absence of a public will to participate, nor in the absence of any understanding that participation in political life is a right, one that must be exercised to ensure that all rights are protected. Thus, widespread civic education programs are a prerequisite for successful development of democratic culture and citizens' capacity to claim their rights. In the first few years following the end of a conflict, the international community has an important role in helping amplify local voices promoting human rights, peace, and democracy and the cultural change that the internalization of these catalyzes in society as a whole. With international support, civic or peace education programs can be implemented that not only provide information on child rights/human rights but build civic-minded solidarity and a national citizen capacity to promote, demand, and defend rights. International actors can support such training through state institutions, media campaigns, churches, schools, indigenous/cultural associations, women's groups and youth groups, chambers of commerce, trade unions, and other civil society organizations.

For children and adolescents, civic education, whether through formal or informal channels, not only increases their understanding of the foundations of a democratic society but helps ensure that behaviors conducive to sustainable peace and a strong democracy are internalized. It is very significant that, in an extensive review of peace practice in Haiti, a country that experiences "lots of conflict without a war" (Pace and Luzincourt 2009, 23), among the most promising programs for advancing peace was the Campaign for the Reduction of Violence that engaged adolescents and youth in nonviolent conflict resolution among their peers and communities in zones at high risk of violence. The Campaign carried out human rights and conflict resolution training in middle and secondary schools, reaching close to five thousand students, a third of whom were girls; it created "peace centers" for adolescents and youth, safe places for them to go both to avoid neighborhood violence and learn life skills to protect them from violent influences; it established youth clubs for peace, involving a thousand children and supporting them in cultural and sporting events; and it trained Carnival Peace Brigades, youth and adolescent volunteers deployed during the normally violent carnival festivities, to urge crowds to remain peaceful and to alert police when dangerous situations developed. That these initiatives with Haitian adolescents and youth from violent communities were "wildly popular" speaks to the pent-up demand of Haitian young people to contribute to peace and nonviolent forms of conflict resolution (Pace and Luzincourt 2009, 29–23). In this, they are not alone, as some of the other examples in this chapter demonstrate.

Conclusion

This chapter began by reviewing the legacy that civil war has left on the adolescents of Guatemala, as emblematic of other civil wars of the past decades. That legacy is one, as the World Bank starkly stated, of crippling distrust and the embedding of devastating violence in society. Adolescents have the potential to power the wings of the phoenix away from the ashes of conflict's devastation, toward a new culture of nonviolence, justice, and democratic participation, yet both international and national policy makers too rarely see or support that potential, despite the universal ratification of the CRC and its provision, in Article 12, that all children have the right to be heard in decisions that affect them. Given the extent of violence prevailing in countries that have suffered civil conflict, the potential of adolescent agency to heal the social wounds of war at least deserves another look by the international community, in its support of postconflict policy and programs.

Yet it is also true that social processes are long-term, and that recovery can take a generation; just returning to their original growth path takes countries that have gone through civil war an average of fourteen years of peace (World Bank 2011, 63). Repairing economic damage is relatively straightforward compared to repairing the sociocultural and political damage of internal conflict on a people. Too often, donors' initial enthusiasm for consolidating peace wears off as violence and insecurity rises, and the difficulty of transforming institutions and society becomes clear. Aid to postconflict and fragile countries is more than twice as volatile as that to stable countries, a volatility that robs reconstruction programs of predictability. For children and adolescents, losing predictability in programs they need and count on for building their dreams undermines their trust in the state and society. Absence of trust fuels despair, which in turn fuels a sense of helplessness that makes participation in violence appear an empowering option for adolescents.

Though international aid to postconflict countries needs to be both more generous and more predictable, so that it does not become another factor fueling an unstable situation, foreign actors can only set the stage for rebuilding a country after war, accompanying the people with discretion, modesty, and evenhandedness. The real work of creating a new society will be done by local actors, who through individual and collective acts of grace and forgiveness reconcile, build trust, and confidence in one another, and hence in a shared future. Adolescents and young people, with their resilience, optimism, and energy, can carry that future forward, if efforts are made to support their psychosocial recovery, their capacity to contribute and be heard, and to build their trust and increase their stake in society.

Notes

Sections of this chapter originally appeared in "Die Schwingen des Phonix—Junge Generationen beim Wiederaufbaunach dem Krieg," in UNICEF, *Guatemala: Der Krieg und die Kinder* (Gottingen: Lamuv-Verlag, 2003).

1. Betancourt, Agnew-Blais, et al (2010) analyze the role that postwar experiences of discrimination played in psychosocial adjustment for former child soldiers in Sierra Leone and find that for those who wounded or killed others, perceptions of discrimination largely explained their subsequent increases in hostility; however, it notes that perceived stigma might not be actual discrimination on the part of the community, and that more research is needed to confirm this finding.

References

Adams, Tani Marilena. 2011. *Consumed by Violence: Advances and Obstacles to Building Peace in Guatemala Fifteen Years After the Peace Accords*. CDA Collaborative Learning Projects. http://www.seguridadcondemocracia.org/.

Africa Barometer. 2008. Online Analysis 2008 surveys. http://www.jdsurvey.net/afro/AnalizeQuestion.jsp.

Alta Comisionada de las Naciones Unidas para los Derechos Humanos. 2010. *Informe de la Alta Comisionada de las Naciones Unidas para los derechos Humanos sobre las Actividades de su Oficina en Guatemala, año 2010*. New York: Alto Comisionado de las Naciones Unidas para los Derechos Humanos.

Betancourt, Theresa S., Jessica Agnew-Blais, Stephen Gilman, David Williams, and B. Heidi Ellis. 2010. "Past Horrors, Present Struggles: The Role of Stigma in the Association Between War Experiences and Psychosocial Adjustment Among Former Child-Soldiers in Sierra Leone." *Social Science and Medicine* 70, no. 1 (January): 17–26.

Betancourt, Theresa, Ivelina Borisova, Timothy Williams, Robert Brennan, T. Hatch Whitfield, Marie de la Soudiere, and Stephen Gilman. 2010. "Sierra Leone's Former Child Soldiers: A Follow-up Study of Psychosocial Adjustment and Community Reintegration." *Child Development* 81, no. 4 (July–August): 1077–95.

Commission for Historical Clarification (CEH). 1999. *Guatemala Memory of Silence*. Report of the CEH, Conclusions and Recommendations.

Gibbons, Elizabeth. 2003. "Die Schwingen des Phonix—Junge Generationen beim Wiederaufbaunach dem Krieg." In *Guatemala: Der Krieg und die Kinder*. UNICEF. Gottingen: Lamuv-Verlag.

Latinobarometro: Opinion Publica Latino Americana. 2010. "Online Analysis, Guatemala, Question A102." http://www.latinobarometro.org/latino/LATAnalize.jsp.

Leaning, Jennifer. 2008. "Human Security and Conflict." In *Risking Human Security: Attachment and Public Life*, edited by Marci Green, 125–50. London: Karnac Books.

Lunde, Henriette, and Ketty Luzincourt. 2010. "'Politics Is Dirty': The View of Haitian Youth." Norwegian Peace-building Center. http://www.peacebuilding.no/var/ezflow_site/storage/original/application/c030c21239d6dfead2ed18b22896e609.pdf.

Machel, Graca. 1996. *Impact of Armed Conflict on Children: Report of the Expert of the Secretary General*. UN General Assembly A/51/306.

———. 2000. *Impact of Armed Conflict on Children: A Critical Review of Progress Made and Obstacles Encountered in Increasing Protection for War-Affected Children*. International Conference on War-affected Children, Winnipeg, Canada, 2000.

McKay, S., and D. Mazurana. 2004. *Where Are the Girls? Girls in Fighting Forces in Northern Uganda, Sierra Leone, and Mozambique: Their Lives During and After War*. Montreal: International Center for Human Rights and Democratic Development.

Morales, Sergio. 2012. *Informe Anual Circunstanciado de la Procuraduría de Derechos Humanos de Guatemala*. January. Guatemala City: Procurador de los Derechos Humanos.

Moser, C. *Assets, Livelihoods and Social Policy*. Edited by C Moser and A Dani. World Bank, 2008. eScholarID: 4b1494.

Novelli, Mario, and Alan Smith. 2011. *The Role of Education in Peacebuilding: A Synthesis Report of Findings from Lebanon, Nepal and Sierra Leone*. UNICEF NY.

Pace, Marie, and Ketty Luzincourt. 2009. *Haiti's Fragile Peace: A Case Study of the Cumulative Impacts of Peace Practice*. CDA Collaborative Learning Projects. http://www.seguridadcondemocracia.org/.

Pederson, Silje Vik. 2012. "UNICEF-Supported Summer Camps Are Helping Syrian and Lebanese Children Integrate into Public Schools in Lebanon." Last modified July 6. UNICEF. http://www.unicef.org/infobycountry/lebanon 65234.html.

SOPORTE. 2000. *Conocimiento y Percepción de Derechos Humanos de la Ninez en Guatemala*. Opinion poll of thirty-two hundred people ages 10–55 on perceptions of democracy, peace, human rights, and child rights. Guatemala City: UNICEF.

Stiefel, Matthais. 1999. *Rebuilding After War: A Summary Report of the War-torn Societies Project*. Geneva: United Nations Statistics Division.

Time Research-UNICEF. 2000. *Enquesta Regional "Voz de los Niños, las Ninas y los Adolescentes en America Latina y el Caribe."* Bogota: UNICEF.

Torres-Rivas, Edelberto, and Bernardo Arevalo de Leon. 1999. *From Conflict to Dialogue: The WSP Guatemala Way*. Guatemala City: Facultad Latinoamericana de Ciencias Sociales

Tortora, Bob. 2008. "Sierra Leoneans, Liberians Want Charles Taylor Convicted." Gallup World, December 19. http://www.gallup.com/poll/113491/sierra-leoneans-liberians-want-charles-taylor-convicted.aspx.

Truth and Reconciliation Commission of South Africa. 1998. "Special Hearing: Children and Youth." In *The Truth and Reconciliation Commission of South Africa Report*, vol. 4, chap. 9. www.justice.gov.za/trc/report/finalreport

UN Secretary General for Children and Armed Conflict and UN Focal Point on Youth. 2007. "Will You Listen: Young Voices from Conflict Zones." UN Department of Economic and Social Affairs.

UNICEF. 1996. *State of the World's Children Report, 1996: Children in War*. http://www.unicef.org/sowc96/1cinwar.htm.

———. 2004. "Return to Happiness (Retorno de la Alegria) in Colombia." In *Adolescent Programme Activities During Situations of Conflict and Post-Conflict*. New York: UNICEF.

UNICEF, OECD, and Save the Children. 2011. *Child Rights and Governance Roundtable Report*. London.

Weinberger, D., B. Elvevag, and J. Giedd. 2005. *The Adolescent Brain: A Work in Progress*. National Campaign to Prevent Teen Pregnancy www.thenationalcampaign.org/resource/adolescent/brain.

World Bank. 2011. *World Development Report 2011: Conflict, Security and Development*. Washington, D.C.: World Bank.

CHAPTER 9

Adolescents in the Colombian Armed Conflict: Recruitment Realities and Important Lessons for Their Successful Reintegration

Katie Naeve

All illegal armed groups participating in Colombia's armed conflict recruit and use children as soldiers. Half of all combatants join armed groups when they are under the age of eighteen (Human Rights Watch 2003, 4). Unlike the phenomenon of kidnapping child soldiers witnessed in many past and present conflicts, most child soldiers in Colombia *voluntarily* chose to join armed groups (UNICEF 2006, 74). While the concept of a child's voluntary involvement in armed groups is nuanced, this chapter identifies voluntary as not physically forced by any other individual.

As Volkmann notes in an earlier chapter in this volume, there are many reasons why Colombian youth choose to enter armed conflict, including a lack of economic opportunities, poor role models, to protect themselves from sexual violence, and the desire to be a member of a group. Voluntary recruitment represents a new reality in the recruitment of youth into illegal armed groups—a new reality that necessitates a critical review of not only prevention initiatives, but also of reintegration services to address the needs of children that demobilize.

Examining the Age Cutoff Impact on Demobilized Child Soldiers: Methodology and Data

Although approximately one in four illegal armed combatants in Colombia at any given point is under the age of eighteen, the most important characteristic that the government of Colombia uses to determine an ex-combatant's path of reintegration is the age at which he or she *demobilizes*: under eighteen years of age and the child is characterized as a victim of illegal recruitment and receives benefits and services for demobilized children through the Colombian Institute for Family Welfare (ICBF); over eighteen years of age and the individual is characterized as an illegal ex-combatant and receives benefits and services for adult ex-combatants through the Colombian government's reintegration program, the Colombian Agency for Reintegration (ACR). This cutoff dangerously underestimates the needs of adolescents who were used as child soldiers by armed groups and are now adults, attempting to reintegrate with all of the issues they faced when they mobilized, plus the added trauma from their time with armed groups.

Child soldiers who demobilize after their eighteenth birthdays face a fractured legal and policy response to their demobilization and reintegration. Under Colombian and international law, they were illegally recruited and thus victims of the armed conflict. Their age at demobilization, however, restricts them from receiving reparations and reintegration services provided to former child soldiers who demobilized prior to their eighteenth birthdays. All ex-combatants who legally demobilize in Colombia have the right to government reintegration programs through the ACR when they are at or above eighteen years of age, so long as there is no warrant for their arrest for crimes against humanity. Those who demobilize before eighteen years of age, however, receive distinct treatment, reparations, and rehabilitation for being child soldiers, including mandatory education and specialized psychological and social services through the ICBF.

The purpose of the study on which this chapter is based was to measure the cutoff impacts in reality, especially in light of the needs of these adolescents. The study sought to understand whether there were measureable differences in key reintegration outcomes between those child soldiers who demobilized under eighteen years of age and those who demobilized over eighteen years of age, and if so, how they could be addressed through appropriate reintegration services, holding constant key ethnogeographic, mobilization, and conflict experience characteristics.

The data in this chapter were collected through a survey administered to 112 randomly selected demobilized child soldiers, currently aged 18–27, who are active participants in the Colombian government's reintegration program. All participants were interviewed at one of six of the twenty-nine ACR service centers in Colombia in late 2011. The six service centers selected provided a sample of interviewees with significant heterogeneity, which improves the robustness of the data. The participants interviewed are from twenty-two of Colombia's thirty-two departments and fought in twenty-three departments and Ecuador.

The survey instrument administered to participants contained a series of demographic questions related to the individual's experience entering, participating in the conflict, and demobilizing from the armed group, asked about services received and the length of time in the reintegration processes, and outcome indicators focused on economic well-being, educational attainment, social integration, mental health, self-esteem and self-confidence, drug and alcohol use, and criminal activity. It also solicited self-reported participation in the ACR, in addition to perceptions of and attitudes toward the reintegration programs, and their recommendations for services—information that had never previously been asked of this population. For the full methodology, questionnaire, and information about data analysis, see Naeve (2012).

The data collected from the survey was aggregated to produce key summary statistics on the population, in addition to a rigorous empirical analysis of the impact of the reintegration program on these youth, using a regression discontinuity design to examine the effect of the government-mandated cutoff for youth-specific reintegration services.

Recruitment

Significant literature and policies that address the prevention of child soldier recruitment focus solely on the aspect of forced recruitment into armed groups, leaving dangerous gaps in both the understanding of voluntary youth recruitment and prevention measures. Preventing child recruitment in Colombia is key to protecting the fundamental rights of Colombian children and necessary for ending the decades-long conflict that has depended on the exploitation of children as soldiers. It is without a doubt a daunting task. Colombian illegal armed groups recruit children without regard to age, race, gender, or location. Efforts to end child recruitment must address the root causes of children's vulnerability, including poverty, harsh child labor practices, marginalization of minority or indigenous groups, poor educational and health services, and domestic and street violence. Physical protection by police and national armed forces, in addition to antipoverty and family support services, will be required to address the fundamental needs of children that are neglected when children are forced or invited to join armed groups.

The findings illustrated in this chapter undermine the conventional understanding of youth who enter armed conflict, and show that adolescents are not merely submissive children, but misguided young adults capable of making dangerous decisions in attempts at improving their circumstances.

As children's rights expert Mike Wessels asserts, the recruitment of child soldiers is not only a practice of violent forced labor but also one, sadly, of opportunity for youth who find themselves with no alternative livelihood (Wessels 2006, 32). He explains that children who *choose* to join armed groups are not always "passive victims" but "active agents" who understand the economic and power opportunities that come with joining an armed group, while at the same time being largely ignorant of the fate that awaits them when they are recruited (Wessels 2006, 32). This is especially true of adolescents, highly influenced by their surroundings and circumstances, who look toward adulthood with skepticism and disappointment at their lack of opportunity.

This chapter does not explore why children join armed groups in order to transfer blame away from the leaders of armed groups that recruit these children, or suggest that any form of illegal recruitment is less harmful than another. It simply aims to identify the new realities of youth who enter armed conflict and to argue for a new policy framework for prevention, demobilization, and reintegration programs. All recruitment of children under the age of eighteen into combat is illegal, and the use of children in armed conflict is one of the most egregious forms of child abuse, regardless of the way in which it began or the role a child has with an armed group (United Nations 1989, 3; United Nations 2007). Understanding the dynamics of why adolescents are joining armed groups is crucial to designing policies that prevent this phenomenon and all of its negative consequences for them and their societies, and to constructing policies that effectively return these youngest members of society to their societies as peaceful, integrated, rights-holding citizens.

According to the data collected for this study, 70.5 percent of demobilized children joined armed groups voluntarily, and 28 percent were forced to do so by the armed group or their families. The reasons adolescents cited for joining armed groups voluntarily include the appeal of weapons and uniforms (41 percent), to earn money or other resources (22 percent), and because friends and family also joined the group (17 percent). As one interviewee explained, he joined "because I didn't have a job or money to help my family and my family was and is very poor and I was getting along really bad, and because I was already involved somehow in this group, I went, or I had to go."

While joining an armed group because one likes weapons and uniforms can be interpreted a number of ways, following Wessel's argument it could be used as a proxy for an attempt to create a meaningful life or in recognition of the opportunities that may be associated with joining a powerful illegal armed group like the Revolutionary Armed Forces of Colombia (FARC) or United Self-Defense Forces of Colombia (AUC). Further evidence to support this explanation is that less than 5 percent of the former child soldiers interviewed had completed primary school (while the World Bank estimates that over 90 percent of the general Colombian population has completed secondary education), and most were working as child laborers before entering the armed group, leaving them few visible opportunities outside the armed group.

Similarly, a smaller empirical study in 2003 in Colombia found that girls joined armed groups primarily because they were looking for a way out of abusive family or social environments, and because the life of a combatant (uniform, status, and opportunity to see new places) looked attractive to them (Keairns 2003, 11).

These statistics paint a complex picture of child recruitment. They describe adolescents as active mobilizers seeking a new, or different, identity than that defined by poverty and lack of prospects, although they were taking unguided and dangerous decisions to do so. According to these statistics, youth not only need to be physically protected from kidnapping and abduction, they need education, role models, opportunities, and the chance to form a constructive identity. This has significant implications for the prevention of child recruitment as well as reintegration programs.

Reintegration

Evidenced in the changing face of youth recruitment and participation in Colombia's armed conflict, the unique needs of adolescents must be met by government services for these young people to promote their economic, social, and physiological needs in order to peacefully and successfully return them to their societies once they demobilize from armed groups. Since 2002, the government of Colombia has made significant progress in bringing its decades-long internal conflict to an end by instituting disarmament, demobilization, and reintegration processes for illegal armed combatants—including programs for child soldiers.

The Colombian government instituted what is now the ACR, which seeks to legally return Colombia's demobilized population to their communities to contribute to the peace, security, and reconciliation of Colombian society (High Presidential Council for Reintegration 2012a). Together, Colombia's demobilization and reintegration programs have encouraged over fifty thousand armed combatants to hand in their weapons and return to civilian life. Nearly four thousand of these individuals were children when they demobilized (High Presidential Council for Reintegration 2012b).

There are legal, normative, economic, and political rationales both for and against the cutoff of intensive services for child soldiers who demobilize after age eighteen. The data show that both of these groups of youth (those who demobilize under eighteen years of age, and those who demobilize after eighteen years of age) face the same dilemmas in reintegration that they faced in deciding to join armed groups: a lack of economic opportunity, low educational attainment, marginalization, and poor social connections. Youth who demobilized after their eighteenth birthdays, however, encountered added difficulties.

Only 43 percent of respondents indicated having jobs. This figure is quite low compared to the general population of Colombians aged 15–24, of which 77 percent are employed (World Bank 2008). The unemployed respondents reported the reason for their unemployment as an insufficient number of jobs in their city (33 percent); not being qualified (22 percent);

other reasons (20 percent), which include being pregnant or disabled; not having time to work the hours necessary (14 percent); and lack of interesting jobs (10 percent).

The high unemployment figures could be explained through various phenomena. First, this is a highly immobile population due to the security risks they continue to face after demobilization and their need to maintain their participation in reintegration programs in order to benefit from the services and receive the associated stipend. Another reason could be their very low level of education.

Although the ACR's education program has improved basic education for participants—13 percent of those interviewed had no education prior to joining an armed group, whereas less than 4 percent report having received no education to date—very few participants have gained higher levels of education. There are more participants who have now received two or three years of education more than they had prior to mobilization; however, there seem to be very few participants who receive four or more years of education to date after demobilization. Furthermore, those participants who demobilized prior to eighteen years of age, and thus received specialized services for children, are 17 percent more likely to have achieved fifth grade (the last grade in primary school), as compared to their counterparts who demobilized after their eighteenth birthdays, representing a large gap in educational services provided to those who did not qualify for child services due to their age at demobilization.

This finding demonstrates the disparity in educational attainment of these two groups, but also signals key implications of not finishing primary school, a point that chapters in the next section of this volume explore in detail. In order to be eligible for job training courses at the ACR, participants must first complete primary school; primary school completion is also the minimum standard in the Colombian job market. Therefore, because participants who demobilized at or above eighteen years of age are significantly less likely to have completed primary school, they are also less likely to be eligible for job training courses, and less likely to be qualified for employment.

Education, Training, Employment, and Incentives

There are several policy adjustments the reintegration program in Colombia can undertake to better ensure that the needs of demobilized adolescents are met so that they can return safely and productively to their communities.

Under the current reintegration program, most participants attend school during the workday. Many participants reported facing a trade-off between working and going to school, because the two overlapped during the day. Furthermore, participants felt that since they were receiving a stipend to attend school, they could forgo working. Schooling should not be a trade-off for work for these youth, or a constraint, but a complement to employment. Offering evening or weekend courses, for example, for those that work during the day would reduce participants' need to choose between school and work.

In addition to making both work and school feasible for participants, the ACR could better focus on each participant's individual educational needs and goals. Although the ACR's psychosocial services help participants identify their appropriate educational grade level and ensure that participants have a school to join, little support is provided educationally to ensure that participants succeed in reaching their academic goals. There is more involved in the educational success of these young participants than simply providing them a seat in a classroom. While a seat in an appropriate-level classroom is an important first step, once the participants are in the classroom, it is important to recognize the diverse academic needs of each student and provide adequate services to ensure their success, including out of the classroom tutoring and success monitoring.

Other than the six and a half year maximum for receiving the education stipend, there are no concrete mechanisms in place to ensure that participants' individual academic needs are met and that they are indeed proceeding through school rather than merely sitting in a classroom. This improvement in educational quality to ensure outcomes is especially crucial to those participants who did not receive ICBF care and subsequently seem to be less likely to have completed higher levels of education to date.

Due to the requirements of the Colombian job market, and the constraint that ACR participants must complete primary school (fifth grade) to participate in job training courses, the ACR needs to facilitate attainment of this level of education. To do this, the ACR should gradually increase financial assistance for those receiving primary school education to give them an incentive to graduate. Then, when participants finish fifth grade, they should receive decreasing financial assistance while attending high school. Once a participant completes primary school, he or she is eligible to receive compensation for attending government vocational training (Servicio Nacional de Aprendizaje, or SENA) courses. Together, the compensation awarded for attending high school courses and the compensation for attending SENA courses will equal the payment received up until primary school completion. This will provide incentives for completion of primary school, increase the incentives for secondary school and job training, help participants reduce their dependence on ACR stipends, and provide them an economically sustainable future of employment.

It is important to note, however, that this change in financial compensation for education must be delivered to active participants in a transparent manner so that they do not feel that their benefits are being restricted unfairly, as many commented had happened in the past. Furthermore, actions should be taken to ensure the new compensation schedule does not reduce the motivation of participants to attain postprimary education.

In addition to improving access to and success in educational programs, the ACR must improve efforts to help participants become gainfully employed. Less than half the participants interviewed were currently employed, and almost half of those employed do not work full-time. Furthermore, of those unemployed, 62 percent report currently looking for but being unable to secure employment. While the ACR is consistently working with employers to find positions for ACR participants, this significant effort has been largely unfruitful, often resulting in only one or two ACR jobs per employer (according to a spring 2011 presentation by Frank Pearl, former high commissioner for peace and reintegration). The ACR should look to multinational corporations and solicit positions for ACR participants as part of the plan for Colombia's future economic growth. Because significant amounts of Colombian defense ministry funds come from the United States, the Colombian Ministry of Defense and the ACR should collaborate to involve North American economic actors, such as businesses, in the effort to bring peace to the country.

As a resource, the ACR could look to learn best practices for employing young adults in adversity from U.S. organizations such as YearUp that work to provide meaningful job experiences to at-risk young adults. In addition to providing employment opportunities and relevant experience for the populations they serve, job placement services for young, at-risk adults can also reduce stereotypes, misperceptions, and discrimination often faced by these groups by giving them a positive presence in their communities and in their places of employment. Careful measures must be in place, nonetheless, to protect their identities from former armed groups—highlighting these youth as success stories without proper care can cause unwanted and dangerous attention.

Furthermore, the ACR could employ the skills and experience these adolescents already have. Because participants only receive compensation for up to two job training courses to help prepare them for economic reintegration, it may helpful to build those courses upon the current skills of each participant. When asked, 90 percent of participants stated they gained a useful skill while in the armed group (such as cooking, sewing, security services, or nursing) and of those, 80 percent stated they would be interested in using a skill they gained for a job. Therefore, the ACR could use participants' current skill-sets to help them find appropriate employment, or build upon those skills in job training courses. As clothes manufacturing and restaurant jobs are currently the most common form of employment for those interviewed, the cooking and sewing skills learned could be particularly worthwhile to utilize when the unemployed look for employment.

The ACR promotes entrepreneurialism through their Proyecto Productivo grant for participants to start their own business, but most of those receiving the grant only create jobs for themselves. Furthermore, only seven of the 112 participants interviewed had received a grant. Most recipients who use the grant for entrepreneurial activities purchase carts from which to sell food or handcrafts, or open their own small shop or bakery.

Extra incentives should be provided to ACR participants receiving the grant for hiring other ACR participants. This not only further enhances the ACR's support of entrepreneurship and economic sustainability; it promotes appropriate collaboration among participants.

Participation and Social Integration

Nearly all those interviewed stated that they did not have personal relationships with individuals other than their family members or partner. Because the ACR seeks to reintegrate individuals economically *and* socially, in addition to psychosocial services, opportunities for relationship building should be added to participants' path to reintegration. Collaboration and relationships among participants is crucial to foster a sense of community and solidarity.

During group interviews, participants openly shared their experiences with one another, asked each other questions, and listened attentively when each participant was sharing their opinions or experiences. Furthermore, few participants knew the others in the room. This experience demonstrates that participants would benefit from social activities, both to connect with others who have and are experiencing similar difficulties and successes, and also to relearn how to manage social relationships. This is especially important for those who did not receive ICBF services, have had no civilian social relationships since they were young children before they entered the conflict, and, in many cases, primarily had relationships before they entered the armed conflict that were filled with violence, distrust, and manipulation. Social activities could include group job training; specialized educational services provided in groups; community service projects such as building infrastructure, painting murals, or planting gardens; or merely social activities. The ACR currently facilitates community projects for participants that seek to gain community trust and reconciliation—these same projects can be used to foster relationships and support among young participants.

In addition to social isolation and a lack of personal connections, another significant setback to the social reintegration of ACR participants is their inability to reconnect with their families. Studies have shown that discrimination against former child soldiers is inversely associated with family and community acceptance, and that family acceptance is associated with decreased levels of hostility (Betancourt et al. 2010). While families often live in areas still occupied by armed groups, thus making it unsafe for participants and their families to be in contact, this is not the case for all demobilized child soldiers in Colombia. The ICBF program for demobilized child soldiers as well as several NGOs attempt to connect children to their families when possible. Thus, the ACR could utilize the same initiatives used by the ICBF to safely reunite these young participants with their families when possible.

While the ACR seeks to place participants in services that meet their educational, economic, and psychosocial needs, the services offered are largely one-size-fits-all. In order to meet the needs of each unique demobilized child soldier, the ACR should take into account each participant's background, including experience in the conflict, gender, education level, employment goals, mental health status, family relationships, number of children, native language, and whether the individual belongs to an indigenous group.

Each of these and other identifying characteristics of demobilized child soldiers affect their ability to successfully reintegrate and the issues they face on their path to economic and social reintegration. Identifying and understanding the uniqueness of each participant's background and experiences will allow the ACR to better target their needs and ensure their success in the program and in their postconflict lives.

Constant feedback from participants is important to the successful reintegration of participants and the sustainability of the ACR reintegration program generally. ACR needs to understand whether participants' needs are being met and what services they feel they could benefit from. This study was the first time this population of ACR participants had ever been asked to provide feedback to the ACR on their needs and the services they feel would benefit them in their reintegration. Asking participants what they wanted from the ACR gave them a sense of empowerment and forced them to think critically about their needs as demobilized child soldiers. The three needs that the large majority of participants articulated were increased financial support, greater transparency in services offered and changes in service provision, and improved access to job training courses, along with improved job placement services.

These points, as well as other information the ACR could collect on a regular basis through short questionnaires or small focus groups, would help ensure the ACR hears the needs of the participants. It will give the participants a sense of agency and ownership in their path to reintegration. It is important, however, that the ACR also uses the feedback gained from participants to formulate its programs. Without clearly incorporating the suggestions or needs articulated by participants into the design of programs, they will feel their voices are unheard and may become reluctant to provide their opinions.

Learning from Demobilized Youth

The use of child soldiers remains a tremendous problem in Colombia and a significant roadblock to peace. Yet, dangerous misunderstandings exist about the role of adolescents in armed conflict. Understanding that adolescents more often than not *choose* to join armed groups, and more important understanding why, will be the key to successfully undermining the illegal recruitment of these youth into violence. Furthermore, there are important lessons to be learned from the circumstances surrounding youth who mobilize that should inform demobilization and reintegration programs that seek to effectively return these youth to their communities. Knowing that young adults seek a sense of agency and identity—often from dangerous sources in the absence of peaceful opportunities—is crucial to preventing the recruitment of these youth into armed groups and ensuring that, when they demobilize, they are provided the opportunities and improved circumstances they lacked when they decided to mobilize.

References

Betancourt, T. S., J. Agnew-Blais, S. E. Gilman, D. R. Williams, and B. H. Ellis. 2010. "Past Horrors, Present Struggles: The Role of Stigma in the Association Between War Experiences and Psychological Adjustment Among Former Child Soldiers in Sierra Leone." *Social Science and Medicine* 70 (1): 17–26.

Betancourt, T. S., S. Simmons, I. Borisova, S. E. Brewer, U. Iweala, and M. de la Soudiere. 2008. "High Hopes, Grim Reality: Reintegration and the Education of Former Child Soldiers in Sierra Leone." *Comprehensive Education Review* 52, no. 4 (November 1): 565–87.

Coalition to Stop the Use of Child Soldiers. 2008. *Child Soldiers Global Report 2008*. London: Coalition to Stop the Use of Child Soldiers.

High Presidential Council for Reintegration. 2012a. "Historical Brief." www.reitegration.gov.co.

———. 2012b. "Reintegration in Colombia: Facts and Figures." www.reintegration.gov.co.

Human Rights Watch. 2003. *You'll Learn Not to Cry*. New York: HRW.

Keairns, Yvonne. 2003. *The Voices of Girl Child Soldiers*. New York: Quaker United Nations Office.

Machel, G. 1996. *The Impact of Armed Conflict on Children*. New York: UNICEF.

Naeve, Katie. 2012. "Right, Duty, or Privilege: An Evaluation of the Impact of Government Reintegration Programs for Former Child Soldiers in Colombia." Policy analysis exercise. Cambridge, Mass.: Harvard Kennedy School of Government.

Singer, P. W. 2004. "Talk Is Cheap: Getting Serious About Preventing Child Soldiers." *Cornell International Law Journal* 37:561–586.

———. 2005. *Children at War*. New York: Pantheon.

Theidon, Kimberly. 2009. "Reconstructing Masculinities: The Disarmament, Demobilization, and Reintegration of Former Combatants in Colombia." *Human Rights Quarterly* 31:1–34.

United Nations. 1989. "Convention on the Rights of the Child, November 20, 1989." UN, Treaty Series, vol. 1577, 3. http://www.unhcr.org/refworld/docid/3ae6b38f0.html.

———. 2007. "Optional Protocol to the Convention on the Rights of the Child on the Involvement of Children in Armed Conflict." May 25. http://www.unhcr.org/refworld/docid/47fdfb180.html.

UNICEF. 1996. *The State of the World's Children 1996*. New York: UNICEF.

———. 2006. *The State of the World's Children 2006*. New York: UNICEF.

———. 2011. *The State of the World's Children 2011: Adolescence, an Age of Opportunity.* New York: UNICEF.
Wessels, Michael. 2006. *Child Soldiers: From Violence to Protection.* Cambridge, Mass.: Harvard University Press.
———. 2012. "Child Soldiers." In *The Encyclopedia of Peace Psychology.* 1st ed. ed. Daniel J. Christie: Oxford, Blackwell.
World Bank. 2008. "World Databank." www.worldbank.org/ Accessed March 5, 2012.

PART III

Social Interventions: Strategic Approaches to Adolescent Rights

CHAPTER 10

Young Arabs and Evolving Realities: Linking Social and Economic Rights

Jocelyn DeJong and Mary Kawar

Generalizations about adolescence are difficult to make across an area as diverse as the Arab region, which hosts some of the richest and the poorest countries in the world. Although they share similarities in their linguistic, cultural, and religious composition, the Arab countries that stretch from Morocco in the west to Iraq in the east diverge in many respects, not least in their colonial history, current political regime, and endowment of natural resources. The presence of oil in the Middle East has attracted strong geopolitical interest. In the oil-rich countries of the Persian Gulf, the state is characterized by its "rentier" nature—able to rely on revenue from oil rather than on taxation from its own citizens, which in turns affects the nature of political accountability (Beblawi and Luciani 1987). Even countries without oil, however, have benefitted from remittances from migrant workers and foreign aid from the oil-producing countries, as well as from Western foreign aid related to a second defining feature of the region—the Arab-Israeli conflict. The long-term and wider repercussions of this underlying conflict have in many cases exacerbated or ignited wars, such as the fifteen-year civil war in Lebanon, and led to major refugee flows to neighboring countries. Palestinian refugees in countries such as Jordan, Lebanon, and Syria now represent some of the longest-standing populations of refugees in any area of the world.

The Arab countries of the Middle East and North Africa can be divided into subregions of broadly similar countries. In the first grouping are the wealthy, oil-producing countries of the Gulf—otherwise known as countries of the Gulf Cooperation Council (GCC). In the second grouping are the middle-income countries of North Africa, or Maghreb, from Morocco to Libya to which can also be added the lower middle-income country of Egypt. The third group is another middle-income grouping, including the so-called Mashreq countries of the eastern Mediterranean and the occupied Palestinian territories (the West Bank and Gaza). Finally, there is a miscellaneous category of the poorer countries, including Sudan, Yemen, and Djibouti. While it is not possible to apply this typology to aspects of adolescence in region, we provide country examples as a means to avoid generalizations.

The so-called Arab Spring,[1] which started in Tunisia in December 2010 and in 2011 spread to Egypt, Yemen, Bahrain, Libya, and Syria, has transformed the political and social space not only of these countries but of countries across the whole region. Significantly, it began with the self-immolation of a young Tunisian street vendor, Muhammed Bou 'Azizi, in protest again the harassment and humiliation inflicted on him by the arbitrary behavior of government officials, rather than a massive deterioration of economic conditions. Though it is risky to derive generalizations from such a distinct incident, one can associate it with the lack of other channels for expressing "voice." Indeed, the experience of active citizenship, or lack thereof, at a young age has formative and lasting effects on the extent and kind of political and social participation of a young person throughout his or her life cycle.

At the same time, the Arab popular uprisings should be seen in light of a long history of protest beginning before independence and continuing during the postindependence period in the Arab region. It has been argued that this history of protests is rooted in a moral economy of rights and responsibilities influenced by Islamic notions of justice, anticolonial nationalism, and developmentalism (Burke 1986). Violation of this set of norms has sparked cycles of unrest, such as the so-called bread riots in North Africa beginning in the late 1970s (for further discussion, see Walton and Seddon 1994).

What distinguishes the Arab popular uprisings that began in 2010 from earlier protests is the role of social networking in linking people across social class and religious divides, the predominant role of young people, and the emergence of a renewed public sphere. It is primarily unarmed young people—often inspired by their counterparts in other Arab countries—who, at great personal risk, have sustained the uprisings (such as the almost year-long mass protests in Yemen and recurrent demonstrations in Egypt). Women, such as the Yemeni 2011 Nobel Prize winner Tawakkul Karman, have also been at the forefront of collective action, even in the most conservative cultural settings.

As Syria descends into full blown armed conflict, it is important to highlight three factors; one is that this crisis was sparked by children and adolescents from a school in a town in the south, Dera'a, who were tortured by local police for writing antiregime graffiti on their school's walls. A second factor is that despite the numbers of Syrians who have fled the country, or those who are internally displaced, as the country becomes fractured by sectarianism, young Syrian activists are giving a voice to those who sparked the uprising. While one cannot assess their impact right now, it is clear that many young activists are indeed working toward developing alternative messages through print, Internet, and social media avenues.[2] A third factor is that young boys between fourteen and sixteen years of age are increasingly drawn into the conflict as fighters.[3]

This chapter focuses on this intersection of multiple layers of social exclusion among Arab youth that the popular uprisings and conflict brought to worldwide public attention. It focuses on young people's social, economic (particularly employment), and health rights. While not ignoring the underlying importance of political rights, and their evolving context in the region, we argue that it is imperative to link the health, economic, and social rights of adolescents because they have been too often ignored or compartmentalized in past policy making and programs. At this crucial political juncture, the need for underscoring their interrelatedness is all the more timely.

We begin by looking at some of the recent demographic changes affecting young people and the role of the family. We then move to a discussion of social rights, including education and the health status of and health services for young people. The next section on economic rights analyzes employment and employment-related youth policies in the region. Finally, we conclude with some observations on the need to link economic, health, and social rights and to strengthen the participation of young people in Arab societies.

Demographic Trends Affecting Young People and the Role of the Family

Notwithstanding the diversity of countries in the region, demographic trends affecting young people have played a significant role in the transformation of adolescence. First and foremost is the rising age at marriage for young people (Singerman 2007; Salem 2012). While early and universal marriage used to characterize the region, this has changed a great deal with the current generation of young people. This is a particularly marked trend in North Africa; in Tunisia, for example, the average age at marriage had risen to just over thirty-two years for men and twenty-seven years for women by 2010. The reasons behind the rising age at marriage have been underresearched. Singerman (2007) argues that the rising cost of housing and of getting married, in addition to rising educational levels, are key factors. Salem's study (2012) on Jordan national data, however, found that, contrary to popular perception, the costs of marriage have not increased in Jordan. It is likely, however, that rising levels of youth unemployment, to be addressed further below, is a major contributor to this trend.

This rising age at marriage is accompanied by the persistence of early marriage in some countries such as Yemen, where one in ten girls marry before the age of fifteen and 32 percent of women twenty to twenty-four were married before age eighteen, or Iraq, where 6 percent of girls marry before the age of fifteen and 25 percent before the age of eighteen (Roudi-Fahimi and Ibrahim 2013). Early marriage also persists in pockets of other societies, such as the underprivileged Palestinian refugee camps in Lebanon (Meyerson-Knox 2009). As the most populous country in the region, Egypt has the highest number of child marriages among all Arab countries (Roudi-Fahimi and Ibrahim 2013). UNICEF (2011) estimates the rate of child marriage for the period 2000 to 2008 was 15 percent in the Middle East and North Africa region (hereafter MENA) as a whole.[4] There is agreement, however, that early marriage is generally declining (Roudi-Fahimi and Ibrahim 2013), although the effects of recent conflicts and refugee movements on early marriage have not been explored. Anecdotal evidence suggests a higher rate of early marriage among the hundreds of thousands of Syrian refugees in Jordan, for example (*Jordan Times* 2013). While there has been legal reform in some countries on the legal age at marriage raising it to eighteen (such as Morocco), in others (such as Yemen) there has been resistance to raising the minimum age of marriage for girls, which remains as low as fifteen in Kuwait, the West Bank, and Yemen and sixteen in Egypt.

A second demographic feature that has received a great deal of international attention, particularly during the media coverage of the Arab popular uprisings, is the youth bulge. Fertility in the region started to decline in the 1970s, somewhat belatedly given the region's social and economic indicators

(Assaad and Roudi-Fahimi 2007). Through population momentum, this led to a surge in the population—first in the age group of children under fifteen and subsequently in young people aged ten to twenty-four. This "bulge" in the population moved its way through subsequent age cohorts, even as fertility declined. Now with half of its population under age twenty-five, the MENA region has the second youngest population in the world after sub-Saharan Africa (Roudi-Fahimi 2011).

This demographic reality is no doubt a main factor explaining the fact that the Arab region boasts, according to the ILO, the highest youth unemployment rate of all regions, as we discuss below. Nevertheless, as we argue, there is a danger of "demographic determinism" that focuses on demography to the exclusion of political factors—such as the subordination of social policy to the prerequisites of political survival—and deficiencies in the quality of education and health services that have contributed to these problems. Simplistic associations are sometimes made between the youth bulge, high youth unemployment, and political disenfranchisement on the one hand with political instability and even terrorism on the other. Among others, Anne Hendrixson (2004) of Corner House (an organization that supports democratic and community movements for social justice) has criticized this view, arguing that particularly in the aftermath of September 11, focus on the youth bulge tended to homogenize young people and reinforce stereotypes of the image of "the angry young man and the veiled young woman" (Hendrixson 2004). As she notes, "Contesting 'youth bulge' theory and its practical effects also requires questioning more general theories that blame social problems on overbreeding or demographics, as well as the determinism that insists that political instability inevitably follows from numbers" (Hendrixson 2004, 16). This focus on the threat posed by adolescents, rather than on their potential, has unfortunately reinforced both external and internal stereotypic views of adolescence as a time of potential deviance. Sahar El-Tawila (2000), a researcher on youth in Egypt, distinguishes between this "deviant" paradigm of youth with its negative expectations of youth that has characterized much research on youth both outside and inside the region, and the new youth development approach, which argues for recognizing the potential contributions of young people to their societies and their rights to full participation within them. Arguably an important outcome of the Arab popular uprisings is that they have given young people in particular a pride in their own collective identity as Arabs and their potential to stimulate change in their societies.

In the literature on the "youth bulge" in the region, the increased proportion of youth who are educated is often described optimistically, with reference to a potential demographic "dividend" (Assaad and Roudi-Fahimi 2007; Bloom, Canning, and Sevilla 2003). However, this potential can only be realized through greater attention to the quality of health and education for young people, and to providing adequate employment opportunities for them. As Assaad and Roudi-Fahimi (2007) note, "The extent to which this large group of young people will become healthy and productive members of their societies depends on how well governments and civil societies invest in social, economic, and political institutions that meet the current needs of young people." Higher education levels among young people, as compared to previous generations, also contribute to rising expectations (Assaad and Roudi-Fahimi 2007, 1). As the demographer Philippe Fargues (1995) has argued, Arab young people are much more highly educated than their parents, yet the latter retain moral authority and political authority. Combined with exposure to global norms through social networking and other media, this creates a pronounced generation gap.

Social Rights

Health Status of Young People

Fundamental to young people's ability to enjoy their rights to participate in society and live full lives is to be free of avoidable morbidity and to avoid early death. Health is therefore a fundamental aspect of social policy. It is difficult to provide a comprehensive picture of the public health status of young people in the Arab region given that the research base in this area is relatively weak, although rapidly growing (Afifi et al. 2012; DeJong and El Khoury 2006; DeJong et al. 2005, 2007). Until the last decade, population-based surveys in the region have tended to focus almost exclusively on married women, because of a prevailing interest in fertility reduction and maternal health.[5] Egypt was among the first countries in the region to conduct a nationally representative survey of adolescents aged ten to nineteen and it has fielded an updated national survey of young people aged ten to twenty-nine that included some biological markers and provides a broader picture of health status (Egypt Institute of National Planning 2010). In addition, the

Arab League initiated youth surveys in a number of countries, but data from these are not always comparable since the governments of the countries concerned decide on the questions that will be permitted. Moreover, the latter surveys have relatively few questions on health-related behaviors. In general, more data is available on young people's attitudes and knowledge than on their health status, health-related behaviors, and health-care seeking.

Even for the relatively less sensitive topic of the health of young, married women there is a limited literature, despite the known fact that a young age at marriage raises the risk of morbidity and mortality (UNICEF 2011; Viner et al. 2012). An early community-based study in Egypt showed that even young women aged fifteen to twenty-four bore a heavy burden of reproductive morbidity, including reproductive tract infections and genital prolapse (Khattab, Younis, and Zurayk 1999).[6] More recently, the first nationally representative study on reproductive morbidity in the region was conducted in Oman. It found that among the ever-married women of reproductive age in the sample, 25 percent suffered from reproductive tract infections and 10 percent from genital prolapse. Although it does not provide the prevalence among young women, it found age to be the most important risk factor for sexually transmitted infections; ever-married women under age twenty-five were twice as likely to have an sexually transmitted infections as women ages twenty-five and older (Mabry, Al-Riyami, and Morsi 2007).

More comprehensive data is available on the prevalence of female genital mutilation or cutting. Only four countries of those included within the Arab League practice some form of female genital mutilation. In Egypt, the first nationally representative survey in 2005 found the prevalence of the first type of female genital mutilation, according to the WHO classification, to be almost universal (El-Zanaty and Way 2006). Subsequent population-based surveys have found the practice has become less prevalent as public support for it has decreased with greater NGO and governmental action against it. Sudan has the earliest population-based data where it has also found to be near universal, and in a more severe form than in Egypt. The practice is also found in Djibouti among all ethnic groups and in Yemen mainly in the coastal areas.

There have been major barriers to conducting studies exploring young people's sexual behavior in the region, and the relatively recent surveys of adolescents in the region (such as the one in Egypt mentioned above) have been prohibited from asking questions relating to sexual behavior (personal communication, Ghada Barsoum, responsible for the Egypt 2010 national survey). As one report summarizes the situation, "Data on initiation of sexual intercourse and frequency of premarital sexual activity are almost nonexistent for countries in this region" (International Women's Health Coalition 2007). Nonetheless, there exists evidence of a rise in sexual relations among unmarried young people. For example, among a sample of Lebanese university students, nearly three-quarters of male students and over a fifth of female students reported previous sexual relations (Barbour and Salemeh 2009).

Given the above evidence of increasing sexual relations among youth, there is an urgent need in the region for interlinked health and education programs to prevent sexually transmitted infections and HIV. According to the 2011 UN Millennium Development Goals Report, nearly 23 percent of people living with HIV globally are under the age of twenty-five and young people aged from fifteen to twenty-four account for 41 percent of new infections among those aged fifteen or older. Relatively little is known about the incidence of HIV among young people in the Arab region. The 2011 State of the World's Children report on adolescence reports an HIV prevalence rate of 0.2 percent in the region among young people fifteen to twenty-four years old. The relatively recent introduction of voluntary counseling and testing centers, where people can obtain an HIV test free of charge and without having to provide their name, is likely to encourage young people who perceive themselves at risk to get tested.

Drug and tobacco use is receiving increasing research attention because of its public health significance. While cigarette smoking among youth is a growing concern in the region, young people are also exposed to the potentially more harmful *nargileh* (or water pipe) for tobacco use (Nakkash and Khalil 2010). According to a recent situation analysis of youth in the region (Issam Fares Institute 2011, 45), the most commonly used substances in the region are cannabis, sedatives, opiates, and stimulants, and there is increasing evidence that young people are using these from an early age. A study in Egypt among street children, for example, found high levels of substance abuse (Khaled and El Daw 2010).

Another critical but underresearched issue in the region is the mental health of young people, which is an underemphasized health problem worldwide (Sawyer et al. 2012). Given high levels of political conflict and of youth unemployment in the region, this is a pressing issue. Yet worldwide there has been relatively little research on these types of linkages although the limited available research does point to mental health costs from youth unemployment (Viner et al. 2012). UNICEF (2011) has also pointed to the urgent need for a focus on youth mental health. Some interesting action research at a micro level has been conducted in the region, however. For example, a project to address the mental health of young people aged ten to twelve in a Palestinian refugee camp in Lebanon included the development and validation of a research tool to assess the mental health of adolescents in the region, the Arab Youth Mental Health Scale (Makhoul et al. 2011).

Health Services for Young People

If we went to ask a nurse or a doctor, they would laugh at us and tell us to wait till we get older.

—Fifteen-year-old Jordanian girl[7]

As elsewhere, young people in the Arab region are falling through the gaps in health service provision. Health services in the region are only beginning to adapt to the changing health needs or potential risk behaviors of adolescents, such as smoking. Nor do they adequately provide sexual and reproductive health services in a confidential manner respecting their evolving capacities.

Beyond this gap in services there is a growing crisis situation with refugee populations. For example, in the crisis in Syria, which started in 2011, young women face added risk. Syrian refugees cited rape as a primary reason their families fled the conflict, yet there is an alarming lack of medical and counseling services to help them recover in the countries to which they have fled (Jordan, Turkey, and as internally displaced people, in Syria itself). They face unsafe conditions in camps and elevated levels of domestic violence, while reports of early and forced marriages of young women and girls are increasing.[8]

Internationally, young married women have been found to have less decision-making power concerning health-care seeking than older women (Jejeebhoy 1998; Barua and Kurz 2001; Rani and Bonu 2003). They may also face higher social costs in revealing morbidity conditions seen to affect their fertility as they begin their married and reproductive lives (Rani and Bonu 2003).

The rising age at marriage noted above in the region has occurred in a context where premarital sexuality is morally rejected, where the provision of sexuality education and information is minimal, and where health services largely do not recognize the special needs of adolescents. Youth-friendly services have become an increasing focus, but these tend to be pilot, small-scale activities encouraged by the United Nations Population Fund and other international organizations—not policy commitments for implementation on a national scale. In many cases, the private sector and NGOs are filling some of the gaps on a piecemeal basis.

Those population-based surveys that do exist on young people's knowledge about their sexual and reproductive health indicate a severe lack of information on these issues (Hanafy et al. 2012). For example, the 2010 nationally representative survey in Egypt found that 60 percent of female respondents reported being shocked or afraid when they reached menarche. Moreover, less than a quarter of young people reported having talked to their parents about the changes associated with puberty.

Tunisia presents an interesting exception, having developed a school health system with institutionalized referrals to health services (World Health Organization 2002). Moreover, as the only Arab country that has legalized abortion on demand, referral services also include access to abortions (although the legal status of abortion has been contested within the context of postrevolution political changes in Tunisia). A social policy focused on gender equity and a sophisticated health-care infrastructure both played a key role. In general in the region, however, school health programs are not well linked to health-care services. Nor are they fulfilling the role of providing sexuality education to young people. While some countries have developed sexuality education curricula, in most it tends to be restricted to extracurricular activities such as anti-AIDS after-school clubs (Montasser Kamal, Ford Foundation, Regional Office for Middle East and North Africa, personal communication). There are many barriers to introducing and teaching sexuality education within the curriculum although promising examples of extracurricular activities have been established in many places. All of the above health needs require intersectoral action, with close collaboration between ministries of education and ministries of health to address the health needs of adolescents. Unfortunately, however, there are precious few examples of such cooperation in the region.

Education

> I work so hard here for nothing. I want to get an education, I want to do a master's degree, but the degrees here are not regarded anywhere else—the courses here are worth nothing.
> —*Guardian*, February 14, 2011

Significant Progress in Levels of Education

Young Arabs today are relatively highly educated. Rising education rates have been the fastest growing in the world since the 1980s (Yousef 2003). Most Arab countries have achieved universal or near universal primary level enrollment for both boys and girls. Seven countries are close to achieving the Education for All Goal[9] for universal primary education by 2015. Secondary enrollment rates in the MENA region (65 percent) are above the world rate (figure 10.1). Significant progress has also been made in tertiary education. As many as 80 percent of postsecondary students are in universities (International Finance Corporation and Islamic Development Bank 2011, 10).

These achievements are a result of strong governmental commitment and high public education spending, which amounted to 19 percent of total government expenditures in 2008 (Salehi-Isfahani and Dhillon 2008, 16). Likewise, parents and students also invest in education. Arab families spend billions on private schools, test preparation courses, and private tutors for their children (Salehi-Isfahani and Dhillon 2008, 23).

Closing Gender Gaps in Education?

Girls comprise 47 percent of total students in primary and secondary education (UNESCO 2011, 16). In sharp contrast to the situation in South Asia, discussed in the following chapters of this volume, Arab women have overtaken men in educational attainment in universities in some countries (notably Jordan, Kuwait, Saudi Arabia, and Syria) (World Bank 2007, 11). Nevertheless, if one looks at national averages it is obvious that gender gaps persist and that the

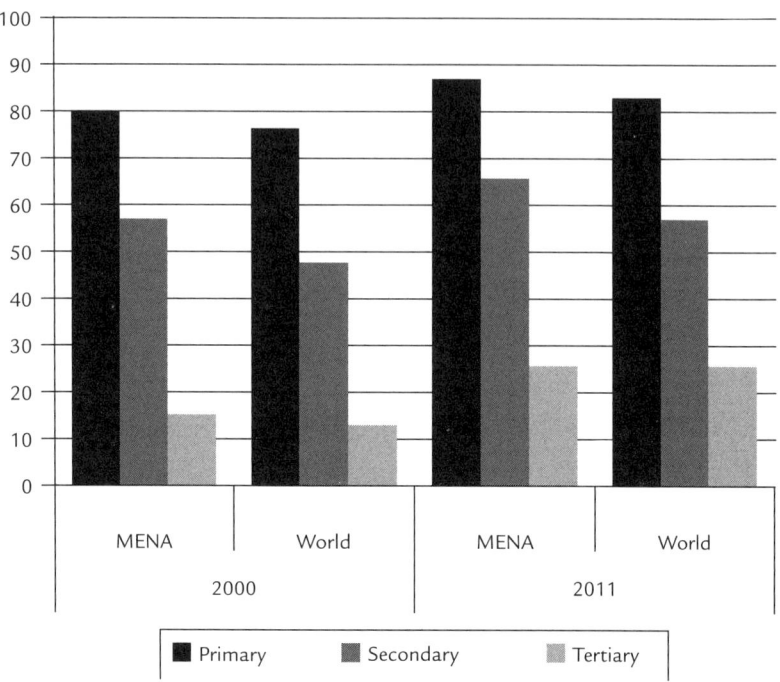

Figure 10.1. Enrollment rates in primary, secondary, and tertiary education, 2000 and 2011 (world and Middle East and North Africa [MENA]).

Source: UNESCO Institute for Statistics Database, September 2013, http://stats.uis.unesco.org/unesco/TableViewer/document.aspx?ReportId=143&IF_Language=eng.

contrast with South Asia is much less stark. In Yemen, primary school enrollment rates are 79 percent for boys but 66 percent for girls. Moreover, within countries, girls from poorer families are more likely to drop out. In Egypt one quarter of girls from the poorest households had less than four years of education. Another issue is that education is perceived as being linked to women's potential to marry upward, rather than as a means to advance economic participation (on Egypt, Assaad and Elbadawy 2006).

Learning Outcomes Are Weak

The quality of education has been implicated as a cause for the frustrations of unemployed Arab youth in the recent social unrest (for example, Watkins

2011). Arab students do indeed have low scores in international tests that reflect some qualitative deficiencies in the education system. As many as 84 percent of Arab students scored below the low international mathematics benchmark in the Trends in International Mathematics and Science Study 2007 results.[10] This reveals that while Arab countries have invested heavily in education this has not led to high standards of educational quality. According to some sources the quality of education has been deteriorating in some countries as a result of traditional teaching methods, outdated curricula, and the poor quality of teaching staff (European Training Foundation 2009, 27, 28). In recent years teachers have experienced a decline in their traditional social status (European Training Foundation 2009, 30) and in several countries, including Bahrain, Jordan and Lebanon, teachers have been mobilizing to contest low pay and poor working conditions.[11] Young people themselves express doubts about the quality of the education they receive, with only 36 percent believing that their education prepares them for a job (International Finance Corporation and Islamic Development Bank 2011, 32).

Inequality of opportunity in education is another issue. A recent study that analyzed the Trends in International Mathematics and Science Study results accounting for family and community characteristics found that not everyone who attends school achieves the same amount of learning. Parents' education and ability to pay for extra tuition to supplement low-quality education are some of the reasons (Salehi-Isfahani and Dhillon 2008, 21; Assaad 2010). Geographic disparity is another aspect. An estimated 30 percent of rural children in the Arab states are out-of-school compared with 18 percent of those living in cities (UNESCO 2011, 22). In Morocco, for example, net enrollment in primary education is 10 percentage points lower in rural areas than in urban. In Algeria and Tunisia, education is less accessible in the inland regions of the countries. Children from poor families are also often obliged to work. In 2005, some six hundred thousand children between seven and fourteen years old were working in Morocco (European Training Foundation 2009, 25). There is indeed a causal relation between poverty and education where in some cases ongoing poverty across generations is due to a failure of parents to send children to school. Nevertheless, when education, which is a fundamental right, is not provided equally for all then the state is partially responsible for regenerating socioeconomic stratification.

Failures in education systems in terms of quality and unequal access are related to wider challenges linked to weak governance. While most countries have instituted programs to advance educational reform, change has not been perceptible to date. Among the many reasons are limited accountability systems where mismanagement is rife. Another explanation for the lack of notable education progress, advanced by some Arab youth, is that their education systems are not a source of learning and opportunity but a vehicle to limit critical thinking and undermine freedom of speech (Watkins 2011). For some, bureaucracy and autocratic political systems are the culprits explaining low educational outcomes.

Economic Rights

> Selma is typical of the aspirational urban Damascene youth . . . [who] is determined to live independently. But after working 13-hour night shifts as a nurse, earning just 9,000 Syrian pounds (£125) a month for the last three years, she is pessimistic about the future.
> —*Guardian*, February 14, 2011

High Unemployment Rates Coupled with Low Economic Activity Rates

Youth unemployment rates in MENA are among the highest in the world with 25 percent unemployment (International Labour Organization 2011). Disaggregating the region, unemployment is 30 percent for the Middle East excluding GCC countries, 20 percent for GCC countries, and 23 percent for North Africa (International Labour Organization 2011). Youth unemployment in the region is almost four times the adult rate. Young women find it even harder than men to find a job. Out of ten economically active women, almost four are unsuccessful at finding a job (International Labour Organization 2011).

Countries in the region tend to focus on the educated unemployed, probably because they are more vocal and have higher expectations. However, there are country variations (table 10.1). In some countries, such as Jordan and Syria, unemployment is higher among the less educated, and in Morocco and Tunisia it is higher among the university graduates. In other countries, such as the Occupied Palestinian Territories and the United Arab Emirates, unemployment is widespread across the board.

Table 10.1. Unemployment rates by educational attainment for selected Arab countries

Country	Total (%)			Male (%)			Female (%)		
	Primary	Secondary	Tertiary	Primary	Secondary	Tertiary	Primary	Secondary	Tertiary
Algeria (2004)	19	22.4	22.8	19.9	21.1	16.5	13.7	27.8	35.4
Morocco (2003)	8.8	24	30.3	9.5	21.6	24.4	6.9	30.7	41.3
OPT* (2006)	24.7	20.8	21	27	21.3	15.3	8.4	15.6	31.8
Oman (1996)	7.3	18.6	2.1	7.1	10.5	1.8	9.6	47.2	3
UAE (2005)	2.4	2.4	2.8	3.9	2.8	9.9	4	2.3	9.5

*OPT: Occupied Palestinian Territories
Source: International Labour Organization 2011.

Moreover, the focus on youth unemployment rates does not reflect the whole picture. A significant number of Arab youth are out of school and out of work. This economically inactive population comprises 20.8 percent of young men and as much as 41.5 percent of young women (International Labour Organization 2011).

Unemployed and economically inactive young Arabs are frustrated. According to a Gallup World Poll in 2009, as many as 58 percent of respondents were unsatisfied with the availability of quality jobs. Most dissatisfied, at 75 percent, were young people in Egypt, Jordan, Sudan, and Yemen (Sitte and Rheault 2009). It is well known that the transition from school to work typically entails some period of unemployment as one undertakes a job search. Yet it seems that young Arabs face additional challenges. International Labour Organization School-to-Work Transition Surveys in Egypt and Syria (before the evolving uprisings and conflicts in both countries) reveal that a very low percentage of young people succeed in this transition. Most are either unemployed or employed in temporary or unsatisfactory jobs. Many are inactive but planning to look for work (El-Zanaty and Associates 2007; Alissa 2007), suggesting that a significant proportion of young Arabs are simply "discouraged" from even seeking work. The tradition of strong family support allows them the option to "wait" for the right opportunity. If one looks at the wage structure in the region this "waiting period" is not surprising. In Jordan, for example, two-thirds of working men earn just above the minimum wage (Jordanian Ministry of Health 2012, 19). This creates a disincentive to seek work.

Where Are the Jobs?

A large part of the youth employment challenge is due to structural issues related to labor market demand. In most of the region the public sector remains the largest employer representing 29 percent of all employment (International Labour Organization 2010). For educated youth the public sector is still the first employment choice due to the relatively high wages and job security that characterize public sector jobs. The role of the public sector as the main employer and protector has been difficult to change. For example, in response to the increasing pressures spurred by the recent social unrest in the region, some governments have actually opted to create even more new jobs as a means to offset the citizens' dissatisfaction.[12] As governments continue to play this role young educated people will continue to seek education geared toward public sector jobs.

In comparison, the formal sector outside government employment is small. Private sector investments in the region flow into sectors that are creating either few or low quality jobs. The share of overall private formal employment, where workers are entitled to social security, remains low and can reach levels below 5 percent of overall employment in countries such as Yemen and Morocco (World Bank 2009, 3–10). Bureaucratic government regulations have offset incentives for the creation and expansion of a competitive private sector. They have also pushed activity toward the informal sector, which is estimated to employ two-thirds of the labor force and produce one-third of GDP in non-GCC countries, based on the definition of the informal economy "as the share of all employment with no access to social security" (Angel-Urdinola and Tanabe 2012, 15). As shown in figure 10.2, data from Yemen, Egypt, and Syria indicate that adults are less likely to work in the informal sector than young people (Angel-Urdinola and Tanabe 2012, 16).

With these choices, it is not surprising that the region is experiencing one of the highest rates of skilled emigration. Across most countries young people are looking elsewhere to access opportunities. Thirty percent of young people in the region would like to migrate permanently to another country (Silatech 2009, 55). The most likely individuals to express a desire to migrate are those who are the most educated, are already employed, and aspire to start their own businesses (for example, in Egypt, Elbadawy 2011).

The structure of the labor market, with its divergent working conditions, affects young people's willingness to work, how they search for jobs, or whether they decide to migrate. While improved education and skills can increase young people's assets, a major issue here is creating jobs with decent working conditions. So far many existing governmental efforts focus on the work readiness of young people themselves (for example, career guidance, job intermediation services, and so on). However, efforts to increase employment opportunities need to address the structural imbalances inherent in labor demand. This includes economic policies that create incentives for investments with high social benefits rather than for low quality jobs. Another issue is to improve labor market governance.[13]

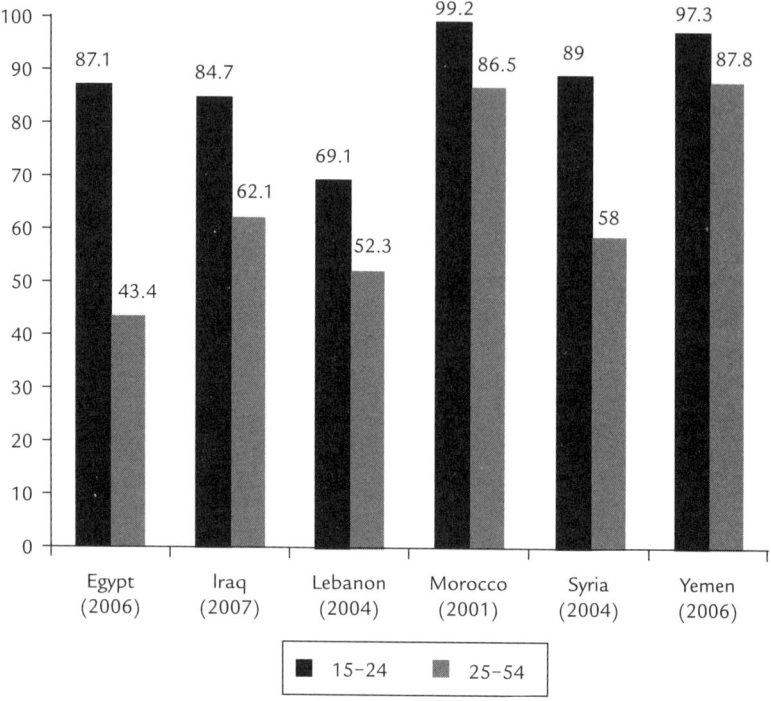

Figure 10.2. Percentage of informal employment in selected Arab countries, by age group.
Source: Angel-Urdinola and Tanabe 2012.

Measures could include improving social protection, especially for workers in the informal economy, and upgrading informal economy enterprises so that they are more productive and able to provide career jobs for their workers.

Young Arab Women and Work

Arab women's low economic participation, usually attributed to "social norms," has been changing, with an impressive 47 percent increase since 2001 (Tzannatos, Haq, and Schmidt 2011). Yet, the gender gap persists. Women's participation is only one-third of male participation, as shown in table 10.2.

Table 10.2. Unemployment and youth unemployment rates by gender, 2010

Country	Total %			Youth %		
	M	F	Total	M	F	Total
Algeria (2010)	8.1	19.1	10	18.7	37.5	21.5
Bahrain (2010)	2	9	4.3	7.6	27.5	14.3
Egypt (2010)	4.9	22.6	9	16.8	53.9	25.4
Jordan (2010)	10.4	21.7	12.5	48.1	51	50.1
Morocco (2010)	8.9	9.6	9.1	18.1	16.1	17.6
Syria (2009)	5.7	22.3	8.1	12.1	43	16.7
Yemen (2010)	12.6	23.1	15	52.2	54.6	52.9

Source: International Labour Organization 2011.

Unemployment rates among young Arab women are alarmingly high in some countries, and higher than men in the same age groups. This indicates that many women want jobs but are unable to secure them.

While country-specific research and data reveal that young women's participation varies across and within countries, young women seem to face more challenges than young men. Gendered perceptions of women's roles and workplace suitability affect both the supply of and demand for women's employment. Women are crowded in a limited number of sectors given their preference for the public sector, but there they join long waiting queues (Tzannatos 2010). Finding socially accepted jobs in the private and informal sectors results in overcrowding, which reduces opportunity and depresses wages (Salehi-Isfahani and Dhillon 2008, 23). In conservative societies, fear of sexual harassment in small work settings is one of the main reasons women prefer to stay at home or work in government jobs (Salehi-Isfahani and Dhillon 2008, 23; Kawar 2000, 158). Labor market discrimination exists with employers believing that women have less attachment to work (on Jordan, Kawar 2000, 92; on Egypt, Salehi-Isfahani and Dhillon 2008, 24, and Assaad and Elbadawy 2006). This is also obvious in wage disparities where young women earn less than young men, especially in Egypt, Jordan, and Syria (European Training Foundation 2009).

Most Arab countries have antidiscrimination laws, regulations, and programs to promote women's employment. More are needed, however. Enabling women to have greater access to economic opportunities and security requires a political commitment to remove barriers, including the adoption of policies on equal wages, maternity benefits, child care, part-time work, and home-based work.

Youth Policy and Participation

In Tunis, Ghazi Megdiche says that the psychological impact of two decades of repression run deep. "What defined us was not lack of job prospects, but lack of the most basic freedoms: being a teenager in a police state," Megdiche says.

—*Guardian*, February 14, 2011

Starting well before the recent social unrest, most Arab countries have been working to establish mechanisms and reform systems for addressing youth development. The institutional platforms are diverse and include youth councils (for example, Egypt, Jordan); youth ministries (for example, Egypt, Iraq, Sudan, Palestinian Territories, Algeria); national youth strategies (for example, Jordan, Egypt, Bahrain, Morocco); and youth parliaments (for example, Lebanon, Tunisia, Morocco). Often, such governmental mechanisms are not sufficiently empowered in terms of institutional capacity and budget. This particularly applies to ministries of youth, which remain ineffective if not marginalized in most countries. In fact, the Jordanian Ministry of Youth and Sports was dismantled after a new government took office in the spring of 2012. In terms of youth councils and policies, there are often gaps between planned youth initiatives and reality. For example, a youth policy can become an end in itself without realistic targets, commitment of financial and human resources, and attention to setting up proper implementation procedures for monitoring progress. Moreover, most of these mechanisms remain outside mainstream social and economic policy making.

Young people themselves are usually excluded from participation in the parliaments. Only four countries (Egypt, Jordan, Tunisia, and Yemen) have established specialized youth-related legislative committees. The majority of Arab countries tend to address youth issues by proxy, through committees on sport, culture, or family affairs. Entrenched institutional arrangements, dated governing procedures, and inadequate accountability mechanisms have contributed to limited youth participation in all forms of decision making (UN Programme on Youth 2011). As a recent situation analysis on youth in the region expresses it, governments are ill-prepared to encourage youth participation, even where there is willingness (Issam Fares Institute 2011, 46).

Political leadership in the region is dominated by an older generation that seems to be out of touch with the needs and aspirations of young people. Yet, more than ever before, young Arabs are aware of the importance of participation. According to recent surveys a significant 42 percent have no confidence that their national elections will result in positive change, and half of all Arab youth do not see them as being honest (Issam Fares Institute 2011, 17). One poignant example is the decision in the autumn of 2011 of younger members of the Muslim Brotherhood in Egypt to take to the streets of Tahrir (Liberation) Square to protest the reluctance of the military to relinquish power despite the professed wishes of the older generation of the Brotherhood that they not demonstrate. After some time of discontent in Egypt, young leaders through a movement called Tamarud, led by the twenty-eight-year-old Mohammed Badr, managed to initiate a massive online petition and later street demonstrations against the Morsi government, which ultimately resulted in its removal by the military in early July 2013.[14]

Despite young people's exclusion from the political process, they are quite positive toward citizen participation and democratic reform. Young Arabs put a high value on democracy (93 percent in Jordan, 84 percent in Egypt, 85 percent in Morocco, 91 percent in Iraq, and 75 percent in the United Arab Emirates), and most desire the right to vote (Issam Fares Institute 2011, 17). Finally, there are increasing cases of women leading social movements, particularly in countries such as Lebanon, Jordan, Egypt, Morocco, and Kuwait. New media and communications technologies are narrowing some of the gender divides in public participation (Issam Fares Institute 2011, 17).

Conclusion: The Imperative of Linking Health, Economic, and Social Rights

We have argued in this chapter that to understand the situation of young Arab people and the frustrations they face, one needs to take a broad, cross-sectoral approach linking both economic and social rights in addition to political and civil rights. Young people, no more than any other age group, do not compartmentalize their lives yet policies and programs addressing them tend to do so. To further the strategic goals discussed in this chapter, and in particular to advance the rights of Arab adolescents today so that the demographic dividend generates vibrancy and fulfillment at home rather than through the aspiration of migration abroad, more holistic and dynamic policy development and implementation are needed. This applies across the various sectors of public services that are relevant to adolescents, from health to education, and from employment to social integration, political participation, and empowerment

In terms of social rights, we have seen that health policy and health services have not kept pace with demographic change in the region and particularly with the needs of unmarried young people. The scope of health services is generally not adequately addressing priority public health issues, such as drug use and mental health. Moreover, neither health services nor education are fulfilling their role of providing critical information on sexuality and health to young people, or providing the needed links between these services.

When it comes to education and employment young people's needs and hopes are thwarted when faced with low quality education and limited decent job opportunities. Individuals and parents have made schooling decisions with an eye on the types of employment choices and earning power. Yet, low quality education or inequality of access prevail, which means that the economic returns from education have been low as the jobs they hoped for are not there. Indeed, youth employment is among the most pressing challenges that many Arab countries have faced, starting well before the current regional unrest. The major constraints can be identified: insufficient labor demand or low quality jobs in the private sector, insecure jobs in the informal economy, and a diminishing number of secure public jobs that young people are willing to wait for. The result has been a growing cohort of young people in the region who wish to migrate.

All of the above contributes toward social discontent among young people. While this chapter has demonstrated that policy makers in Arab countries have attempted to address youth-related issues, young people still remain disenchanted with these efforts and have the sense of being excluded from mainstream policy making and the political process. Perhaps one reason is the countries' lack of experience in developing the appropriate sustainable structures, methods, and resources.

A further contributing factor to existing discontent is that many young people in the region are in an extended waiting period for a number of interrelated reasons—waiting to be able to afford a home and to get married; waiting for a good quality, secure job; and not yet able to avail themselves of health services that are more designed for children or married couples (Dhillon and Yousef 2009). This chapter also underscored the crucial role of strong families in this context—for it is the recourse to the family's economic and social support that makes such waiting possible. Nevertheless, this extended coresidence is not without its tensions. We have shown that many have pointed to an increasing generation gap between the younger, more highly educated generation exposed through global media and social networking to higher standards of consumption and lifestyle, and the older generation that, socially and politically, commands authority.

In the face of such constraints, however, young people in the region have shown themselves to be resourceful. A resurgence in nonconventional forms of marriage, for example, such as *'urfi* (or customary) marriages, primarily among university students, shows that young people have found ways to circumvent constraints on traditional marriage. Although they are not without problems, and without legal and social protection, such marriages are reported to become increasingly common although their actual numbers are not known (Rashad and Osman 2003; Singerman 2007). Moreover, young people's use of the Internet and social networking has provided information on a full range of topics, even sensitive questions around sexuality and relationships, which have not been provided through formal means.

We have also argued that to attribute the frustrations of Arab youth deterministically to the demography of the "youth bulge" ignores the evidence on the many deficiencies in social and economic policy we have outlined—such as the poor quality, or inappropriateness, of education, the lack of comprehensive and accessible health services, and the lack of quality jobs. In some cases, we have shown that governments are either failing to address or inadvertently exacerbating or even creating inequalities. We have also shown that it is generally not lack of investment in education and health in the region that explains the lack of positive outcomes for young people, but rather the failure to adequately involve and reach out to this generation and to offer appropriate, high-quality services. This, ultimately, is a question of governance. Good governance does not necessarily mean extra public expenditures, which are already stretched in most countries. It simply means a redirection of the current development paradigm, which has been taken a top-down opaque form, toward a more efficient, equitable, accountable, and participatory form.

We have also pointed to many research gaps on young people in the region. Studies on the perceptions and aspirations of young people themselves that look at these issues comprehensively across a range of sectors are sorely lacking. We have acknowledged that countries of the region, while sharing many similarities, are also diverse and therefore in-depth national studies as well as regional comparisons using comparable research tools are needed. Moreover, rather than homogenizing young people, understanding inequities across social class, gender, and other dimensions is critical.

The Middle East and North Africa's globalized young people share similar aspirations to those of young people worldwide—decent employment, being able to afford housing, and starting and maintaining a family in good health. Yet they by and large find themselves trapped in a cycle of high unemployment, poorly paid employment, poor quality education with little correspondence to labor market needs, and in a context of few avenues for political participation.

Whether the Arab popular uprisings will ultimately succeed in improving this situation depends both on their political outcomes (still very much in flux) as well as the capacity of administrations that have ignored such issues for too long to develop a strategy to involve young people as assets to their societies. There are many reasons to be optimistic given the high levels of education of young people in the region as well as both the courageous leadership and resourcefulness they have amply demonstrated.

Notes

1. Different terms have been used to refer to the popular uprisings that began in Tunisia. Rather than the "Arab Spring," given that they are no longer confined to the spring of 2011, the preferred terminology used in the region is "Arab popular uprisings," which is the term that will be used in this paper.

2. See, for example, http://www.neurope.eu/article/young-syrian-activists-only-hope-post-conflict-syria (accessed on July 15, 2013).

3. http://www.hrw.org/news/2012/11/29/syria-opposition-using-children-conflict (accessed on July 15, 2013).

4. Child marriage is defined here as the percentage of women aged twenty to twenty-four who were married or in a union before they were eighteen years old.

5. These have typically been under the aegis of the Demographic and Health Surveys in countries with significant U.S. Agency for International Development funding or under the Arab League, such as the PanArab Project for Child Development or, in the Gulf Cooperation Council, the Gulf Family Health Surveys.

6. Pelvic organ prolapse is defined as "the downward descent of the pelvic organs that result in a protrusion of the vagina, uterus or both" (Jelovsek, Maher, and Barber 2007).

7. From a qualitative study of young people ten to twenty-four in Jordan that found that young people tend to equate reproductive health with maternal health and

that health centers are mainly for mothers and babies (quoted in DeJong and El Khoury 2006).

8. International Rescue Committee, "Syria: A Regional Crisis," January 2013.

9. Education For All is a UNESCO-led global movement aiming to meet the learning needs of children, youth, and adults by 2015. Education for All contributes to the Millennium Development Goals.

10. In 2007 the International Association of Educational Achievement carried out its fourth survey with forty-nine participating countries.

11. http://jordantimes.com/teachers-go-on-strike-to-protest-fuel-price-hikes, http://www.teachersolidarity.com/blog/teachers-strike-in-bahrain, and http://www.teachersolidarity.com/list/LB. All accessed on July 15, 2013.

12. For example, during 2011 the Jordanian government announced the creation of twenty-one thousand jobs, the Yemeni government sixty thousand jobs, and the Omani government fifty thousand jobs.

13. Labor market governance covers the range of policies, regulations, and institutions that influence labor demand and supply. It includes wages, work hours, social security, anti-discrimination, and so on.

14. For more, see, for example, http://www.huffingtonpost.com/2013/07/08/mahmoud-badr-tamarod-protest-leader-egypt_n_3559487.html.

References

Afifi, Rima, Jocelyn DeJong, Krishna Bose, Manal Benkirane, Tanya Salem, and Amr Awad. 2012. "The Health of Young People: Challenges and Opportunities." In *Public Health in the Arab World*, edited by Samer Jabbour et al., 236–48. Cambridge: Cambridge University Press.

Alissa, Sufyan. 2007. "The School-to-Work Transition of Young People in Syria." *ILO*, no. 2007/3. http://www.ilo.org/emppolicy/pubs/WCMS_113894/lang—en/index.htm.

Angel-Urdinola, Diego, and Kimie Tanabe. 2012. "Micro-Determinants of Informal Employment in the Middle East and North Africa Region." *Social Protection and Labor: The World Bank*, no. 1201 (January). http://www-wds.worldbank.org/servlet/WDSContentServer/WDSP/IB/2012/02/01/000333038_20120201032926/Rendered/PDF/665940NWP00PUB0Box365795B0SPDP01201.pdf.

Assaad, Ragui. 2010. "Equality for All? Egypt's Free Public Higher Education Policy Breeds Inequality of Opportunity." *Economic Research Forum* Policy Perspective. http://www.erf.org.eg/cms.php?id=publication_details&publication_id=1309.

Assaad, Ragui, and Asmaa Elbadawy. 2006. "Education Returns in the Marriage Market: Does Female Education Investment Improve the Quality of Future Husbands in Egypt?" Paper presented at the Thirteenth Annual Conference of the Economic Research Forum, Kuwait, December 16–18.

Assaad, Ragui, and Farzaneh Roudi-Fahimi. 2007. "Youth in the Middle East and North Africa: Demographic Opportunity of Challenge." *Population Reference Bureau*. http://www.prb.org/Publications/PolicyBriefs/YouthinMENA.aspx.

Barbour, Bernadet, and Pascale Salemeh. 2009. "Knowledge and Practice of University Students in Lebanon Regarding Contraception." *Eastern Mediterranean Health Journal* 15, no. 2: 387–99.

Barua, Alka, and Kathleen Kurz. 2001. "Reproductive Health-Seeking by Married Adolescent Girls in Maharashtra, India." *Reproductive Health Matters* 9, no. 17 (May): 53–62.

Beblawi, Hazem, and Giacomo Luciani. 1987. *The Rentier State.* Kent: Istituto Affari Internazionali, Italy.

Bloom, David E., David Canning, and Jaypee Sevilla. 2003. *The Demographic Dividend: A New Perspective on the Economic Consequences of Population Change.* Santa Monica, Calif.: Population Matters: A RAND Program of Policy-Relevant Research Communication. www.rand.org/pubs/monograph_reports/2007/MR1274.pdf.

Burke, Edmund. 1986. "Understanding Arab Social Movements." *Arab Studies Quarterly* 8:333–45.

DeJong, Jocelyn, et al. 2005. "The Sexual and Reproductive Health of Young People in the Arab Countries and Iran." *Reproductive Health Matters* 13, no. 25 (May): 49–59.

———. 2007. "Young People's Sexual and Reproductive Health in the Middle East and North Africa Region," *Population Reference Bureau.* www.prb.org/pdf07/menayouthreproductivehealth.pdf.

DeJong, Jocelyn, and Golda El Khoury. 2006. "Reproductive Health of Arab Young People." *British Medical Journal* 333 (October: 849).

Dhillon, Navtej, and Tarik Yousef, eds. 2009. *Generation in Waiting: The Unfulfilled Promise of Young People in the Middle East.* Washington, D.C.: Brookings Institution.

Egypt Institute of National Planning. 2010. *The Egypt Human Development Report 2010: Youth in Egypt, Building Our Future.* New York: United Nations Development Programme; and Cairo: Institute of National Planning.

Elbadawy, Asmaa. 2011. "Migration Aspirations Among Young People in Egypt: Who Desires to Migrate?" *Economic Research Forum* working paper no. 619. http://www.erf.org.eg/cms.php?id=publication_details&publication_id=1417.

El-Tawila, Sahar. 2000. *Youth in the Population Agenda: Concepts and Methodologies.* West Asia and North Africa MEAwards Regional Papers, no. 44. Cairo: Population Council.

El-Zanaty, Fatma, and Associates. 2007. "School-to-Work Transition: Evidence from Egypt Employment Policy Papers." *ILO*, no. 2007/2. http://www.ilo.org/emppolicy/pubs/WCMS_113893/lang–en/index.htm.

El-Zanaty, Fatma, and Ann Way. 2006. "Egypt Demographic and Health Survey 2005." Cairo: Ministry of Health and Population, National Population Council, El-Zanaty and Associates, and ORC Macro. www.measuredhs.com/pubs/pdf/FR176/FR176.pdf.

European Training Foundation. 2009. "Human Capital and Employability in the 14 Partners of the Union for the Mediterranean." Background paper for the EUROMED

Employment and Labor High Level Working Group Meeting, Brussels, November 26–27.

Fargues, Philippe. 1995. "Changing Hierarchies of Gender and Generation in the Arab World." In *Family, Gender and Population in the Middle East: Policies in Context*, edited by Carla Makhlouf Obermeyer, 179–98. Cairo: American University in Cairo Press.

Hanafy, Sara A., et al. 2012. "Minding the Gap in Alexandria: Talking to Girls in Schools About Reproductive Health." *Population Reference Bureau*. http://www.prb.org/pdf12/girls-egypt-schools-workingpaper.pdf.

Hendrixson, Anne. 2004. "Briefing 34: Angry Young Men, Veiled Young Women: Constructing a New Population Threat." *Corner House* (December). http://www.thecornerhouse.org.uk/resource/angry-young-men-veiled-young-women.

Ibrahim, Barbara L., et al. 1999. "Transition to Adulthood: A National Survey of Egyptian Adolescents [Arabic]." Population Council. http://www.popcouncil.org/arabic.asp.

International Finance Corporation and Islamic Development Bank. 2011. "Education for Employment: Realizing Arab Youth Potential." *Education for Employment* (April). http://www.e4earabyouth.com/.

International Labour Organization (ILO). 2010. "G20 Country Briefs: Saudi Arabia's Response to the Crisis." Paper presented at the meeting of the Labour and Employment Ministers, Washington, D.C., April 20–12.

———. 2011. *Key Indicators of the Labour Market*. 7th ed., October. http://www.ilo.org/empelm/pubs/WCMS_114060/lang-en/index.htm.

International Labour Organization and UN Development Programme. 2013. *Rethinking Economic Growth: Towards Inclusive and Productive Arab Societies*. ILO and UNDP, Geneva.

International Women's Health Coalition. 2007. "A Just and Health Life: Every Woman's Right. Annual Report." http://www.iwhc.org/index.php?option=com_content&task=view&id=2368&Itemid=82.

Issam Fares Institute for Public Policy and International Affairs. 2011. *A Generation on the Move: Insights into the Conditions, Aspirations and Activism of Arab Youth*. Beirut: American University of Beirut.

Jejeebhoy, Shireen J. 1998. "Adolescent Sexual and Reproductive Behavior: A Review of the Evidence from India." *Social Science and Medicine* 46, no. 10 (March 20): 1275–90.

Jelovsek, J. Eric, Christopher Maher, and Matthew D. Barber. 2007. "Pelvic Organ Prolapse." *Lancet*, 369 (March 24): 1027.

Jordan Times. 2013. "Early, Forced Marriages Haunt Syrian Refugees in Jordan." June 13. http://jordantimes.com/early-forced-marriages-haunt-syrian-refugees-in-jordan.

Jordanian Ministry of Health. 2012. *Jordan's National Employment Strategy 2011–2020*. http://www.google.com.lb/url?sa=t&rct=j&q=jordan%20national%20employment%20strategy&source=web&cd=6&sqi=2&ved=0CDsQFjAF&url=http

%3A%2F%2Fesc.jo%2FPDFDownloader.aspx%3FFileName%3D837dad1b-e6e1-451a-b4a2-57347dcb5e7f.pdf%26FileTitle%3DNational%2520Employment%2520Strategy&ei=o29EUO3dBqGH0AWByIGIAQ&usg=AFQjCNEkGbskC1BJV9Ebuza29SgZmK36ww.

Kawar, Mary. 2000. *Gender Employment and the Life Course: The Case of Working Daughters in Amman Jordan.* Amman: Jordan Studies Series.

Khaled, Nada H., and Suliman A. El Daw. 2010. "Violence, Abuse, Alcohol and Drug Use, and Sexual Behaviors in Street Children of Greater Cairo and Alexandria, Egypt." *AIDS* 24, supplement 2 (July).

Khattab, Hind A. S., Nabil Younis, and Huda Zurayk. 1999. *Women, Reproduction, and Health in Rural Egypt: The Giza Study.* Cairo: American University of Cairo Press.

Mabry, Ruth, Asya Al-Riyami, and Maqdi Morsi. 2007. "The Prevalence of and Risk Factors for Reproductive Morbidities Among Women in Oman." *Studies in Family Planning* 38, no. 2 (June).

Makhoul, Jihad, et al. 2011. "Development and Validation of the Arab Youth Mental Health Scale." *Community Mental Health Journal* 47, no. 3 (June).

Meyerson-Knox, Sonia. 2009. "Early Marriage in Post-Conflict Nahr el Bared Refugee Camp." MS thesis, American University of Beirut.

Nakkash, Rima, and Joanna Khalil. 2010. "Health Warning Labeling Practices on Narghile (Shisha, Hookah) Waterpipe Tobacco Products and Related Accessories." *Tobacco Control* 19: 235–39.

Rani, Manju, and Sekhar Bonu. 2003. "Rural Indian Women's Care-Seeking Behavior and Choice of Provider for Gynecological Symptoms." *Studies in Family Planning* 34, no. 3 (September): 173–85.

Rashad, Hoda, and Magued Osman. 2003. "Nuptiality in Arab Countries: Changes and Implications." In *The New Arab Family*, edited by Nicholas S. Hopkins, vol. 24, nos. 1–2, 20–50. Cairo: American University in Cairo Press.

Roudi-Fahimi, Farzaneh. 2011. "Youth Population and Employment in the Middle East and North Africa: Opportunity or Challenge?" Paper presented at the UN Expert Group Meeting on Adolescents, Youth and Development, New York, July 21–22.

Roudi-Fahimi, Farzaneh, and Shimaa Ibrahim. 2013. "Ending Child Marriage in the Arab Region." Population Reference Bureau Policy Brief. http://www.prb.org/pdf13/child-marriage-arab-region.pdf

Salehi-Isfahani, Djavad, and Navtej Dhillon. 2008. "Stalled Youth in Transitions in the Middle East: A Framework for Policy Reform." *Middle East Youth Initiative*, no. 8 (October). http://www.shababinclusion.org/content/document/detail/1166/.

Salem, Rania. 2012."Trends and Differentials in Jordanian Marriage Behavior: Marriage Timing, Spousal Characteristics, Household Structure and Matrimonial Expenditures," *Economic Research Forum* working paper no. 668. http://www.erf.org.eg/CMS/uploads/pdf/668.pdf.

Sawyer, Suzan, et al. 2012. "Adolescence: A Foundation for Future Health." *Lancet* 379 (April):1630–40.

Silatech. 2009. "The Silatech Index: Voices of Young Arabs." *Gallup* (June): 55. http://www.gallup.com/poll/120758/silatech-index-voices-young-arabs.aspx.

Singerman, Diane. 2007. "The Economic Imperatives of Marriage: Emerging Practices and Identities Among Youth in the Middle East."*Middle East Youth Initiative*, no. 6 (September). http://www.shababinclusion.org/content/document/detail/559/.

Sitte, Adam, and Magali Rheault. 2009. "Arab Youth Perceived Many Barriers to Economic Opportunity: Shortage of Good Jobs Perceived by Many as the Chief Obstacle." *Gallup World*. http://www.gallup.com/poll/120755/arab-youth-perceive-barriers-economic-opportunity.aspx.

Tzannatos, Zafiris. 2010. "Decreasing the Gender Gap in Employment and Pay in the Arab World: Measuring the Gains for Women, Youth and Society." Kuwait: Arab Planning Institute. http://www.connectsouth.org/~research_papers/Decreasing%20the%20gender%20gap%20in%20employment%20and%20pay%20in%20the%20Arab%20World:%20Measuring%20the%20gains%20for%20women,%20youth%20and%20society.

Tzannatos, Zafiris, Tariq Haq, and Dorothea Schmidt. 2011. "The Labour Market in the Arab States: Recent Trends, Policy Responses and Future Challenges." In *The Global Crisis: Causes, Reponses and Challenges*, edited by the International Labour Organization, 51–66. Geneva: ILO.

UNESCO. 2011. *Education for All: Regional Report for the Arab States*. Beirut: UNESCO.

UNICEF. 2011. "Adolescence: An Age of Opportunity, the State of the World's Children 2011." UNICEF. http://www.unicef.org/sowc2011/pdfs/SOWC-2011-Main-Report_EN_02092011.pdf.

UN Programme on Youth and UN Economic and Social Commission for Western Asia. 2011. "Regional Overview: Youth in the Arab World." United Nations Programme on Youth fact sheets 4. http://social.un.org/youthyear/.

Viner, Russell M., et al. 2012. "Adolescence and the Social Determinants of Health." *Lancet* 379 (April): 1641–52.

Walton, John K., and David Seddon. 1994. *Free Market and Food Riots: The Politics of Global Adjustment*. Oxford: Blackwell.

Watkins, Kevin. 2011. "Education Failures Fan the Flames in the Arab World." February 23. http://efareport.wordpress.com/2011/02/23/education-failures-fan-the-flames-in-the-arab-world.

World Bank. 2007. *The Road Not Traveled: Education Reform in the MENA Region*. Washington, D.C.: World Bank.

———. 2009. "MENA Development Report: From Privilege to Competition: Unlocking Private-Led Growth in the Middle East and North Africa." Washington, D.C.: World Bank.

World Health Organization. 2002. "Growing in Confidence: Programming for Adolescent Health and Development. Lessons from Eight Countries." WHO. http://whqlibdoc.who.int/hq/2002/WHO_FCH_CAH_02.13.pdf.

Yousef, Tarek M. 2003. "Youth in the Middle East and North Africa: Demography, Employment, and Conflict." In *Youth Explosion in Developing World Cities: Approaches to Reducing Poverty and Conflict in an Urban Age*, edited by Blair A. Ruble et al., 9–24. Washington, D.C.: Woodrow Wilson International Center for Scholars.

CHAPTER 11

The Challenges Facing India in Advancing Secondary Education Attainment Among Adolescent Girls

Orla Kelly and Elizabeth A. Newnham

Improved levels of national educational attainment result in considerable social and economic gains (Dreze 1993; Benhabib 1994; Barro 2001). Conversely, educational deficits, particularly in the context of a growing adolescent population and increased skill requirements for employment, produce negative "downstream" consequences, including increased poverty and criminality, mass unemployment, civil unrest, and poor health outcomes. Evidence establishing the significant impact of education on social and economic growth has fueled global efforts for increased educational access as exemplified in the Education for All (EFA) movement and the subsequent education goals of the Millennium Development Goals (MDG).[1]

The attention of the EFA, MDG, and related national programs has not only been focused on increasing states' gross enrollment levels but also on addressing the gender gap in educational attainment: "Eliminate gender disparity in primary and secondary education, preferably by 2005, and in all levels of education no later than 2015" (MDG Target (a); EFA Goal 5; UN General Assembly Resolution A/57/270).

Improved rates of female educational attainment have so far proved to be the most effective mechanism for correcting historic gender inequality and enhancing female empowerment (Schultz 1993; Klasen 1999). They are linked to reductions in exposure to violence, human trafficking, and sexual harassment, and generate long-term intergenerational health benefits such as lower infant mortality rates, lower rates of HIV/AIDS infection, and lower fertility rates (Subbarao and Raney 1995; Dreze and Murthi 2001; Gokhale et al. 2004).

As the previous chapter noted, over the last two decades there has been tremendous international progress toward achieving universal enrollment and closing the gender gap at the primary level (UNESCO Institute for Statistics 2011). This intergenerational shift is the product not only of increased international and national resource allocation but also of growing domestic demand (Baker and LeTendre 2005). The movement towards higher educational attainment at the primary level is an essential first step.[2] Achieving increased enrollment at the secondary level is more challenging, complicated by a host of factors, some universal, some country or region specific. These include economic constraints, the opportunity costs of lost labor, discrimination and segregation (both perceived and real), lack of school accessibility, language barriers, teacher absenteeism, corporal punishment, and the absence of materials and exams in the mother tongue. For young women in many parts of the developing world including South Asia, these barriers are further compounded by societal expectations of early marriage, burdensome housework, familial concerns about adolescent girls' safety and virginity, and concurrently low expectations of economic returns to women's education (World Bank 2009). Strict gender roles and discrimination are significantly associated with the development of psychological disorders among girls and young women (Pillai et al. 2008). Thus social restrictions have a significant impact not only on education and economic access but also on health outcomes. As DeJong and Kawar point out in their chapter on the multifaceted interconnections between social and economic rights impinging on Arab adolescents, national education programs aimed at achieving gender parity at the secondary level need to take stock of this social ecology to support young women as they navigate this complicated path to educational success.

India has made significant progress toward improving educational provision and achieving gender parity at the primary school level, through large-scale legislative and programmatic reform. However, as Sinha discusses in her chapter, progress at the secondary level has been slower and gender discrepancies remain pronounced particularly in poor, rural areas. In 2009, the Indian government operationalized its fiscal commitment to overhaul the secondary education system through the Rashtriya Madhyamik Shiksha Abhiyan (RMSA) or National Secondary Education Campaign, a central government program also supported by the World Bank and others, with the goal of achieving universal secondary school enrollment by 2017. The scheme aims to improve access, equity, and the quality of the education system. Key components of the policy specifically outline goals and programs that target the participation of adolescent girls, particularly girls from disadvantaged backgrounds, through measures such as infrastructural improvements, teacher training, scholarships, and the provision of hostels for those from disadvantaged and or remote communities.

In a nation where exclusion from secondary schooling can be classified as a manifestation of intense gender discrimination,[3] simply removing supply-side barriers[4] may not be enough to generate the support necessary to enable young women to make the critical transition to sustained engagement with secondary education, a point made in several chapters in this volume. Of particular concern is the lack of policy consideration concerning the family and societal dynamics. These factors play out as increasing numbers of young women assert their right to education beyond the primary level. A transition to gender equity in higher education also has the potential to generate both positive and negative mental health effects, and the implications of these should be carefully considered as adolescent girls are supported in their critical drive for access to secondary schooling.

This chapter will outline the current landscape in Indian secondary education and explore the psychosocial implications, including increased stress and interpersonal tension that may arise as adolescent girls resist societal expectations and traditional gender roles to pursue their education. Findings from the Shanu Project, a mixed methods study of factors impinging on adolescent girls' educational attainment in rural Gujarat, illustrate societal gender expectations, the girls' experience of education (or lack thereof), and their hopes for the future. The study highlights the potential for both mental health difficulties and resilience as girls act to attain their rights, and in doing so alter the terrain for future generations. Finally, the chapter draws attention to opportunities for government to facilitate equitable access to education by supporting vulnerable adolescents through holistic education policies that integrate adolescent mental health and family support initiatives. The importance of linking health and educational interventions, a point emphasized by the preceding chapter, is one that we will return to.

The Evolving Landscape of Secondary Education

In recent years, governments across the developing world, including India, have made considerable progress in improving educational provisions and achieving gender parity at the primary school level.[5] In India this focus on primary education came in the legislative form of the Right of Children to Free and Compulsory Education (RTE) Act, 2009. The Act grants the right to education for children through fourteen years of age but stops at the threshold of secondary education (at class nine where students are generally fifteen years of age). The focus on primary education has resulted in a intergenerational shift from illiteracy to large scale enrollment in primary education; in 2010 primary school net enrollment rates were 89 percent for males and 87 percent for females, up from 84 percent and 73 percent, respectively, in 2002.[6] Further, gender parity at the lower primary level (Standards 1–5) has been achieved. (UNESCO Institute for Statistics 2011). The programs' success, coupled with a growing population of adolescents, has resulted in increased domestic pressure to provide an accessible secondary system to ensure that the swelling number of primary graduates have a path for continued education. According to the World Bank, the number of students finishing upper primary education has been increasing at more than 5 percent per year since 2001; and this is projected to continue through 2014 with increased elementary enrollments linked to the push for primary education (World Bank 2009). A universally accessible secondary education system is essential for India, a country poised for further growth, as shortages in educated labor hinder national economic growth and social development, and deter international investment (World Bank 1991, 2009; Tilak 1993; Filmer 2005; Lewin 2011, 53).

Female participation at the secondary level in India is increasing. According to UNESCO (2011), the gender parity index lay at 0.88 with gross enrollment rates of 64 percent and 56 percent for males and females, respectively. This is a marked increase from the 1991 participation rates: up from 51 percent and 36 percent. While improvement is being made, these participation figures lie well below those of the countries with which India is regularly compared economically. In China, the gender parity index is 1.07 and gross enrollment rates are 76 percent for males and 81 percent for females. Russia has a gender parity index of 0.97 and gross enrollment rates of 86 percent for males and 84 percent for females. It is clear from these figures that secondary education is out of reach for many Indian adolescents, but the problem is more acute for girls.

The Indian government's eleventh and twelfth Five-Year Plans (the most recent for years 2012–17) declare secondary school a major focus, with the intention that educational infrastructure will keep pace with a more populous generation of youth. The eleventh Five Year Plan report stated that "in view of the demands of rapidly changing technology and the growth of knowledge economy, a mere eight years of elementary education would be grossly inadequate for our young children to acquire necessary skills to compete in the job market." In 2009, the government operationalized this commitment to overhaul the secondary education system through the previously mentioned RMSA scheme, estimated to cost more than fifteen billion U.S. dollars by 2020. The scheme aims to make the secondary education system available, accessible, and affordable to all young persons aged fourteen to eighteen, with the ambitious goal of achieving universal enrollment by 2017 and universal retention by 2020. The main objectives of the scheme, more specifically, are "to achieve a Gross Enrollment Rate of 75 percent for standards IX–X within the next five years by providing a secondary school within 5–7 kms [kilometers] of every habitation; improve quality of education by making all secondary schools conform to prescribed norms; remove gender, socio-economic and disability barriers; and achieve universal access to secondary education by 2017."[7]

At present, attaining a secondary education is a challenge for many adolescents, male and female alike. However, broader issues specific to gender further contribute to females' exclusion. The eleventh Five-Year Plan (Planning Commission Government of India 2008) highlighted the correlation between gender and graduation rate, noting that as of 2005, 63.9 percent of girls who began secondary school did not finish it, compared to 38.7 percent of boys.[8] The slower pace at which India is closing the gender gap at this level is particularly notable because in many countries, particularly in Latin America, girls' educational attainment in secondary school is on par with that of their male counterparts (Fiske 2012).

Contributory supply-side factors to this disparity include large populations, overburdened infrastructure, poor quality schools, and teachers absenteeism (Kremer et al. 2005; World Bank 2009). The increased investment through RMSA should help to remedy the impact of these factors on girls (Andrabi et al. 2007, xvii). Girls' participation in secondary education up to now has also been hindered by demand-side issues, many of which are compounded by discriminatory gender norms such as disproportionate domestic burden (Reddy and Sinha 2010), unequal family resource allocation (Lancaster et al. 2008; Azam and Kingdon 2011), parents' perception that there is little benefit from girls' education (Siddhu 2011), and early marriage (Moore et al. 2009). As noted by Sinha in her chapter, child labor in agriculture and in the home-based handicraft industry are both permitted by law. There is also a prevalent practice of girls engaging in arduous household work from a very young age.

Challenges to these gendered expectations and norms may increasingly occur in the national drive for an equitable secondary education system. The findings of the Shanu Initiative illustrate complex social issues that determine the familial and personal demand for secondary education.

The Shanu Project: Education and Traditional Gender Roles

The Shanu Adolescent Agency Initiative explored the intricate barriers to educational attainment in five villages in North Western Gujarat. The study, undertaken as a collaboration between the Indian Self Employed Women's Association (SEWA) and the François-Xavier Bagnoud Center for Health and Human Rights (FXB Center) at Harvard University, documented the factors impinging on educational access for adolescents in five remote villages.[9] Focus groups with adolescent girls in school (n=40, ages 10–12), not in school (n=30, ages 10–15), and their mothers (n=36, ages 30–50), together with key informant interviews conducted with teachers (n=10, 40 percent female), provided insight into the daily lives of adolescent girls and the personal and social barriers that they face in accessing education.

The findings of the Shanu project highlighted several well-established, yet enduring, obstacles impinging on adolescent girls' access to school. Factors frequently emphasized by girls and their parents included a lack of facilities (including schools within or near the village, clean toilets at schools, reliable transportation); a lack of resources to fund school fees, uniforms, and books; and concerns for the safety of adolescent girls traveling to and from school outside the village. Further, economic duress within families, in the face of unequal and rapid economic development, translated into pressure on girls to assist with farming and domestic duties, limiting their ability to attend school regularly or at all. These factors are serious and real threats to girls' right to education on a nondiscriminatory basis. However, many of the study participants suggested that even if these issues were overcome, and should "rights" to education be more diligently enforced by the government, girls' access to education would not be guaranteed. In other words, rights alone do not deliver social justice within an effective route to implementation. A more radical embrace of nondiscriminatory entitlements is required. As long as society makes different demands of boys and girls, the challenge of translating constitutional or other legal entitlements into realities on the ground will remain, a point also made in the chapters by Sinha and Burra in this volume. Beyond tangible barriers, three main themes emerged from the data: the role of gender expectations, family dynamics, and girls' personal sense of responsibility that restricted them from attending school beyond the primary level. These themes, emerging as interconnected threads in both the literature and our data, are discussed in what follows.

Gender is a major organizing factor in India, and cultural ideals not only define the socially regulated codes of behavior but also the emotional experience of individuals (Mahalingam and Jackson 2007). Culturally defined roles, particularly hypermasculine and hyperfeminine notions of gender, resonate with notions of family honor in patriarchal societies and act as a scaffold that guides and controls behavior (Mahalingam and Jackson 2007; Tiwari and Ghadially 2009). In these settings, girls maintain an identity that relates purely to their position in the family: as obedient daughter, dutiful wife, caring mother, and powerful mother-in-law (Tiwari and Ghadially 2009). Their sense of self-worth is dependent, in part, on their ability to meet these gender ideals. Women's financial dependence on men produces a constriction of roles, an asymmetry maintained by girls' restricted access to education (Dreze 1999). Thus the development of identity and gender roles among adolescent girls in rural India is strictly controlled by societal norms, enacted by the family. Adherence to this identity has tremendous implications for girls' future relationships, economic livelihood, and autonomy.

An emerging understanding of their gender and household position is evident in the reports of the adolescent girls who participated in the Shanu Initiative focus groups. Many discussed parental and societal expectations of girls' domestic responsibilities and the competing demands on their time and energy.

One girl reported, "There are fewer girls [in school] because they have to stay home and do the work. That is not expected of the boys. Parents often scold girls for going to school and doing their homework rather than helping out on the farm. Boys do not have any work."

Another said, "Often my mother would say: stop doing homework and start doing housework, there are much more important things than learning to be done right now. But if we were not doing homework, our teacher was beating us."

Mothers concurred, and one outlined the stark difference in gender roles: "Boys cannot work like girls, for example if our daughter is out of the village for some reason then we call our neighbor's daughter for household work."

Mothers reported great benefits from education, and on occasion this was expressed as an opportunity to bring value to their future-in-laws. However, they maintained conflicting positions between wanting to encourage their daughters' schooling and acknowledging that the daughter's primary role was within the home. This was exemplified in one mother's description of the short-term benefits but long-term cost: "If a daughter is educated, then she can also teach her mother, younger sister. My daughter keeps the financial accounts. But the problem is that [after marriage] she leaves for the in-laws' house."

Once girls became married, they were expected to leave school, and the family no longer benefits from the investment in education. Education was often referenced as just one of many skills that would be important for the girls' future as wives and mothers. One mother suggested, "We wish our daughters study well and make us and their in-laws proud. But we want our daughters to retain our traditional business too."

This conflict between education and traditional gender roles arose throughout the focus groups and reflected the obstacles to girls' ongoing attendance at school beyond the primary level. The adolescent girls saw many benefits in education, but their lack of exposure to female role models and aspirational figures was evident. When asked about their personal ambitions, few named professional roles. One girl stated, "I don't know but I know my parents will not let me go beyond the village." Opportunities for females to work in the village included needlecraft, farming, and domestic work, none of which required literacy.

Parents were the primary influence in girls' short- and long-term ambitions; one girl, currently in school, stated, "I will be whatever my parents decide I should be, if it is a doctor then I will be a doctor, if they wish for me to stay at home then I will stay at home and that is fine too." Highly structured and narrowly defined gender roles were thus promoted and maintained by the family.

Girls suggested that if change was to occur in enabling girls' access to school, it was needed at the parental level: "But decisions on education are not made by the society or community, what the parents want is final." One girl who was not attending school asked the interviewer to "encourage mothers; tell them that they will arrange the necessary arrangements to enable us to continue our studies." The role of parents, and mothers in particular, may be critical in enabling educational attainment for adolescents, yet this dynamic is often overlooked in research and policy. Further investigation is needed to explore the impact of household needs, parents' desires, and their role as aspirational figures in girls' education attainment.

There is great potential for female role models to improve adolescent agency in rural areas, to increase the impetus behind and the awareness of women's rights. A recent study conducted in rural India demonstrated that villages that assigned a female council leader for two election cycles erased the gender gap in educational attainment and reduced the amount of time that girls spent on domestic duties (Beaman et al. 2012). In contrast, this initiative had no effect on adolescent boys' schooling or domestic work, suggesting that their access is not compromised by the presence of girls in school. It is possible that positive female role models can counteract gender disparities in the community and influence parents' views of the value and potential of girls' agency. As rapid economic development and resulting urbanization occurs in India, exposure to the wide realm of economic opportunities available to girls will increase drastically. This transition has the potential to broaden perspectives on female roles in society and within the household.

Intertwined with gender expectations, family dynamics were an underlying current that ran throughout the girls' descriptions of educational attainment. One girl, not attending school, explained: "Out of duty to her family and family members, girls are leaving school early. It is much easier for parents if there is a girl to do housework and the other reason [for leaving school] is her marriage."

In a different village, the allegiance to parents was echoed: "Once a girl reaches a certain age then she must care for her siblings and do her embroidery and go to the fields. It is a girl's responsibility to her parents." Repeated assertions that these decisions were out of the girls' hands were common.

These findings are in keeping with national data on the vulnerable position of rural adolescent girls in India, indicating that educational exclusion is occurring against a backdrop of other abuses. Across the country, adolescent girls from poor, rural backgrounds are the most likely to be out of school and at high risk of early marriage, with 53 percent of rural women married before the legal age of eighteen (Moore et al. 2009). Studies have shown that parents' preference for girls' early marriage is a contributing factor to early school leaving (Shahid 2007), and conversely that participation in education raises the marriage age and reduces birth rates (Lewis and Lockheed 2007). Currently nearly half (43 percent) of women aged twenty to twenty-four in India were married before the age of eighteen[10] (UNICEF 2011). Protecting family interests over those of the individual occurs not because the individual is not valued, but because it is believed that girls' interests are best protected in a stable family system (Bano 2009).

Adolescence is a critical period for the development of role expectations, a coherent sense of identity, mental health, and moral compass. These psychological processes develop within a complex and dynamic framework of family, peer, community, societal, cultural, and religious influences (Bronfenbrenner 1986; Betancourt 2012; Viner et al. 2012). In adolescence, and particularly in more collective societies where the family unit plays a strong role in economic and social support, the child's social ecology provides a framework for development and well-being (Pillai et al. 2008; Tiwari and Ghadially 2009; Betancourt et al. 2012). Children's relationships to parents, siblings, extended relatives, peers, and the community have the potential to shape their individual development. Accordingly, in the Shanu study, we found that the family dynamic was intricately related to girls' sense of responsibility and personal agency. Beyond the need for girls to leave school if required by the parents, some elaborated on the sense of shame inherent in pursuing one's education: "For girls it is shameful to continue once you reach a certain age. It is embarrassing to continue with your own studies rather than helping your parents at home."

It follows that enabling access to secondary education will not be sufficient for the empowerment of young women in rural India. To translate girls' entitlement to education into a new reality on the ground, additional complementary implementation strategies are essential. These include a cultural shift toward supporting girls' education and vocational aspirations through role models, awareness campaigns, family support, and economic empowerment. Although many girls demonstrated a sense of personal agency and aspiration, cognitive dissonance about their value and role within the family prevented them from pursuing further schooling. One said, "Of course, if we learn, we can get ahead; then we do not have to be stuck in the same place. . . . My mother even admitted to me that education would have helped me, but that she had no choice but to take me out [of school], that it would mean that I am stuck in the fields."

Across India, gender identity is changing at a much faster pace for girls than it is for boys (Tiwari and Ghadially 2009). Yet, those who engage in "nontraditional" lifestyle choices (characterized by social excursions, shopping for fun, and romantic interactions with the opposite sex) are at greater risk of psychological distress (Pillai et al. 2008). In practice, a girl does not even have to be sexually active to be labeled promiscuous. Simple contact and platonic friendships with the opposite sex can be enough to damage her reputation (Lindenbaum 1981; Caldwell et al. 1983, 1998).

Throughout adolescence, girls and boys take increasingly divergent developmental paths, with strength and autonomy encouraged in males and dutiful obedience molded in females (Tiwari and Ghadially 2009). Resistance to traditional gender norms and lifestyle rules has a potential for backlash through impairing mental health and interpersonal relationships. Those girls who act to attain their rights are likely to do so at a cost. Challenges to these social norms can result in backlash in the private and public sphere. The event of the December 16, 2012 Delhi gang rape, where a young student was brutally assaulted by five men and subsequently died from her injuries exemplify how brutal this backlash can be.

Encouraging adolescents to continue their education beyond primary school level is of critical importance. However, targeting these young individuals without the support of their parents and community is unlikely to succeed. Changes occurring in the cities have enabled a smoother transition for girls seeking to enter and stay in the education system and workforce and delay marriage (Tiwari and Ghadially 2009). A multifaceted approach that addresses the girls' social ecology, exposure to broader economic opportunities, and strong female role models will empower girls to express agency without experiencing shame. Governmental and local organizations must therefore work to support girls within the context of their family through more integrated community- and family-based approaches, while addressing cultural attitudes. Recognition of the vital role that family and community play in restricting or advocating access to rights will increase the likelihood of success for a range of education and empowerment programs. It is therefore important that policies be nuanced and multifaceted to achieve sustainable change that does not place the most vulnerable at risk.

The Case for an Integrated Approach

Efforts to deliver bold changes to human rights and female empowerment in other settings have had mixed results. One example is the implementation of microfinance programs to reduce poverty through the enfranchisement of women. Microfinance loans to women have been heralded as the "magic bullet" for female empowerment (Kabeer 2005). Through the distribution of small loans that enable women to start a business or join local organizations, a virtuous spiral of improvements in child health, reduced child marriage, increased education, and economic freedom for women has been established (Kabeer 2005; Kim et al. 2007). However, some efforts to empower women through economic autonomy have had unintended negative consequences (Mayoux 1999). On occasion, access to loans was accompanied by reported increases in stress, family dysfunction, and domestic violence (Goetz and Sen Gupta 1996; Leach and Sitaram 2001; Kabeer 2005). In these cases, women secured financial independence and begin to assert influence in household decision making, which disrupts traditional hierarchies and results in interpersonal difficulties. Challenging the balance of power and unseating traditional hierarchies for decision making within the household has potential to disrupt the unity and coherence of the family unit, with severe physical and mental health risks for affected girls and women (Goetz and Sen Gupta 1996; Leach and Sitaram 2001). Unfortunately, these adverse outcomes have undermined a number of economic programs designed to support women in attaining their rights. Even though education and economic empowerment programs are tremendously important, emerging evidence suggests that their implementation must enable women to strengthen their economic options within a network that supports and protects them. Social change requires thoughtful action. These adverse consequences thus highlight the need for holistic and comprehensive rights implementation strategies, and the inadequacy of one-dimensional interventions to target gender discrimination.

Family and community support play an important role in programs designed to transition gender roles (Leach and Sitaram 2001). Bano (2009) argues that the failure of some female empowerment programs (especially those established in largely Islamic societies) is due to two key problems. First, the programs do not do enough to address a core unwillingness to accommodate and respect alternative notions of femininity within the community; and second, that programs do not enable women to negotiate increased space for themselves within existing societal structures at an incremental pace. Fortunately, more recent initiatives have successfully demonstrated that coordinated household engagement (incorporating roles for both men and women) in microfinance lending programs results in reducing intimate partner violence and improving family unity (Kim et al. 2007; Fiske 2012). Working to empower women within currently existing structural norms or processes (such as engaging with local madrasas, or Islamic religious schools) will create a more sustainable and accessible opportunity for women who are constrained by socioeconomic limitations and strict gender expectations (Bano 2009). Policies targeting adolescents need to take a similarly integrated approach with a particular focus on mental well-being if universal enrollment is to be achieved and the rights of vulnerable youth protected. The feelings of hopelessness, shame, and lack of control raised by the adolescents in the Shanu Initiative are indicative of a broader mental health crisis facing marginalized youth across the country.

The rates of common mental disorders among adolescents and youth in the region have become an alarming issue. Suicide is now a leading cause of death for young people in India (Caldwell et al. 1983; Patel et al. 2007). A longitudinal study of 108,000 young people in a rural community in South India revealed that suicide was the cause of a quarter of deaths among boys, and one-half to three-quarters of deaths among girls aged ten to nineteen years (Caldwell et al. 1983). Most mental disorders begin during adolescence and early adulthood, but are often not detected or treated until later in life (Patel et al. 2007). Social determinants (the economic and social conditions in which people are born, live, grow, and work) have significant impact on adolescent health (Viner et al. 2012). And although poverty has been demonstrated to be a significant predictor of mental disorder (Lindenbaum 1981), Indian data suggest no difference in the prevalence of mental disorders among children living in urban, middle-class, slum, or rural settings (Caldwell et al. 1998).

Growing evidence suggests that girls who face gender discrimination report a higher prevalence of mental disorders (Pillai et al. 2008). This discrimination is perpetuated by an ongoing discrepancy in access to rights, and lack of opportunity to step out of poverty through education and economic agency. These findings are consistent with evidence from the Shanu Initiative that suggests that competing life choices, lack of control over their future and access to resources, together with a sense of shame inherent in continuing their education, led girls to drop out of school. Family support is a critical factor in adolescent mental health (Pillai et al. 2008), and the current findings indicate the vital role of girls' social ecology in determining their educational success. Integrating secondary education policies with programs that target adolescent mental well-being provides the Indian government with a unique opportunity to not only reach their goal of an accessible and equitable education system but also to provide much-needed mental health support to an extremely vulnerable cohort, two inextricably linked objectives.

India's recent focus on secondary education is concurrent with a broader move to expand and develop its social infrastructure. This presents the Indian government with a chance to spearhead sustainable and holistic approaches to improving adolescent rights, by integrating its education policy with programs that support mental health. The Ministry of Health and Family Welfare's newly appointed Mental Health Policy Group has proposed innovative promotion of community mental health through capacity building of lay mental health workers and engagement with local communities to develop sustainable and effective mental health care (Ministry of Health and Family Welfare Mental Health Policy Working Group 2012). Mental health needs are often unmet, even in high-resource settings. It is vital that the mental health policy addresses the vast and underacknowledged need for mental health promotion and intervention for adolescents (Patel et al. 2007; Pillai et al. 2008). Through a coordinated and collaborative approach, and recognition of the intricate relationship between family support, adolescents' well-being, and access to secondary education, it may be possible to support young people in ultimately reaching their potential. Recognition of the rights of India's large adolescent population and the development of integrated and comprehensive programs to support their potential will be key to India's ongoing economic and social development.

Conclusion

India is undergoing a period of rapid transformation, economically, socially, and culturally. Adolescents, particularly girls from underprivileged backgrounds, are at the leading edge of this rapid modernization. On the one hand, development has opened up new opportunities and expectations including secondary and tertiary level education. On the other hand, many settings demand that girls maintain a significant number of the traditional, more restrictive gender roles such as sibling care and household work. These gender norms are reinforced through restricted access to education, sexual and physical violence, and child marriage. There is no disputing that accessing secondary education is essential to adolescents' development and a prerequisite for participation in the modern economy. However, education policies such as the RMSA and implementation thereof need to go beyond the goal of promoting access and take a holistic approach to ensuring adolescent girls' well-being as they shape new expectations for their role within the family and society. Alarming data on adolescent mental health needs across the country, such as the increase in rates of adolescent suicide, demonstrate the complex dynamic between adolescent development, interpersonal relationships, well-being, and education that need to be addressed in concert through coordinated response. As the government expands its social and political infrastructure it is presented with a unique opportunity to spearhead an integrated and innovative approach to adolescent advancement. It is time to address the vast gender inequalities and guide adolescent girls on a fulfilling, realizable, and safe path to secondary education and, beyond that, to a rights-respecting adulthood.

Notes

1. The EFA movement was launched at the World Conference on Education for All in 1990 by UNESCO, UNDP, United Nations Population Fund (UNFPA), UNICEF, and the World Bank. Participants endorsed an "expanded vision of learning" and pledged to universalize primary education and massively reduce illiteracy by the end of the decade. Ten years later, the international community met again in Dakar and affirmed their commitment to achieving Education for All by the year 2015.

2. The quality of education the children are receiving at both primary and secondary levels is still very much an ongoing issue of concern but beyond the scope of this chapter.

3. Other manifestations include sex-selective abortion, malnutrition, early marriage, the dowry system, unequal distribution of household resources, a disproportionate domestic burden, and violence.

4. Although it should be noted that the infrastructural deficit is certainly an issue that also needs to be addressed.

5. In India, efforts have included opening new schools; strengthening existing school infrastructure through provision of additional teachers, classrooms, toilets, and drinking water; more maintenance; and school improvement grants.

6. However, gains begin to be lost as children progress through the primary and particularly upper primary levels: Statistics of School Education 2007–08 shows that 52.47 percent of girls dropped out before completing class eight.

7. Education for All webpage, http://www.educationforallinindia.com/SEMIS.html.

8. Five-Year Plan, 15.

9. The principal investigator in this research was Prof. Jacqueline Bhabha (editor) and program manager Orla Kelly (coauthor).

10. Forty-eight percent of women aged twenty to twenty-four- in rural areas vs. 29 percent of women aged twenty to twenty-four in urban areas.

References

Andrabi, T. J. Das, A.I. Khwaja, T. Vishwanath, and T. Zajonc. 2007. "Pakistan: Learning and Education and Achievements in Punjab Schools (LEAPS)." World Bank Discussion Paper. Washington, D.C.: World Bank.

Azam, M., and G. Kingdon. 2011. "Are Girls the Fairer Sex in India? Revisiting Intra-Household Allocation of Education Expenditure." *Working Paper Series 2011–10*. Oxford: Centre for the Study of African Economies, Department of Economics, University of Oxford.

Baker, D., and G. LeTendre. 2005. *National Differences, Global Similarities: World Culture and the Future of Schooling*. Stanford: Stanford Social Sciences.

Bano, M. 2009. "Empowering Women: More Than One Way?" *HAGAR Studies in Culture, Policy and Identities* 9:5–23.

Barro, R. J. (2001) Human capital and growth, American Economic Review (Papers and Proceedings), 91, 12–7.

Beaman, L., E. Duflo, Pande, R. and Topalova, P. 2012. "Female Leadership Raises Aspirations and Educational Attainment for Girls: A Policy Experiment in India." *Science* 335:582–86.

Betancourt, T. S. 2012. "The Social Ecology of Resilience in War-Affected Youth: A Longitudinal Study from Sierra Leone." *Social Ecology of Resilience*:347–56.

Betancourt, T. S., McBain, R.K., Newnham, E.A., Brennan, R. 2012. "Trajectories of Internalizing Problems in War-Affected Sierra Leonean Youth: Examining Conflict and Postconflict Factors." *Child Development, 84(2)*, 455–470.

Bronfenbrenner, U. 1986. "Ecology of the Family as a Context for Human Development: Research Perspectives." *Developmental Psychology* 22:723–42.

Caldwell, J. C., Caldwell, P., Caldwell, B.K., and Pieris, I. 1998. "The Construction of Adolescence in a Changing World: Implications for Sexuality, Reproduction, and Marriage." *Studies in Family Planning* 29:137–53.

Caldwell, J.C., Reddy, P.H. and Caldwell, P. 1983. "The Causes of Marriage Change in South India." *Population Studies* 37:343–61.

Dreze, J. 1999. "A Surprising Exception: Himachal's Success in Promoting Female Education." *Manushi* 112:12–17.

Dreze, J., and M. Murthi. 2001. "Fertility, Education, and Development: Evidence from India." *Population and Development Review* 27, no. 7:33.

Filmer, D. 2005. "Gender and Wealth Disparities in Schooling: Evidence from 44 Countries." *International Journal of Educational Research* 43:351–69.

Fiske, E. 2012. *World Atlas of Gender Equality in Education*. Paris: UNESCO.

Goetz, A. M., and R. Sen Gupta. 1996. "Who Takes the Credit? Gender, Power and Control over Loan Use in Rural Credit Programmes in Bangladesh." *World Development* 24, no. 1: 45–63.

Gokhale, M., K. Kanade, A.N., Rao, S., Kelkar, R.S., Joshi, S.B., Girigosavi, S.T. 2004. "Female Illiteracy: The Multifactorial Influence on Child Health." *India Ecology of Food and Nutrition* 43, no. 4: 4543–5237.

Kabeer, N. 2005. "Is Microfinance a 'Magic Bullet' for Women's Empowerment? Analysis of Findings from South Asia." *Economic and Political Weekly* 40:4709–18.

Kim, J. C., Watts, C. H., Hargreaves, J.R., Ndhlovu, L.X., Phetla, G., Morison, L.A., Busza, J., Porter, J.D.H., and Pronyk, P. 2007. "Understanding the Impact of a Microfinance-Based Intervention on Women's Empowerment and the Reduction of Intimate Partner Violence in South Africa." *American Journal of Public Health* 97, no. 10: 1794–1802.

Klasen, S. 1999. "Does Gender Inequality Reduce Growth and Development? Evidence from Cross-Country Regressions." Policy Research Report on Gender and Development. Washington, D.C.: World Bank.

Kremer, K., Chaudhury, N., Rogers, F.H., Muralidharan, K., and Hammer, J.. 2005. "Teacher Absence in India: A Snapshot." *Journal of the European Economic Association* 3, no. 2: 658–67.

Lancaster, G., Maitra, P., and Ray, R., 2008. "Household Expenditure Patterns and Gender Bias: Evidence from Selected Indian States." *Oxford Development Studies* 36, no. 2.

Leach, F., and Sitaram, S. 2001. "Microfinance and Women's Empowerment: A Lesson from India." *Development in Practice* 12, no. 5: 575–88.

Lewin, K. 2011. *Beyond Universal Access to Elementary Education in India: Is it Achievable at Affordable Costs?* CREATE Pathways to Access Research Monograph No. 53. Sussex, UK: University of Sussex, Center for International Education.

Lewis, M., and M. Lockheed. 2007."Social Exclusion: The Emerging Challenge in Girls' Education." In *Exclusion, Gender, and Education: Case Studies from the Developing World*, edited by M. Lewis and M. Lockheed, 1–27. Washington, D.C.: Center for Global Development.

Lindenbaum, S. 1981. "Implications for Women of Changing Marriage Transactions in Bangladesh." *Studies in Family Planning* 12.

Mahalingam, R., and B. Jackson. 2007. "Idealized Cultural Beliefs About Gender: Implications for Mental Health." *Social Psychiatry and Psychiatric Epidemiology* 42:1012–23.

Mayoux, L. 1999. "Questioning Virtuous Spirals: Microfinance and Women's Empowerment in Africa." *Journal of International Development* 11:957–84.

Ministry of Health and Family Welfare Mental Health Policy Group. 2012. XIIth Plan District Mental Health Programme. New Delhi: Government of India.

Moore, A., Singh, S., Ram, U., Remez, L. and Audam, S. 2009. *Adolescent Marriage and Childbearing in India: Current Situation and Recent Trends*. New York: Guttmacher Institute.

Patel, V., Flisher, A. J., Hetrick, S. and McGorry, P. 2007. "Mental Health of Young People: A Global Public-Health Challenge." *Lancet* 369:1302–13.

Pillai, A., Patel, V. Cardozo, P. Goodman, R. Weiss, H.A. and Andrew, G. 2008. "Nontraditional Lifestyles and Prevalence of Mental Disorders in Adolescents in Goa, India." *British Journal of Psychiatry* 192:45–51.

Planning Commission Government of India 2008. *Eleventh Five Year Plan (2007–2012): Social Sector*. Vol. 11. New Delhi: Oxford University Press.

Reddy, A., and S. Sinha. 2010. "School Dropouts or Pushouts? Overcoming Barriers for the Right to Education." CREATE Pathways to Access Research Monograph 40. Sussex, UK: University of Sussex, Center for International Education.

Schultz, T. 1993. "Returns to Women's Schooling." In *Women's Education in Developing Countries: Barriers, Benefits, and Policy*, edited by E. King and M. Hill, 48–87. Baltimore: Johns Hopkins University Press.

Shahid, A. 2007. "Socioeconomic Determinants of Female Education in a Muslim Family: An Econometric Analysis." *Indian Economic Journal* 54, no. 4.

Siddhu, G. 2011. "Who Makes It to Secondary School? Determinants of Transition to Secondary Schools in Rural India." *International Journal of Educational Development* 31:394–401.

Subbarao, K., and L. Raney. 1995."Social Gains from Female Education." *Economic Development and Cultural Change* 44, no. 1: 105–28.

Tilak, J. 1993. "Economic Reforms and Investment Policies in Education." *Perspectives in Education* 9, no. 2.

Tiwari, N., and R. Ghadially. 2009. "Changing Gender Identity of Emerging Adults." *Journal of the Indian Academy of Applied Psychology* 35: 313–21.

UNESCO Institute for Statistics. 2011. "UIS Statistics in Brief: Profiles: Education (All Levels) Profile—India 2010." http://stats.uis.unesco.org/unesco/TableViewer/document.aspx?ReportId=121&IF_Language=eng&BR_Country=3560.

UNICEF 2011. "Child Marriage Information Sheet." New York: UNICEF.

Viner, R.M., Ozer, E.M., Denny, S., Marmot, M, Resnick, M., Fatusi, A. and Currie C. 2012. "Adolescence and the Social Determinants of Health." *The Lancet* 379:1641–52.

World Bank. 1991. "Gender and Poverty in India." World Bank country study. Washington, DC: World Bank.
———. 2009. *Secondary Education in India: Universalizing Opportunity.* Vol. 1. Washington, D.C.: World Bank. http://documents.worldbank.org/curated/en/2009/01/10567129/secondary-education-india-universalizing-opportunity-vol-1-2.

CHAPTER 12

Rights and Realities for Vulnerable Youth in Urban Brazil: Challenges in the Transition to Adulthood

Irene Rizzini and Malcolm Bush

This chapter contrasts the rights guaranteed young people in Brazil by law and the realities of their lives. We note the large improvements made in the situation of some young people and the plight of the many youth living in situations of vulnerability. The chapter pays special attention to the most vulnerable group of young people, those who either spend their days or their days and nights on the street. Many of the points made here echo reflections on the rights-implementation gap and on the problematic legacy of a silo-based approach to social problems ably discussed in the preceding chapter on girls' secondary education in India. The commonalities and differences provide a useful basis for reflection on the global challenges of realizing adolescent rights.

Brazil is a country with exceptionally strong constitutional and legal protections for children and youth and an increasing number of policies and programs to fulfill those rights in practice. In modern times, the critical event in the development of the contemporary rights language was the long struggle to overthrow the military dictatorship that seized power in 1964 and ended in 1985. The new guarantees are enshrined in the 1988 Constitution and the 1990 Statute on the Rights of the Child and the Adolescent, which itself was inspired by the United Nations Convention on the Rights of Children (1989). The current Brazilian Constitution was adopted in 1988 and contains a sweeping clause about the rights of all children. Article 227 of the Constitution states: "It is the duty of the family, society and the state to assure with absolute priority the rights of children and adolescents to life, health, food, education, leisure, occupational training, culture, dignity, respect, freedom, and family and community life, and in addition to protect them from all forms of negligence, discrimination, exploitation, violence, cruelty and oppression."[1]

The 1990 Brazilian Statute on the Rights of the Child and the Adolescent marked a major step forward in the establishment of legal rights for children.[2] It was the result of years of mobilization on behalf of children. The critical change the statute made was to provide that children and adolescents were, henceforth, to be "the subject of rights" and citizens, albeit citizens with additional rights to protect their full development.[3] The statute made a clean break with the former legal status of children that, to the degree it was spelt out in law, was concerned with those children the state found a challenge under the "Doctrine of [children in an] Irregular Situation," that is, a situation that required judicial intervention. This former status labeled the children as sources of danger to the public order, not as persons with rights.

Just as the Constitution contained a sweeping statement of children's rights so did the Statute. Articles 3 through 5 of the Statute established the basic principles of the law.[4]

> Art. 3. Without prejudice to the full protection treated of in this Law, the child and adolescent enjoy all the fundamental rights inherent to the human person and, by law or other means, are ensured of all opportunities and facilities so as to entitle them to physical, mental, moral, spiritual and social development, in conditions of freedom and dignity.
>
> Art. 4. It is the duty of the family, community, society in general and the public authority to ensure, with absolute priority, effective implementation of the rights to life, health, nutrition, education, sports, leisure, vocational training, culture, dignity, respect, freedom and family and community living.

The notion of rights is the context in which Brazil thinks, talks, and acts about social issues. The language of rights is, in short, the key discourse for setting out the need for social change. However, despite the clear progress in the discourse of young people's rights in Brazil, there is still a considerable gap between those rights guaranteed in law and the realities of their lives throughout the country (Kaufman and Rizzini 2009; Secretaria de Direitos Humanos 2010). This chapter will use demographic and other empirical data to discuss some of the major challenges and opportunities in the process of implementing adolescents' rights in the past two decades with a special focus on street children, one of the most vulnerable groups of children.

Challenges Facing Youth in Brazil

Half the population of Brazil is under twenty-four years of age.[5] They live in a country where after centuries of massive income disparities, those disparities are slowly beginning to lessen due to a variety of factors including an expanding economy, steady increases in the minimum wage, and a family income supplement called Bolsa Família. In the period 1990 to 2010, the number of Brazilians in extreme poverty measured by a per-capita household income[6] of less than 25 percent of minimum wage decreased to 8.9 million people. Those almost nine million people, however, have incomes of less than R$127 or US$78 a month. The official poverty line in Brazil is currently a per diem, per capita income of R$6.80 or about US$3.40.[7] Between 1997 and 2008, the percentage of newborns to seventeen year olds below the poverty line declined from 43 percent to 36 percent but that decline leaves over a third of all Brazilian children and youth living on tiny amounts of money.[8]

Low-income youth in urban Brazil face many difficulties in accessing the mainstream, formal job market. These difficulties include poor educational preparation and discrimination based on race and on living in low-income communities. The existence of high per-employee taxes on employers that inhibits employment in the formal sector, and a climate of violence that makes many routine tasks of daily life difficult to accomplish, add to the difficulties youth face.

Part of the current challenge facing young people is caused by the very disparate impact of certain harms by race and geography. As in any other mixed-race country, the manifestations of racial discrimination in Brazil take their own particular national form. It is true that the darker one's skin in Brazil the greater the likelihood of being poor. It is also true that after slavery was finally abolished in 1888 the race problem was considered "solved" by the ruling elites and thus swept out of sight in official discourse. However, unlike, for example, the United States, perhaps most Brazilians regard Brazil with pride as a mixed-race country. In the 2010 census 38.5 percent of the population identified themselves as brown or mixed race, 6.2 percent as black, and 53.7 percent as white.⁹ In general, the arid northeastern states of the country are much poorer than the prosperous southeast. There are also large differences in living conditions and access to the mainstream economy among low-income communities in the same city. In Rio, for example, the *favelas* (shantytowns) close to middle-class neighborhoods offer many more economic opportunities than the low-income communities on the periphery of the city. Whatever their color, many youth who live in low-income communities feel discriminated against when they enter middle-class sections of their cities.

A major threat to youth in many countries is high rates of violence. In general the low-income communities or favelas suffer high rates of violence. International comparisons in youth homicides show a vast difference between northern and southern hemisphere countries. The publication *Mapa da Violência, Os Jovens da América Latina* (Map of violence, the young people of Latin America) showed 2008 homicide rates for "youth" (young people aged ten to twenty-nine) of 51.6 per 100,000 in Brazil, 73.4 in Colombia, 1.7 in Portugal, 12.9 in the United States, and 10.4 in Mexico (Rede de Informação Tecnológica Latino Americana 2008). In Brazil, the appalling rates of death by homicide among young black men and the lack of appropriate measures to prevent this tragedy as well as high levels of violence in society in general have caused some commentators to refer to the phenomenon as the *banalization* of violence (Secretaria de Direitos Humanos 2010, 11). In 2007, for example, in Rio de Janeiro, the murder rate of youth aged twelve to eighteen was 24.1 per 100,000 and for black youth a horrifying 300 per 100,000.¹⁰

Favela violence has several sources in addition to concentrated poverty. The iron grip of heavily armed and violent drug traffickers is a reality in many favelas. This phenomenon and the counterviolence of vigilante "militias" and the violence of the police when they raid low-income communities create a reality of constant violence and the threat of violence.

There are, however, signs of change in the levels of violence in Rio. When the current governor of the state of Rio de Janeiro came into office on January 1, 2007, he declared that a state of genocide existed in the city of Rio both on account of the violence and the terrible state of the public hospitals that provide medical care for a large majority of the population. One of the reforms he introduced was a new policing program with the unfortunate name of Police Pacifying Units (Unidades de Polícia Pacificadora or UPP) that constituted the first ever attempt at regular policing of the low-income communities.

Given the decades of police, trafficker, and militia violence in the lower-income communities of Rio, with the police paying attention only when the traffickers took their violence to surrounding middle-class communities, and then responding by shooting and killing indiscriminately, it is not surprising that there are mixed feelings about UPP in the neighborhoods themselves. But the results have been striking. UPP has been installed one favela at a time because of the enormous person power needed to enter the communities in force, secure them, and then establish a permanent police force. In the "pacified" favelas the traffickers have to a large degree been chased out, killed, or arrested. The major news conglomerate *O Globo* regularly reports that over 95 percent of residents in these communities are pleased with the result, with many residents saying that their lives were transformed overnight. Some "unobtrusive" measures of the success of the interventions include significant increases in the property values of surrounding middle-class communities and a reduction of car insurance rates in Rio in 2010 of 37 percent compared to a 7 percent reduction in the rest of the country as carjacking diminishes.

Questions about the program include whether the program is only international window dressing for the 2014 World Cup and the 2016 Olympic Games, both of which will be held in Rio; whether it will be systematically extended to all favelas especially those outside the middle-class southern zone of the city; whether more attention will be paid to the militias since most of the initial attention has been paid to the traffickers; how the police will deal with casual crime, forbidden by the traffickers and now increasing in "pacified" favelas; and whether the attempts at infrastructure renovation, or what Brazilians call "urbanization," education, and social programs will be extensive. There is another set of questions particularly relevant to street children. In an even more unfortunately named city initiative, "the shock of order" (*choque de ordem*), police are adapting the so-called zero-tolerance approach popularized by the former mayor of New York City, Rudy Giuliani, to a variety of "urban nuisances."

Many of the visible signs of *choque de ordem* involve cracking down on the ubiquitous illegal street vendors and to a lesser degree on carefully selected "illegal" housing. But part of *choque de ordem* is picking up street kids from middle-class neighborhoods and taking them elsewhere. In the course of this exercise, street educators (teachers and social workers working with street children) report that the young people suffer high degrees of harassment and abuse. The youth tend to be "expelled" to the periphery of the city and hence are even more hidden and out of reach of some of the helping organizations that are located in more central parts of the city (Rizzini et al. 2012).

Low-income communities in urban Brazil vary significantly but youth in many of them suffer from high rates of school absenteeism, high rates of being behind grade level, inadequate instruction, and pressure to drop out of school to earn small amounts of money to support their family. Most youth who are behind grade level blame their learning difficulties on themselves, rather than on the schools. They report classrooms constantly disturbed by talking, fighting, and playing. Youth whose parents have low-educational achievements, black males, youth in large families, and youth at the bottom of the income distribution do worse than other low-income youth (Bush 2007). While certain key indicators of education in Brazil, most notably formal enrollment, show huge improvements, the reality in low-income neighborhoods is that fundamental problems remain. Children only go to school for half a day because of the shortage of classroom space and teachers. Dropout rates and the rates of children scoring below grade level are very high. For example, in 2009, 51 percent of children and youth eight to fourteen years of age who lived in urban areas were behind grade level.[11]

In these difficult circumstances, many youth struggle to improve their chances by taking educational courses. But the courses typically only last for a short period of time, are inadequately structured, and offered by non profit organizations that do not connect the hard skill training to the demands of employers. These courses do not provide effective training in soft skills, and do not connect enrolled students to existing jobs or to a supportive network in cases where students actually receive job offers (International Center for Research and Policy on Childhood 2010). These problems are similar to problems experienced by workforce development programs in the United States.

While youth who live in low-income communities face difficulties moving into mainstream society, these difficulties are much greater for "children in the situation of the streets." The majority of these children do not sleep on the streets but spend their days there hustling for small change. A recent national census of such children and youth showed that while the majority still lived at home, almost 40 percent of them were living in a variety of other places with no stability of residence (Instituto de Desenvolvimento Sustentável 2011). A majority of this latter group had unstable relationships with their parents. In contrast, 78 percent of those living at home reported good or very good relationships with their parents(s). Twenty-four percent of those sleeping outside their homes had been on the streets for between two and five years. Just about all the children and youth on the street hustled constantly for small amounts of income with 16 percent of the girls admitting to prostitution. Despite this constant hustling, almost 30 percent of the national sample said they did not eat every day. Their future prospects are also grim. Only 24 percent of the sixteen and seventeen year olds had completed elementary school and only 2 percent had graduated from secondary school.

Opportunities and the Challenges of Implementation

Despite the challenges described in the last section, Brazil has achieved some major successes in children and youth policy over the last decade. The rate of infant mortality, for example, dropped from 53.7 per 1,000 live births in 1990 to 22.8 in 2008 (Secretaria de Direitos Humanos 2010). Between 1982 and 2008, the rate of illiteracy among fifteen-seventeen year olds dropped from 13.1 percent to 1.7 percent (Secretaria de Direitos Humanos 2010, 92). In 1992, 60 percent of adolescents were attending school, a figure that increased to 84 percent in 2008 (Secretaria de Direitos Humanos 2010, 91). Recent initiatives for young people that mark important advances include the National Policy for Youth and the creation of the National Secretariat for Youth, the National Council of Youth, and the National Program for the Inclusion of Youth: Education, Training, and Community Action. In 2000, the president signed into law the Program of Youth Apprenticeship, which requires companies with a minimum of seven employees to hire 5–15 percent of their workforce from young people between the ages of fourteen and twenty-four on a contract lasting between fourteen and twenty-four months.[12] The problem, as in other areas of Brazilian life, is the difficulty of implementing rights and programs. Centuries of imperial and oligarchic rule and the comparatively recent end of the military dictatorship have left little tradition of citizen action to advocate for the passage and implementation of reform programs.

One key phenomenon that supports the development of youth capacities is the space that exists for young activists to sharpen their leadership and advocacy skills by participating in organizations that permit young people to express their citizenship. This phenomenon recalls the points made by

Pineda, in an earlier chapter in this volume, in the context of civic engagement and adolescents with disabilities. In a study of activist youth in Rio de Janeiro, Mexico City, and Chicago, the authors discovered the ways in which a variety of organizations including churches and cultural, political, and advocacy organizations gave the next generation of leaders the room to express and develop their proclivity for civic engagement (Rizzini, Torres, and Rio Lugo 2009). Youth became involved through family, friends, and community institutions such as schools, churches, and youth organizations. Some youth were sought out by these organizations; others described themselves as having an inner restlessness that drove them to seek involvement outside the home. The Brazilian young people's involvement was fired by a sense of the deep disparities in Brazilian society, of the physical danger that threatened young people in the cities, but also by a sense of optimism that key aspects of Brazilian society were improving or were capable of improvement. The young people were quite aware of the risks of participation including getting labeled as an activist and having to sacrifice time with family and friends for their activist work. The importance of social solidarity as a facet of social existence and as a vehicle for change seems to be much stronger in Brazil than in the United States or Europe. The critical condition for participation was the presence of organizations that encourage youth participation.

Brazil also has a unique tool for tackling children and youth issues. As part of the return to democracy, a serious attempt has been made to include citizens in the ongoing task of government decision making. One vehicle was the establishment at the federal, state, and municipal levels of councils, half of whose members were composed of public officials and half of elected civil society members, with federally mandated powers to debate public policy. Many countries have commissions of various kinds that oversee aspects of public life, but the executive or legislative branches of government usually appoint such commissions. The Brazilian Children's Rights Councils spring from a more general provision contained in the Brazilian Constitution known generically as Oversight Councils for Social Policy (Conselhos Gestores de Políticas Sociais). The civil society members are elected by a very select electorate, civil society organizations that are registered by the councils as organizations that provide services to children and youth.

What is unusual about the Children's Rights Councils is that they are one of two oversight councils that have the power to formulate policy as well as consult on policy.[13] This power is spelled out in Article 88 of the Statute on the Child and the Adolescent that states that the Children's Rights Councils are decision-making and monitoring organs (*órgãos deliberativos e controladores*).[14] (The Portuguese adjective "deliberativo" translates here as decision making.) The same article enumerates the guidelines of the enforcement policy for the provisions of the statute and these (with original paragraph numbers):

- I – municipalization of enforcement;
- II – creation of municipal, state and national councils of child and adolescent rights, which will be deliberative and controlling entities of actions at all levels, in which equal popular participation is ensured through representative organizations, according to the terms of federal, state and municipal legislation;
- IV – maintenance of national, state and municipal funds connected to the respective councils of child and adolescent rights;
- VI – mobilization of public opinion so as to achieve the essential participation of the different segments of society.

Thus the crucial locus for implementation is the municipality, and Children's Rights Councils are a key democratic tool for monitoring enforcement of rights. While these councils exist at the three levels of government, it is the municipal councils that have the day-to-day responsibility for implementation at the municipal level. We should note, however, that the councils are but one part of a theoretically comprehensive system in Brazil for implementing rights known as the System for the Guarantee of Rights (Sistema de Garantia de Direitos). This system encompasses all the public and nonprofit sector actors responsible for guaranteeing the rights of all citizens.[15]

The authors were recently part of a multiyear project to assist the Children's Rights Council in the municipality of Rio de Janeiro in formulating for the first time a policy for street children aimed at giving them the variety of supports they needed. The process of the Rio council in formulating and adopting a policy on street children demonstrated both the possibilities and challenges of Children's Rights Councils. The attempt was a success, and in June 2009 the council adopted a policy to assist street children, encouraged by strong pressure from the major children's network in Rio, Rede Rio Criança (Rio Child Network), and critical technical support from the International Center for Research and Policy on Childhood.[16] The policy contained concrete and, therefore, actionable instructions for eight municipal departments regarding street children. The Rio process reinforced the principle of civil society-public sector parity by maintaining parity of membership of both sectors in the working group that was charged with developing a draft policy. To the extent that data were available (the national census on street children was only completed after the council had adopted the policy), the working group and the council used those data. Once the council had adopted the policy it established an implementation committee that in turn adopted an implementation agenda. The policy adopted by the council represented a dramatic change from seeing street children mainly as threats to public order, a change in perception advocated by Zermatten in the opening chapter of this volume. Thus, the council adopted provisions to protect street children from violence, and to guarantee them access to schools and public services.

The Rio experience also underlined some of the national challenges in making and implementing policy changes through Children's Rights Councils. While the Brazilian system of councils is an adventurous step in participatory democracy, the reality falls short of the promise. This reality in some ways reflects tensions in the actual powers of councils that resulted from the massive struggle to legislate their existence. In law, there is a gray area between the authority of councils and the powers of elected municipal governments. There are precedents in Supreme Court rulings stipulating that municipalities are obliged to follow the resolutions of the councils. There could, for example, be grounds for a class-action lawsuit against a municipality refusing to implement a policy. But there are also theoretical arguments questioning this possibility on the grounds that such actions would give the councils more power than the elected legislative bodies. In practice, in the judgment of one eminent jurist, councils act in the gaps in state and municipal law.

The civil society members of councils are unpaid and, therefore, have little time for their council duties. In the Children's Rights Councils, most of the councils' time was spent on their federally mandated duty of registering all nonprofit groups that work with children. Many of the public sector councilors were junior employees without the authority to act on behalf of their departments. Many councilors lacked any experience of policy making. While Brazil has a complex, centralized system for monitoring public budgets at all levels of government, budgets are opaque and in municipal budgets lump sum allocations make it hard to discover a budget allocation and budget expenditure for a particular program. In Rio de Janeiro, some combination of disinterest and the opposition of the current city administration to the policy on street chlldren means that the work of implementation has essentially come to a halt.

A 2005 study of the Children's Rights Councils gives a national perspective on this mixed picture (Secretaria de Direitos Humanos 2005). That study, aptly titled *Good Councils: Understanding the Reality* (*Bons conselhos: Conhecendo a realidade*), paints a very mixed picture of the functioning of the councils yet still it is a picture of real advances for citizen participation despite all the inherent difficulties. That study reported that there were 5,084 councils in operation, covering 91 percent of the territory of Brazil. Of these 13 percent were not policy decision-making bodies while 63 percent acted as consultative bodies, 49 percent as norm-setting bodies (*normativos*), and 75 percent fulfilled their function of approving the disbursement of certain funds for children and youth. The same study judged that 49 percent of the councils were operating "regularly" with 47 percent displaying an absence of effective action.

A number of strategies might help municipal Children's Rights Councils to fulfill their responsibilities more effectively. These include more practical assistance via training and support services for civil society members; the development of model policies that councils could adapt to their particular circumstances; and the development of effective sanctions for councils that do not fulfill their responsibilities and municipalities that do not respect the policies developed by the councils.

The councils' effectiveness is, not surprisingly, partly a matter of local politics. A number of observers said that other types of federally mandated oversight councils had some success in implementing council actions because of the particular context in which those councils worked. Councils on Social Assistance were said to be effective because all the social assistance budgets passed through the councils. Health Councils exercised considerable power because the doctors' unions often shaped and supported their activities and because these councils developed a tradition of vigorous action to combat the HIV/AIDS crisis. Some Environmental Councils have the support of well-organized advocacy groups.[17] A council's power appears, therefore, to be relative to its subject matter and the forces aligned with it. For this reason, the proper implementation of the policy will depend on more strategic choice of candidates for the councils, the appointment of more committed public servants to head public departments, and the use of other tools such as the forced implementation of the policy through the

Public Prosecutor, a public functionary with responsibility to prosecute criminal cases but also act on behalf of civil society more generally.

Apart from the councils, there are other avenues for better implementation of existing laws, policies and plans. As mentioned earlier, the councils are but one part of the System for the Guarantee of Rights, encompassing all the public and nonprofit sector actors responsible for guaranteeing the rights of all citizens.

We have noted that public budgets in Brazil are opaque and lack critical detail. But the development, adoption, and implementation of budgets are major opportunities for shaping public policies. Since Brazil lacks a history of advocacy and of nonprofit groups examining these processes, it will take time to develop the interest and expertise in these groups' capacities to analyze budgets. But efforts are being made to make public budgets and public expenditures more transparent; nonprofit groups are beginning to develop an interest in those budgets as a tool for shaping and monitoring public policy. In some cities and states political alliances have been built between reform-minded elected officials and leading civil society groups.

Conclusion

Challenging conditions for Brazilian low-income young people persist despite exceptionally strong constitutional and legal protections for children and youth and an increasing number of policies and programs to fulfill those rights in practice. These guarantees are enshrined in the 1988 Constitution and the 1990 Statute on the Rights of the Child and the Adolescent, which itself was inspired by the United Nations Convention on the Rights of Children (1989). In the struggle to help low-income young people enter the mainstream economy and the mainstream world in urban Brazil certain transformational events stand out. These include the passage of the Statute on the Child and the Adolescent in 1990, the impact of this Statute and the efforts of the International Labor Organization to reduce child labor, successful attempts to increase adolescent enrollment in high school, the reduction in teenage pregnancy, and the actual and potential effects of new policing efforts in low-income communities in Rio de Janeiro. Many activists in Brazil are aware of this discourse on rights that is much more a touchstone for action in Brazil than, for example, the discourse on rights is in the United States.

Some priorities for assisting youth in Brazil have reached scale. Formal secondary school enrollment has increased substantially although the quality of the schools, actual attendance, and the proportion of students at grade level remain major problems. Recent attempts to bring peace to the slums of Rio are unprecedented in their scale and impact. Such peace is a sine qua non for the full development of young people. Brazil has a developing nonprofit sector, parts of which have roots in the massive organizing that was necessary to overthrow the military dictatorship. The nonprofit sector that provides opportunities for youth and advocates on their behalf is, however, fragile and seriously underfunded. Many of the nonprofit organizations that exist have effectively become operating subsidiaries of public ministries and departments. Strengthening and extending an independent nonprofit sector devoted to youth would bring major returns. By the same token, providing this sector with tools to analyze the problems facing youth and developing and implementing strategies for change would also make the sector more effective.

Finally, Brazil has now enjoyed three presidents in a row with strong commitments to social reform and is enjoying a period of unprecedented economic growth. The persistence of the difficulties facing vulnerable young people that we have described reflect the entrenchment of inequalities and the legacy of imperial, oligarchical, and dictatorial rule that stretch over the five hundred years of Brazil's existence, and the comparatively recent development of a democratic society. But the founding documents of the new democracy guarantee young people the strongest commitment to the full development of all citizens. The implementation of those guarantees remains very much a work in progress.

Notes

This chapter was first presented as a paper at the conference "Adolescents Rights: What Progress? Exploring Transitions to Adulthood," the FXB Center, Harvard School of Public Health, December 8–9, 2011. We are grateful to our past and present colleagues at the International Center for Research and Policy on Childhood (CIESPI) at the Pontifical Catholic University of Rio de Janeiro (PUC-Rio) for assistance in much of the work on which this chapter is based and to the recent funders of CIESPI, including the Oak Foundation, Geneva, Switzerland, and the Brazilian National Council for the Rights of Children and Adolescents (CONANDA).

1. Constituição da República Federativa do Brasil de 1988, Capítulo VII, Art, 227.
2. Law 8.069 enacted July 13, 1990.
3. Ibid, pp 30–32.

4. Taken from an English language version of the Statute at www.eca.org.br/ecai.htm on March 18, 2011.

5. In Brazil, the term youth includes young people up to the age of 24. Some of the statistics in this text use that definition of youth.

6. Note that the most common measure of poverty in Brazil is the monthly per capita income per family, a figure that controls for family size.

7. This exchange rate reflects that of 5/21/2012.

8. The different time periods used in this section and the different age groups of children reflect the different ranges used by different sources of data.

9. See http://www.ibge.gov.br/english/estatistica/populacao/censo2010/default.shtm.

10. The murder rate in Rio is exceptionally high due to the extreme concentration of poverty in low-income communities.

11. See the CIESPI data resource at www.ciespi.org.br, Table 14.

12. Law 10.097/2000, the Law on Apprenticeship.

13. The following material on the current Children's Rights Councils comes from *Twenty Years of the Statute* (SDH 2010, 166–174). Some of that material in that section is taken from Secretaria de Direitos Humanos e CONANDA (2005). We are also grateful to Eduardo R. Melo for his responses to our questions on the Councils' powers.

14. http://www.planalto.gov.br/ccivil_03/Leis/L8069.htm.

15. The System for the Guarantee of Rights as it relates to children is described in detail in a publication of the Brazilian Association of Magistrates, Prosecutors and Public Defenders of the Child and the Adolescent (ABMP 2010).

16. For a full account of the process of the Rio Children's Rights Council adopting a policy on street children see Bush and Rizzini (2011).

17. We are grateful to Cristina Ventura for responding to our questions on other federally mandated Councils.

References

Associação Brasileira de Magistrados, Promotores de Justiça e Defensores Públicos da Infância e da Juventude (ABMP). 2010. *Organização de Eduardo Rezende Melo: Cadernos de fluxos operacionais sistêmicos. Proteção integral e atuação em rede na garantia dos direitos de crianças e adolescentes* [A guide to the protection of rights system: Full protection and the operation of the network for the guarantee of rights for children and adolescents]. São Paulo: ABMP.

Bush, Malcolm. 2007. *Barriers to Youth Connections to Work: The Case of Young People in the Low-Income Neighborhood of Caju in Rio de Janeiro*. Chicago: Woodstock Institute.

Bush, Malcolm, and Irene Rizzini. 2011. *Closing the Gap Between Rights and Realities for Children and Youth in Urban Brazil: Reflections on a Brazilian Project to Improve Policies for Street Children*. Rio de Janeiro: CIESPI-PUC-Rio.

International Center for Research and Policy on Childhood (CIESPI). 2010. *Juventude e elos com o mundo do trabalho. Retratos e desafios* [Youth and connections to the world of work: Overview and challenges]. A. B. Soares, coordinator. São Paulo/ Rio de Janeiro: Cortez Editora, CIESPI.

Instituto de Desenvolvimento Sustentável. *Pesquisa Censitária de Crianças e Adolescentes em Situação de Rua*. 2011. Rio de Janeiro.

Kaufman, Nathalie, and Irene Rizzini. 2009. "Closing the Gaps Between Rights and Realities of Children's Lives." In *Handbook of Childhood Studies*, edited by Jens Qvortrup, William Corsaro, Michael-Sebastian Honig, and Gill Valentine, 422–32. London: Palgrave Macmillan.

Rede de Informação Tecnológica Latino Americana 2008. *Mapa da violência. Os Jovens da América Latina*. Brasilia:. RITLA.

Rizzini, Irene, Maria de los Angeles Torres, and Norma del Rio Lugo. 2009. *Youth and Civic Engagement in the Americas: Preliminary Findings from Three City Study: Rio de Janeiro, Chicago, and Mexico City*. South Bend, Ind.: Helen Kellogg Center for International Studies, Notre Dame University.

Rizzini, Irene, Marcelo Princeswal, Paula Caldeira, and Malcolm Bush. 2012. *A efetivação de Políticas Públicas no Brasil. O caso das políticas para crianças e adolescentes em situação de rua* [The implementation of public policies in Brazil: The case of children and adolescents living on the streets]. Rio de Janeiro: CIESPI-PUC-Rio.

Rizzini, Irene, and Malcolm Bush. Forthcoming. *Affirming the Young Democracy: Youth Engagement in Rio de Janeiro*. In *Citizens in the Present*, edited by Maria de los Angeles Torres, Irene Rizzini, and Norma del Rio Lugo. Champaign: University of Illinois Press.

Secretaria de Direitos Humanos e CONANDA. 2005. *Bons Conselhos: Conhecendo a Realidade*. Brasilia: SDH-CONANDA.

Secretaria de Direitos Humanos. 2010. *Direitos Humanos de Crianças e Adolescentes: 20 Anos do Estatuto*. Irene Rizzini, coordinator. December. Brasília: SDH.

CHAPTER 13

Youth Unemployment: Facing and Overcoming Obstacles in Partnership

Glaudine Mtshali

The most cursory look at youth unemployment uncovers a complex story of intersecting social, economic, and political dynamics. Political instability in various parts of the world has shown the risk of leaving unattended the challenges faced by an escalating number of unemployed young people. Although the situation is daunting, the interconnectedness of world societies and the transfer of knowledge, risks, and opportunities across national boundaries provide a platform for creative solutions to address youth unemployment in places as different as the United States, Lebanon, and South Africa.[1]

The Link That Binds: Education and Employment

In 2011, the Center for Universal Education at the Brookings Institution in Washington, D.C. raised the alarm: children and youth around the world are facing a serious learning crisis. The report estimates that more than sixty-seven million children in low-resourced countries are not attending primary school (Robinson 2011). Of those in school, many occupy a seat but do not learn basic reading, writing, and math skills. The following chapters by Sinha and Burra concur with this assessment, although with reference to South Asia rather than the African examples covered in the Brookings report. Many developing countries have made great strides over the past decade to improve *access* to schooling but have become outliers in providing *quality* education. The report calls for all parties involved—the United Nations system, governments, nongovernmental organizations, corporations, civil society, parents, and youth—to work in a compact that ensures all learners are adequately prepared to lead productive lives.

It seems reasonable to presume a more advantageous situation exists in well-resourced developed countries. However, a different picture emerges from a 2011 Harvard University study that evaluates reasons why the United States has been unable to prepare all its children to effectively participate in the world of work. The evidence for this is in the large number of high school and college dropouts with only 30 percent of young adults having a bachelor's degree by the age of twenty-seven, factors that all contribute to current youth unemployment rates similar to the immediate aftermath of World War II era (Symonds, Schwartz, and Ferguson 2011). The report suggests that the narrow educational focus on an academic, classroom-based approach to facilitate entrance to four-year colleges may have missed the mark. The study proposes a broad vision of multiple pathways to make it easier for students to transition from school to work, through a consistent multi-pronged approach. The facets of this approach include greater emphasis on high-quality career counseling, apprenticeship programs, two-year community colleges as feasible options to finding well-paying jobs, and offering students more flexibility and support in the last two years of high school on linking learning and work. The report encourages the private sector to work with schools to create experiential opportunities for students to learn work-based skills and to offer them jobs after training. It asks civil society to collaborate with the country's youth to encourage and ensure learning that attains the education, skills, and experience needed for successful lives as adults. The report recognizes the centrality of the business sector to creating job opportunities, as well as that of the government to developing the necessary policy options and programming to support this initiative.

The report offers startling information about employment prospects among various races and income levels. Only 9.2 percent of black youths in lower income households (less than US$20,000) are employed, implying that 90 percent are unemployed. Even in higher income brackets the comparative percentages of employed black and Hispanic versus white youth are strikingly low. A report from Northeastern University in Boston concludes that from 2000 to 2010 the summer employment rate of US teens dropped from 45 percent to 26 percent, a historic low (Sum and McLaughlin 2011, 3). The severity of job losses most significantly affected the youngest teens in the study (16–17 years), black males, low-income, and inner city youth. The report adds the cautionary note that "those who need work experience the most, get it the least." (Sum and McLaughlin 2011, 6). The unemployment rate for black youth in the United States is higher than that for youth in North Africa, which the International Labour Organization (ILO) has cited as having the world's highest youth unemployment rate (27 percent).

The vulnerability of certain subpopulation groups to unemployment raises a tantalizing question. Do these unemployment statistics perhaps reveal an inconvenient truth about the subtle practices we use to exclude "others" from opportunities, occasionally changing in name and content the reigning laws and policies in order to "do the right thing" but in reality setting the stage to achieve the same outcome? Some examples may be instructive.

The U.S. Department of Education reported in March 2012 that minority students, particularly African American males, are three and a half times more likely to be disciplined, suspended, or expelled from school than white students. Teachers at predominantly black schools are paid at lower rates than their counterparts and have fewer qualifications. These schools also offer less challenging subjects (US DOE 2012). It stands to reason that if students are suspended or expelled they cannot be in school learning—automatically contributing to differential academic achievement. How did a country famed for equal opportunity get here?

The U.S. Congress passed the "No Child Left Behind" Act (NCLB) in 2001. In 2007, then Senator Barack Obama, speaking to the largest teachers' organization in the country, the National Education Association (NEA), called the act "one of the emptiest slogans in the history of politics" because it left behind the money to make its admirably described goals a reality (Obama 2007). The NEA, in a 2011 communication to the U.S. Department of Education, referred to the federal mandates imposed under NCLB as "punitive" and "counterproductive"; it appealed to "the need for foundational fiscal support for schools in lieu of overly promoting competition that can leave some districts unable to compete, resulting in students who continue to be left behind" (NEA 2011).

In 2012, at the tenth anniversary of the Act, Diane Ravitch, a New York University professor and education historian, dissected the Act's impact and concluded that it has been destructive to schools, teachers, families, and communities. In her assessment the children who were left behind a decade ago are the same ones who are still being left behind: children from poor, minority, and recent immigrant households (Ravitch 2012). Here is a major contributor to the disastrous employment prospects for teenagers and young adults from poor and minority families. They are the same children who were educationally "left behind," despite legislative terminology and political exhortations to the contrary.

To Congress's credit, the NCLB focused on differential educational achievement rates and developed a linear solution (changed the name of the existing law, added a couple of new requirements, required accountability, measured the outcome, and took action like closing poor performing schools). However, in addition to not adequately funding the law, they also forgot to look at the larger pattern created by multiple root causes. They failed to recognize that the problem (academic underachievement) is an interdependent part of a socioeconomic pattern. Rather than this cause-and-effect short-term fix, they would have been more effective in the long term with a more durable "systems-thinking" approach to the numerous interlinked political, sociocultural, and economic determinants of educational outcomes (Senge 1990; Friel 2003).

Unemployment as a teenager and young adult has long-term consequences on an individual's wage rate and the potential of future employment. Young people's consistent exclusion from the ranks of the employed creates a risk of never gaining employable skills. Helping young people to get a job, any job, irrespective of duration, may increase their prospects of future employment—the "employment occurrence dependence" phenomenon (Moore 2003, 62). Otherwise the disproportionate impact of unemployment on adolescents and young adults, combined with an inability to process feelings of inadequacy in living up to society's expectations, offer fertile ground for sliding into behaviors and actions with untoward consequences. As Robert Merton's strain theory posits: "It is only when a system of cultural values extols, virtually above all else, certain common symbols of success for the population at large while its social structure rigorously restricts or completely eliminates access to approved modes of acquiring these symbols for a considerable part of the same population, that antisocial behavior ensues on a considerable scale" (Merton 1938, 680).

The Picture from Geneva: Youth in Numbers

On January 24, 2012, the Geneva-based ILO released its much-anticipated annual survey, *Global Employment Trends* (International Labour Organization 2012). The report's subtitle, *Preventing a Deeper Jobs Crisis,* is a dead giveaway; its content confirms the foreboding subtitle. The problem is deep. Unless massive effective action is taken, the slide will be only one way: downwards. The report paints a discouraging picture for employment prospects for 2012 and the following four years, based on economic and employment trends since the global financial crisis started in 2007. Worldwide, the current job deficit (the number of jobs needed to employ all those in need of work) is two hundred million, with little sign of improvement. The global unemployment rate is at 6 percent. Youth in the age range of fifteen to twenty-four years are most severely affected; they are three times more likely than adults to be unemployed (International Labour Organization 2012, 33). During 2011, 78.4 million youth were jobless. Since 2009, an estimated 6.4 million have dropped out of the labor market, having lost all hope of finding a job. Regional youth unemployment statistics are equally gloomy. The Middle East and North Africa recorded the highest unemployment rate during 2011 at 26.2 percent and 27.1 percent, respectively. Young women's unemployment rate in North Africa was 41 percent. The job prospects for youth in the developed economies are not much better with unemployment at 17.9 percent (International Labour Organization 2012, 45–47). Despite all the government-supported financial stimulus packages to shore up big banks and major industries, only Germany and Australia managed to increase employment opportunities to precrisis levels. Youth unemployment almost doubled In Ireland, Greece, and Spain during 2011 with Spain's rate at 40 percent. In the developed world, protracted unemployment has dimmed young people's hopes that expensive university degrees would automatically lead to jobs.

In sub-Saharan Africa, many low-income African countries have managed to survive the global economic crisis based on their limited exposure to the global economy (International Labour Organization 2012, 77). But this has not improved their job situation. The employment picture is dismal for most of these countries. In South Africa, one of the region's economic powerhouses, the unemployment rate in 2010 was 24.9 percent. More than half of the economically active youth during that year were jobless. The region's poor labor market performance is attributed to a shift in employment distribution from agriculture to the service sector and technology-based industries where jobs, digitally proficient workers, and supportive infrastructures are limited.

The ILO expects that minimal job creation globally will be a continuing trend. Proposals to help turn the situation around include coordinating global fiscal policies for a more broad-based impact; improving and regulating the global financial system; targeting the real economy to stimulate job growth; and encouraging the private sector to invest (International Labour Organization 2012, 84–87). This is sound advice but the track record for effective global cooperation is discouraging. More likely, additional austerity measures will be implemented without creating much-needed jobs.

What Are Different Parties Doing About the Youth Unemployment Crisis?

The United Nations system has taken active steps and a multifaceted approach to highlight the challenges faced by young people. All UN agencies have mainstreamed youth-focused initiatives in their work with governments and partnerships with the private sector and civil society. Recognizing the double impact of the growing youth population and the jobs crisis, UNICEF has taken the lead in focusing attention on the importance of investing in adolescents to prevent losing the dividend gained from saving lives through early childhood interventions (Ortiz and Cummins 2012). Those whose lives have been saved through childhood vaccinations are now in danger of having their lives made "meaningless" by limited prospects for employment and the associated negative psycho-social consequences of prolonged unemployment including potentially life-threatening risky behavirs. During the July 2011 UN General Assembly's Summit "Youth: Dialogue and Mutual Understanding," the secretary-general noted the many ways in which young people have said that the world they are finding themselves in is not the world they want. He underscored the importance of giving youth an effective voice in matters affecting them contrasted to the high cost of inaction (UN 2011).

The UN member states created the Youth Employment Network within the context of the Millennium Development Goals in 2000. The World Bank and ILO operate in partnership with the UN system to support its work. According to its website, the Youth Employment Network functions as a platform and service provider focusing on policy advice, innovative pilot projects, knowledge sharing, and partnerships, using its core agency partners' know-how and resources to ensure that youth participates in delivering its services. It advances equal employment opportunities for young women and men in recognition that young women face discriminatory policies, structural barriers, and cultural prejudices in the labor market. Youth delegates have access to employers and policy makers attending the annual Youth Employment Summit at the United Nations.

Governments have taken different approaches to survive the economic turmoil but the rewards have been minimal. Few new jobs have been created and many that were available before the crisis are gone. Recognizing that no government has the ability by itself to create sustainable jobs, governments are identifying creative ways to mainstream a youth focus into policies and programs, entering into public-private partnerships to stimulate new job-generating ventures and offering businesses youth-employment-focused incentive schemes (South African National Treasury 2011).

The ILO has issued a practical guide for employers to enhance their understanding of the dynamics associated with the youth unemployment crisis (International Labour Organization, International Training Centre 2011). The guide supplies employers with facts and figures, impact on business operations, success stories, how to use specific perspectives in debates on policy making, and how to effectively integrate young people into the world of work. It reminds employers of the economic benefit they derive from investing in upstream processes to create and hire a cadre of young people with the right skills, knowledge, and experience because such young people earn a livable wage, stimulate the consumption of goods and services through spending, and build capital flow through savings and investing.

What Are the Factors Contributing to Youth Unemployment?

There are undoubtedly not enough jobs. As mentioned earlier, the job deficit is two hundred million. However, youth's significant susceptibility to labor market conditions merits a closer look. Among the multiple reasons there is an evident mismatch between the youthful jobseeker's skill-sets and the employer's expectations. Businesses look for knowledge and skills that are not found in the typical academic curriculum (International Labour Organization, International Training Centre 2011). Soft skills, such as workplace-appropriate behaviors and attitudes, a disciplined work ethic, and the ability to apply theoretical teachings to practical situations, are in much demand. Employers increasingly expect workers to know how to multitask, deal effectively with interpersonal issues, work in teams, negotiate, address customer concerns, and manage complex assignments.

Most educational systems still teach using traditional rote methods. They do not strategically integrate critical thinking, problem solving, self-reliance, and balanced risk-taking skills into the curriculum. In the current lean labor market, these are essential job survival skills. Matters are further complicated by suboptimal integration of theory with structured on-the-job experiential learning, combined with a lack of accurate labor market information about current types of job and their sensitivity to economic fluctuations; remuneration; and future prospects. Without such information supported by appropriate career guidance, students make career choices that do not correlate with labor market realities, a tendency compounded by families' preference for traditional careers in medicine, finance, and law. Less tangible obstacles include lack of sponsoring networks to access internships or suitable work opportunities; suboptimal skills in job searches, curriculum vitae preparation, and interviewing techniques; and an inability to relocate to job-rich places due to financial constraints. However, solutions are built into these challenges.

In 2011 the International Finance Corporation and the Islamic Development Bank issued a report entitled "Education for Employment: Realizing the Arab Youth Potential." The report reflected on the question of academic and vocational career pathways, contrasting the high percentage of Arab youth attending universities (80 percent of postsecondary students) with the high youth unemployment rate (more than 25 percent). Only one-third of job-seekers indicated their education provided them with sufficiently relevant skills to be successful in the workplace. When asked which careers they regard as "most exciting," they chose engineering, medicine, and finance far more than service and vocational jobs (marketing and sales representatives, social workers, health-care technicians, electricians, and car mechanics). Comments indicate students regard vocational jobs as "bad or shameful," which may explain why only 20 percent of Arab secondary school students attend vocational educational training institutions with one- to two- year programs aimed at preparing participants for specific technical and manual occupations. Surveyed employers deemed only one-third of university graduates as "work-ready" for these available types of jobs (International Finance Corporation and Islamic Development Bank 2011, 32).

To alleviate youth unemployment, the report and its sponsors strongly encourage Arab countries to align educational preparedness with the realities of the labor market. The report calls on different players to contribute to this effort from a system perspective. It calls for creating an enabling environment for educational standard setting; funding streams for students; and matchmaking between secondary schools, universities, and employers to support an integrated theoretical and workplace-based experiential learning process. To counteract negative perceptions about vocational training, the report recommends using the media to promote the benefits of a vocational education degree, such as recognition by employers, job availability, a good salary, and career path prospects.

The ILO has also raised concerns about a misalignment between educational tracks, work preparedness, and youth unemployment rates when contrasted against available jobs: "Employers require technicians, but too many young people are choosing an academic education" (International Labour Organization, International Training Centre 2011, 63). It notes that the European Union has experienced dramatic escalation in youth unemployment during the past ten years despite a significant number of unfilled jobs.

"Education for Employment" also discusses a positive example from Latin America. Latin American companies also found that the work readiness of young people was suboptimal (International Finance Corporation and Islamic Development Bank 2011, 52). However, they proactively took steps to collaborate with educational institutions to provide a more balanced mix of theory and practical skills relevant to the labor market: sponsoring industry-specific courses (for example, mining) and offering internships and hiring trainees.

Since technical knowledge constantly evolves, the ILO is advocating "Reflection Learning," a new approach enabling vocational learners to take charge of their own continuous on-the-job-learning, without overdependence on trainers or repeat classroom visits for skills upgrading (Axmann 2004, 7). The ILO's Employment Sector director, Jose Manuel Salazar-Xirinachs, stresses the importance of skills development and training: "Education makes a person trainable, training makes the person employable, and attitude and continuous learning keep the person employed: Education, skills development and lifelong learning are at the center of all innovative and high productivity economies" (International Labour Organization Youth Employment Programme 2011).

Against the Odds: "Youth Making It Happen"

Although adults say they value young people, they use words (immature, impulsive, naïve, reckless) that tend to marginalize and problematize the young. Yet, young people have demonstrated their desire and potential to influence social justice, political ideologies, and larger decision-making processes (Watts and Flanagan 2007) as evidenced by their importance to the U.S. civil rights movement, the antiapartheid struggle, the Arab Spring, and most recently the Occupy Wall Street movement, to name just a few examples. They maintain their interest in community and civic issues when given real responsibility and a say in matters affecting them, along with having their opinions taken seriously. Adults may be more helpful when leading from behind—partnering with young people and finding avenues for dialogue and coaching. Adults can identify and create structural opportunities that provide youth access to people and organizations that offer mentoring, role models, and job opportunities.

There are many examples of young people taking part in community initiatives and opening communication lines between community leaders and marginalized groups. The U.S. Agency for International Development's country profile on Lebanon includes various youth-led initiatives in local matters (traffic and waste management) and broader social issues (racism, discrimination, democracy, and youth advocacy). Lebanese youth often use theater as a form of self-expression and as an interactive tool to mobilize discussion on sensitive issues in their communities (U.S. Agency for International Development 2011). Fatima Abu Said, a young Lebanese actor, had this to say: "Youth should start by changing themselves. We should believe in our capacities and unite our efforts. Just like wooden sticks, you cannot break them if they are assembled."

South Africa's disadvantaged black youth have taken this approach for many decades. United in their efforts, they played a critical role in removing the stranglehold of the apartheid system, a system that used discrimination to ensure that the education of most black children prepared them only for menial jobs. Then and now, with the educational system still struggling to find a solid foothold, young people have continued to find ways to make contributions to society, seeking outlets for their creative energies and promoting collaborative training and job creation with the public and private sectors. Success stories abound about young black South Africans who strove against the odds to make it in this world (Buthelezi 2011). Others yearn for long-denied quality education, for which many died during the struggle against apartheid. In January 2012 hundreds of students waited in long lines to register for admission at an oversubscribed college. When the gates opened, the students stampeded to get in. They crushed someone to death and injured many others in their quest to claim what they thought should be available: a higher education offering the opportunity to progress beyond societal and structural limitations (Polgreen 2012). The minister of education conceded the dire shortage of seats in public universities, but noted that thousands of seats were available at vocational training institutions. In an interview one student expressed skepticism about the value that employers attach to such a qualification, an observation reminiscent of the Arab youth report. This reaffirms the need to publicize the value and relevance of vocational training to students, institutions of learning, parents, and employers. With more than 50 percent of South African youth unemployed, this is long overdue.

A transferrable example of multipartner collaboration is the Community and Individual Development Association's establishment of an almost-free university in Johannesburg. The university provides a fully accredited bachelor of business administration degree emphasizing entrepreneurship (Community and Individual Development Association 2006). It targets disadvantaged students who receive intensive academic coaching and engage in experiential learning. Students design microenterprises and pursue structured internships, which are required to graduate. The efforts have paid off. Before entering this program, most of these students would never before have heard of a stock exchange, yet they posted the highest scores in the National Stock Exchange Exams on such subjects as bonds, equities, and the regulation of financial markets. CIDA facilitates work placements; most graduates are currently employed at notable financial firms and blue chip multinational companies.

Youth Empowerment Through the Arts

Life's challenges can inspire creativity. South Africa's vibrant art community has used the power of prose, poetry, music, and dance to speak of resilience under apartheid, aspirations during the postapartheid societal transformation, and survival strategies needed to live in a globalized village where international economic forces keep jobs and opportunities at bay. The misery of politics, unemployment, and employment, and the way in which that misery affects individuals, families, and communities have received their fair share of attention on the stage, with stories built around familiar characters such as:

"The Mother" rushing off in the predawn hours to take care of "the Madam" and her children while reluctantly leaving her own parent-bereft children to fend for themselves in a survival-of-the-fittest setting;

"The Father" existing on odd jobs doled out and withdrawn at the pleasure of "the Boss," leaving him without the dignity that society has determined can only be acquired through a paying job.

The family's story is often portrayed through a youth lens showcasing young people's efforts to fashion a life beyond the chains of politics, poverty, violence, joblessness, and parents absent by necessity. An exquisite example is the musical *Sarafina!* that originated in the Market Theater in Johannesburg, had 597 performances on Broadway, and became a film success, with both the young female lead actor and the production nominated for Tony awards in several categories (Maslin 1992). The storytelling has continued, encouraged by local, national, and international structures.

With appropriate guidance, youth participation in the arts, culture, and sports provides an opportunity for personal evolution and local socioeconomic development, thus contributing to vibrant, self-reliant, and healthy communities. Exemplifying this approach, the South African Department of Arts and Culture entered into a partnership arrangement with the National Youth Development Agency in January 2012 to support young South Africans who have an interest in the field of arts and culture (South African National Youth Development Agency 2012a). The Trendsetter Initiative is a twelve-month apprenticeship and trade skills-building program created to improve young people's employability in the arts, culture, and heritage sector. Apprentices are recruited from community art centers and given basic training in the visual and performing arts, along with advanced training in project and financial management, personal development, and other life skills. Each Trendsetter is expected to recruit and mentor fifteen other interested youth, thus creating a self-sustaining outreach network. The program facilitates employment opportunities through collaborative public-private partnerships. Many of the fruits of this initiative are still to come but it is safe to say that it has much potential.

Private citizens have created ventures that constructively channel despondent youth's artistic expression and nurture self-discovery. The Bokamoso Youth Center in destitute Winterveld in South Africa offers three-month programs that help build the mostly out-of-school youth's life skills including leadership and entrepreneurial initiative (Bokamoso Youth Foundation website, http://www.bokamosoyouth.org). Through a collaborative partnership St. Andrew's Episcopal School and George Washington University, both located in Washington, DC, cultural exchanges with the United States allow the young artists to reflect on their lives through original poetry, plays, and traditional songs and dances (George Washington University 2012). They shared the hardships they face and the opportunities they create to survive in a February 2012 performance of their play, *Take off the Masks,* at George Washington University. GWU professor of theater Leslie Jacobson, who has worked with the Bokamoso Youth Center since 2003, expressed the value of this effort: "Performance is both a way to build confidence and self-esteem for these young men and women who often feel forgotten and voiceless and a way of giving respect and honor to their culture. The acts of helping to create and perform these plays about the challenges in their community allow the youth to model behavior that can promote change, as well as exposing behavior that is self-destructive. Audiences learn through watching these situations and modeled behaviors as well" (George Washington University 2012).

The theme of building hope through acting resonates in many other initiatives throughout South Africa. According to its website, the Lalela Project in the Western Cape aims to empower children and adolescents through art. It offers interactive community-relevant art curricula to at-risk youth during the after-school and weekend hours, engaging them in the art of creative thinking, problem solving, and self-expression. It also finds innovative ways to guide their educational and career paths, having established partnerships with a number of corporations that offer internships to high school students. The Lalela Project provides a safe haven during those vulnerable after-school and holiday hours, guiding students away from falling prey to substance abuse, gang violence, and health risks. It has also reached out to thousands more students through a partnership with the South African National Gallery by distributing guided lessons about current museum exhibits to schools in disadvantaged communities. Additional opportunities have been created to exhibit the students' artwork and get others interested in art and culture through partnerships with the Cape Town Jazz Festival, a mural photography initiative focusing on social awareness, and a youth center focusing on HIV/AIDS prevention strategies.

Sport as a Social Change Catalyst

The popularity of soccer (called football in many countries) across the global South and Europe has given it a reputation of having the power to unite different cultures and age groups; cut across gender barriers; promote an understanding of rule-based decision making; and teach about tolerance, peacemaking, and dealing with defeat. The hosts of the 2006 and 2010 World Cup, Germany and South Africa, recognized soccer's value to educate. They entered into a five-year collaborative partnership, Youth Development through Football (Youth Development through Football 2012; Deutsche Gesellschaft für Internationale Zusammenarbeit 2012). The project demonstrates the potential of sport as a vehicle to teach adolescents and young adults enduring skills when it is systematically incorporated into existing processes of social change. The carefully coordinated strategy involves the German Ministry for Economic and Cooperation Development, the South African Department of Sport and Recreation, schools, sports coordinators, artists, and NGOs already involved in community-building initiatives. The concept shows instructors and youth coaches how to integrate social competencies into the game of soccer and emphasizes the coaches' role-modeling responsibility to the players.

To date, education and training initiatives targeting health, environmental management, and social engagement have reached thousands of in- and out-of-school youth: youth soccer leagues have been established; more than one hundred instructors are disseminating the message of sport as a tool for youth development; and five hundred youth coaches (many formerly unemployed) serve as role models for the groups they train. They receive a stipend for their efforts. Two NGOs have tapped into the creative skills of youth, using the performing arts as a platform to spread the word about the socially transformative power of soccer. The project's sustainability has been boosted by being integrated into existing government-supported youth development initiatives, subjected to regular monitoring and evaluation, and adapted to local needs. The National Youth Development Agency, on behalf of the millions of distressed youth in South Africa, is lobbying Parliament and government to recognize the value of collaborative partnerships as an essential tool for youth development (South African National Youth Development Agency 2012b). Clearly, these partnerships provide part of the solution to helping young people acquire the knowledge and skill to survive life's challenges (including unemployment) while encouraging job creation.

Conclusion

Youth unemployment statistics are staggering and require urgent structured interventions by all relevant parties to reignite hope among despairing young persons. The good news is that young people have joined the search for solutions, assertively seeking a voice and participation in decision-making structures at international and local levels. They are also promoting problem solving through collaborative partnerships. They have identified creative outlets to channel their frustrations and aspirations, simultaneously using these avenues to fill knowledge and skill gaps, and as a transition to self-reliance and community strengthening. Youth must be included in the discussion of potential solutions, along with parties that can create jobs and provide the enabling environments to help young people acquire employable and survival life skills for a positive future. Finding the right balance in preparing learners with the necessary theoretical and practical know-how for "life after school" is a priority and necessitates cross-sector participation in collaborations that all interested parties can readily participate in.

Efforts to address youth unemployment require a systems-based approach to manage the intersecting dynamics that affect employment, as other contributors to this volume point out. These dynamics include global economic forces that create and decimate jobs; regulatory factors impacting the labor market; the supply and demand chain for jobs; the opportunities and exclusivity presented by new discoveries including the digital environment; and challenges with political, economic, and sociocultural factors affecting families' access to effective education systems that adequately prepare their children for work and life.

Effectively addressing unemployment will require not only system-based approaches to problem solving but also a repositioning of economies, along with sustainable and innovative job creation efforts. These are not easy tasks. When we as individuals and communities feel overwhelmed by the challenges that unemployment present, we may gain sustenance from a wise man, locked away for life for his beliefs, who regained his freedom after almost three decades through his own unwavering principled approach to life, supported by local and global collaborative partnerships efforts. This is an approach worth emulating in unshackling young people from the chains of unemployment.

> I have walked that long road to freedom. I have tried not to falter; I have made missteps along the way. But I have discovered the secret that after climbing a great hill, one only finds that there are many more hills to climb. I have taken a moment here to rest, to steal a view of the glorious vista that surrounds me, to look back on the distance I have come. But I can rest only for a moment, for with freedom comes responsibilities, and I dare not linger, for my long walk is not ended.
>
> Nelson Mandela (1994, 625)

Note

1. Concept derived from a framework for global health dynamics developed by Professor Sue Goldie, director of the Harvard Global Health Institute (2012), personal communication.

References

Axmann, Michael. 2004. "Facilitating Labour Market Entry for Youth Through Enterprise-Based Schemes in Vocational Education and Training and Skills Development." Geneva: International Labour Organization. http://www.ilo.org/youth makingithappen/pdf/wp48-2004.pdf.

Buthelezi. 2011. "From a Tiny Shack to the Big Apple." Timeslive. Accessed January 4, 2014. http://www.timeslive.co.za/local/article964195.ece/From-a-tiny-shack-to-the-Big-Apple.

Community and Individual Development Association. 2006. "Welcome to CIDA City Campus, Africa's First Virtually Free University." Accessed July 31, 2012. http://www.cidafoundationuk.org/assets/cms/files/1/1192107376_AboutCIDA2006.pdf.

Deutsche Gesellschaft für Internationale Zusammenarbeit. 2012. "Youth Development Scores a Goal." Accessed December 11, 2012. http://www.giz.de/themen/en/24660.htm#.

Friel, Brian. 2003. "The Big Picture." *Government Executive*, October 1. Accessed July 31, 2012. http://www.govexec.com/magazine/2003/10/the-big-picture/15197.

George Washington University. 2012. "Latest Collaboration Between Professor of Theatre Leslie Jacobson and the Bokamoso Youth Centre Premieres Friday." *GW Today*, February 1. http://gwtoday.gwu.edu/south-african-youth-perform-gw.

International Finance Corporation and Islamic Development Bank. 2011. "Education for Employment: Realizing Arab Youth Potential." http://www.e4earabyouth.com.

International Labour Organization. 2012. "Global Employment Trends 2012: Preventing a Deeper Jobs Crisis." Accessed July 31, 2012. http://www.ilo.org/global/publications/books/global-employment-trends/WCMS_171571/lang-en/index.htm.

International Labour Organization, International Training Centre. 2011. "An Introductory Guide for Employers' Organizations: Tackling Employment Challenges." Turin, Italy: International Training Centre. http://www.ilo.org/public/english/dialogue/actemp/downloads/projects/youth/tackling_ye_guide_en.pdf.

International Labour Organization, Youth Employment Programme. 2011. "Youth Employment: Making It Happen." Accessed December 12, 2012. www.ilo.org/youthmakingithappen/home.htm.

Mandela, Nelson. 1994. *Long Walk to Freedom: The Autobiography of Nelson Mandela*. New York: Little, Brown and Company.

Maslin, Janet. 1992. "Sarafina! Torture and Hope in a Clash." *New York Times*, September 18.

Merton, Robert. 1938. "Social Structure and Anomie." *American Sociological Review*, 3, no. 5: 672–82. As quoted in Eric Pelser, "Learning to Be Lost: Youth Crime in South Africa," discussion paper presented at the HSRC Youth Policy Initiative, Cape Town, South Africa, 2008. Accessed January 4, 2014. www.cjcp.org.za/articlesPDF/70/HSRC-Youth-Crime-Discussion-Paper.pdf

Moore, Jack. 2003. "Long-term Consequences of Youth Unemployment." Undergraduate economics thesis, Stanford University. http://economics.stanford.edu/undergraduate/current-major/honors-program/honors-theses-2003.

National Education Association. 2011. "Request for Regulatory Relief for K-12 Schools." Letter to U.S. Department of Education, May 27. Accessed July 31, 2012. www.nea.org/assets/docs/o05-27-11_NEA_regulatory_relief_letter.pdf

Obama, Barack. 2007. "Remarks to the National Education Association Annual Meeting in Philadelphia." July 5. Accessed July 31, 2012. http://www.presidency.ucsb.edu/ws/index.php?pid=77006.

Ortiz, Isabel, and Matthew Cummins. 2012. "When the Global Crisis and Youth Bulge Collide: Double the Jobs Trouble for Youth." Social and Economic Policy Working Paper, February. New York: UNICEF. http://www.unicef.org/socialpolicy/files/Global_Crisis_and_Youth_Bulge_-_FINAL.pdf.

Polgreen, Lydia. 2012. "Fatal Stampede in South Africa Points Up University Crisis." *New York Times*, January 10. http://www.nytimes.com/2012/01/11/world/africa/stampede-highlights-crisis-at-south-african-universities.html.

Ravitch, Diane. 2012. "NCLB: The Death Star of American Education." *Bridging Differences* (blog), January 10, 2012. Sponsored by *Education Week*. Accessed December 12, 2012. http://blogs.edweek.org/edweek/Bridging-Differences/2012/01/nclb_the_death_star_of_america.html.

Robinson, Jenny Perlman. 2011. "A Global Compact on Learning: Taking Action on Education in Developing Countries." Washington, D.C.: Center for Universal Education, Brookings Institution. Accessed July 31, 2012. http://www.brookings.edu/reports/2011/0609_global_compact.aspx.

Senge, Peter M. 1990. *The Fifth Discipline: The Art and Practice of the Learning Organization*. New York: Doubleday.

South African National Treasury. 2011. "Confronting Youth Unemployment: Policy Options for South Africa." Discussion paper for public comment. Accessed July 31, 2012. http://www.treasury.gov.za/documents/national budget/2011/Confronting Youth Unemployment-Policyoptions.pdf.

South African National Youth Development Agency. 2012a. "NYDA Promotes Career Guidance Through Ster-Kinekor Cinemas." February 14. Accessed July 31, 2012. www.nyda.gov.za/index.php? . . . nyda . . . career-guidance . . . ster-kinekor.

———. 2012b. "NYDA Presentation to the Standing Committee on Appropriations: NYDA 5 Year Strategic Plan and Annual Performance Plan." May 2. Accessed July 31, 2012. d2zmx6mlqh7g3a.cloudfront.net/cdn/farfuture/mtime:1336555448/files/docs/120502nydastrat_0.pdf.

Sum, Andrew, and Joseph McLaughlin. 2011. "The Steep Decline in Teen Summer Employment in the U.S., 2000–2010, and the Summer 2011 Teen Job Market Disaster: Another Bummer Summer." Boston: Center for Labor Market Studies, Northeastern University. Accessed July 31, 2012. http://www.northeastern.edu/clms/wp-content/uploads/Teen-Summer-2011-Job-Market-August.pdf.

Symonds, William C., Robert B. Schwartz, and Ronald Ferguson. 2011. *Pathways to Prosperity: Meeting the Challenge of Preparing Young Americans for the 21st Century*. Pathways to Prosperity Project report, February. Cambridge, Mass.: Harvard Graduate School of Education. http://www.gse.harvard.edu/news_events/features/2011/Pathways_to_Prosperity_Feb2011.pdf.

UN High Level Meeting on Youth. 2011. "Youth: Dialogue and Mutual Understanding." Accessed July 31, 2012. http://www.un.org/sg/statements/?nid=5432.

U.S. Agency for International Development. 2011. "Snapshot: Providing a Stage for Youth Advocacy." July. USAID Transition Initiatives: Lebanon webpage. Accessed December 12, 2012. http://transition.usaid.gov/our_work/cross-cutting_programs/transition_initiatives/country/lebanon2/topic0711.html.

US Department of Education, (2012) "*New Data from U.S. Department of Education Highlights Educational Inequities Around Teacher Experience, Discipline and High School Rigor;*" http://www.ed.gov/news/press-releases/new-data-us-department-education-highlights-educational-inequities-around-teache; March 6, 2012.

Watts, Roderick J., and Constance Flanagan. 2007. "Pushing the Envelope on Youth Civic Engagement: A Developmental and Liberation Psychology Perspective." *Journal of Community Psychology* 35, no. 6 (August): 779–92.

Youth Development through Football. 2012. Website for joint project between the Department of Sport and Recreation South and Deutsche Gesellschaft für Internationale Zusammenarbeit. Accessed July 31, 2012. http://www.za-ydf.org/pages/home/.

CHAPTER 14

Confined by Narrow Choices: The Stories of Roma Adolescents

Margareta Matache and David Mark

Roma adolescents in Romania get excited or gloomy; they fall in love; they are fans of football teams, singers, and actors like any other adolescent. But, their lives differ dramatically from their non-Roma peers. Lower participation in secondary and tertiary education, stigmatization, higher rates of poverty, lack of access to the Internet and social media, discrimination in public places (pubs, clubs, and so forth), and higher health risks (especially for Roma girls) are all phenomena that affect and ultimately define the worldview and experience of many Roma adolescents. This chapter discusses the determinants of Roma adolescents' opportunities and choices in Romania, looking at their daily challenges and at their developmental environment at home, within the community, at school, or in society.

The Roma are a very heterogeneous ethnic group, with communities often based on kinship or bloodline and structured according to ancestral heritage, traditional crafts, and occupation. Social structure, customs, and celebrations are common to the various groups defined by the Roma identity. Worldwide there are more than fourteen million Roma or people in Roma-related groups (known by names such as Sinti, Gypsie, Gens due voyage, Travellers). Most Roma, about ten to twelve million, live in Europe (European Commission 2011). Romania is the country with the largest Roma population, with about one and a half to two million Roma. However, even in Romania, a country of twenty-one million people, they are still an ethnic minority. Adolescents between ten and nineteen years old (the official UNICEF definition of adolescence) represent almost one-fourth of the Roma population (National Institute of Statistics Romania 2012), part of the first generation to be born and grow up in the young Romanian democracy. Romanian Roma are composed of various subgroups, with varying degrees of assimilation.

Roma: A Traumatized People

Historical events created the foundation for the inequalities faced nowadays by Roma adolescents. Slavery has had a major effect on generations. The predecessors of the Romanian state, the principalities of Walachia and Moldova, enslaved the Roma population from 1385 to 1856 (Fraser 1995). Often, entire villages were bought and sold.

Slavery has had a very significant impact on the social structures of the Roma, especially on the Roma family, which was not perceived as a community structure, but rather as a means to increase the number of slaves. Roma girls and women at a fertile age were called "breeding females" (Grigore, Neacsu, and Furtuna 2007). Roma families were torn apart through the sale of individual members. Separated from their parents, both boys and girls were exploited for labor, and girl adolescents were often subjected to sexual abuse by the "owners."

Roma slavery ended after almost five hundred years, but it was not followed by policies, programs, or measures aimed at diminishing the inequalities and deprivations caused by the legacy of slavery. The prolonged period of slavery defines the beginnings of the Roma presence and the starting point of continuing inequality in relation to ownership of property, income generation, education, health, and the protection of family and culture in the territory of the Romanian principalities. The history of slavery has also contributed greatly to the perception of Roma as an inferior ethnic group.

Another seminal point in the history of the Roma community in Romania is the Holocaust. The Romanian state under the pro-Nazi administration of Marshal Antonescu initiated the deportation of Roma people in June 1942 (Wiesel Commission 2004). Families were forced to leave their homes, moved to concentration compounds, and then transported to the barren lands in the border region of Transnistria. Deportations and restriction of movement led to the extermination of thousands of Roma people through starvation, malnutrition, diseases, and exposure to harsh weather (Wiesel Commission 2004; Petcut n.d.). The Roma orphans who returned from Transnistria had been exposed to malnutrition and were affected by disease, as well as depression and anxiety and other vulnerabilities. Under the subsequent communist regime they did not benefit from any postdeportation measures aimed at improving their health and their social and emotional development or leading to their reintegration into society.

In the second half of the twentieth century, the policy of Romania's communist government regarding the Roma changed to one of forced assimilation. The Roma were considered a group with complex social issues, rather than a distinct ethnic minority. Consequently, they were treated like working-class communities in Romania. Most urban Roma were enrolled as unqualified workers in industrial plants and factories while those from the rural areas were integrated into centralized agricultural collectives.

Although officially there was no discrimination in schools, Roma youth continued to be treated differently by teachers and staff. Roma children were largely ignored, placed at the back of the classroom, and routinely mistreated. Some Roma continued education in vocational schools or graduated high school but very few went on to study in universities or colleges. Those who did and moved up the social ladder did so by renouncing their identity, avoiding the stigma associated with being Roma, and, in essence, reacting to the conscious assimilation policy of the state (Marushiakova and Popov n.d.).

The wider effects of those oppressive and assimilationist policies are still reflected in the denial of ethnic identity by many Roma families, including adolescents, nowadays. Young children and adolescents learn to deny their ethnicity from their elders who experienced the Holocaust and, unfortunately, from their own negative experiences interacting directly with their peers and teachers, and indirectly with mass media and the values promoted in society.

These historical elements constitute the foundation for the dismal situation of the present-day Roma (including adolescents); they can also constitute the basis for envisioning more appropriate policies. Building fair integration policies implies, in our opinion, taking into account the exploitative and oppressive state policies that led to the current inequalities. Improving and extending existing reparatory actions (affirmative action in high schools and universities) should be considered as fair and just intervention rather than an injustice done to the majority or a special benefit awarded to Roma by the state.

Ethnic Identity Under the Influence of Stigmatization

The social and emotional development of adolescence relies not only on the biological processes described in earlier chapters but also on other factors, including the behavior and attitudes of those they interact with—parents, adults, peers around them—and, from a broader perspective, the contexts they live in. The social and emotional development of Roma adolescents is therefore closely connected to their relationships with peers and non-Roma people. How the latter choose to relate to them, treating them with (or without) prejudice, generates (or prevents) a lack of confidence and the feeling of inferiority.

Across the centuries a large set of stereotypical generalizations about the Roma have been constructed. These pose, even today, a real obstacle for understanding Roma communities and Roma culture. Criminality, lack of interest in education—these are stereotypes that more than 72 percent of the Romanian population share about Roma (National Council for Combating Discrimination 2009). Even though few if any have had tense interactions with Roma, 45 percent of Romanians believe Roma to be aggressive (National Council for Combating Discrimination 2012).

A recent video project documents what Bucharest high schoolers think about the Roma and, in the process, illustrates some frequent stereotypes. The following are some excerpts from statements of Roma and non-Roma adolescents concerning widespread images of Roma.[1]

A common stereotype is that all Roma marry off their children early, while still virgins, and that they practically sell them, as two different teenagers report: "Of what I know, Roma sell their daughters in marriage," and, "A well-behaved Roma girl stays a virgin until the age of 18 or until she marries" (Petri and Serban 2011).

Another idea is that the Roma are lazy and do not want to integrate into society. Some adolescents share this opinion: "There are Roma who have an ugly character," or "There are Roma who go in France and Italy and steal" (Petri and Serban 2011). According to an opinion poll conducted in 2012 (National Council for Combating Discrimination 2012), 46 percent of Romanians share the opinion that Roma are lazy. Although the reality of Roma poverty is very visible and demonstrated through research studies, many Romanians believe that Roma are rich and have villas. One of the young girls interviewed said, "You know that most Roma are well off . . . with a lot of small towers on their houses."

These perceptions become strong determinants in Roma adolescents' lives, influencing the development of their social and emotional skills. Surrounded by negative prejudice, lacking positive examples of Roma who declare their ethnicity, Roma adolescents and children lack models to look up to. Adolescent victims of prejudice have their own reactions, feelings, and protective strategies.

Lighter-skinned Roma, as well as Roma who are able to hide easily identifiable specific Roma cultural markers, will often hide their ethnic identity to avoid the stigma and related disadvantages. Some even develop anti-Roma discourse and attitudes. This strategy plays into the nature of stereotypes that associate Roma with darker skin, traditional "gypsy" clothing, uncleanliness, and linguistic deficiencies. As a teacher in a focus group reports, "When in school, they [Roma children] change the situation. We love them, we help them, yet, in the school, their skin color begins to count; children begin to separate, Roma are marginalized, no one wants to share the desk with them" (Mark and Matache 2010a).

Many Roma adolescents shut down and avoid their peers, preferring life within the Roma community. Roma adolescents become adults with inferiority complexes as a result of dealing with ostracism, and may also hide their ethnic identity, as this former student explains: "Eight years in the primary and middle school I suffered a lot because, as I was the only Roma pupil there, the other children couldn't stand me. The day I would be handed the flower crown at the end of the year awards ceremony, as it was the custom back then, I think I was the saddest girl in the whole room because when I got on stage no one would applaud me. Because of this, during the following four high school years I hid the fact that I was Roma" (Surdu, Vincze, and Wamsiedel 2011).

Some others make huge efforts to integrate: "I am a Roma child and I am proud of it! I get along very well with my mom my dad and my teacher. I like to have many friends, and I do have many, not only Roma, Romanians as well. I talk nicely with all the people, it does not matter if they are like me, that is if they are Roma or Romanians" (Mark and Matache 2010b) or, "I was ashamed to say I am gypsy, but not anymore" (Mark and Matache 2010b).

And finally, others cannot take the pressure and choose to skip classes or to drop out, unable to cope with the preconceptions and negative attitudes of Romanian peers or teachers. The phenomenon is especially noticeable in the case of Roma adolescents who attend high school through affirmative action measures and therefore can easily be identified as Roma and are treated as such. They often become very isolated or depressed. Although the affirmative action program is designed to create equal opportunities, in many situations it generates negative effects because neither high school staff nor students are informed about and prepared to handle cultural differences.

Little attention is given to trying to change perceptions and to diminishing prejudices held against Roma. Without public policies to combat prejudice, the stigmatization continues and is perpetuated, and there are risks that the underlying conflict will escalate. Structural changes in educational policies, as well as broadly in the values of the Romanian society, are needed.

Romanian schools could contribute more to help Roma youth. The school system remains very monoculturally centered. It still does not encourage cultural diversity, acceptance, or respect for the values of those who may be different. It has a negative impact on the development of children belonging to a different group, especially a socially excluded one: "The kids would always call her nigger and gypsy and, at some point, she came home and said, 'I am not going to school anymore . . . rub me harder to make me whiter'" (Mark and Matache 2010b). Many incidents like this occur between Roma adolescents and their non-Roma peers or teachers.

Social and Economic Determinants in Roma Adolescents' Choices and Access to Education

A significant proportion—39 percent—of Romanian Roma adolescents over eleven years old do not enroll in school, compared to 9 percent of for their non-Roma peers. Only 9 percent of young Roma have secondary education and 2 percent tertiary education, compared with 41 percent and 27 percent, respectively, of the majority population (Fleck and Rughinis 2008). The Roma's status as a marginalized minority group, with all that entails—poverty, exposure to discrimination, the minor investment of the state in policies supportive of the Roma, some cultural practices and taboos different from the majority population, lack of support or empathy from the majority population—contributes to lower participation in education and fewer opportunities in life.

Sixty percent of Roma Romanian communities live in poverty and 23 percent of Roma communities lack adequate access to electricity or drinking water, or both (Sandu 2005). Although Romania is considered a developed country as a member of the European Union, many Roma adolescents, regardless of the Roma subgroup they belong to, share some of the characteristics and the challenges of adolescents belonging to families with very low socio-economic status from developing countries. Aside from low income, other factors prevent the access of Roma to education, factors that are common to other marginalized communities discussed in this book.

As most of the high schools and universities are in the big cities, lack of necessary resources such as transport or accommodation, decreases the participation of poor Roma (and Romanians living in rural areas). Families without hope for secondary education for their children do not invest their time and resources in the educational performance of their children, starting with primary school. The rationale is simple: If the children will not continue to high school, why they should try to do well in primary school? However, in those Roma families where for the first time children have studied at a higher level, the family's economic status improves as does the participation of younger siblings in the education system: this generation becomes one of the agents for social mobility.

The poverty of Roma families drives adolescents to work, and consequently to drop out of school. Both boys and girls are involved in work inside or outside the house, helping their parents or raising their smaller siblings. More than half of parents who have children who dropped out of schools stated that the respective child was doing occasional or frequent work in the household and almost a quarter declared that they were working outside the household (Surdu, Vincze, and Wamsiedel 2011). Roma adolescents become income providers for the families. Many of them make the sacrifice of giving up school, fully conscious of the consequences for themselves as individuals, but aware of the family constraints and needs. Their early transition to adulthood is precipitated by these factors.

More than half of the Roma families have members who go to sleep hungry at least once per month (Fleck and Rughinis 2008). But even in these socioeconomic conditions, the percentage of Roma adolescents enrolled in higher education has been increasing over the past ten years, from 6 percent to 9 percent in high schools and from 0.2 percent to 2 percent in universities (Surdu and Szira 2009). Many of these first-generation students find inner resources, power, resilience and motivation to cope with the challenges. A teenager sums up some of the issues: "My name is Letitia and I belong to a large family. I have 6 brothers, 5 go to school, one is of preschool age, a toddler. I live together with my family in the Roma community in a house made of clay with a kitchen and a room. My father is a day worker and my mom takes care of my brother. My elder sister, Melinda, helps my mom. Our only source of income is the student allowance and the social aid. I try to learn well, to become a music teacher" (Mark and Matache 2010b).

The low level of education of parents and of previous generations has a negative impact on the participation of Roma youth in education. The intergenerational transmission of poverty and lack of education in the case of Roma is highlighted by the fact that 23.1 percent of Roma parents who did not attend school at all declared that their own parents did not go to school either (Surdu, Vincze, and Wamsiedel 2011); another 48.8 percent cited economic reasons (poverty) as the main cause of their children dropping out of school. Behind these numbers there are stories of parents who do not own any books following a pattern set by their parents or grandparents. These parents may not notice the meaning of motivating their children to read regularly. There are parents who cannot afford to buy a pair of shoes for their children so that they can go to school just as their own parents could not provide basic goods for them (Matache 2012). Many Roma youngsters remain stuck between the intergenerational and intragenerational transmission of poverty and lack of education.

A significant number of Roma parents have very low expectations regarding the future career path of their children: more than a quarter of the parents interviewed in a study conducted by Roma Center for Social Intervention and Studies- Romani CRISS, a leading Romanian Roma nonprofit organization, declared that they would like their children to become drivers /mechanics (Surdu, Vincze, and Wamsiedel 2011) or another type of manual laborer. These low career path expectations for Roma adolescents are an indicator of how families have internalized the stigma and the idea of "Roma inferiority." With such expectations, the fight against the perpetuation of economic and social deprivation in Roma communities becomes very difficult, especially when these young adolescents and their parents lack role models that could guide and motivate them and show them that it is possible for Roma to be successful.

Structural discrimination in education is a major concern for Roma youth; it often takes the form of *de facto* segregation. The educational opportunities in segregated Romani schools are much lower than those provided in mainstream schools (Surdu, Vincze, and Wamsiedel 2011). In Roma primary schools, for example, teachers' absenteeism is higher than in non-Roma schools (Surdu 2012). The schools where Roma learn are poorly equipped; they often lack laboratories for physics, chemistry, biology, or computer science. Lower quality of education, poor infrastructure, insufficient investment by local authorities, and lower quality of teaching are all phenomena that hinder the ability of Romani youth to develop their skills, knowledge, and abilities. It also reduces their chances to attend high school or universities.

One program for increasing the access to education for Roma adolescents is the affirmative action program for higher education, introduced in 1992 at the initiative of the Romanian Ministry of Education and the University of Bucharest. The program reserved places for Roma candidates for tertiary education at the Faculty of Sociology and Social Work. A few years later the program was extended to a larger number of tertiary education institutions. In 1998, the program was expanded to select secondary education institutions and in 2000 to the entire secondary education system (Surdu and Szira 2009). Two reserved places per class are allocated at the secondary education level. During the 2000–2006 period, 10,300 Roma students were enrolled in secondary and vocational education on subsidized places for Roma people, and 1,420 students benefited from education in universities (Surdu and Szira 2009). This institutional program was supported by scholarships and mentorship programs offered by several foundations.

Roma Adolescents and Migration

Another aspect worth discussing in relation to Roma adolescents is the participation of Roma in Europeanization, namely the mobility of Roma within the EU borders.

The mobility of young Roma is on the increase for a range of reasons. These include socioeconomic pressures, including financial debt, the daily pressures of discrimination and stigmatization, the absence of viable employment options as a result of their lack of appropriate skills and qualifications, the pursuit of opportunities fueled by the dream of higher incomes as for many other young people described in this volume, and finally, the power of example. Like other young people, Roma adolescents have discovered that exercising their European citizenship rights can lead to new possibilities; they see the apparently successful outcomes of migration decisions taken by their peers and aspire to similar Western European success.

Although the Roma are generally not connected to global means of communications such as the Internet and satellite TV, news of better opportunities flows fast in close-knit Roma communities. Young people learn or imagine that life "outside" is better. The exploitation of this phenomenon by trafficking networks is a major concern. Often, young Roma become victims of criminal or trafficking networks, involved in begging (sometimes linked to debt bondage), prostitution, and forced labor (European Roma Rights Center 2011).

The consequences of migration for Roma adolescents can be seen as both positive and negative, depending on the context and the influences exerted by different factors. These include the existence of qualifications and skills, the presence of another member of the family in the country of destination, the presence of accompanying parents, knowledge of the local language, enrollment in school, employment of other members of the family who accompany the adolescent, relations with local NGOs, institutions, and type of residential accommodation available. Roma adolescent migrants living in irregular camps face multiple disadvantages compared to those able to secure rental accommodation within the destination town or city.

The outcome of the migration experience for young Roma migrants is therefore quite mixed. Some benefit from migration, where for example their parents find jobs and they are able to access better and safer schools. One recent success story presented by the mass media is that of Anina, a girl who left Romania together with her family when she was nine years old. Although she was supposed to have a certain level of educational proficiency at that age, her Romanian school experience had left her functionally illiterate. Moving to France with her family changed her educational path. After some years in the French school system, she was admitted to the prestigious University of Sorbonne (B1 TV 2012). Our fieldwork shows examples of Roma children and adolescents enrolled in French and Italian schools who performed better than they would have done in their home countries, learned the local language, and later integrated in those societies (Mark and Matache 2006, 2008, 2010a, 2010c).

At the other extreme are the situations of adolescents living in "camps" or in unsafe environments, lacking protection and rights. Their chances to benefit from good health decrease to the extent that they lack good shelter, access to drinking water, access to a family doctor, and sometimes even access to education. The risks increase in these locations. During the past years, there have been some tragic events involving Roma adolescents from Romania who travel to wealthier EU countries. Consider the story of Marioara Rostas, an eighteen-year-old Roma girl who traveled to Ireland. She had fourteen siblings and an extremely poor family, and ended up begging on the streets of Dublin. One day, having been offered a McDonald's burger, she got into a fancy car and ended up raped and killed (Cusack 2012). Marioara's death remains a tragic example of the dangers that many Roma adolescents face.

There are also cases of Roma adolescents who accompany their parents to western EU countries and back to Romania as part of a so-called seasonal migration, several times per year. This migration pattern makes it impossible for the adolescents to enroll in school, particularly in Romania, where the system is rigid, particularly with regard to Roma students (Mark and Matache 2010c).

Another aspect of the migration phenomenon is the case of young Roma adolescents who remain at home while their parents travel abroad. Although there is no systematic data on the phenomenon of left behind Roma children, a study on Romanian migration reveals that migration, when children are left at home, has negative effects on their educational outcomes and on their emotional and social behavior (Fundatia Soros Romania 2007).

Vulnerability of Roma Girls

Not unlike the case of Indian girls discussed elsewhere in this volume, Roma girls' health and maternal mortality rates are highly influenced by socioeconomic factors (such as poverty and inadequate nutrition) as well as by cultural models (early marriage, early childbirth) and discriminatory access to health care. Pregnant girls, especially those who become pregnant at a very early age, face considerable health risks. The age of women at first birth is less than eighteen years of age for 55 percent of Roma women, compared to 14 percent for non-Roma Romanian women (Matache 2012).

Lack of access to information and insufficient family planning expose many Roma women to greater risk (Fleck and Rughinis 2008). There is no data available on the number of Roma adolescents seeking abortions. However, UNICEF underlines that throughout the world many girls use this method due to the lack of resources, lack of contraception, or lack of information about sexual and reproductive health (UNICEF 2011).

Early arranged marriages is a practice in some Roma communities, especially in traditional, wealthier communities (including Romani-speaking Roma groups). The practice affects participation in school for around 6.6 percent of the Roma youth, mostly girls (Surdu, Vincze, and Wamsiedel 2011). The phenomenon of dropping out of school due to marriage has decreased in recent years compared to the previous generation: 14 percent of today's parents (Surdu, Vincze, and Wamsiedel 2011) dropped out of school due to early marriage.

Some Roma families have put a stop to the education of their children, especially their daughters, around the fifth and sixth grades, essentially contributing to premature childbearing and to health risks for the girls, who are usually ignorant about their health needs and sexuality. Traditional families are known for a strategy of maintaining the family wealth and goods by setting up arranged marriages with Roma families coming from the same Roma group and with similar socioeconomic status. There are those who argue that since families can provide a better socioeconomic status for young couples than they could on their own, the risk factors for the adolescents decrease. Some Roma anthropologists argue that girls married at an early age are treated by the boy's family as their own child; they are loved and cared for. One of the most important protective factors contributing to the harmonious emotional and social development of young Roma children is the social capital, the safe environment of the Roma family, based on the warm relations and affection of parents, sisters, brothers, and of the larger family. In the case of early marriage, young adolescents are deprived of this important protective factor, namely the affection of their natal family and, equally important, they are deprived of the opportunity to be educated, to have choices.

There are some exceptional situations when very young girls are married. One such case, reported by the *Guardian*, is that of Marghioala, married to a boy when she was only eleven in 2011. The parents justified this by arguing "that way we can all be sure that no other boy touches the girl" (Radu 2011). Critics decried the protection failure on the part of child protection agencies, religious bodies, and state institutions and argued for more vigorous monitoring (Radu 2011). This approach recalls the argument advanced earlier in this volume by Rozzi in her discussion of the Italian authorities' rights enforcement failures vis-à-vis the needs of the migrant Roma community. Sometimes the adolescents react against forced marriages. In one reported case, a twelve-year-old adolescent girl sold into marriage tried to run away and was caught and held in chains by the boy's family (Hera 2011).

Not yet researched in the case of Roma girls, though found elsewhere, is the direct relationship between pregnancies at an early age and a high level of maternal mortality, child malnutrition, and negative psychological effects for both girls and boys. As McNeely and Bose discuss earlier in this volume, young adolescents are not equipped physically or mentally to have intimate relations, and the consequences may be devastating. Early pregnancies may make girls powerless and dependent (UNICEF 2011). For a child at the age of puberty, it is hard to take on the role of mother or father: she or he lacks sexual education and information, has missed some critical development stages and may easily fall into depression. As Roma health mediators (Romani

CRISS 2011) stated, "They barely start having menstruation and they make a child."

This problem needs to be addressed by people from the community who present different models or promote girls' education as an alternative to the traditional pattern of socialization. Burra discusses an interesting example of a strategy to challenge child labor in her chapter, a strategy that could also be applied to the prevention of child marriage. Adolescence is a period of serious physical, social, and emotional development. Early marriages and lack of proper sexual information and counseling may have a significant impact on Roma adolescents' development, contributing to the perpetuation of disadvantage and exclusion.

Interests of Roma Adolescents and Accessibility

The use of the Internet for entertainment and communication is very limited within the Roma community as a significant percent cannot afford regular electricity, let alone an Internet connection and a computer. Less than 8 percent of Roma families own a computer (Fleck and Rughinis 2008) and probably even less have access to the Internet.

For the 23 percent of the Roma families who lack electricity, these technology tools are pure utopia. In the winter, Roma children who learn only in daylight or by candlelight have problems at school. In addition, they do not have access to any other source of information (Internet, TV, books). Eighty-six percent of children from Roma households where at least one child dropped out of school did not have access to any books in the dwelling (Surdu, Vincze, and Wamsiedel 2011).

Since access is very limited, it remains to be seen whether the Internet can be a tool for increased social integration. Private initiatives and public policies targeting educational development and integration should consider the large spectrum of possibilities that wider access to the Internet may provide for Roma adolescents and for all adolescents.

The availability of the Internet to Roma families has the potential to change behavior and habits. Communication technology is one of the best ways to provide adolescents with information, with more exposure to education and literacy, and with motivation and resources. Access to information technology should be considered when designing programs and policies for those most deprived, in our case, Roma adolescents. Social networks, e-mail, and messaging software also blurs the racial divide, allowing Roma youth to express themselves in the wider Internet community and interact more easily with non-Roma peers.

Recently, and only in better off families, interaction through messaging software and use of video-sharing websites has started to gain ground. The phenomenon indicates the level of penetration of information technologies in some Roma communities. As parents start to use the Internet for economic activities (for example, advertising merchandise), the younger members of the family get access to entertainment and communication opportunities beyond the traditional ones. As in the case of traditional social events, the Internet tends to be more available to boys, with access somewhat restricted for girls.

Roma adolescents have very few alternatives and choices while growing up in compact rural communities or in urban ghettoes. Usually, life revolves around events that take place within the community: baptism of the newborn, marriages, and funerals. Socializing among the young in traditional communities is often controlled by adults. Usually, boys enjoy more freedom and are able to interact with the "outside," but, even so, preference is given to life within the community. Going to the cinema, watching TV, visiting the mall for shopping, and meeting with friends outside the Roma community are ways of spending time that occur more often than in the past, but are still largely unavailable to most Roma adolescents. Interaction with non-Roma peers is also more readily available for adolescents who have access to the Internet and to other communication tools.

These new—however limited—trends for the current generation of adolescents often create clashes within the family as both girls and boys opt for more independent decision making. They also create opportunities for informed personal decisions of Roma adolescents. This is precisely why programs, projects, and state measures should consider giving the Roma youth access to information, a right they deserve.

Conclusions and Perspectives

As we have seen, the participation of Roma adolescents in secondary and tertiary education remains very low due to many factors, but most basically because the minimum conditions for an adequate life are missing: permanent residence, employment, access to services, and steady incomes.

One of the most effective ways to combat extreme poverty and inequity is to invest in adolescents. Breaking the intergenerational transmission of poverty in Roma communities should be a priority to stop the cycle, since "poor adolescent girls give birth to impoverished children" (UNICEF 2011). As UNICEF concludes, effective governmental policies include not only access of minorities or poor adolescents to education but also attention to creating a supportive environment for adolescents' development, encompassing the factors mentioned in this chapter.

In the long run, the insignificant investment of the government in Roma education-related policies bears an increasing economic cost. One argument for taking action is provided by a 2010 World Bank survey, showing that the annual economic cost of Roma exclusion—caused by low levels of employment, low wages, and lack of adequate education to participate successfully on the labor market—is about 887 million euro for Romania. The study cites several reasons for the economic cost, the most important being the loss of labor force productivity that educated and qualified young Roma could provide to the Romanian economy. The average earnings of Roma who complete secondary education are 144 percent higher than those who complete only primary education. Roma are one of the youngest demographic groups in the country and, if invested in, could offset the losses caused by the aging of the general population. According to the study, further economic losses include, among others, the costs of social security provided to the unemployed youth and the poorest people (World Bank 2010). Conventional support interventions are costly, and often create a situation of dependency; the future requires government policies that adapt measures and interventions to changing contexts and patterns of behavior, encouraging positive developments and tackling the negative.

If we aim to develop an independent, skilled, trained, and competitive Roma youth generation, but also a more self-confident one, strategic and early investment has to target Roma children and youth, in terms of their performance, as well as in terms of comfort with their own identity. Early childhood development programs followed by investments in adolescents would decrease significantly the costs of social assistance programs and would increase productivity. Such programs would have a greater impact on the emotional, social, cognitive, physical, and linguistic development of Roma children and youth, preparing a more skilled and educated labor force for tomorrow.

Another solution that could positively affect the education prospects of Roma adolescents involves the family and community resources available. This includes adults, parents, and others who can invest time and effort to support children, and, at the community level, resources and strong networks able to support youth. In this context, school and community workers and mediators have been and may continue to represent relevant networks in Romania. Similarly, good interactions with non-Roma and "acceptance" from non-Roma leaders can build the trust of Roma parents in the educational and labor market system and in more optimistic future prospects for their children.

The investment in the infrastructure of the schools, in creating computer labs, offering access to information, to the Internet, for Roma and non-Roma poor youth should become a priority of the state, so that all children have equal opportunities, irrespective of their social status or ethnic origin.

> The challenge of early marriages, as well as other so-called cultural issues, requires increased attention from the members of the Roma community, on the one side, and a more integrative attitude from mainstream actors that would bring closure to the sensitive issue of Roma women and girls, on the other. Investing more in girls' education must become a priority of public policies but also of the Roma movement, bearing in mind that "educated girls are less likely to get pregnant as teenagers, more likely to have correct and comprehensive knowledge of HIV and AIDS and more likely to have healthy children when they eventually become mothers.
>
> (UNICEF 2011)

The "new" Roma leaders need to come up with an alternative identity and cultural offering to the traditional Roma, one that combines the values of Roma traditions and strengthens Roma identity, without further segregating Roma from the rest of the society. Such a set of values could enable the next generation to be proud of their roots while enjoying the universal freedoms and rights we share as human beings. The challenge for Roma elites is to reach out to the thousands of Roma adolescents. The mechanisms and mediums for debating and promoting such an offering among adolescents are not in place and need to be created. The Internet is one attractive instrument that can be used, but it cannot replace direct interaction and more focused campaigns.

Some interesting recent trends within several Roma groups could constitute the topic of future research and analysis. In the first case, children and adolescents belonging to better-off families, such as Lăutari[2] (a subgroup of traditional musicians) are becoming increasingly competitive in formal education, especially in arts schools. These modern Lăutari parents have started to value and pay for formal musical education and enroll their children in renowned musical schools and conservatories, expecting them to become fully fledged "artists." The environment in those schools is more welcoming than the average, as generations of educated Roma musicians from other groups have attended those schools and gained the acceptance of teachers and peers. The number of Roma students attending is higher than in other schools, a factor that diminishes, in these specific circumstances, the likelihood of stigmatization. The income of some of these families is better than that of many other Roma. They already have some social mobility; the next step is investment in good education for young children.

In the second case, youth belonging to traditional Roma groups that have converted to Christian evangelical denominations are benefitting from educational and moral support provided by their churches (Romania Libera 2010). Parents become increasingly motivated by their spiritual leaders to hope for a better future for their children and invest more in their education. Some of these churches are attended by both Roma and non-Roma and, from what we could tell in recent visits,[3] relations between the two are better than in Romanian society in general. Respect and trust among Roma and Romanian church goers seems high. We believe that this respect motivates Roma families to integrate further as part of society since in this context they are not met with rejection.

In the third case, the Rudari group has higher participation in high school education than other Roma groups. Around 22 percent among the Rudari have graduated from high school compared to only 4 percent of the two most traditional Roma groups (Fleck and Rughinis 2008). The Rudari are considered one of the most assimilated[4] Roma groups, while other more traditional groups are more visible in their clothes and language, and also in the pride they take in their ethnicity.

We identified common patterns in these three cases: good interactions with non-Roma (building social capital), trust (which also entails likely or promised acceptance from the "outside" by religious leaders and fellow churchgoers), and acknowledgment of the importance of investing in education of young Roma (building human capital).

In a country where the transition from communism to democracy also produced a series of instances of interethnic conflicts between Roma and non-Roma population and where negative prejudice toward the Roma remains pervasive, more policies are needed to ensure a multicultural school environment. One of the solutions offered by the Ministry of Education was the introduction of legal provisions allowing for an optional course on history and culture in one's mother language. Although policy makers seem content to affirm that the recognition of cultural rights is being realized through such legal provisions, in practice the measure is only sporadically implemented. Offering Roma youth the opportunity to attend an optional class dedicated to learning about their culture and language while many are avoiding declaring their ethnic identity is, in practical terms, rather ineffective. As a consequence, the reduction of prejudice and the development of self-esteem among Roma adolescents in the school environment remains an objective to be achieved.

One of the most concrete recommendations is the insertion of cultural elements and historical facts about Roma and the other minorities living in Romania into the mainstream curricula of primary and secondary education. It is a loss for all children and youth of Romania that information about slavery or the Holocaust is missing from the history books of the country. Every minority adolescent should have access to his or her own historical background, but Romanians in general should better understand the social and economic situation of their peers belonging to different minorities, including Roma. If Roma history was included in the curriculum, it might help diminish the obstacles to the social inclusion of Roma. It could become a factor in changing negative perceptions about Roma among non-Roma Romanians; it could also increase self-esteem and provide a sense of belonging for Roma children and adolescents. Furthermore, we believe that more open and warm attitudes of teachers toward Roma families would lead to improved results in the educational participation and performance of Roma children and youth. Romani activists, including the authors, have called for policy measures that provide more inclusive teaching, for valuing cultural diversity and equality in curricula at all levels.

Apart from the needed systemic changes, we believe Roma youth need an impressive "Roma character," "Roma story," or "Roma idea"—one that is modern, interesting, and that can become their inspiration for success and pride, as well as having the power to open the minds of their Romanian peers to diversity while stirring their curiosity about the Roma. Such characters could be imagined through movies, cartoons, books, and so forth, but she or he could also be real, loved by the society, loved by adolescents. Such an idea was imagined by Roma and non-Roma adolescents involved in the "Youth Civic Engagement and Dialogue Program" of the Roma Center for Social Intervention and Studies-Romani CRISS and IREX project.[5] One of the youth groups, asked to develop a local project based on existing needs, proposed opening a radio station for their high school. The school was very negatively perceived at the county level and the interactions between Roma and non-Roma students were very limited. In a short time, a small adolescent team, supported by their mentors, succeeded not only in starting the radio station but in significantly improving the image of the high school at the county level. From a school considered poor and underperforming, the high school was transformed to a place adolescents wanted to become part of; from a place where Roma students were isolated and marginalized, it became a place where it is cool to hang out with them, where it is cool to reject racism.

There are other examples of small but great ideas proposed and implemented by adolescents themselves in the same program that led to similar results: changes in the attitudes of non-Roma, increased self-esteem of Roma. One of the non-Roma girls involved in the program stated:

> Before I started participating in this project, I considered the Roma vulgar. But after I became involved in this project, I understood that they are humans. I made a Roma friend that changed all my opinions about the Roma. I knew her before, but did not have a good opinion of her. I didn't really know her, and knowing she was Roma, I thought she was like all the other Roma. . . . Now I have a different opinion of the Roma in general. I realized that they are also human, that they have the same reactions as I have. Like every other person, they go home and cry in their pillow.[6]

To address the deficiencies related to identity and self-esteem, creating the framework where strong elites can emerge—able to act as role models for a young generation and able to motivate parents—should be advocated for by Roma civil society. As the educational system is not very welcoming for Roma youth and the quality of education in general is decreasing, Roma individuals who have succeeded through education should be more visible publicly, providing motivation and paths to follow.

The main achievements of the postcommunist generation of Roma activists over the past twenty years of work relate to the inclusion of Roma in targeted policies, laws, and resolutions by the state and by intergovernmental bodies. But those policies have been superficiality implemented at the community level; they have also not addressed the need to change the attitudes and combat the prejudices of the majority.

A new vision is needed to increase the chances of Roma children and adolescents to have the same opportunities as the majority population in their transition to secondary or tertiary education, and in their transition from adolescence to adulthood. Social and economic inclusion of Roma will happen, in our opinion, if decision makers, intellectual elites, and eventually communities and the larger public acquire a new perspective.

Policies need to pursue not only repairing the effects of exploitation and past oppression that led to current inequality but also the creation of the basis for equal opportunities by building trust, encouraging and stimulating internal developments that have proven their worth. Only when Romania and other European states have developed and implemented policies seriously reflecting the "European values" of human rights, equity, and diversity will Roma integration move ahead. Those principles are essential pillars in shaping all public policies and in preventing the emergence of other social and economic inequalities between the majority and the minority population in the future.

Notes

1. Vlad Petri (a young Romanian cinematographer investigating present realities and social transformations) and Alina Serban (a young Roma actress and activist) created this video report to investigate high school students' prejudices about Roma. They made it available via YouTube (Petri and Serban 2011).

2. Roma subgroup who used to play instruments and sing for noblemen, weddings, and baptisms on Romanian territory. In the text we refer specifically to the modern "turbo folk" ones who did not get a music education; it's important to note that there are well-educated families of musicians that had a tradition of learning at music schools before.

3. Bucharest, Buzau, Ilfov, Timisoara are all cities where the authors visited evangelical churches or met with evangelical traditional Roma.

4. They do not speak the Romani language, plus many of them would argue that they do not have a Roma heritage.

5. A project started in Romania and Republic of Moldova in 2011 with the aim of mobilizing adolescents in improving community life and fostering intercultural understanding.
6. Information gathered from Romani CRISS and IREX project reports.

References

B1 TV. 2012. "Povestea de Succes a Unei Tinere de Etnie Romă Din România, În Presa Franceză: Din Satră, Studentă la Sorbona." Accessed August 27, 2012. http://www.b1.ro/stiri/externe/povestea-de-succes-a-unei-tinere-de-etnie-roma-din-romania-in-presa-franceza-din-atra-studenta-la-sorbona-35927.html.

Badescu, Gabriel, Vlad Grigoras, Cosima Rughinis, Malina Voicu, and Ovidiu Voicu. 2007. *Barometer of Roma Inclusion*.Bucharest, Open Society Foundation.

Cusack, Jim. 2012. "Young and Vulnerable, Her Last Days Spent in Fear." *The Independent* January 29. http://www.independent.ie/opinion/analysis/young-and-vulnerable-her-last-days-spent-in-fear-3003027.html.

European Roma Rights Center. 2011. *Breaking the Silence: Trafficking in Roma Communities*. Budapest, European Roma Rights Center and People In Need.

European Commission. 2011. "EU Framework for National Roma Integration Strategies." Accessed March 3, 2012. http://ec.europa.eu/justice/policies/discrimination/docs/com_2011_173_en.pdf.

Fleck, Gabor, and Cosmina Rughinis. 2008. *Come Closer: Exclusion and Inclusion of Roma in Present-Day Romania*. Bucharest, Human Dynamics.

Fraser, Angus. 1995. *The Gypsies*. 2nd ed. New Jersey, Blackwell Publishing.

Friedman, George. 2010. *The Next 100 Years: A Forecast for the 21st Century*. New York, Anchor Publishing House.

Fundatia Soros Romania. 2007. *Copiii Ramasi Acasa* [Children left home]. http://www.soros.ro/ro/publicatii.php?cat=15&pag=2#.

Grigore, Delia, Mihai Neacsu, and Adrian-Nicolae Furtuna. 2007. *Romii . . . In Căutarea Stimei de Sine-Studiu Introductiv*. UNICEF and Amare Rromentza.

Hancock, F. Ian . 2012. "ROMA [GYPSIES]." Handbook of Texas Online. Texas State Historical Association. Accessed March 26, 2012. http://www.tshaonline.org/handbook/online/articles/pxrfh.

Hera, Mona. 2011. "Caz Socant la Constanța." *Mediafax.ro*. Accessed March 11, 2012. http://www.mediafax.ro/social/caz-socant-la-constanta-fetita-de-12-ani-tinuta-in-lanturi-dupa-ce-fusese-vanduta-de-parinti-pentru-casatorie-8536906.

Mailat, Maria. 2005. *Evaluation Report of the Health Mediation Program.*, Bucharest, Roma Center for Social Intervention and Studies- Romani CRISS.

Mark, David, and Margareta Matache. 2006. Unpublished Reports of Field Visits to Roma Camps in Paris, France.

———. 2008. Unpublished Reports of Field Visits to Roma Camps in Rome, Milan, and Naples.

———. 2010a. Unpublished Report of Focus Group with Teachers in Bucharest.
———. 2010b. Unpublished Reports of Field Visits to Roma Summer Camp.
———. 2010c. Unpublished Reports of Focus Group with Roma Parents from Craiova, Mofleni, in Paris, France, June.
Marushiakova, Elena, and Veselin Popov. N.d. *Politica de Stat în Țările Comuniste*. Consiliul Europei. http://romanikultura.ro/docs/Istorie/6.1_Comunismul_RO.pdf.
Matache, Margareta. 2012. "Early Childhood Development of Roma Children: Ideas, Policies, Instruments." PhD diss., University of Bucharest.
Maximoff, Mateo. 2005. *The Price of Liberty*. Cluj, The Center for Roma Resources.
National Council for Combating Discrimination. 2012. "Perceptions and Atitudes Concerning Discrimination in Romania." Bucharest, NCCD.
National Council for Combating Discrimination and INSOMAR. 2009. "Discrimination Phenomena in Romania: Perception and Attitudes." Bucharest, : NCCD and The National Institute for Opinion Surveys and Marketing-INSOMAR.
National Institute of Statistics Romania. 2012. Accessed June 15, 2012. http://www.insse.ro/cms/files/RPL2002INS/vol1/tabele/t43.pdf.
Petcut, Petre. *Holocaustul Romilor în România* [The Roma Holocaust in Romania]. http://www.idee.ro/holocaust/pdf/rromilor.pdf.
Petri, Vlad, and Alina Serban. 2011. "Investigatie: Roma." YouTube video. Uploaded April 2011; accessed March 16, 2012. http://www.youtube.com/watch?v=4cPFMTf1Dsg.
Radu, Roberta. July 19, 2011. "Romania's Child Brides." *The Guardian*. Accessed March 5, 2012. http://www.theguardian.com/journalismcompetition/roberta-radu-short list-2011.
Romania Libera. 2010. "Cine este Pastoral Care." Accessed October 7, 2012. http://www.romanialibera.ro/exclusiv-rl/reportaj/cine-este-pastorul-care-a-oprit-hu litele-casatorii-dintre-copii-187655.html.
Roma Center for Social Intervention and Studies- Romani CRISS. 2008. "Drepturile Copilului sunt Negociabile?" Accessed March 5, 2012. http://www.romanicriss.org/Mariajele%20timpurii%20in%20comunitatile%20de%20romi.pdf.
———. 2011. *Roma Health: Perspectives of the Actors Involved in the Health System—Doctors, Health Mediators and Patients*., Bucharest, Roma Center for Social Intervention and Studies-Romani CRISS.
Sandu, Dumitru. 2005. *Roma Communities from Romania: A Map of Community Poverty Though PROROMI Survey*. Bucharest, World Bank.
Surdu, Laura. 2008. *Monitoring the Application of the Measures Against School Segregation in Romania*. Bucharest, UNICEF and Romani CRISS.
Surdu, Laura, Eniko Vincze, and Marius Wamsiedel. 2011. *Roma School Participation, Non-Attendance and Discrimination in Romania*. Bucharest, Romani CRISS and UNICEF.
Surdu, Mihai, coordinator. 2012. *Teacher Absenteeism, Roma Pupils and Primary Schools in Romania*. Budapest, Roma Education Fund.

Surdu, Mihai, and Judit Szira. 2009. *Analysis of the Impact of Affirmative Action for Roma in High Schools, Vocational Schools, and Universities.* Budapest, Roma Education Fund and Gallup Romania.

UNICEF. 2011. *The State of The World's Children. Adolescence: An Age of Opportunities.* New York, UNICEF.

Wiesel Commission. 2004. "Wiesel Commission on Anti-Semitism." Accessed August 21, 2012. http://www.antisemitism.ro/uploads/283/comisia-wiesel-raport-final-ro.pdf.

World Bank. 2010. *The Economic Costs of Roma Exclusion.* World Bank.

CHAPTER 15

Beginning in the Middle: Ending the Exploitation of Adolescents in India

Shantha Sinha

Adolescent Participation in Labor and the Workforce

Many of the adolescent laborers who are in the workforce today began as child laborers. According to the 2001 India Census, out of a total population of 250 million children in the 5–14 years age group, 80 million children were out of school, of which 12.6 million were employed in child labor and 0.12 million children were engaged in hazardous occupations (India Census 2001). A decade later all those children are likely to have become adolescent workers. Over this period there appears to have been a 45 percent decline in child labor: according to the National Sample Survey Office the number of working children in India has decreased from 9.75 million in 2004–05 to 4.9 million in 2009–10 (India NSSO). Yet the survey also found that millions of children are "out of school" and "school dropouts."

As adolescent laborers, they carry with them the scars of exploitation and a lost childhood. According to the National Family Health Survey (Parasuraman et al. 2009), 33.4 percent of girls and 50.4 percent of boys (in the 15–24 years age group) are engaged in labor. Among boys, 60.9 percent of the workforce is in the rural sector and in productive occupations; 88 percent of employed adolescent boys earn wages in cash. Significantly, 70.5 percent of urban boys are engaged as workers. In contrast, only 22.2 percent of girls are employed in the rural sector: 64 percent of young women engaged in agricultural work are employed by a family member, 28 percent are employed by a nonfamily member, and 7 percent are self-employed. More than half of the girls engaged in agricultural work (54 percent) are employed seasonally. Unlike boys, less than two-thirds of them earn cash for their work. Eleven percent of employed adolescent girls are paid only in kind. Twenty-six percent are not paid at all; they are unpaid family workers. Only 39.5 percent of urban girls—about half the proportion of boys—are in the workforce. Adolescent boys are in the labor market as wage earners on long- or short- term contracts or as daily wage earners. Girls continue to be predominantly engaged in hidden and invisible work, most of which is nonwage work provided for their families and not accounted for in government or other statistics.

Instead of going to school, very sizeable numbers of Indian children have been forced into a routine of drudgery and suffering at the cost of realizing their fullest potential. They are gradually edged out of active participation in any economic activity that involves skilled labor. They have no claim to any system of security or insurance; thus, they are unable to take advantage of state programs and policies as well as market interventions. Ultimately their fate is sealed by their lack of access to education.

Child Labor—Critical Gaps in Policy and Legal Framework

When we begin to look at adolescent children and their rights, we have to consider that most adolescents in the workforce are child laborers subject to violence and victimization. There is no specific law that governs and protects adolescent child labor (children between fourteen and eighteen years of age). Therefore the work provided by adolescents in the 14–18 years age group is legally permitted. They can claim their fair share of wages through the Minimum Wages Act 1948, which enforces payment of minimum rates of wages and hours of work for a normal working day for all kinds of employment.

The Child Labour Prohibition and Regulation Act 1986 (CLPRA) covers children only up to fourteen years of age. It reflects a targeted and priority-based approach of prohibiting child labor only in certain identified processes and occupations (currently child labor is prohibited in eighteen occupations and sixty-five processes). Child labor in agriculture is not prohibited and thus large numbers of children in this sector are legally exploited as wage earners and also are trafficked. Child labor in household units is also permitted by law, thus increasing its invisibility. For example, carpet production units that previously engaged children, a practice prohibited by law, have shifted their looms to households. Work is then subcontracted to home-based workers, creating a growing trend of "child laborization" of the workforce[1] (India Census 2001). Most such children belong to scheduled castes (SC), backward castes (BC) and minority communities. Since the work is rendered under the guise of household units, all such work remains out of the purview of CLPRA and children remain unprotected.

Some argue that children engaged in home-based work, such as traditional crafts, sewing, or other occupations, are going through apprenticeships and therefore their work should not be seen as child labor. However, incorporating children into the family occupation at an early age takes away the possibility for them to choose other avocations under the pretense of providing skills and apprenticeship. Even if they are at work in their own family, children are exploited, foregoing their education in the process.

Much of the work done by girls is also permitted by law. Girls are largely engaged in running the household from a very early age, even before they are capable of wage-earning activities. At home, they become available for work in many of the sectors that have been prohibited from employing child labor by law.

CLPRA is based on the temporal premise that it is impractical to address all children in the short term. Thus it makes a distinction between labor that is prohibited and labor that can be allowed. Due to this nonuniversal definition of child labor, large numbers of children are available for the labor market and the legal exploitation of millions of children continues unabated.

Children cannot be asked to wait endlessly for their turn because the system is not yet ready for them. Experience has also shown that only when there is an uncompromising stand toward elimination of child labor in all its forms have there been results. As discussed in the chapter by Burra, the M. Venkatarangaiya Foundation (MV Foundation, www.mvfindia.in) has succeeded in withdrawing one million child laborers from work and mainstreaming them into formal schools based on the nonnegotiable principle that "no child shall work and all children must attend fulltime formal day schools." Thus a rights-based perspective is not only a moral and politically correct imperative but also the only way in which the child labor issue can successfully be addressed.

According to the rights-based perspective enshrined in the CRC and the Indian Constitution, and binding on the Indian government, the state has an obligation to guarantee children all their rights without discrimination based on principles of universality, equity, and justice. Adolescents under the age of eighteen are entitled to these rights. If the state were to enforce its obligations, rights-enhancing results would ensue. Children enjoying full-time education do not get exploited as child laborers. But this is not the case. The National Child Labour Program of the Ministry of Labour and Employment runs 7,311 special schools in 266 districts for children engaged in labor prohibited by law, with a view to implementing the Child Labour Prohibition legislation. But in its twenty-three years between its establishment in 1988 and 2011, the NCLP only withdrew eight hundred thousand child laborers from work and sent them to mainstream schools. In all these years the National Child Labour Program has failed to eliminate child labor. Children can be kept out of child labor only by getting them into schools. The removal of child labor is inextricably linked to full-time formal education during the day. Accommodating child labor by adapting the school schedule to fit working hours denies children their right to education. As a remedy for the protection failures for younger children, the Ministry of Labour and Employment offers a Skill Development Initiative Scheme for early school dropouts, unemployed adolescents, children previously involved in child labor and their families, and other existing workers in the unorganized sector. The minimum age limit for persons to take part in the scheme is fourteen years with no upper age limit. The scheme is not specific to adolescents nor does it target their skill development exclusively.

To summarize the argument so far: given the flaws in the legislative framework, out-of-school children have perforce grown up to become disempowered adolescents.

Child Marriage

The exploitation of adolescents is further compounded by children being married at an early age, a point also made in the previous chapter by Mark and Matache. The age at which child marriage takes place varies from marriages being contracted between families when a boy and girl are infants (as in the state of Rajasthan) to being married before/just before eighteen years of age, which is officially the legal age of marriage for women (Srivastava and Rao 2012; Innocenti Research Centre 2007). According to a survey conducted by the Ministry of Health and Family Welfare, 0.9 percent of children in the ten-fourteen years age group are married (India MHFW 2008). According to the 2001 census there are 1.5 million girls in India under the age of fifteen who are already married. Of these, 20 percent or approximately 300,000 are mothers to at least one child.

At the national level, one in every five girls aged 15–17 years is married in comparison to one in every seventeen boys of age 15–20. There is a sharp increase in the proportion of girls married in the 17–18 age bracket[2] (Parasuraman et al. 2009). The risk of domestic violence, abuse, and exploitation inherent in child marriages is well known. Being married young, they conceive young. There were 90 births per 1,000 adolescents aged 15–19 years and 209 births per 1,000 women age 20–24, the highest of any age group (Parasuraman et al. 2009, 55). Early marriage also impacts adolescent health, causing reproductive health problems, including complications that come with teenage pregnancies. The likelihood of girls aged 10–14 dying in pregnancy and child birth is five times higher than that of women aged 20–24 (Patil 2011). Nearly six thousand adolescent mothers die every year in India. Further, children born to adolescent mothers are much more likely to die in infancy than children born to older mothers. The National Family Health Survey -III shows that the infant mortality of children born to mothers who are not yet twenty is 77 deaths per 1,000 live births (Parasuraman et al. 2009, 76). Adolescents also experience an increased incidence of sexually transmitted infections and diseases as well as an increased risk of HIV. The emerging trends in new HIV cases in India show that nearly two-fifths of new infections are reported among people below twenty-five years of age (Parasuraman et al. 2009).

As discussed in the Kelly-Newnham chapter, there is an inverse correlation between achievement in education and risk of child marriage. The higher the education the lower the odds that a woman age 15–17 will be married and the lower the odds that a woman age 18–24 will have been married before age eighteen (Parasuraman et al. 2009). Strikingly, the proportion of women with no education who have begun childbearing is about three times as high as women with ten or more years of education (Parasuraman et al. 2009, 56).

Child Protection Legal and Policy Framework: Gaps in Implementation

Under the Child Marriage Prohibition Act 2006, eighteen years is the permissible age of marriage for girls and twenty-one years for boys. A child marriage is void if the child is taken away from his or her lawful guardian by enticement, force, or use of deceitful means, or is sold or trafficked for the purpose of marriage. The courts have the power to issue injunctions to prevent child marriages from taking place (HAQ Centre for Child Rights 2006). Parents' approval of child marriage is recognized as a serious offense under Indian law, meriting arrest and the refusal of bail pending trial. Yet the Act has limitations because it fails to declare that all child marriages are illegal. The law makes child marriages voidable only when children or guardians seek annulment of the marriage. In this sense, it presumes that the child is able to exercise her agency to say "no" to child marriage and that there are appropriate support systems and institutions to enable a child to defy marriage and also to rehabilitate her. In reality it is unlikely that the guardian will take the initiative and risk of terminating a marriage. The number of child marriages stopped under the Child Marriage Act has been negligible.

The overarching legal framework for protection of children up to the age of eighteen is the Juvenile Justice Care and Protection Act of 2000.[3] In practice it has been found to cover a miniscule set of children. The Integrated Child Protection Scheme, launched in 2009, offers shelter homes and other forms of institutional support to those rescued from child labor and trafficking, street children, and victims of abuse and violence. There are not enough homes and the quality of care in all such homes has been found to be grossly inadequate, including reported incidents of abuse and violence (Loveleen, Varadon, and Kumar 2007). These homes operate in isolation from the community and even the children's guardians and families. In many cases the process of institutionalizing is one of disempowerment, and labels the child as a victim.

Along with institutional support, noninstitutional options such as foster care, sponsorship, and adoption are also envisaged as part of the Integrated Child Protection Scheme. However, at present these noninstitutional options are operational only in a few areas and have yet to evolve into a comprehensive nationwide program. Effective implementation of the Juvenile Justice Care and Protection Act also importantly requires that children be heard and enabled to take informed decisions regarding their lives. This is more honored in the breach than in practice.

Under a scheme called Ujjwala, the Ministry of Women and Child Development of the government of India funds NGOs to prevent sexual exploitation of adolescents. It is estimated that there are about three million prostitutes in the country of whom 40 percent are children (India MWCD 2008). There are seventy-three rehabilitation centers so far in sixteen states in the country under the Ujjwala scheme. Considering the vast number of children in such a predicament, this is just a drop in the ocean.

Another program for adolescent girls is the Rajiv Gandhi Scheme for Empowerment of Adolescent Girls commonly known as SABLA, established in 2010. It addresses the nutritional and health status of girls 11–18 years old in two hundred identified districts and aims to equip them with life skills as well as vocational skills while encouraging children below fourteen years to go to school. By the end of 2011 a total of 11,149 adolescent girls were provided vocational training as part of SABLA and 4,212 adolescent girls were mainstreamed into the school system (India MWCD 2012, 7). SABLA also provides supplementary nutrition and gives health and nutritional training to adolescents. It is reported that 6.7 million adolescents were covered by these nutritional programs in the year 2011–12 (India MWCD 2012, 23). SABLA emphasizes reproductive health programming, including information on safe sex in which the objective of delaying marriage becomes part of reproductive health interventions.

Interventions that link financial incentives with raising the age of marriage have been developed.[4] Programs involving conditional cash transfers, vouchers, and scholarships aim to enable girls to transition from primary to secondary and higher education and such incentives are linked to the girls' continuance of schooling without getting married.[5]

However, these programs are mainly driven by the supply side. They assume that adolescent girls are in a position to avail themselves of the services automatically. But, as the chapter by Kelly and Newnham explains in detail, adolescent girls have to negotiate barriers of power and authority within the family, gender and caste discrimination, patriarchy, and the nexus of economic exploitation before they can take advantage of the programs offered. Existing schemes do not address these barriers to enable meaningful access by adolescents. Nor do they provide the spaces, support structures, and shelter required to enable girls to defy traditions and cultures of domination, to exercise their agency and say no to child labor, early marriage, servitude, violence, and abuse. None of the interventions for protection of children weave education in as an indispensable component for empowering adolescents.

Access to Education—Real or Illusory?

For most children the completion of primary school education, let alone elementary and secondary school education, is a herculean task. There are innumerable challenges in access to education. An indication of the enormous demand for education today is the 98 percent initial enrollment of children in schools. However, the statistics on retention tell a different story: in 2007–08, 30.09 percent of children dropped out before completing class (grade) five; 52.47 percent dropped out by class eight; and 68.42 percent of children dropped out of school before completing class ten[6] (India MHRD 2008, 102). According to the NFHS-III (Parasuraman et al.2009) only 41 percent of youth in the 15–17 years age range were attending school. School attendance in rural areas was 37 percent while in urban areas it was 51 percent. School attendance was lower among girls (34 percent) than boys (49 percent). At age 15–19 the girls' literacy rate lagged behind the literacy rate of boys by 15 percentage points (Parasuraman et al. 2009, 10). Thus, more than half of adolescents are school dropouts. Those who survive and complete their schooling are the lucky ones. The cumulative effect of not being in school is reflected in statistics for the educational achievement of 15–19 year olds. At that age, there is substantially greater school attendance of children from rich households (68 percent) than of children from poor households (13 percent).

Although there is an explosive demand for education and primary schools are bursting at their seams with overcrowded classrooms, there has been no corresponding increase in the numbers of schools and places at middle and high school levels. This fundamental mismatch between the expectations of parents and the system's capacity to respond with equal seriousness results in children losing the battle for formal education. The education system contains an underlying structural logic that keeps children away from schools.

At every step, poor children receive the message that education is not in the realm of possibility for them. Adolescent dropouts suffer low self-esteem and feel ashamed to be branded as failures. Their track record of failing to graduate from primary school or high school continues to haunt them throughout their life.

The Path to Realizing Education Entitlements—Policy and Legal Framework

Indian authorities have hesitated to plan for simultaneous universalization of education for all age groups up to eighteen years. As early as 1966, the Education Commission under the chairmanship of Daulat Singh Kothari emphasized universalization of free and compulsory education up to the age of fourteen. However, when it came to rolling out policy the Kothari Commission preferred to focus on some children with particular merit for the time being, "to ensure that the brighter children from all strata of society receive the best education possible." It gave financial constraints as a reason for this prioritization.

During the 1990s the government focused on universalizing primary education through the District Primary Education Program followed by the Sarva Shiksha Abhiyan, a broadly based national program. In concrete terms, the government was unwilling to make investments in education beyond class five, underlining the gross unjustness of its treatment of the country's child citizens.

Finally, with the enactment of the Right of Children to Free and Compulsory Education Act of 2009 (RTE Act), education was guaranteed as a fundamental right for all children in the 6–14 years age group. Children now have a right to education up to the elementary school level (class eight). The RTE Act sought to remedy the structural deficiencies that have pushed children out of schools. It mandates improving infrastructure and facilities to address the situation of overcrowded government schools[7] (National University of Educational Planning and Administration 2007). It explicitly addresses discrimination on the basis of caste, gender, disability, ill health, and other grounds, providing that "no child shall be subjected to physical punishment or mental harassment." The Act also promotes a child-friendly pedagogy.

However, all of these guarantees exist only for children in the 6–14 years age group. There is no constitutional obligation to provide education for children in the 14–18 years age group. After completion of class eight the child cannot claim secondary school education as a matter of right. In line with this limitation, the otherwise well-crafted policy of providing residential schools for girls who have dropped out of school through the Kasturba Gandhi Balika Vidyalaya program provides schooling only up to class eight. Many girls who wish to pursue their education beyond class eight cannot access residential facilities such as hostels and so drop out of school. Currently over 200,000 children are studying in the Kasturba Gandhi Balika Vidyalaya program.

While the government of India has recently been emphasizing universalization of secondary education through the Rahtriya Madhyamik Shiksha Abhiyan program (Scheme for Secondary Education for All), it is still in a rudimentary stage. It does contain provision for hostels, but the numbers still do not correspond to demand.

Other education programs for adolescents include the adult education program, Sakhshar Bharat–National Literacy Mission, covering all citizens age fifteen years and above. The National Institute of Open Schooling or the National Open School also offers courses for school dropouts enabling them to achieve parity with their peers in the mainstream formal schools. According to its website (http://www.nios.ac.in/default.aspx), the National Institute of Open Schooling provides a number of vocational, life enrichment, and community-oriented courses besides general and academic courses at secondary and senior secondary level. It also offers elementary-level courses through its Open Basic Education Programmes. The government has vested the National Institute of Open Schooling with the authority to examine and certify learners registered with it up to predegree-level courses. However, each year only one million students in the 15–25 years age group graduate from the Open School system from the potential pool of the nearly one hundred million school dropouts in this age group. There are no special efforts made to enable adolescent children to access these facilities.

Right to Education—the Adolescent Perspective

Indian education policy has always been fragmented. Planning for all levels of education simultaneously—from class one to university or to other education streams—was regarded as impractical. The movement of children from one stage to the next has never been seen as a seamless organic progression enabled by sufficient investments at every stage. Plans to provide education have been short-term without considering the enormity of the costs of delay, which are far greater than timely investment in education delivery.

The task of providing education and locating it in the specific context of adolescents' life patterns is a significant challenge. There is diversity in their education attainment levels. Some may have never been to school, or may be school dropouts from primary school, with little memory of what they have learned; some may have dropped out from elementary school; and most children have dropped out before they have completed the class ten examination. There is also diversity in the occupational patterns that trap them in a relationship of exploitation with their employers. Many of them are married and have the encumbrances that come with being a family person, posing yet another challenge. As well, they are mostly from families living in extreme poverty; many of them face social exclusion because of caste, gender, and other biases.

In spite of this complexity and diversity, providing adolescents with an education is not an impossible task. Children and adolescents yearn for education; they can catch up with their peers. These two ideas provide a foundation for meaningful outcomes in interventions such as adult literacy programs, open school programs, skill development, or even special tuitions and coaching classes for adolescents to join formal schools. All such programs need to be sensitive to what adolescents experience, physically, mentally, and in terms of role definition. These programs need to be informed by reality in the field and the testimonies of young men and women. They must build from empathy with the anxieties of adolescents regarding the commitments and responsibilities they undertake for their family and survival. These programs must recognize that children are fully cognizant of their unjust childhood experience, and so take into account the repressed anger of adolescents against perceived or actual injustice. This deep-seated resentment against their oppression in society is especially marked in the boys and girls of socially excluded castes. Having lost their self-identity and positive self-esteem they require confidence building. Their innate capacity to learn and understand has to be trusted while they are being motivated to accept another chance to be integrated into the world of mainstream education.

Such empathy for adolescents needs to be complemented by intensive short-duration interactions, long-duration residential training camps, or a continuous forum to create platforms for adolescents to come forward and receive peer support for education. Adolescents who wish to pursue formal education and appear for the class ten or class twelve board examinations should be encouraged.[8] Safe and secure residential spaces for children, especially girls, are important to the delivery of education, life skills, and activities that allow these children to catch up with their lost childhood and build friendships.⁹ Children should be encouraged to act autonomously; this would require creation of spaces for adolescent children to meet, discuss, and act. These interventions need to be creative and imaginative; they could also include activities such as sports or forums for theater. For those who require affirmative action, provision for scholarships—waivers of school fees, examination fees, hostels, and other costs—need to be made.

Ultimately restorative education policies and programs must address what has been the gross denial of fundamental rights to these adolescents— their very right to survival, development, dignity, and protection. To enable all out-of-school children to reclaim what they have lost as children, we have to begin in the middle and build from there.

Braving the Way to Freedom and Liberty

There is an inextricable link between adolescents' right to education and their empowerment. They are two sides of the same coin. An enabling environment and a groundswell of community support are necessary to encourage adolescents to claim their right to education. It is a matter of reconfiguring power relations and societal values in favor of child rights. It is creating new traditions and cultures that respect children.

When children know that they have allies in adults who are willing to vouch for them and take up their cause, they gain courage to defy authority. With this support, children exercise their agency, and refuse to go to work or even be married. Once an enabling environment is created, the success of a child being rescued depends largely on the child's innate strength. As oppressed children stand their ground and exercise their agency in not relenting to pressure, more and more adults are also empowered and inspired to take a stand.[10] In this charged atmosphere adolescents begin to find ways out of the traps of being prematurely part of the labor force, of being drawn into oppressive domestic situations and of being burdened with the family responsibilities that come with being a married person. These children can stand firm and take the risk to walk out of their past. Anchored by a ray of hope given by the changed atmosphere and some voices in their support they can brave their way to freedom and liberty. It becomes the responsibility of all—the state and society, community and family—to respect the capacity of children to exercise autonomy and take decisions that would enhance their dignity. In doing so, girls and boys are encouraged to take part in sports, children's clubs, theater, public activities, and enjoy being young. Communities might begin to realize that youth are not just boys but are also girls. In fact, taking the decision to embark on a journey for education is a defining moment. It begins the process of discovering a lost childhood to fully realize adolescence and to move ahead to the next step.

Education as Empowerment

The importance of education in bringing about transformation in the lives of adolescents cannot be overstated.[11] The very act of joining the education stream integrates these children into a web of interaction, encouraging them to utilize the modes of thinking and pursuit of knowledge that have gained currency and acceptability. They are able to transcend their local environs and locate themselves in the context of a larger society and its complexities. This equips them to gain confidence and acquire a body language that demands that they be addressed not as anonymous workers but as students seeking to join the cultural milieu. Education gives them compelling ammunition not to yield to pressures of marriage and even gives them access to reproductive health care and life skills as informed and literate persons. While this continues to entail a struggle at every stage, in the process of going to school poor children no longer endure hardships for the sake of others but for their own development and growth. Education becomes the first step toward equity and bridging the gaps in the social and cultural hierarchies surrounding these children. All children aspire to a similar kind of learning regardless of their class or cultural background. In this sense education is a great leveling process.

Adolescents from disadvantaged backgrounds who have completed secondary school education are the real heroes, keeping alive the hope of the poor for education. They are the change makers for communities that have been trapped for generations in the vicious cycle of immobility, poverty, and illiteracy. They show that even for the poor, things can be different and better. Their success has far-reaching consequences for the growth and development of India's democracy.

Notes

1. Census 2001 data shows a sharp decline in the number and percentage of children classified as regular workers from 4.3 percent in 1991 to 2.3 percent in 2001. But

there was a substantial increase in marginal workers in every category of worker irrespective of sex and residence. As a result, despite the number of regular workers declining from 9.08 million in 1991 to 5.78 million in 2001, the total number of children in the work force increased from 12.86 million in 1991 to 16.35 million in 2001. A large part of the increase was accounted for by the increase in marginal workers, from 2.2 million in 1991 to 6.89 million in 2001 (India Census 2001). Most of the children employed as marginal laborers are employed in agriculture and the increase in marginal workers compared to regular workers could also be related to the growing demand for children in agricultural processes.

2. According to the NFHS-III survey, 47.3 percent of women aged 20–24 were married by age eighteen. Of these, 2.6 percent were married before they turned thirteen, 22.6 percent were married before they were sixteen, and 44.5 percent were married when they were between sixteen and seventeen.

3. Other relevant legislation includes the Protection of Women from Domestic Violence Act, 2005; the Dowry Prohibition Act, 1961 (28 OF 1961); Immoral Traffic Prevention Act, 1986.

4. There have been several programs for girls implemented by individual state governments. For example, Apni Beti Apna Dhan (1994–2005) of the Haryana government where a fixed deposit is made in a bank in the name of the girl to be given to her after she is eighteen and on condition that she continues her education. Balika Samridhdhi Yojana (1997–2004) from the Indian government has similar objectives.

5. There is a Delhi Voucher Project that includes a School Choice Campaign & School Vouchers for Girls pilot project for Economically Weaker Sections and minorities. There are several others, most importantly Rahtriya Madhyamik Shiksha Abhiyan. Some are very creative, such as those providing bicycles to girls so they can get to middle and secondary schools have made a remarkable difference. For example, the Mukhyamantri Balika Cycle Yojana in Bihar, a project that gives school girls two thousand rupees to purchase a bicycle, has so far resulted in 871,000 schoolgirls cycling to school, the number of girls dropping out of school has fallen, and the number of girls enrolling has risen from 160,000 in 2006–07 to 490,000 in 2013.

6. Primary school is from class one to five for children in the 6–11 years age group; elementary school is up to class eight for children up to fourteen years of age, secondary school is up to grade ten for adolescents up to sixteen years of age, and higher secondary school or junior college is up to eighteen years of age.

7. Enrollment at the primary stage increased by 11.5 percent from 1.18 million in 2004–05 to 1.32 million in 2006–07 and that of upper-primary level increased by 26 percent from 380,000 to 480,000 students between 2004 and 2006. There are 1.64 million schools of all types, with the student-classroom ratio equal to or more than sixty (National University of Educational Planning and Administration 2007). The RTE Act mandates that teachers are appointed for every thirty children at the primary stage and thirty-five children at the upper primary stage. In practice there are significant unfilled teacher vacancies, particularly in unpopular remote areas, and a dearth

of facilities for enabling adolescents from rural areas to access teacher training opportunities themselves.

8. The National Commission for the Protection of Children's Rights's program of social mobilization in areas of rural insurgency where disruption is pervasive enough that students cannot attend school has thus motivated hundreds of such adolescents and enabled their taking the examination as private candidates. In the state of Maharashtra the government was persuaded to pay for their examination fee and also arrange for residential tuition and coaching classes.

9. For example, the residential bridge course camps of such organizations as MV-Foundation, Doosra Dashak, Aman Biradari, and others.

10. This has been borne out by the experiences of NGOs in India such as MV-Foundation (described in more detail in the Burra chapter), Doosra Dashak, Aman Biradari (http://www.amanbiradari.org/dilse.html), Sandhan (http://www.sandhan.org), the Meena Manch program of UNICEF (http://www.unicef.org/india/children_corner_4118), and many others.

11. This section has been drawn from field notes of the author collected over two decades while interacting with NGOs such as MV Foundation, Pratham, Doosra Dashak, Action Aid, Plan, Save the Children, and other partners across the country.

References

HAQ Centre for Child Rights. 2006. *Handbook on the Prohibition of Child Marriage Act, 2006*. Delhi: Ministry of Women and Child Development, Government of India, and UNICEF India. http://www.unicef.org/india/Child_Marriage_handbook.pdf.

India Census 2001 (Government of India: Ministry of Home Affairs). 2001. http://censusindia.gov.in/.

India MHFW (Government of India: Ministry of Health and Family Welfare). 2008. *District Household and Facility Survey 2007–08*. Delhi: Government of India.

India MHRD (Government of India: Ministry of Human Resource Development). 2008. *Tables of Statistics of School Education, 2007–08*. Delhi: Government of India. http://mhrd.gov.in/sites/upload_files/mhrd/files/SES-School-2007-08.pdf.

India MWCD. 2008. *India Country Report: To Prevent and Combat Trafficking and Sexual Exploitation of Children and Women*. Report to the World Congress III Against Sexual Exploitation of Women and Adolescents, Rio De Janeiro, Brazil.

———. (Government of India: Ministry of Women and Child Development). 2012. *Annual Report 2011–12*. Delhi: Government of India. http://wcd.nic.in/publication/ar201112e.pdf.

India NSSO (Government of India: National Sample Survey Office, Ministry of Statistics and Program Implementation). 2010. National Sample Survey Office. http://mospi.nic.in.

Innocenti Research Centre and UNICEF. 2007. "Early Marriage: Child Spouses." *Innocenti Digest*, March. Vol.7. http://www.unicef-irc.org/publications/pdf/digest7e.pdf.

Loveleen, Kacker, Srinivas Varadan, and Pravesh Kumar. 2007. *Study on Child Abuse: India 2007.* Delhi: Government of India, Ministry of Women and Child Development.

National University of Educational Planning and Administration. 2007. "Flash Statistics, 2006–07." www.dise.in/ . . . /Publication%202006-07/Flash%20Statistics%202006-07.

Parasuraman, Sulabha, Sunita Kishor, Shri Kant Singh, and Y. Vaidehi. 2009. *A Profile of Youth in India*. National Family Health Survey (NFHS-III) India, 2005–06. Mumbai: International Institute for Population Sciences; Calverton, Md.: ICF Macro.

Patil, Justice Shivraj, and the Core Committee. 2011. *Prevention of Child Marriages in the State of Karnataka*. Delhi: Government of India, Ministry of Women and Child Development.

Srivastava, Anupam, and Jyoti Rao. 2012. "Early Marriage: A Childhood Interrupted." Webpage, UNICEF India. Accessed December 18, 2012. http://www.unicef.org/india/child_protection_1536.htm.

CHAPTER 16

Indian Adolescence and Its Discontents: Transformational Solutions Through Education, Skill Development, and Employment

Neera Burra

The Concept of Adolescence

The concept of adolescence, as usually understood, does not seem to have a cultural or even a legal correlative in India. According to the Constitution of India, the cut-off date for childhood is fourteen years old.

The Indian Constitution says that children below the age of fourteen should not work and also that all children up to the age of fourteen should be given free and compulsory education. The Right of Children to Free and Compulsory Education (2009) applies to children up to the age of fourteen years. However, the National Policy for Children (2005) refers to all persons below eighteen years as children. Other laws specify different ages: for example, the minimum legal ages for girls and boys to be married are eighteen and twenty-one, respectively. The National Youth Policy (2005) of the government of India covers persons between the ages of twelve and thirty-five! In some writings, youth are defined as those between fifteen and twenty-nine.

In the absence of the notion of adolescence as a period that characterizes the life cycle between childhood and adulthood, significant proportions of young girls and boys move directly into the world of adulthood in terms of the responsibilities they are forced to undertake by family, community, and society.

Child Marriage and Its Consequences

According to the National Family Health Survey-3 (Parasuraman et al. 2009, vol. 1, xxxi–ii), more than 50 percent of adolescents are married before the legal minimum age. Teenage pregnancies are common and one in six adolescents in the 15–19 age group have begun childbearing. At the time of the survey (2005), 12 percent were mothers and another 4 percent were pregnant with their first child. All this happened in spite of a law that prohibits child marriage and sets the minimum age for marriage for girls at eighteen and for boys at twenty-one. The NFHS-3 survey data showed that 6 percent of girls in rural areas and 2 percent of girls in urban areas in the 6–17 age group dropped out of school because of marriage (Parasuraman et al. 2009, vol. 1, 34). There are, of course, wide regional variations as well as urban and rural differences (UNICEF 2011, 23).

Underage anemic mothers produce low-birth-weight, stunted babies; this explains both high maternal mortality and high under-five mortality and infant mortality. Assuming the responsibilities of motherhood and of running a household at a very young age also leads to girls dropping out of the educational system.

Child Labor and Its Consequences

Boys are under far greater pressure to do wage work as compared to girls. Thus 8.8 percent of boys as compared to 3.3 percent of girls were required to work for a living (Parasuraman et al. 2009, vol. 1, 34). According to NFHS-3, 12 percent of children between the ages of 5–14 years, or one in every eight children, worked either for their own household or for somebody else (Parasuraman et al. 2009, vol. 1, 49), trends described in greater detail in the previous chapter by Sinha. This category of working children is not considered child labor under the law as it only prohibits child labor in hazardous industries and occupations that are listed in the schedule attached to the law.[1] Expectations for male children to support the family at a young age have adverse consequences for their health, their wages, and their future prospects.

Case Study 1: A Transformational Solution for Getting Children out of Work and into School—Child Labor Eliminated Through Education

Illiterate adolescents have traditionally been ignored by the educational system and were treated as a lost generation because no one had any idea how to get a ten or twelve year old back into school.[2] It took an NGO, the M. Venkatarangaiya Foundation (MV Foundation) in the state of Andhra Pradesh, to develop a methodology of accelerated teaching for adolescents who had never been to school or had dropped out of school and then help them to enter school in classes appropriate to their age. This transformational strategy is now popularly known as the "Bridge Camp Approach." There are both residential and nonresidential bridge camps. Residential bridge camps (RBCs) are for older children and nonresidential bridge camps are for younger out-of-school children. The latter are run on school premises. Several hundred thousand children who would have remained illiterate have been able to get back into formal, full-time schools and complete their tenth or twelfth grade examination (table 16-1 shows the results thus far). Many went on to get technical education and now have decent jobs.

MV Foundation was successful because they have a nonnegotiable approach to child labor and education. They believe that every child out of school must be defined as a child laborer. They worked with schools to see that lack of birth certificates does not result in children being denied admission. Many children of school-going age would drop out of school and join the ranks of child laborers because poor parents did not know how to prepare a child for school. Child absenteeism due to illness or any other factor could mean that the child would have to leave school forever.

They lobbied to change government policy at every level while at the same time remaining engaged with officials and community leaders, local landlords who employed child labor, youth volunteers, adolescents, and the children themselves. This is the centerpiece of their strategy. Thus, for instance, landlords employing bonded child laborers were asked to be chairpersons of school education committees and they were publicly feted for having released bonded child laborers. This put moral pressure on other landlords to voluntarily release bonded child laborers working on their farms. When some of them refused to release the children, the Bonded Labor Abolition Act of 1976 was used to file cases against recalcitrant landlords till the message went out that no child was to be employed as a bonded laborer.

School teachers were organized into a forum against child labor and they were encouraged to visit the homes of children who were absent from school. Children and adolescents were and continue to be organized into Child Rights Protection Forums along with local leaders. It is these fora that provide information to youth volunteers—supported by MV Foundation—on violations of rights such as plans of parents to marry underage children, child sexual abuse and violence cases, child trafficking, and so on. These cases are discussed with the concerned families and there are many instances where community pressure has prevented child marriage, for example. The approach developed by MV Foundation is one of consensus-building and getting everyone on board to the extent possible. But the NGO did not hesitate to use the prevailing laws when parents or employers did not listen.

MV Foundation youth volunteers now work in many districts across India using the strategy they developed in the state of Andhra Pradesh. They have been working in the states of Bihar, Chhattisgarh, Madhya Pradesh, and Tamil Nadu. They are being asked to work in districts affected by the Maoist guerilla insurgency, where organizing the community is a challenge. It is a slow process but it is beginning to show results. The table below provides details of their achievements as of October 2011.

The figures in table 16.1 are for the work that has been directly implemented by MV Foundation. They do not include the work done in the states of Bihar, Chhattisgarh, Madhya Pradesh, and Tamil Nadu where they have worked either with *panchayats* (elected assemblies at village level), state governments, or local NGOs as support organizations. Today, the Bridge Camp Approach has been mainstreamed and become an integral part of the government of India's flagship education program, Sarva Shiksha Abhiyan (Education for All Campaign).

Nonnegotiable principles have certain advantages. Once it is decided that something has to be done, then solutions follow and the results are self-evident. At a time when illiterate adolescents were seen as a "lost generation," the MV Foundation proved everyone wrong by experimenting continuously and developing a curriculum that could take illiterate adolescents from grade one to grade seven in one year, and then ensured that these children

Table 16.1. M. V. Foundation's achievements, as of November 2011

- 490,023 child laborers mobilized out of work and into full-time, formal, government day schools[1]
- 52,448 child laborers put through nonresidential bridge course camps and 30,000 education activists mobilized to liberate children
- 80,000 youth volunteers and members of Child Rights Protection Forum encouraged to protect child rights
- 25,000 adolescent girls assisted to get admission to schools and 8,000 child marriages stopped
- 1,500 *gram panchayats* (village elected bodies) made child-labor free
- 1,500 *gram panchayats* kept watch over child rights through their health and education subcommittees
- 50,000 children mainstreamed into formal schools through residential bridge camps
- 25,000 bonded child laborers released and sent to schools

Source: MV Foundation (http://www.mvfindia.in/).
[1] The total number of children withdrawn from work and mainstreamed into the formal school system is 1,008,214. This includes children in Bihar, Chhattisgarh, Madhya Pradesh, and Tamil Nadu.

were mainstreamed into formal, full-time schools by lobbying governments to change their school enrollment policies. MV Foundation also proved that it was possible to mainstream out-of-school children into the formal government schools without setting up parallel structures. The bridge camps are only transitional facilities so that children can reach the age-appropriate grades and then continue their education with other children.

India's Demographic Dividend and Skill Development

While the work of MV Foundation has affected significant numbers of youth, it is important to remember the sheer scale of India's demographics as far as adolescents are concerned.

India has the largest population of adolescents in the world. If India is to reap greater benefits from its demographic dividend, then large-scale skill development will have to be undertaken across the country, both in rural and in urban areas.

With low levels of education and poor learning outcomes, there is fear among policy makers that India's demographic dividend could easily become a demographic nightmare, with large numbers of adolescents and young adults unemployed or underemployed and therefore liable to become prey to antisocial elements. Formal skill-development programs target young adults in the age-range of twenty years and above.

The training provided by industrial training institutes—run by the government—and industrial training centers—managed by the private sector—is not very effective and does not necessarily match the skills required by the labor market. The age group is twenty years and above and trainees need to have a tenth grade education. A tracer study commissioned by the World Bank showed that the majority of workers (60 percent) with vocational qualifications did not have marketable skills. Those who were employed were largely working in trades other than the ones they had been trained for (Tan, Goyal, and Savchenko 2007, 4). Three major reasons were cited by the tracer study for this situation. First, the quality of training provided was poor. Second, there was a mismatch between the skills acquired and the demands of the labor market. Third, there was a mismatch between the skills acquired and the aspirations of the graduates.

Vocational training for adolescents in the 15–19 age group is almost nonexistent and such programs face all the problems cited above. Moreover, the aspirations of adolescents have changed in the last decade or so. They are no longer interested in following in their parents' footsteps and working at low wages in the informal economy. The growth of the Indian economy, the easy availability of consumer goods even in smaller towns and larger villages, greater mobility because of better connectivity, and the expansion and impact of electronic media have all affected the aspirations of the poor, particularly the adolescents among them.

The case studies described below are both examples of a transformative strategy for linking educated unemployed youth with the job market. Even though the targets of these efforts were older age groups, the approach would be relevant for adolescents as well (Burra 2012).

Case Study 2: Transformative Solutions for Skill Development and Employment for Rural Youth

This is a case study of a partnership between the government of Andhra Pradesh (GOAP) and the District Rural Development Agencies, the Society for Elimination of Rural Poverty, and the Andhra Pradesh Rural Poverty Reduction Programme—all government entities/programs—along with women's self-help groups (SHGs) and the private sector to provide skill development and organize placement for rural youth belonging to the poorest families in the state of Andhra Pradesh. Self-help groups are collectives of women, usually of ten women or more, that are organized around savings and credit activities with the purpose of enhancing their incomes. These SHGs were first organized by the government of Andhra Pradesh in partnership with the UN Development Programme and later with assistance from the World Bank.

In 2005, the GOAP set up the Employment Generation and Marketing Mission (EGMM). With the help of a network of approximately half a million SHGs and their federations they identified poor rural youth between eighteen and thirty-five years old who were educated up to the tenth grade, organized a three-month training program for them, and then placed them with the retail sector in the major cities and towns of Andhra Pradesh. What is unique about this training program is that it does not stop at training but also provides placement and postplacement mentoring and guidance. Of the 368,218 youth trained up to March 31, 2011, 270,183 or 73.38 percent have been placed in the service sector. More than 450 EGMM training centers have been established in rural and tribal areas. Thirty-four percent of the trainees are girls and 43 percent belong to scheduled caste (SC) and other minority communities.[3] Training costs are paid by the government.

This impressive achievement is based upon a systematic collection of information about unemployed youth by job resource persons who are volunteers. They are paid an honorarium by the GOAP to help identify potential candidates for the skill development and placement program. The data collected with the help of the job resource persons depends upon the network of SHGs and their federations. Job resource persons visit every household in their area, and the information about eligible youth is fed into the software prepared by EGMM. This data is used to identify potential trainees.

Unlike most government training programs, which provide training and then leave it to the trainee to find a job, this particular government program works on a market-led principle. The training programs are designed keeping in mind the needs of the market.

Officials of EGMM systematically scan the market with a view to identifying the kinds of needs employers have and the sorts of qualifications sought. This is the first step in deciding the kinds of training programs required and their contents as well as in making a match between the jobs on offer and the backgrounds of individual youth. Scanning the market involves studying a wide range of potential employment sources, including retail sales, security, restaurants, data entry, electrical operations, plumbing and sanitation, carpentry, painting and decoration, heavy equipment driving, and making and selling garments.

These training centers offer training not only in particular job skills but also for personality development and soft skills such as time and money management. Personnel from the private sector help in designing the curriculum and also teach.

Central to the success of the EGMM strategy is the role played by the private sector and the stakes they develop so as to ensure a fit between demand and supply. There is a close partnership between the government and the private sector in the EGMM. While the EGMM is a government entity, it has a core team of private sector people who have the freedom to build up partnerships with private sector entities.

By liaising with well-known chains such as the retail markets of Aditya Birla, McDonalds, Café Coffee Day, Hindustan Unilever, Apache, and Adidas, EGMM supplies about 80 percent of new recruitment in these companies. Over a period of time, EGMM has sensitized private companies about its vision and mission and holds "job melas" or "job fairs" in rural locations to ensure placements. This link with market demands is key to its positive impacts.

Training at EGMM does not end with placement. Candidates are given orientation training at their new workplace; they are also helped through counseling to transition from a rural background to an urban work environment. The initial experience of EGMM was that many youth left their employment in the first month. This was because they did not have the money to pay for rent, food, and so on, for the first month due to placements away from their home villages and towns. EGMM then started giving these trainees stipends so that they could manage their expenditure till they got their first paycheck. EGMM has used this strategy in training programs conducted in remote and tribal areas with equal success.

However, as the former executive director of EGMM told me, many of the really bright trainees wanted to move up the corporate ladder but hit the glass ceiling very quickly. Inadequate educational qualifications often get in the way. Many young people left their jobs after a few years to improve their educational qualifications so that they could get better jobs.

Case Study 3: Transformative Solutions Skill Development and Employment for Disabled Girls

The same approach has been used for skill development of disabled youth in the state of Andhra Pradesh by the team, which has now set up their own NGO called the Youth 4 Work. Using the partnership model described above, they use the job resource persons and the self-help groups to identify disabled youth with hearing impairment and neuromotor disorders. They then identify potential employers, provide training at their Centre for People with Disabilities Livelihoods in the city of Hyderabad and then monitor the progress of the youth. They help them solve problems with their new employers.

Another source of information is a database kept by the government called Software for Assessment of Disabled for Access, Rehabilitation and Empowerment. This database provides information about all disabled people in the state including their age, gender, type of disability, educational qualifications, and social background. Since the focus of the Centre is to serve the poorest and the most marginalized among the disabled and place them in jobs, this database is used extensively for identifying potential candidates. Telephone calls are made and text messages are sent to potential candidates and they are encouraged to go to their local Mandal Mahila Samakhya (Federation of Women's SHG Groups) offices or to local government offices to get more information about the training programs.

This is a relatively new program that started in January 2010, but it has shown that even the disabled can get productive employment and become financially independent. As of June 2011, 1,001 disabled youth in the age range of 22–29 years have been trained and placed, of which 331 are girls (there are currently plans to identify disabled adolescents in the 17–19 years age range by working with local high schools). I interviewed thirty-two disabled girls at the training center and also in the hostel provided by their employer in June 2011. Some of their common experiences are described below.

Interviews with Disabled Girls

Thirty-two disabled girls were interviewed in Hyderabad city over a two-day period. They belonged to different districts of Andhra Pradesh. Except for one girl who had suffered from severe burns, all of them said that they were survivors of polio. Four out of the thirty girls used long sticks to support themselves while walking as their legs were of different lengths. One girl walked with the support of her hand as her leg had shrunk after polio.

All the girls interviewed had finished their tenth grade exam and several of them had completed grade twelve. Some were high school graduates. Most reported that they had to face considerable difficulties in completing their education as high schools were far away from their villages. Except for two trainees, who had considerable difficulty finishing their education because of lack of family support (especially from brothers), in all other cases the girls reported that their parents were very supportive and encouraged them to study. Of the parents, it was primarily mothers who had supported the girls. Many girls were brought to the Centre by their mothers. At the time when the girls were studying, there did not seem any hope that they would be able to get jobs; yet, parents felt that educating their children was important as they hoped that they would have to pay a smaller dowry if they got married.

Twelve of the thirty-two girls interviewed were trained by the Centre. Ten of them were still undergoing training. The girls still receiving training said that when they first came to Hyderabad, they were really scared and were not sure if they would be able to cope. As Kavita said, "I was too scared to open my mouth when we were asked questions, but our Sir (customary Indian polite term for teacher) said, 'Do not worry about making mistakes. That is the only way you will learn. You must talk.' So that is how my confidence increased. Now we are learning to speak English and we practice English in the hostel. If I know English, I can manage anywhere. The English training is the best and I want to improve my language skills."

Other girls said they had never touched a computer keyboard before and were scared to do so the first time they had to. But the trainers helped them to get over their fear, and many girls had a good typing speed now.

The girls said that the most important part of their training was to help them build their confidence. The course curriculum was designed such that the first two months were spent in helping the girls deal with low self-esteem. They were trained in soft skills in addition to English and were given basic computer knowledge.

Twenty disabled trainee girls interviewed said that the training was essentially on-the-job training. While the work was monotonous and sometimes they would get very tired sitting in one place for long hours, the salary was good. As one girl said, "The main value of this kind of work for us is that there is no danger of falling and injuring ourselves. Even tea and snacks are sent to us at our workstation while the others have to go to the canteen. Then the factory provides transport, accommodation, and food. After the training we have an assured job."

Impact of Training and Placement on Families and Others

The girls said that the best thing that happened to them was the impact this training and placement had on their families and other villagers. The girls got more respect when they went home because they were working and earning money. Most girls sent money home to their parents. As one girl said, "We are no longer dependents. We are providers! We are supporting our parents in their old age."

More important, the girls were working in Hyderabad city! Villagers, who would earlier taunt them for their disability, no longer did so. Parents were relieved that the girls could now be independent and would not be a burden on their brothers or families. Girls reported that they were treated better by their siblings now. The girls also said that apart from the salaries they were getting, the good thing about working and living together in a hostel was that they did not feel isolated. At home when everyone left for work, there was no one to talk to and they would feel lonely.

Future Plans

All of the thirty-two girls interviewed said they would work for a few years and then go back to completing their education. Some of them wanted to improve their English language skills so as to start providing English language classes in their village. One girl said, "Till we came to the Centre and started learning English, we had no idea how important it was for our self-confidence and well-being. In our schools, teachers conduct classes to teach English in Telugu [the regional language of Andhra Pradesh] so of course we could not speak the language. Now when I go home to my village and speak English so well, everyone is surprised and they treat me differently." Other girls wanted higher level jobs that required better qualifications.

Lessons Learned

There are several important lessons to be learned from this model. First, it is an unusual partnership of government and a group of committed team members with a private sector background. The vision, strategy, and face of the program have been crafted by the private sector team of the Centre, whose salaries are paid by a private foundation. The government pays for the training costs. The private sector team works independently and innovates as it moves along. Since the government does not pay their salaries, the relationship of the team with their government counterparts is not hierarchical. This promotes cooperative functioning.

Second, disabled youth are identified through the established network of SHG groups and the local district offices as well as the Software for Assessment of Disabled for Access, Rehabilitation and Empowerment database. Since many states now have SHG networks, a similar strategy could be pursued in other states as well.

Third, it is a competency-based model in that all placements are made after an assessment is done of the competency of the youth by the recruiting company. No special concessions are made for the disabled (other than workplace adjustments). Companies have realized that there is less attrition in this group and persons with disabilities are able to work hard and be productive.

Any employment based on a welfare approach would not last long if the persons employed did not serve the company's interests. Furthermore, it is important for the self-esteem of disabled youth to know that they have been hired for their competency and not for their disability or out of a sense of charity.

Certain elements of this model deserve to be underlined. Strong private sector linkages were needed in order to convince senior management of the need to make workplace adjustments and also of the viability of offering employment to the disabled. In the case of skill development and placement for both disabled and nondisabled youth, a system was put in place from identification of candidates to training, placement, and postplacement mentoring so that the persons did not drop out of the program. When it was found that poor persons did not have the money to stay in the city without a salary, the team negotiated with the GOAP to provide a stipend for the first month to tide them over and this dramatically reduced the problem of dropouts.

Core Principles for Scalability and Replicability

The three case studies described in this paper draw attention to the links between education and skill development. The importance of bridging administrative and policy silos emerges here as a critical issue, as it has done in previous chapters in this volume, including those by Betancourt, Hann, and Zombo and by Kelly and Newnham. All three case studies are complementary to one another. The effort of getting children out of work and into formal full-time schools paved the way for skill development. The core principles for MV Foundation were social mobilization and community empowerment. Social mobilization was the first critical step in consensus-building around the issue of abolition of child labor. The struggle was to forge a consensus on the need for the abolition of child labor. It was difficult but the organization believed that without consensus within the community, child labor elimination would be an uphill task. They developed partnerships even with employers of child bonded laborers so as to put moral pressure upon them to release these children and to pay for their education. Government school teachers initially resisted the idea of more children in their already large classrooms. Partnerships were built up over the years with formal school teachers around the elimination of child labor so that they would see it as their duty to ensure that every child was in school. Government officials were invited to visit the bridge camps and see for themselves the transformation of a child bonded laborer into a school-going child. These partnerships helped take this initiative to scale.

In the other two case studies on skill development and employment, the core principle was forging partnerships. The issue of upgrading skills of youth for improving their employability was raised among organized women's SHGs. Since the women were already mobilized around issues of thrift, credit, and the need for improving incomes, taking up the issue of skill development for youth was not difficult and they took upon themselves the work of identifying educated, unemployed youth from the poorest families. The new partnership was developed with the private sector in order to ensure placements. The skill development programs piggybacked on an existing large network of women's SHGs supported by the GOAP and added another dimension, the partnership with the private sector.

Economic Growth and Changing Aspirations

Economic growth has brought new opportunities for both boys and girls in India. Notwithstanding levels of extreme poverty and inequality, parents are investing in the future of their children. The 2011 World Development Report notes that the rise in outsourcing has brought new opportunities for women and this has, in turn, led to an increase in parental investments in girls' education. The report cites research undertaken randomly in selected villages where business process outsourcing recruiting services informed parents and girls alike about the possibilities of wage work for educated girls. This information had wide-ranging impact. Three years later, it was found that girls in the 5–15 age group in the villages where work was provided were 3 to 5 percentage points more likely to be in school, had a higher body mass index (a measure of health), and were 10 percent more likely to have jobs. Other factors such as the mother's educational levels or the poverty of the family did not seem to have made a difference. The possibility of market returns on education alone seemed to be sufficient to increase enrollment of girls and to improve outcomes (World Bank 2011, 110). Clearly, parents were investing in their girls because there was the possibility of future work opportunities. Thus, according to the report, "evidence of greater returns was enough to stimulate greater human capital accumulation" (World Bank 2011, 67).

My interviews with adolescents over a period of twenty years have brought out how deeply they valued education and aspired for good jobs. Girls and boys, when asked how far they wanted to go in their studies, always spoke about going to college and later becoming doctors, engineers, district collectors (civil servants in charge of districts with considerable power and authority), or senior police officers. Many would not have been able to fulfill their dreams for a variety of reasons described earlier. But some adolescents have fulfilled their dreams because their parents invested in their education in spite of adverse financial circumstances. This is evident from the fact that literacy levels are going up even among vulnerable and marginalized communities such as the scheduled caste and scheduled tribe parents are investing in private schools and in English language courses so that their children have a better future.

The Debate About Compulsory Schooling and Quality Education

There are divergent views among academics and others on the issue of compulsory education for all children. The Right of Children to Free and Compulsory Education Act 2009 mandates compulsory education for all children between the ages of six and fourteen years in age-appropriate classes. Even so, there is an argument to the effect that India is churning out millions of children from its classrooms whose learning outcomes are extremely poor. In turn, it is argued that these children will have very low levels of skills and will therefore be unemployable in the labor market. Lant Pritchett, an American academic working on Indian education, has made a scathing attack on the Act, which, according to him, is the "most massively ill-conceived thing that happened"[4] to Indian education policy. Pratap Bhanu Mehta (2011), a prominent Indian scholar and writer, argues that, first of all, schooling is not the same thing as education, just as having a degree is not the same thing as having skills. He goes on to say, however, that the relationship between education and unemployment is uncertain. Kerala, a state with high educational achievements, also has higher unemployment rates than the Indian average. Eric Hanushek (2004, 2) has pointed out that while it is common to consider education and schooling to mean the same thing, it is important to make a distinction between knowledge and skills, on the one hand, and schooling, on the other, because cognitive skills can also be developed outside the schooling system—within the family and the community. Hanushek and Woβmann (2007, 2) have suggested that without quality education, economic outcomes will not be significant. They argue that the thrust should be to improve quality rather than just ensuring adequate infrastructure, putting in place the required number of teachers, and making sure books are available.

It can be nobody's case that quality education is not a desirable goal. However, quality does not improve by itself. There has to be public pressure and creative strategies for improving the quality of education. Empty classrooms will not lead to quality education.

If the argument is made that quality should be improved before education is universalized, it faces many objections. For one thing, when we think of education as a human right, it must be available and accessible to all, as Sinha cogently argues in the preceding chapter. Second, we do not have to assume that learning outcomes or quality will forever and necessarily be poor. The Annual Status of Education Reports (ASER 2010) indicate that there has been an improvement in learning outcomes—at least in some states—and the relevant question would then be how to scale up and replicate these successes. The experience of MVF and its impact—both on learning outcomes in different states and on public policy—is an outstanding example of a transformational solution to the problem. Lastly, the argument fails because even when learning outcomes are poor, training programs, as described in the latter two case studies, can help improve skills and therefore the prospects of employability, provided there is at least some basic level of education. Even if the improvements are modest and are to be found in some regions and not in others and even if these improvements have taken a considerable amount of time, it is important that we do not underestimate the potential for change.

Notes

1. A bill for a complete ban on child labor has been introduced in Parliament.

2. This case study is based on this researcher's field visit to the MVF over a period of fourteen years from 1993 to 2007.

3. This information was provided by the executive director, EGMM, on June 14, 2011.

4. "People can't believe the same economy that produces 100,000 students a year in global top 10% also churns out millions with zero skills": Lant Pritchett, quoted in "Interview with Lant Pritchett," *Indian Express,* November 8, 2011.

References

Annual Status of Education Reports. 2010. ANDHRA PRADESH. District Institute of Education and Training.

Burra, Neera. 2012. "Developing Women's Skills for Improving Economic Prospects." New Delhi: South Asia Sector for Education, World Bank.

Hanushek, Eric A. 2004. "Economic Analysis of School Quality." Paper prepared for the *Education for All Global Monitoring Report,* on file with the author.

Hanushek, Eric, A. and Ludger Woβmann. 2007. "The Role of School Improvement in Economic Development." National Bureau of Economic Research working paper no. 12832. http://www.erf.org.eg/cms.php?id=publication_details&publication_id=1417.

Mehta, Pratap Bhanu. 2011. "The Education Wars." *Indian Express*, November 10.

Parasuraman, Sulabha, Sunita Kishor, Shri Kant Singh, and Y. Vaidehi. 2009. *A Profile of Youth in India*. National Family Health Survey (NFHS-3) India, 2005–06. Mumbai: International Institute for Population Sciences.

Tan, Hong, Sangeeta Goyal, and Yevgeniya Savchenko. 2007. "2006 Baseline Study of India's Industrial Training Institutes: Institutional Performance and Employment of ITI Graduates." On file with the author.

UNICEF. 2011. *The State of the World's Children 2011: Adolescence, an Age of Opportunity*. New York: UNICEF.

World Bank. 2011. *World Development Report: Gender Equality and Development*. World Bank. New York.

CHAPTER 17

Emerging from the Shadows: Adolescents with Disabilities Claim Their Rights Under International Law

Kerry Thompson

For too long, children and youth with disabilities have grown up in the shadows—excluded from society and hidden out of shame or fear. But, as the youngest generation of the twentieth century comes of age in the twenty-first century, the field of human rights is witnessing its emergence from the shadows into a role and place of its own. Though children and youth with disabilities continue to face violations of their human rights, yesterday's victims are becoming today's advocates as a new generation of self-advocates enters the fight against violence. This chapter will review some salient issues relating to the human rights circumstances of children and youth with disabilities. The focus will then shift to violence to which this population is subjected before turning to measures taken, particularly by young people themselves, to address this and advance their human rights.

Approximately one billion people or 15 percent of the world's population, its largest minority, have a disability (World Health Organization 2011). Eighty percent of this population lives in a developing country (UN Enable *Factsheet 2013*). Children and youth with disabilities constitute a significant portion of people with disabilities worldwide: 150 million children (UNESCO 2013) and between 180 and 220 million youth (United Nations Programme on Youth 2011) are estimated to have a disability. This circumstance is associated with significant rights deprivations and dramatic quality of life impacts starting from birth and continuing through childhood and adolescence into adulthood.

International acknowledgement that violence against young people with disabilities is a human rights violation is long standing. A critical milestone was set in 1989, when the UN General Assembly adopted the Convention on the Rights of the Child, the first human rights treaty to address the issue of disability. Article 2 of the CRC states (emphasis added): "States Parties shall respect and ensure the rights set forth in the present Convention to each child... without *discrimination* of any kind, irrespective of... *disability*." This represents the first inclusion of the word "disability" in a human rights instrument and the first acknowledgement of the correlation between *disability* and *discrimination*. *Disadvantage*, the Convention implies, is not a fact of life inherent in disability but a consequence of discriminatory attitudes and behavior toward disabled persons. In addition to the above contributions to disability rights, the CRC designated an article solely for the rights of children with disabilities (Article 23).

These developments represented important milestones for the disability rights movement in general and for children and youths with disabilities in particular. But progress following the coming into force of the CRC, both in terms of the implementation of treaty mandates and increases in young people's participation, has been limited. Though the Convention's articles apply to all children, initiatives taken by countries to comply with its provisions have not tended to address children and youth with disabilities. Many countries have made strides toward implementation of Article 28, which stipulates that "primary education [should be] compulsory and available free to all" and that it must be "accessible to all." For example, Tanzania's school enrollment rates had "doubled to 99.6 percent by 2008, compared to 1999 rates" (United Nations *We Can End Poverty* 2013). However, 47.6 percent of disabled Tanzanians are illiterate compared to 25.3 percent of those without disabilities (Tanzania National Bureau of Statistics 2010). Despite pronouncements to the contrary, governments rarely appropriate education funds to the needs of disabled children. As a result, 98 percent of children with disabilities in the developing world still do not get a full education (Child Rights International Network).

Doctrinal issues too give rise to concern, as Pineda points out in an earlier chapter in this volume. As Article 23 makes clear, the CRC approach to the needs of disabled children is based on an outmoded, medical model of disability, focused on the inherent detriments that flow from impairment rather than the contingent obstacles caused by lack of social accommodation. Emphasis is placed on "special needs," on "medical" and "social" treatments, and on "rehabilitation" rather than on nondiscriminatory provision of services and opportunities. The excerpt from paragraph 2, 3, and 4 within the CRC's Article 23 is shown in the footnote,[1] with terms of concern italicized. A more appropriate policy approach, based on a social model of disability, would distinguish between the impairment itself and the disabling effects of prevailing social norms, rather than simply equating disability with impairment. It would place the central human rights principle of equality at the core of programmatic interventions, rather than ignoring it as Article 23 does. It affords youth with disabilities education, health-care services, training, and enjoyment but only on the basis of "available resources" or "whenever possible." This prioritization reflects the Convention's language and hierarchical approach to entitlement, predicated on the assumption that youth with disabilities, far from being equal to other children or entitled to services that require inclusive reach, have needs that are subordinate to resource allocation constraints. The CRC thus implicitly gives states permission to provide for and protect the disabled child's rights on a conditional basis.

The attention to disability issues afforded by the CRC is expanded on in the UN Convention on the Rights of Persons with Disabilities (CRPD), which entered into force in 2008. The CRPD does not establish new human rights, but rather clarifies the legal obligations of states to respect and ensure the equal enjoyment of all human rights by persons with disabilities. The CRPD uses a social model and a rights-based approach; it "takes to new heights the movement from viewing persons with disabilities as 'objects' of charity, medical treatment and social protection towards viewing persons with disabilities as 'subjects' with rights, who are capable of claiming those rights and making decisions for their lives based on their free and informed consent as well as being active members of society" (UN Enable *Convention* 2013). By contrast with the CRC, equality is emphasized as a core starting point for policy; Article 7 of the CRPD requires states to "take all necessary measures to ensure the full enjoyment by children with disabilities of *all* human rights and fundamental freedoms on an *equal* basis with other children" (emphasis added).

Despite this doctrinal progress, children and youth with disabilities continue to face many rights violations, especially violence, one of the most inhumane but common acts against children whether disabled or not. Both the CRC and CRPD hold states accountable for protection against violence.[2]

The World Health Organization estimates around 150 million girls and 73 million boys under eighteen years of age experience sexual violence. Children with disabilities are twice as likely to encounter physical and sexual abuse as those without disabilities. Homicide of children is also widespread, particularly in low-income countries (World Health Organization 2004). High-income countries tend to have a lower risk of violence against children *without* disabilities compared to low-income countries, but violence against children *with* disabilities is nearly equal in low- and high-income countries. In the United States, which ranks fourth in the 2011 UN Human Development Index rankings (UN Development Programme 2011, 17–20), 30 percent of children with disabilities were abused, and these children were three to four times more likely to be abused than children without disabilities (Sullivan and Knutson 2000). Across the U.S. border, Canada (ranked sixth) also shows a high incidence of abuse against children with disabilities, five times greater than for the general population (Burin Peninsula—Voice Against Violence 2013). Even in top-ranked Norway, 80 percent of deaf adults reported being abused in their childhood (UN Secretary General 2005, 5). Compare these statistics with those of countries on the lower Human Development Index range: In Kenya (ranked 143rd), 15–20 percent of young people with disabilities experience severe levels of physical and sexual abuse (Handicap International and Save the Children 2011, 4). In India (ranked 134th), 25 percent of those with an intellectual impairment were raped (Handicap International and Save the Children 2011, 4). Underreporting in the developing world is likely to be a significant factor in the disparity just noted. Other forms of violence against individuals with intellectual impairment are pervasive, estimated at 80–90 percent in both the developed and developing world (UN Secretary General 2005, 5).

Effective legislation is considered an important step in the prevention of violence against those with a disability and yet many countries do not have such legislation in place: according to UN Enable only forty-five countries (out of 193 states parties to the CRPD) have antidiscrimination and other disability-specific laws, most of them developing countries (UN Enable *Factsheet* 2013). Some states have preexisting disability legislation that addresses concerns similar to those articulated by the CRPD. An example is the United States' Americans with Disabilities Act (ADA) that protects the rights of persons with disabilities.

When persons with disabilities are denied recognition under the law, their vulnerability to violence is exacerbated. According to a 2004 British study, persons with disabilities are less likely to obtain police intervention, legal protection, or preventive care than their nondisabled counterparts (UN Enable *Factsheet* 2013). Long-standing discriminatory attitudes within legal systems plus inaccessible investigative and testimonial procedures lead to a denial of justice and perpetuate the climate of violence.

In spite of the obstacles just discussed, there is some encouraging evidence suggesting that youth with disabilities are beginning to stand up for their rights, acting on the rally cry of the disability rights movement, "Nothing about us without us." In the past four years, since the coming into force of the CRPD, the number of registered disabled persons organizations (DPOs) has been rising, as has the number of youth disabled persons organizations run by and for youth with disabilities. Most DPOs focus on disability as it affects the community as a whole or on a specific type of disability; as a result disabled youth have complained of exclusion from the disability rights movement. Despite the CRC's injunction twenty-one years ago that children should have a voice in decisions and policies affecting them, it was not until 2005 that young people with disabilities were given a chance to be part of treaty negotiations. Prior to the negotiations, more than two hundred youths with disabilities from twelve countries took part in focus groups to provide feedback on issues of most concern to them. Representatives from these focus groups were invited to witness the drafting of the CRPD and provide feedback to the authors of the Convention (United Nations 2007). Today, youth DPOs are successfully advocating for changes. In Uganda, the Youth with Physical Disability Development Forum has been promoting educational rights for youth with disabilities. As a result of their advocacy, they have successfully lobbied their government to provide sixty-four university scholarships to youth with disabilities: ten of these recipients have gone on to receive a law degree. Another youth DPO in Uganda, Action for Youth with Disabilities, pushed for educational reforms at several universities and succeeded in getting Kyambogo University to implement a disability policy to better accommodate students with disabilities. Liberian youth with disabilities who lobbied for a disability bill were eventually invited by the House of Representatives to witness the signing of the bill in 2005.

The impact of youth DPOs has not been confined to promoting legislation and education. Violence has also been a target of their activism. In 2010, a group of young females with disabilities marched to the Bangladeshi parliament to protest sexual abuse. Their action increased attention to the issue and sent an encouraging message to other victims to come forward.

Deaf youth, who have successfully pushed their countries to accept sign language as a national language, are paving the way for deaf victims of violence to be able to report in sign language the violations against them. Disabled youth activism enhances participation of this constituency not just on disability specific issues but also on more comprehensive development issues affecting young people as a whole. In Uganda, Legal Action for Persons with Disabilities, a youth DPO established by a group of young lawyers, has been providing legal aid to people with disabilities, enabling them to access justice, and in the process stimulating reporting and prosecution of a greater number of human rights violations.

In addition to youth-led activism, institutional developments also suggest encouraging progress. These include attention to disability rights issues affecting young people in the regular periodic country submissions to UN monitoring mechanisms. To correct past neglect of disability issues, a general comment by the Committee on the Rights of the Child notes "that the implementation of the Convention with regards to children with disabilities should not be limited to these articles (2 and 23)" (Committee on the Convention on the Rights of the Child 2007). Now, more countries are including disabilities within their reports. The sixtieth session of the Committee on the Rights of the Child met in June 2012 to review reports submitted by Algeria, Australia, Cyprus, Greece, Turkey, and Vietnam. All six countries' reports included references to children with disabilities. At its seventeenth session in June 2011, the Human Rights Council passed a resolution, calling on the UN Office of the High Commissioner for Human Rights to do "a thematic analytical study on the issue of violence against women and girls and disability." The HRC resolution stressed the importance of a "coordinated multisectoral approach" to combating violence against women and girls with disabilities, one that also included youth. The HRC's statement illustrates the progress made by the youth with disabilities movement.

The voices of youths with disabilities are finally being heard. No longer silenced, they stand before government and civil society to demand their rights. In turn, governments and civil society are beginning to recognize youth with disabilities not simply as victims, but instead as partners and equal participants in the fight against violence and other human rights violations. In the last few years, more NGOs and DPOs have been working together to present alternative reports to the UN monitoring mechanisms, with youth DPOs contributing and emerging from the shadows. In 1998, former United Nations secretary-general Kofi Annan addressed the World

Conference of Ministers Responsible for Youth as follows: "A society that cuts itself off from its youth severs its lifeline; it is condemned to bleed to death." No words ring truer when it comes to the role that youth with disabilities must play in the disability rights movement.

Notes

1. Article 23 of the CRC states (the emphasis is added) that "(2) States Parties recognize the right of the disabled child to *special care* and shall encourage and ensure the extension, *subject to available resources*, to the eligible child and those responsible for his or her care, of assistance for which application is made and which is appropriate to the child's condition and to the circumstances of the parents or others caring for the child.

"(3) Recognizing the *special needs* of a disabled child, assistance extended in accordance with paragraph 2 of the present article shall be provided free of charge, *whenever possible*, taking into account the financial resources of the parents or others caring for the child, and shall be designed to ensure that the disabled child has *effective* access to and receives education, training, health- care services, rehabilitation services, preparation for employment and recreation opportunities in a manner conducive to the child's achieving the fullest possible social integration and individual development, including his or her cultural and spiritual development

"(4) States Parties shall promote, in the spirit of international cooperation, the exchange of appropriate information in the field of *preventive health care* and of *medical, psychological and functional treatment* of disabled children, including dissemination of and access to information concerning methods of *rehabilitation*, education and vocational services, with the aim of enabling States Parties to improve their capabilities and skills and to widen their experience in these areas. In this regard, particular account shall be taken of the needs of developing countries."

2. Article 19 of the CRC states that "States Parties shall take all appropriate legislative, administrative, social and educational measures to protect the child from all forms of physical or mental violence, injury or abuse, neglect or negligent treatment, maltreatment or exploitation, including sexual abuse." Article 15 of the CRPD calls for states to take "effective legislative, administrative, judicial or other measure to prevent persons with disabilities, on an equal basis with others, from being subjected to torture or cruel, inhuman or degrading treatment or punishment."

References

Burin Peninsula—Voice Against Violence. *Disability Abuse*. www.bpvav.com/disabilityabuse.htm. 2013.

Child Rights International Network. *Disability*. www.crin.org/themes/ViewTheme.asp?id=5. 2013.

Committee on the Convention of the Rights of the Child. 2007. General Comment No. 9. CRC/GC/2007/9. New York: United Nations.

Handicap International and Save the Children. 2011. *Out from the Shadows: Sexual Violence Against Children with Disabilities*. London, Handicap International and Save the Children.

Sullivan, P. M., and J. F. Knutson. 2000. "Maltreatment and Disabilities: A Population-Based Epidemiological Study." *Child Abuse and Neglect* 24, no. 10 (October): 1257–74.

Tanzania National Bureau of Statistics. 2010. *Tanzania 2008 Disability Survey*. www.Nbs.go.tz/tnada/index.php/catalog/5.

UN Enable. 2013. *Convention on the Rights of Persons with Disabilities*. http://www.un.org/disabilities/default.asp?id=150.

———. 2013. *Factsheet on Persons with Disabilities*. www.unn.org/disabilities/default.asp?id=18.

UNESCO. 2013. *Children with Disabilities*. www.unesco.org/new/en/education/themes/strengthening-education-system/includsive-education/children-with-disabilities.

UNICEF. 2002. *Adolescence: A Time That Matters*. New York: UNICEF. http://www.unicef.org/publications/index_4266.html.

United Nations. 2007. *Youth Flash*. Vol. 4. No. 1.

United Nations. *We Can End Poverty 2015 Millennium Development Goals*. http://www.un.org/millenniumgoals/pdf/MDG_FS_2_EN.pdf. 2013.

UN Development Programme. 2011. *Human Development Report 2011, Sustainability and Equity: A Better Future for All*. New York: UNDP.

UN Programme on Youth (UNPY). 2011. *Fact Sheet: Youth with Disabilities*. International Year of Youth (August 2010– August 2011) website. http://social.un.org/youthyear/docs/Fact%20sheet%20youth%20with%20disabilities.pdf.

UN Secretary General. 2005. *Violence Against Disabled Children*. Report on Violence against Children, convened by UNICEF at the United Nations, New York, July 28.

World Health Organization. 2004. *Global Estimates of Health Consequences Due to Violence Against Children*. Geneva, Switzerland: WHO.

World Health Organization and World Bank. 2011. *World Report on Disability*. Geneva, Switzerland: WHO. http://whqlibdoc.who.int/publications/2011/9789240685215_eng.pdf.

LIST OF CONTRIBUTORS

Theresa S. Betancourt is Associate Professor of Child Health and Human Rights in the Department of Global Health and Population at the Harvard School of Public Health and directs the Research Program on Children and Global Adversity (RPCGA) at the François-Xavier Bagnoud Center for Health and Human Rights. Her central research interests include the developmental and psychosocial consequences of concentrated adversity on children and families, resilience and protective processes in child and adolescent mental health, and applied cross-cultural mental health research. She has extensive experience conducting research among children and families in low-resource settings and in adaptation and testing of mental health interventions for children facing adversity due to violence and chronic illness. She is the Principal Investigator of a project to develop and evaluate a Family Strengthening Intervention (FSI) for HIV-affected families in Rwanda, a project to integrate evidence-based mental health interventions into education and employment programs for youth in postconflict settings, as well as a prospective longitudinal study of war-affected youth in Sierra Leone. She has written extensively on mental health and resilience in children facing adversity.

Jacqueline Bhabha is FXB Director of Research, Professor of the Practice of Health and Human Rights at the Harvard School of Public Health, the Jeremiah Smith Jr. Lecturer in Law at Harvard Law School, and an Adjunct Lecturer in Public Policy at the Harvard Kennedy School. She received a first class honors degree and an MSc from Oxford University, and a JD from the College of Law in London.

From 1997 to 2001 Bhabha directed the Human Rights Program at the University of Chicago. Prior to 1997, she was a practicing human rights lawyer in London and at the European Court of Human Rights in Strasbourg. She has published extensively on issues of transnational child migration, refugee protection, children's rights, and citizenship. She is the editor of *Children Without a State* (2011), and author of *Child Migration and Human Rights in a Global Age* (2014, Princeton University Press).

Bhabha serves on the board of the Scholars at Risk Network, the World Peace Foundation, the *Journal of Refugee Studies* and the *Anti-Trafficking Review*. She is also a founder of the Alba Collective, an international women's NGO currently working with rural women and girls in developing countries to enhance financial security and youth rights.

Krishna Bose is currently working at the World Health Organization at their headquarters in Geneva, in the Department of Maternal, Newborn, Child and Adolescent Health. She holds a PhD from Carnegie-Mellon University and a Master's in Public Health from the University of Michigan. Her work has mainly focused on improving measurement of the health and development of adolescents and their right to access prevention, promotion, and care. An important focus of her research has been supporting the collation and analyses of epidemiologic data and the availability, accessibility, and acceptability of adolescent friendly health services (AFHS). She has also researched documenting protective factors associated with increased self-efficacy and decreased prevalence of risk behaviors among adolescents across cultures. The importance of connection to and regulation from a trusted adult has been shown to be strongly protective across cultures, as is the respect for individuality shown by trusted adults for adolescents in their lives. She has also worked to build capacities with ministries of health in member states of the United Nations to strengthen adolescent epidemiology, document the prevalence of protective factors and other social determinants, and assess the quality, accessibility, and acceptability of AFHS.

Neera Burra has a PhD in Sociology from the Delhi School of Economics and has worked for over two decades with different UN agencies. She was with the UN Development Programme from 1995 to 2007, first as Assistant Resident Representative and later as Special Advisor, Poverty.

She has done extensive fieldwork on the issue of child labor in India and has published several papers and a book titled *Born to Work: Child Labour in India* (1995). The book was used by the Supreme Court of India as evidence of the widespread prevalence of child labor in India.

She took early retirement from UNDP and now works as a development consultant on issues related to social inclusion and equality, with a focus on gender, education, skill development, employment, and poverty, subjects on which she has written several research papers for the World Bank and various UN agencies. She has edited and contributed to a book on women and wasteland development as well as another on microcredit, poverty, and empowerment.

She continues to work on issues related to children's rights around free and compulsory education. She is currently advisor to the India Programme of the Paul Hamlyn Foundation.

Malcolm Bush is an affiliated scholar at Chapin Hall at the University of Chicago and senior adviser to the International Center for Research and Policy on Childhood at the Pontifical Catholic University of Rio de Janeiro. His many publications include research in the United States and Brazil on community economic development, low-income children and families, affordable housing, and workforce development. He is fluent in Brazilian Portuguese. He is the author of *Children in Distress: Public and Private Responses*. He has been a regular faculty member at Northwestern University and the University of Chicago, and for fifteen years was the president of Woodstock Institute in Chicago, a national economic development think tank. While at Woodstock Institute he served a term on the Community Advisory Council of the U.S. Federal Reserve Board where he chaired the bank regulations committee. He was also awarded one of the MacArthur Foundation's international awards for creative and effective organizations. He holds a BA in modern history from Oxford University, an MA in American History and Economics from the University of Pennsylvania, and a PhD from Northwestern University in Social Psychology and Urban Affairs. He is a longtime board member of the Chicago Low-Income Housing Trust Fund.

Jocelyn DeJong has worked and done research on reproductive health in the Middle East region for over twenty years. She is currently a professor at the Faculty of Health Sciences, American University of Beirut in Lebanon, where she coordinates two regional research networks, the Reproductive Health Working Group in the Arab countries and Turkey (www.rhwg.org) and a four-country research network on maternal health (http://www.aub.edu.lb/fhs/cccc/). During the 1990s she ran a regional grants program in reproductive health for the Ford Foundation regional office for the Middle East and North Africa in Cairo. She has published on youth sexual and reproductive health in the Arab countries and is currently doing research on the health of young, married women in Yemen. She is interested in linkages between reproductive health and development and has published on the application of Amartya Sen's capabilities framework to reproductive health. She holds a BA in Social Anthropology from Harvard University (where she was awarded a Harvard Knox fellowship), an MPhil in Development Studies from the Institute of Development Studies, University of Sussex, and a PhD in Health Policy in Developing Countries from the London School of Hygiene and Tropical Medicine.

Elizabeth Gibbons is currently a Visiting Scientist at the FXB Center for Health and Human Rights at the Harvard School of Public Health and was a 2012 Distinguished Visiting Fellow at the Kozmetsky Center of Excellence in Global Finance at St. Edwards University. Prior to these 2011 academic appointments, Elizabeth Gibbons enjoyed a lengthy career in the UNICEF. Her career in social development and humanitarian affairs spanned almost three decades, during which she lived and worked in Togo, Kenya, and Zimbabwe, and served as head of UNICEF's offices in Haiti and in Guatemala. She also served as strategic regional advisor to UNICEF's Haiti operations following the devastating earthquake of 2010, and held several positions in UNICEF's New York headquarters, including Acting Director, Emergency Operations; Chief, Global Policy; and Deputy Director, Division of Policy and Practice. A graduate of Smith College and Columbia University, Elizabeth D. Gibbons is the author of *Sanctions in Haiti: Human Rights and Democracy Under Assault*, and a contributing author to several other books.

Katrina Hann is Research Manager of the Children and Armed Conflict research portfolio of the Research Program on Children and Global Adversity (RPCGA) at the François-Xavier Bagnoud Center for Health and Human Rights, Harvard School of Public Health. She is also a member of the Sierra Leone Mental Health Coalition and Secretary of the Mental Health Steering Committee, Ministry of Health and Sanitation, Government of Sierra Leone. Her research interests include health systems development and cross-cultural mental health research in low-resource and postconflict settings. She is also interested in research capacity building, mental health policy, and advocacy for the right to health. Hann holds a Master's in Theory and Practice of Human Rights from the University of Essex.

Mary Kawar has worked on employment issues for the past twenty years. She is currently the Senior Employment Specialist at the Arab States Office of the International Labour Organization (ILO) where she supports the development of employment policies and manages employment promotion programs. Previously she worked at the ILO headquarters in Geneva on issues related to employment policy, gender, youth employment, and skills development. She has authored and coauthored research, managed surveys and programs, and developed training materials and policy guidelines in the Arab region and outside on the same issues. Between 2005 and 2006 she served as an advisor to the Minister of Labour in Jordan where she initiated the development of an employment policy, a maternity protection law, and the establishment of a women's department in the ministry, among other things. She holds a BA in Social Anthropology from Tufts University, a MSc in Social Policy and Planning from the London School of Economics (LSE), and a PhD in Development Studies from LSE where she was awarded the Foreign Commonwealth Office Scholarship as well as the Population Council Middle East Research Award.

Since May 2010, **Orla Kelly** has worked as a Research Associate at the François-Xavier Bagnoud Center for Health and Human Rights, Harvard University, where she has been managing the India-based research portfolio. In this role she has designed and managed two research projects. The first is an investigation into the obstacles to secondary school educational access and success for rural adolescents, specifically girls in the northwestern state of Gujarat. The second aims to determine the infrastructural and social triggers that enable disadvantaged girls to successfully complete secondary education and gain access to third-level institutions, using the positive deviance approach and a mixed methodology.

Prior to her position at the FXB Center, she interned at the Human Rights Network in New Delhi and worked as a campaign developer at Google between 2005 and 2007.

Kelly holds an LLM in Human Rights Law and an MBS in International Business from University College Dublin, and an undergraduate degree in European Commerce and German from University College Cork.

Born in Timisoara, Romania, **David Mark** completed his MA studies in International Relations and European Studies at the West University of Hungary.

Mark is a Romani activist and was previously a Roma Initiatives fellow for the Open Society Foundations. He was also the coordinator of the European Roma Policy Coalition (ERPC), an informal coalition of nongovernmental organizations operating at the EU level on issues of human rights, antidiscrimination, antiracism, social inclusion, and Roma rights. Previously, he held the position of Executive Director of the Roma Civic Alliance of Romania (ACRR) and was a member of the staff in the cabinet of Member of the European Parliament Viktoria Mohacsi. Mark is a PhD candidate in Political Sciences at the University of Bucharest.

Margareta Matache is a Romanian Roma human rights activist who joined the François-Xavier Bagnoud Center as a Post-doctoral Research Fellow in September 2012.

She has worked on Roma and minorities issues since 1999 in various local, national, and international environments. From 2005 to 2012, Margareta Matache was the Executive Director of Romani CRISS (www.romanicriss.org), a leading Roma NGO that defends and promotes the rights of Roma.

Previously, Matache served as a youth worker, trainer, and as a short-term observer for several missions in Balkan countries for the Organization for Security and Co-operation in Europe's Office for Democratic Institutions and Human Rights. She has also coordinated and participated in the implementation of multiple regional European projects, including Roma and the Stability Pact in South-Eastern Europe and Roma, Use Your Ballot Wisely" of the OSCE/ODIHR.

She completed her doctoral research work in early childhood development of Romani children at the Faculty of Political Sciences, University of Bucharest, in 2012. Margareta holds a master's degree in European Social Policies from the University of Bucharest.

Clea McNeely, MA, DrPH, has a joint appointment with the Center for the Study of Youth and Political Conflict and the Department of Public Health at the University of Tennessee, Knoxville. She also serves as the Vice President of Programming for the Society for Research on Adolescence. Dr. McNeely researches positive youth development across social contexts, with a particular emphasis on schools. Her current research focuses on how youth make successful transitions to adulthood in regions of political conflict around the globe and in regions of economic and social distress within the United States. As part of this research agenda,, McNeely carries out community-based participatory evaluation of programs and policies to promote the health of young people. She uses multiple research methods including social network analysis, causal models, and qualitative methods. Her work has been supported by the Centers for Disease Control and Prevention, the National Institute for Child Health and Development, the William T. Grant Foundation, the Robert Wood Johnson Foundation, and the Jacobs Foundation. McNeely is coauthor of *The Teen Years Explained: A Guide to Healthy Adolescent Development* (Johns Hopkins University Press, 2010). A free downloadable version of the book is available at http://www.jhsph.edu/adolescenthealth/.

Glaudine Mtshali is a medical doctor and experienced diplomat with a deep-seated commitment to promoting vulnerable groups' health and human rights. She practiced medicine during South Africa's turbulent apartheid era and was appointed Chief Director for National Health Programs at apartheid's abolition. Her work focused on the rights of women, adolescents, children, the elderly, the mentally challenged, and disabled groups. She chaired the multisectoral National Program of Action for Children and represented South Africa on UNICEF's Executive Board.

Mtshali has served as South Africa's Ambassador to the United Nations Office in Geneva, Health Envoy to the Governments of the USA, Canada, and Brazil, and as a Consul-General. She led the Geneva-based African Ambassadors' efforts on the 2009 UN Racism Review Conference resulting in an actionable five-year work plan to address racism. She presented South Africa's progress report on dealing with apartheid's racial legacy to the UN Human Rights Council. She is currently the Executive Director of the Harvard Global Health Institute where she helps build collaborative partnerships to enhance students' experiential exposure to global health education and leadership development.

She holds degrees in medicine (MBBCh), law (LLB), and administration (MBA) from the University of the Witwatersrand in Johannesburg and the University of Massachusetts-at-Amherst.

Katie Naeve is currently Policy Advisor for Oxfam America, where she designs national and global level policy strategies for sustainable community-driven economic development. She also researches innovative antipoverty models that focus on economic empowerment and private sector collaboration for development. Prior to this, Naeve worked in economic development research at Harvard University's Center for International Development, where she was involved in a number of research initiatives and evaluations focusing on improving girls' access to education in Burkina Faso and child protection mechanisms in Sierra Leone that utilized mobile phone technology. More recently at Harvard, Naeve was Research Associate at the Women and Public Policy Program where she worked to link academic research on gender equality to policymakers and practitioners and consulted on the U.S. Paycheck Fairness Act. Naeve serves as advisor to Instiglio, is a board member of the Breath of Life Foundation, is a guide for the Resolution Project, and volunteers with Court Appointed Special Advocates for Children. She holds a Master of Public Policy degree from Harvard University's Kennedy School of Government where her graduate research evaluated the impact of social and economic reintegration programs for former child soldiers in Colombia.

Elizabeth A. Newnham is a postdoctoral research fellow at the François-Xavier Bagnoud Center for Health and Human Rights at Harvard School of Public Health. Her research examines mental health outcomes for children and adolescents living in adverse conditions, and the development and evaluation of evidence-based interventions in disaster and postconflict settings.

Newnham joined the FXB Center in 2010 as the inaugural Morgan Stanley Pediatrics Fellow. She completed her Master of Psychology (Clinical) and PhD at the University of Western Australia, and has conducted work in Australia, Sierra Leone, Hong Kong, China, India, and the United States. Newnham was recently awarded a National Health and Medical Research Council (NHMRC) Sidney Sax Early Career Fellowship to examine the mediating role of daily hardship in posttraumatic stress among war- and disaster-affected children. She holds concurrent positions at the University of Oxford, the Chinese University of Hong Kong, and the University of Western Australia.

Victor Pineda is a globally recognized expert on disability policy. He is the Chancellor's Postdoctoral Research Fellow for Academic Diversity at the University of California, Berkeley, a Lecturer in the Department of City and Regional Planning at the University of California at Berkeley, and an Adjunct Professor at American University's School for International Service. He teaches courses on planning theory, policy evaluation, and international community development. In 2003, Pineda founded the World Enabled Initiative to improve the employment and participation outcomes for youth with disabilities through inclusive research and educational programs. Pineda holds a PhD from the Luskin School for Public Affairs at the University of California at Los Angeles and a Master's in City and Regional Planning from the University of California at Berkeley.

Irene Rizzini is a professor at the Pontifical Catholic University of Rio de Janeiro, Brazil, and the Director of the International Center for Research on Childhood (CIESPI). Rizzini served as the President of Childwatch International Research Network from 2002 to 2009. She held the visiting chair in Brazilian Cultural Studies at the Helen Kellogg Institute for International Studies at the University of Notre Dame in 2006, and was appointed a John Simon Guggenheim Memorial Foundation fellow in 2008. She is the author of several books, including *Globalization and Children*; *The Art of Governing Children: The History of Social Policies, Legislation, and Child Welfare in Brazil*; *Disinherited from Society: Street Children in Latin America*; *The Lost Century: The Historical Roots of Public Policies on Children in Brazil*; *Images of the Child in Brazil: 19th and 20th Centuries*; *Children and the Law in Brazil—Revisiting the History (1822–2000)*; and *The Human Rights of Children and Adolescents: Twenty Years of the Statute*.

Elena Rozzi is a human rights advocate working to promote the rights of migrant and Roma children and youth in Italy through advocacy, social research, and legal counseling. She worked with Save the Children Italy from 2001 to 2007, as coordinator of the Migrant Children National Programme, and within European networks such as the Separated Children in Europe Programme. She has been working with the Turin University Social Sciences Department, the Istituto degli Innocenti Research Centre, the Italian Ministry of Welfare, and the Association of Italian Municipalities in action research projects regarding Roma children's education and Roma integration. She has been working with the Harvard University François-Xavier Bagnoud Center in the design of a transnational participatory action research project with Roma and non-Roma youths. She has been working as a legal adviser and serves on the Board of the Association for Legal Studies on Migration, the main Italian association of legal practitioners engaged in protecting migrants and the rights of minorities that have been discriminated against.

She has published articles and contributions on these subjects, including her essay on "Undocumented Migrant and Roma Children in Italy: Between

Rights Protection and Control" in *Children Without a State: A Global Human Rights Challenge*.

Christian Salazar Volkmann has been working as Deputy Director, Programme Division, at UNICEF's headquarters in New York since the end of 2011. In the Programme Division, he is responsible for UNICEF's Mid Term Strategic Plan, research and knowledge management, climate change and resilience, as well as for the post-2015 debates. He oversees UNICEF's technical sections for child protection, education, and HIV-AIDS, and leads UNICEF's global technical support to humanitarian action and programming in fragile contexts. Before this, Salazar represented the High Commissioner for Human Rights in Colombia and served as Representative of UNICEF in Iran as well as Deputy Representative in Vietnam and Guatemala. He also worked as adviser for the German Society for Technical Cooperation (GIZ) on youth and human rights in Guatemala. He is part of the Resident Coordinator/Humanitarian Coordinator pool of the UN.

Salazar is a German citizen with multicultural roots in Germany, Ecuador, and China. He obtained his PhD in Political Sciences from the University of Marburg (1992) and a Master's degree in Communications, Economics, and Philosophy at the University of Bochum (1988). He has published extensively on issues related to development, poverty reduction, human rights, and good governance, and has taught classes at NYU and the New School University. In 2011, Harvard Law School invited him as a visiting research fellow.

Shantha Sinha is currently a Professor in the Department of Political Science, University of Hyderabad. She served as the first Chairperson of National Commission for Protection of Child Rights (NCPCR) for the Government of India from 2007–13. In this capacity she addressed issues concerning violation of children's rights in relation to child labor and child trafficking; rights of children in areas of civil unrest; children's right to education; the juvenile justice system; corporal punishment, child abuse, and violence to children; and child malnutrition, doing so through public hearings, conducting inquiries and investigations, holding consultations with officials and nonofficials at the Union and State level; drafting laws and policies, and monitoring the implementation of programs and policies governing children and their access to entitlements.

She is India's foremost activist in the field of elimination of child labor. Through the MVFoundation, an NGO for which she held office as its Founder-Secretary Trustee, about six hundred thousand children have been withdrawn from work in the last two decades and mainstreamed into formal schools.

In recognition of her outstanding contribution, she was chosen for the prestigious Ramon Magsasay Award in 2003 for community leadership and awarded the Padma Shri in 1998 by the Government of India.

Laurence Steinberg is the Distinguished University Professor and Laura H. Carnell Professor of Psychology at Temple University. He received his AB in Psychology from Vassar College and his PhD in Developmental Psychology from Cornell University. Steinberg is a former President of the Division of Developmental Psychology of the American Psychological Association (APA) and of the Society for Research on Adolescence, and former Director of the MacArthur Foundation Research Network on Adolescent Development and Juvenile Justice. Steinberg's research has focused on a range of topics, including adolescent brain development, risk taking and decision making, parent-adolescent relationships, school-year employment, high school reform, and juvenile justice. Steinberg was the lead scientist in the preparation of the APA's amicus briefs submitted to the U.S. Supreme Court in *Roper v. Simmons*, which abolished the juvenile death penalty; *Graham v. Florida*, which banned the use of life without parole for juveniles convicted of nonhomicide crimes; and *Miller v. Alabama*, which prohibited the use of mandatory life without parole for all juvenile crimes. In 2009, Steinberg was named the first winner of the Klaus J. Jacobs Research Prize for Productive Youth Development. In 2013, he was inducted into the American Academy of Arts and Sciences.

Kerry Thompson holds a master's degree from Harvard University and is a lifelong disability activist and, for the past five years, a human rights advocate working to advance the UN Convention on the Rights of Persons with Disabilities (CRPD). Much of her work focuses on human rights for children with disabilities and for the deaf-blind community. She has guest lectured at Harvard Law School, Harvard Medical School, and the Massachusetts Institute of Technology, and has served on several panels on human rights. During her employment at Brigham and Women's Hospital, she worked to raise awareness of patients' rights for persons with disabilities. In addition, she was also the cocreator and spokesperson for Text4deaf, a technology company that aimed to bridge the communication gap between the deaf and hearing communities. She serves as the Director and Founder of Silent Rhythms, a dance company for children, youth, and adults with disabilities, which also raises awareness of the importance of inclusion in the arts. She serves on the Board of Directors for Deaf Inc. based in Boston. At a young age, Kerry was diagnosed as profoundly deaf then diagnosed a few years later with retinitis pigmentosa, a progressive blindness disorder.

Jean Zermatten was President and Dean of the Juvenile Court of the Canton of Valais (Switzerland) from 1980 to 2005. From 1994 to 1998, he was the President of the International Association of Youth and Family Judges and Magistrates.

He is the Founder and Director of the International Institute for the Rights of the Child in Sion, Switzerland (www.childsrights.org). Additionally, he is the President of the Swiss Society for Juvenile Judges.

He has initiated and launched the Master of Advanced Studies in Children's Rights in collaboration with the University of Fribourg, where he is a Lecturer, and the Institut Universitaire Kurt Bösch. He has worked in many international settings and is a member of the West Africa Network for children on the move.

He has been a member of the UN Committee for the Rights of the Child since 2005, was Vice-Chair from 2007 to 2011, and the Chairperson from 2011 to 2013.

He was awarded an honorary degree by the University of Fribourg. His most recent publications include *Child Rights and the Business Sector: Urging States and Private Companies to Meet Their Obligations*; *Children in the Context of International Law*; and *Climate Change: Impacts on Children and Their Rights*.

Moses Zombo was born and raised in eastern Sierra Leone in a family of photographers. He first worked as a school teacher until the time of his country's brutal civil conflict in which children were deliberately targeted and crimes against humanity were committed on a large scale. During this time, Zombo worked with the war-ravaged population, providing psychosocial support services in camps for the internally displaced. He cofound Defence for Children International–Sierra Leone Section (DCI-SL) with a group of friends. He provided volunteer services through the organization to children in conflict with the law and child victims of abuse. Afterward, he worked for UNHCR providing protection services to unaccompanied minors and the general population of mainly Liberian refugees. He is the joint longest-serving team member on a longitudinal study by the Harvard School of Public Health on Sierra Leone's youth who had childhood associations with the fighting forces.

INDEX

Note: The letter f following a page number denotes a figure; the letter t following a page number denotes a table

abortion, 66, 196, 280
abuse, 35, 91, 163; of children with disabilities, 329; child soldier recruitment as, 173; effect of, on brain development, 107–10
access: to education, 198, 251–52, 265, 275–77, 279, 294–96, 300–302; to information, 192–96, 282–83. *See also* education; information
access audits, 95
access to basic needs (SAFE model), 136–37, 140–42
accomplishments through supports, 87f
accountability, 15, 187, 200, 254, 328
Action for Youth with Disabilities, 330
"active agents", child soldiers as, 173–74
adaptive strategies, 85–87, 94; and SAFE model, 138
adolescence: and agency deprivations, 84–85; axes of, 14, 15–16, 40; brain structure and function in, 63–67; challenges of, 4–6, 7, 11–12; characteristics of, 24–27; concept of, 309–10; definition of, 1–2, 40, 54nn1, 3; developmental tasks of, 102–4; early, 63, 105; extended, 37, 41–43, 208–9; and gender, 227; importance of focus on, 4–9, 11, 26–27; invention of, 39–40; in Italy, 41–51; lack of consensus on, 2, 309–10; late, 64, 106; legacy of, 2, 107–8; limited, 44; luxury of, 10, 12; middle, 66, 105; rights-based approach to, 1, 3–4, 13–14, 18, 31–32, 44; social meanings of, 79–80;
transformation of, for Arab youth, 189; Western, 37, 40–41
adolescent brain development: and behavioral development, 67–70; not uniform, 65, 157; and policy, 9–10; science on, 63–67; and social policy, 70–74; and U.S. law, 60–63
adolescent deviance, 95n1, 191
adolescent offenders, 72
adolescent rights, 3, 6–7, 10; advancing Arab, 207; agenda for, 13, 16, 78; and brain immaturity, 73; challenges of realizing, 15–17, 236; and the CRC Committee, 33–37; and environmental supports, 115–16; lack of electoral pressure for, 6, 129–30; and limits on driving, 63; and policies, 28; and SAFE model, 138; strengthening, to counter youth violence, 132–33; vs. realities, 236–48
adolescents, 171; as adults, 59, 309–10; as agents, 113–14, 173–74; as change agents, 305; as children, 23, 59; and CRC, 23–24, 28, 33–37; cross-cultural research on, 114–15; as dangerous, 26, 31, 129–30, 191, 237; definition of, 23–24, 59; discrimination vs., 31; disrespect for, 111–12, 260; distinct from adults, 59–60; and distrust of state, 151–53; effects of war on, 134–35, 154–55, 157–58; and empowerment, 162–63; and ethnic identity, 158, 272–75; global statistics on, 11; investment in, 256; mental illness and, 68; migration of, 278–80; need for support in change, 54;

adolescents (continued)
  as neither adults nor children, 72;
  participation of, 164–66; as potential
  demographic dividend, 4–5, 192, 208,
  313–14; prevention of recruitment of,
  142–45, 159–60; prosocial decisions of,
  110–11; as resources, 37, 159–60, 166–67;
  risks of impairments for, 79; Roma, 48–51,
  270–89; separate from family, 12, 53–54;
  support for, from adults, 110–11; survival
  strategies of, 137–38; trapped in work,
  293–305; as vulnerable, 26, 31, 156–57
adolescents with disabilities, 6, 8; as agents
  of change, 95; impediments to adulthood
  for, 78–81; research on, 78–79; structural
  disadvantage and, 81–82. See also
  disabilities; disability rights
adulthood, 103; impediments to, for adolescents
  with disabilities, 78–81; early, brain
  development in, 64; and effects of childhood
  stressors, 110; thresholds to, 40, 42–43
adults, 59–60, 110–11; as youth allies, 260,
  304
advocacy, 4, 62, 326, 330–32; to change
  social norms, 116
affirmative action, 274, 278, 304; as
  reparation, 272
African Youth with Disabilities Network
  (AYWDN), 90–92
age: to be charged as adult, 59, 129;
  biological, 39–40, 55n10; to buy alcohol,
  59; chronological, 72–73; at demobilization,
  171; of majority, strategies for
  deciding, 71–72; of recruitment, 14, 128,
  141, 170; vs. maturity, 10, 28–29
age appropriateness, 112–13
age boundaries: and age-specific regulations,
  59–60; and law, 24, 70–74; match to
  brain science, 71–72
agency, 5, 12, 17, 18, 23, 32–33; assumption
  of, 298; collective, 83, 89–93; and disability,
  82–84, 96n5; enhancement of, 85–93;
  and family dynamics, 226; normative, 82;
  refusal as, 304; Sen's concept of, 78, 87;
  social and cultural, 11; vs. best interests of
  adolescents, 29; of war-affected youth,
  135–36, 141; without shame, 227; of
  youth, 260–61
agency, adolescent, 13, 88–93, 113–14, 138,
  166–67, 304; and child soldier recruitment,
  173–74, 181–82; negative exercise
  of, 96n6; rights and, 10; and role models
  for girls, 224–25; supporting, 142; and
  "voice," 188
agency deprivations, 82, 89, 92–93, 98n22;
  inequality and, 83; parents and, 84–85;
  vs. capability deprivations, 87
agency enabling instruction, 88–89
age ranges: for adulthood, 59–60; for adult
  neurobiological maturity, 71–72
age statuses, 39–40, 53
Albanian youth, 43–48, 43, 55–56n17;
  economic activities of, 47t
alcohol, 66, 72, 104
alienation, 158–59
alternative survival strategies, 141–45.
  See also former child soldiers; survival
  strategies
American Psychological Association, 60–61,
  65–66
Americans with Disabilities Act (ADA),
  329
Andhra Pradesh, 311–12, 314–22
Andhra Pradesh Rural Poverty Reduction
  Programme, 314–15
Annan, Kofi, 331
annulment, 298
Antonescu, Marshal Ion, 271
apprenticeships, 46, 51, 54n4, 242, 262
Arab-Israeli conflict, 187
Arab League, 193
Arab popular uprisings, 188–89; as
  preferred term, 210n1; and pride in Arab
  identity, 191; and youth leadership, 210
Arab Spring, 3, 97n19, 188; as term, 210n1
Arab women's leadership, 207
Arab young women, employment challenges
  for, 200, 204–6t
Arab youth: demographic trends of, 189–92;
  education issues of, 197–200f; employment
  challenges of, 200–206t; frustrations of,
  with educational quality, 199, 208; as
  globalized, 210; lack of health information
  on and for, 192–96, 208; lack of health
  services for, 195–97; participation of,
  limited, 206–7
Arab Youth Mental Health Scale, 195
Argentina, 35
Ariès, Philippe, 40
Aristotle, 67

armed conflicts, 11, 14–15, 127–29, 134–35, 189
art, 261–64
Article 1 CRC (definition), 23, 30
Article 2 CRC (nondiscrimination), 30–31, 327
Article 3 CRC (best interests), 31–32
Article 5 CRC (evolving capacities), 23, 28–30
Article 6 CRC (right to life, development), 32
Article 7 CRC (registration), 30
Article 7 CRPD (human rights on equal basis), 328
Article 12 CRC (right to be heard), 28, 32–33, 166
Article 15 CRPD (protection from cruel or degrading treatment), 332 n2
Article 19 CRC (protection from abuse), 332 n2
Article 23 CRC (children with disabilities), 327–28, 332n1
Article 28 CRC (universal primary education), 327
Article 227 (children's rights), of Brazilian Constitution, 236–37
Assaad, Ragui, 192
Assessment of Disabled (database), 317
assimilation, 158, 272. *See also* ethnic identity
"assisted repatriation," 44–48, 56n18
assistive technology (AT), 85–88
authenticity, 88–93
authorities, 44, 130
authority: of Children's Rights Councils, 245–46; of older generation, 192
autonomy, 9, 25, 28, 33, 223, 227, 304; and agency, 85–87; assisted, 86–93; economic, 228; emotional, 111; lack of, 16; vs. dependence, 2; vs. protection, 7. *See also* agency
"available resources," 328. *See also* Article 23 CRC
axes of adolescence, 14, 15–16, 40

backlash, to challenges of social norms, 6, 227
BACRIM (bandas criminals), 128–29
Badr, Mohammed, 207
"bamboccioni," 41
Bangladesh, 330

Barber, Brian, 111
barriers: to agency of girls, 299; to girls' education, 219, 222–26; as social failure, 95
begging, 11, 49, 50, 279
behavioral research, 62, 109; supported by neuroscience, 68, 70
belonging, 104, 287; and gangs, 128–29, 158; and recruitment, 170; through volunteering, 160
Benin, 36
best interests, 12, 135; conflicts in, 24–25, 28–29, 46–48, 52; criteria for, 31–32; and family conflicts in, 53–54; and Italian authorities, 44–48; and policy makers, 23; vs. agency, 28–29; vs. migration control, 55n16
best interests of adolescents, 7, 13–14, 23, 24–25; intercultural approach to, 51–54; in minority groups, 44–54
bicycles, 306n5
Bigombe, Betty, 143
biological sculpting of brain, 107. *See also* brain development
birth registration, 28, 143
Blos, Peter, 24
Bokamoso Youth Center, 263
Bolsa Família, 238
Bonded Labor Abolition Act, 312
Bou'Azizi, Muhammed, 188
brain development: and behavioral development, 67–70; and biological sculpting, 107; brain plasticity, 68, 108–9, 119; effects on, of abuse, 107–10; match of, to legal age boundaries, 71–72; and policy, 70–74; and practice, 103; and stressors, 107–10;
brain structure, effect on, of human rights abuses, 108–9
Brazil, 8, 236–48
Brazilian Constitution, 243; and children's rights, 236–37, 247
Brazilian Supreme Court, 245
Breyer, Justice Stephen, 62
bridge camp approach, 307n9, 311–13
Brookings Institution, 251–52
Bucharest, Romania, 273
budgets, 152, 164, 206, 245; as opportunities for shaping policy, 247
business. *See* private sector

Cali, Colombia, 127, 130
California, 87–89
California Youth Leadership Forum, 83–84
Campaign for Reduction of Violence, 165–66
camps: refugee, 143–44, 195; Roma, 43–44, 48–51, 56n19, 279
Canada, 329
capability, 77–78, 83, 85–93; Sen's concept of, 78, 85
capability approach, agency oriented, 82, 85–87
capacity building, 165, 230
Cape Town Principles, 143–44
career expectations, 258–59, 277
Caribbean, 131–32
Carnival Peace Brigades, 165–66
case, of teen in felony murder, 68–69
case studies: of elimination of child labor, 311–13; of Indian girls with disabilities in job program, 317–22; Mediterranean model of adolescence, 41–43; of return of unaccompanied minors in Italy, 44–48; of Roma teenage couple in Italy, 50–51; of skill development and jobs for rural youth, 314–17; of transformative learning for those with disabilities, 87–93
castes, 295, 303, 315, 323
Center for Universal Education, 251–52
Central America, 132–33, 157
Centre for People with Disabilities Livelihoods, 317–20
change agents: adolescents as, 305; adolescents with disabilities as, 95
child bearing, early. See early child bearing
child, definition of, 2, 135
child labor, 31, 199; and age, 10, 72; as barrier to education, 222; bill for ban of, 324n1; bonded, 311–12; child soldiering as, 173; classifications of, 305–6; elimination of, 294–96, 311–13, 321; gaps in law and policy for, 294–96; in India, 293–305, 310–13; in Italy, 42, 49–51, 54n6; rural societies and, 40; and survival, 56n25
"child laborization," 295
child marriage, 4, 43–44, 296–300, 310; illegal in Italy, 51, 56n23; rate of, in MENA, 190; statistics on, 11–12. See also early marriage

child protection: municipal boards for, 162–63; policies and laws, 298–300; SAFE model of, 136–38
children, 155, 164; at center of Syrian crisis, 189; with disabilities, violence against, 329; mandated funding for, 164; as subject of rights, 237; as victims, 134, 149
Children's Parliaments, 164
children's rights, 163; in adversity, 136; as priority, 237; progress in, 8
Children's Rights Council of Rio de Janeiro, 244–46
Children's Rights Councils (Brazil), 243–47
Child Rights Protection Forums, 312–13
child soldiers, 14–15, 189; and lack of basic rights, 139; SAFE model and prevention of, 142–45; as survival strategy, 137–38
child soldiers, former, 135; demobilization of, in Colombia, 170–82; and discrimination, 167n1; reintegration of, 140–45; in Sierra Leone, 138–39
child trafficking, 36, 295
China, 220–21
Choco, Colombia, 130
Choi, Jeewok, 108
choque de ordem ("shock of order"), 240–41
Christian evangelicals, 286
citizen security, 129–30, 132–33
civic engagement, 165–66, 242–47
civil rights, 115, 163, 207
civil war legacies, 150–54
class, 188, 252–53
CLPRA (Child Labour Prohibition Act, India), 294
coercion, 92, 105
cognitive abilities, 9, 24, 63–67, 103, 108
cognitive dissonance, 226–27
Cold War, 151
collaborations, 16; for adolescent health needed, 195–97; among agencies, 145–46, 321–22; for job creation, 178; multipartner, 259, 261, 263–64
collective action, 89–93, 188–89
Colombia: and child soldiers, 170–81; Return to Happiness, 159–60; and youth violence, 127–33
Colombia Joven, 131
Colombian Agency for Reintegration (ACR), 171–72, 175–81

Colombian Institute for Family Welfare (ICBF), 171, 177, 180
Colombian Minister of Interior, 129
Colombian Ministry of Defense, 178
comic book, 89–90
Committee on the Rights of the Child (CRC Committee), 13, 27, 331; and adolescent rights, 33–37
community acceptance, 140–41, 156, 180
Community and Individual Development Association, 261
community-based approaches, 230, 304, 311–13; for recovery for war-affected youth, 144–45; for recovery from war trauma, 155, 159–60; to support girls' education, 227–28; to support youth, 284–85
community-building initiatives, 264–65
community engagement: and self-image of teens, 159–60; youth contributions to, 260–61
community service projects, 180
competence, 102–3, 113–14, 320
Complementary Rapid Education for Primary Schools (CREPS), 156
compulsory education, vs. quality education, 323–24
confidence building, 303, 305, 318–20; performance as, 263
confidentiality, 8, 115, 195
conflict resolution, 165–66
conflicts, 190; features of countries affected by, 150; legacies of, 14; over limits, 25; in rights, under CRC, 52
consensus, 4; between political elites and society, 164; on brain development, 63, 67; building of, 311–12, 321; international conventions as, 3; lack of, on adolescence, 1–2
contexts, 39; of support, 109–16
Convention on the Rights of Persons with Disabilities (CRPD), 3, 17, 84, 328; and adolescents with disabilities, 93; disability rights legislation and, 98n21; youth participation in, 330
Convention on the Rights of the Child (CRC), 3, 4, 9, 16, 27–33, 135–36, 236; and adolescents, 10, 23–24; and Colombia, 129; conflict in rights under, 52; and CRPD, 17; and disability rights, 327–28;

332n1; hopes for, 12–13; and juvenile offenders, 162; and participation, 27–28, 55n15, 166; rights under, 46; and SAFE model, 138
Convention on the Status of Refugees, 4
coping strategies, 89, 138
Corner House, 191
corruption, 129, 130
cortex, prefrontal. See prefrontal cortex
cost: (economic) of Roma exclusion, 284; of access to rights, 6; of criminal violence to GDP, 154; of delaying education delivery, 302; of inaction, 1, 7, 8–9; of rights for girls, 227; of shredded social fabric, 153–54
CRC. See Convention on the Rights of the Child (CRC)
creativity, 88–92, 260–65
criminal law, neuroscience and, 68–70
criminal responsibility, 72–73, 129; and developmental immaturity, 60–62; diminished, 69–70
Crocker, David, 82–83
cross-cultural research, on adolescent development, 109–16
cross-cultural understanding, 89–93
CRPD. See Convention on the Rights of Persons with Disabilities (CRPD)
cultural attitudes: to adolescents, 25; changing, to support girls' education, 226; to diversity in sexual identity, 106
cultural diversity, 10, 274–75, 287, 289
"culturally legitimated," 52
cultural relativism, extreme, 44, 48–51, 54, 55n12
curricula, 287, 311–12, 316
cutoff age, 171, 175–76

Dalai Lama, 102
death penalty for juveniles, 60–62, 65–66
decision making, 206; adolescent, 61, 66, 84–85, 283; participatory, 12, 23; prosocial, and adult support, 110–11
definition: of adolescence, 1–2, 40, 54nn1, 3; of adolescents, 23–24, 59; of child, 2, 135; of child labor, nonuniversal, 294–95; of disabilities, 79–80, 95n1; importance of, 1–2, 4; of marriage, used, 54n2; of voluntary recruitment, 170
deformed preference, 85

Delhi Voucher Project, 306n5
demobilization, 7, 171, 175–76
democracy, 154–55, 165–66, 207, 243, 305; participatory, 245; transition to, postconflict, 163–64
Democratic Republic of Congo (DRC), 35
"demographic determinism," 191
demographic dividend: adolescents as, 4–5; potential, 7, 192, 208; vs. demographic nightmare, 313–14
dependence, 223; and parents, 85; vs. autonomy, 2; vs. independence, 12, 24, 26, 28–29
depression, 140–41, 156–57, 281
despair, 152–53, 158, 167; of adolescents, 11
developing countries, 40–41, 78–79, 275; education in, 251–52; and gender, 218–20; people with disabilties in, 78–79, 326
development, adolescent, 8, 32, 136–37; for adolescents with disabilities, 80, 94–95; consistent structure for, 112–13; effect of early marriage on, 281–82; emotional, 102–4; and girls' identity and gender roles, 223–27; human rights as context for, 116; and identity, with trauma, 156–57; lack of investment in, 130; and neuroscience, 106–9; and peace, 248; and resilience, 145; right to, 46–47, 52; and secondary education, 231; of sexuality, 104–6; social ecology of, 226; socioemotional, of Roma, 272–75; support for, 110–11, 119, 284
developmental disabilities, 84
developmental immaturity, and criminal responsibility, 60–62
developmental science: and human rights, 116–19
dignity, 89–93, 90–92, 160; of adolescents with disabilities, 78
disabilities, 24; in Africa, 90–92; children with, as having condtional rights, 328; definitions of, 79–80, 95n1; developmental, 84; nondiscrimination as the issue with, 17–18; rights-based approach to, 326–32; as strengths, 79; violence against children with, 17; youth with, skill development and jobs for, 317–22. *See also* adolescents with disabilities
disabilities, persons with, 320; agency of, through localized supports, 85–93; contributions of, 78; framework for enabling agency of, 85–87
disability: and agency, 82–84, 96n5; and discrimination, 327; labels of, 80, 95n1; perspective of, 77–78; as product of social positioning, 81–82; social meanings of, 79–80; as value neutral, 84
disability rights: CRC as a milestone in, 327; in CRC country reports, 331; legislation for, 98n21, 329; movement for, 17–18, 83–84, 90–92, 330; movement for, and youth with disabilities, 332; policy recommendations for adolescent, 93–95; as social justice, 96
disabled persons organizations (DPOs), 330
disabled superhero, 89–90
discrimination, 36, 49, 205; against poor youth, 239; and disability, 17, 78–79, 327; multiple forms of, 24, 31; policies against, 53, 301; reducing, through job placement, 178
District Rural Development Agencies, 314–15
domestic violence, 195, 228
dopamine, 63–64
drugs, 11, 34–35, 66; trafficking of, 128, 132, 157. *See also* substance abuse
Dublin, Ireland, 279

early adolescence, 63, 105
early child bearing, 43, 280–81, 297, 310; guidelines on, World Health Organization, 118–19; of Roma, in Italy, 49, 51–54
early marriage, 31, 40–41, 231n3, 306n2; as barrier to education, 222; from developmental perspective, 118–19; health risks of, 193; in India, 226; in refugee camps, 195; from rights perspective, 116–18; and Roma community, 49–52, 53, 280–82, 285; urban vs. rural rates of, 232n10. *See also* child marriage
early pregnancy. *See* early child bearing
ecological model with human rights, 116–17f
economic rights, 200–206
economic security/education (SAFE model), 136–37, 141–42
education, 9, 15–16; compulsory, in Italy, 42, 48–51; demand for, 218, 220, 300, 303, 322; difficulties in, 241, 279–80; for economic and social growth, 217, 220;

and employment, 200–202, 251–54; as empowerment, 300, 304–5; funding of, for children with disabilities, 327; and gender, 6, 16, 197–98, 217–18, 222–28, 230, 285, 306n4; high levels of, in MENA, 192, 197–98; integrated with health services, 228–31; lengthening of, 37, 41; and marriage, 226, 282, 297; and minority groups, 253–54, 275, 284–89; policies and laws on, in India, 301–2; poor learning outcomes in, 199, 251–54; restorative, 302–4; right to, 10, 16–17, 46, 296, 324; and skill development, 321, 324; structural discrimination in, 277; as transformative learning for those with disabilities, 87–93; vs. child labor, 295–96, 311–13; and war-affected groups, 140–41, 155, 174–78. *See also* educational quality; quality education; skill development

education/economic security (SAFE model), 136–37, 141–42

educational quality, 231n2, 241, 248, 251–52; concerns about, in MENA, 198–200, 209–10; and rote learning, 258; vs. compulsory education, 323–24

educational reform, 199–200, 253–54

Education Commission (India, 1964), 301

Education for All, 197, 211n9, 217, 231n1

"Education for Employment, Realizing the Arab Youth Potential," 258–59

Education for Peace, 156

Egypt, 18n5, 194, 196, 198; child marriage in, 190; school to work, 202; youth health research in, 192–93; youth movement in, 207

El Salvador, 154

El-Tawila, Sahar, 191

emotions, 9, 63–64; competence with, 102–3

empathy, 7, 103, 111, 303

employment, 10, 16, 262–63; adult, 53; and Albanian youth, 46–48t; and employability, 321, 323–24; and employers, 257, 316; for former child soldiers, 176, 178–79; gender and, 204–6t; informal, 11, 203–4f, 238; lack of preparation for, 7; public sector, 202; specialization of, 41

Employment Generation and Marketing Mission (EGMM), 315–17

"employment occurrence dependence," 254

empowerment, 181, 217–18; of adolescents with disabilities, 94–95; education as, 304–5; risks in programs for female, 228; vs. protection, 29; of women, within norms, 229; of youth, through art, 261–64, 287–88

engagement: with all stakeholders, 311–12, 321; in education, 88–89; new social understandings through, 92

English skills, 318–20

enrollment, 275, 306n7; vs. attendance, 241; vs. educational quality, 251–52; rates in education, 198f; vs. retention, 300

environment: disabling role of, 81–82, 96n5; enabling, 265, 304; low-risk and high-reward, 94; safe and barrier-free, 87–93

environmental supports, 115–19

equality, 17, 287; for people with disabilities, 81, 89–93, 328

equity, 3, 8, 289, 305

ethnic identity, 158, 270; pride in, 285; and stigma, 272–75; and transition to adulthood, 52–54

ethnocentrism, 43–48, 54, 55n11

European Union (EU), 47, 55n8, 278

"European values," 289

evolving capacities, 23, 28–30, 79, 135–36

Evolving Capacities of the Child, 29

exclusion, 16, 284, 303; of Arab youth, 189; through school discipline, 253; of youth with disabilties, 326

executive functions (brain), 84, 94

exploitation, 8, 10, 28, 278; of adolescents, 26; through child marriage, 296–97; of children as soldiers, 172; economic, 32, 35, 295; sexual, 105, 299; of sexuality, 9; third-party, 142

expression, right to, 29

extended adolescence, 37, 41–43, 208–9

extreme behavior, 25, 29

families, 11, 104, 136, 159; dynamics of, in rural India, 223–27; and girls' education, 219, 227; and girls' employment, 319; honor of, and gender, 223; major changes in, 37; renegotiation of roles in, 26, 53–54; Roma, 276, 280–81; support from, 140–41, 202, 208–9, 219, 230; war-affected, 134–35, 159–60, 173, 180; youth

families (*continued*)
  still living with, 42–43t, 55n8. *See also* parental support; parents
family and connection to others (SAFE Model), 136–37, 140–42
family to marriage, 14, 15–16, 40
family unity, 44–48, 52
FARC (Fuerzas Armadas Revolucionario de Colombia), 128, 154, 174
Fargues, Philippe, 192
favelas (shantytowns), 239–42
felony murder, 68–69
female genital mutilation, 193
financial independence, 228, 319
financial support: by children, 43, 46–48, 52–54, 55–56n17, 310–11, 319; by parents, 43, 46–47, 208–9; by state, 56n25, 178, 284, 299
former child soldiers. *See* child soldiers, former
framework: for adolescent rights, 10, 27–33; agency-enabling, for those with disabilities, 85–87; for building capability, 78; for child-friendly local governance, 164; developmental with human rights perspectives, 115–19; for ecological model and human rights, 117f; for reintegration programs, 173–75, 181–82
functional magnetic resonance imaging (fMRI), 64
FXB Center at Harvard, 222

gangs, 128–29, 130, 137, 239; and identity, 153–54
gender, 4, 5–6, 11–12, 16, 303; and education, 197–98, 300; and employment, 200, 204–6; enforcement of norms of, 231; equity, policy for, 196; and family honor, 223; and graduation rate, 221; and hidden work, 293–94; roles of, 106, 222–31; segregation by, 49–50; and technology, 207. *See also* girls; sexual violence
gender discrimination, 218, 219, 229, 231n3, 299; inequality from, reduced by education, 217–18
gender parity, 232n5
gender parity index, 220–21
General Comment on adolescent health, 13, 33–34
generation gap, 192, 209

genocide, 158, 162, 239
geopolitical interest, 187
George Washington University, 263
German Ministry for Economic Development, 264
Germany, 264–65
girls: access to education for, 197–98, 219, 300, 302, 306n4; barriers for, 222–26, 299; as child soldiers, 174; with disabilities, 17; with disabilities, in job program, 317–20; double discrimination of, 31; "girl effect," 13; hidden work of, 294; market returns on education of, 322; and psychological disorders, 218; role models for, 224–25; Roma, vulnerability of, 280–82; in rural areas, 8, 222–28; school dropout rates of, 232n6; and secondary education, 220–31; societal expectations for, 219, 223–27. *See also* gender; sexual violence
global economic forces, 256, 265
Global Employment Trends (ILO), 254–56
globalization, 4–5, 119, 210, 256; and changing norms, 5–6, 209
Good Councils—Understanding the Reality, 246
governance: adolescent, 16, 91–92; of labor market, 203–4, 211n13; problems in, 209
government, 14; and commitment to education, 197; decision making of, and citizens, 243–47; and inequality, 209; lobbying to change policy of, 311–13; partnerships with agencies of, 314–17, 320; and youth focus in policies and programs, 257
government of Andhra Pradesh (GOAP), 314–17, 321
Graham v. Florida, 60–62, 69, 72–73
Guatemala, 36, 159; and civil war, 149; as emblematic of war-affected societies, 151–54; postconflict, 162–64
Guatemalan Commission for Historical Clarification, 149
Guatemalan Peace Accords, 150–51, 152, 163
Gujarat, India, 222–27
Gulf Cooperation Council (GCC), 187–88

Habermas, Jürgen, 97n19
Haiti, 154; Campaign for Reduction of Violence, 165–66; and politics as dirty, 164

"handicap," as functional disadvantage, 81
Hanushek, Eric, 323
hard-wiring of brain, 67, 157–58
Harvard School of Public Health, 139
Harvard University, 222, 252
healing from civil war, 149–50
health, adolescent, 6, 11, 33–35; General Comment on, 33–34; lack of services for, 195–97; needs of Arab youth changing, 195–96, 208; right to, 52, 192; social determinants and, 229
health care, 8, 16; gaps in, for Arab youth, 195–97
health risks: in camps, 279; of early child bearing, 280, 310; of early marriage, 285, 297; of girls' lack of information, 280–81
Hendrixson, Anne, 191
hierarchy of needs (Maslow), 109, 136
HIV, 12, 34, 194, 297
Hodgson v. Minnesota, 66
Holocaust, 271–72, 287
homicides, 127–28, 130, 239, 249n10; increase in, postconflict, 157. *See also* murder; violence
hope, 159–60, 263–64
housework, 49; vs. homework, 224
human capital, 286
humanitarian responses, 143–46
human rights, 1, 6–7, 87–93; abuses of, and brain structure, 108–9; in ecological model, 117f; and female empowerment, 228; implications of developmental science for, 116–19; interrelatedness of, 136–38, 189, 206–7; people with disabilities and, 93, 326–32; and postconflict justice, 160–64; principles of, 3–4, 13; training for, 165–66; universal, 52, 54, 285; for urban youth in Brazil, 236–48. *See also* CRC; CRPD; rights-based approaches; *under* rights
Human Rights Council, 331
human rights discourse, 237, 247
human trafficking, 217–18, 278
Hyderabad, India, 317–20
hypersensitivity to reward, 65–66

ideal speech situation, 97n19
identity, 112, 137, 156–57, 284; denial of, 272; and disability labels, 80; formation of, 174; and gangs, 153–54; and role in family, 223; sense of, 111, 181–82
ideologies, formation of, in social groups, 97n19
illegality: of child marriage, 298; of child soldier recruitment, 173
illiteracy, 220, 231n1, 279, 323, 327; and gender, 4, 300; generation lost to, 311–12
ILO (International Labour Organization), 11, 202, 247, 254–56, 259–60; and Youth Employment Network, 256–57
imaging studies (brain), 64, 70
Impact of Armed Conflict on Children (Machel), 157
impairments, 78–79; vs. lack of social accomodation, 328
impulse control, 65–68, 70
impunity, 129–30, 151
"in accordance with the age and the maturity," 32, 55n15
independence, 15–16; vs. dependence, 12, 24, 26, 28–29
India, 2, 329; child labor in, 293–305, 310–13; education policy of, 302, 323–24; grade levels in, 306n6; hopes of poor in, 314, 322; and secondary education for girls, 218–31; skill development and job placement in, 313–22
Indian Constitution, 296, 309
Indian Five Year Plan (2012–2017), 221
Indian Ministry of Health and Family Welfare, 230
Indian Ministry of Labour, 296
Indian Ministry of Women and Child Development, 299
indigenous people, 24, 36, 151; racism against, 152, 158
individualized approach: to best interests, 31, 53–54; to services for child soldiers, 177, 180
individualized decisions, on adolescent maturity, 72–73
inequality, 78–79, 156, 209; as agency deprivation, 83; entrenchment of, 248; from slavery, 271; visibility of, 11
inequity, structural, 82
infant mortality, 217–18, 297
inferiority, sense of, 273, 277

information: access to, through Internet, 209; development of, on labor market need, 316; on health, lack of for Arab youth, 192–96; lack of access to, for Roma adolescents, 282–83; right to, 9, 29, 115, 282–83
information technology, 11, 265, 314; in job placement, 315
initiatives, to link education and health, 219–20, 228–31
Innocenti Research Centre, 29
integrated approach, to adolescent advancement, 227–31
Integrated Child Protection Scheme (India), 298–99
Inter-American Commission for Human Rights, 129
interface, between individuals and environment, 86f
intergenerational relationships, 40; gaps in, 209; need for changes in, 27
intergenerational transmission, of poverty, 241, 276–77, 284
International Center for Research on Childhood, 244
international community: aid from, for adolescent potential, 166–67; elections as agenda of, 164; role of, in war-affected societies, 150, 161
International Covenant on Civil and Political Rights (ICCPR), 3
International Criminal Court, 161
International Finance Corporation, 258–59
International Rescue Committee (IRC), 139
Internet, 209, 282–83
interrelatedness, 135, 144; and creative solutions, 251–66; of human rights, 136–38, 189, 206–7; and integrated programs and policies, 145–46; of rights and capability, 141
interventions, 131; against violence, success of, 240, 247–48; for child protecton, 300; long-term, 14–15, 142–45; for positive behavior, 284; strategic, 15–17; varieties of, for youth education, 303–4
investments, 130; in education, 197–99, 221–22, 285, 286; in institutions to serve youth, 192; in justice systems, 162; in Roma youth, 284; in youth for social change, 153
Iran, 2

Islamic Development Bank, 258–59
Islamic societies, 229
isolation, 78–79, 179–80
Italian Committee for Foreign Minors, 44–47; and migration control pressure, 56n18
Italian Ministry of Education, 48–49
Italy, 11; and adolescence, 41–51

Jackson v. Hobbs, 61
Jacobson, Leslie, 263
job creation, 179, 211n12, 261, 265–66
job deficit, 255, 257
job placement, 178; through partnerships, 259; programs of, with skill development, 314–22
jobs crisis, 255–56
Johannesburg, 261
Jordan, 190, 202, 210–11n7, 211n12
Jordanian Ministry of Youth, 206
judicial system, 130, 151, 161; restructuring, 72
justice, 84; Islamic notions of, 188; postconflict, 160–64
juvenile death penalty, 60–62, 65–66
Juvenile Justice Care and Protection Act (India), 298–99
juveniles and punishment, 28–30, 60–62, 68–70, 129–30; for war crimes, 162

Karman, Tawakkul (Nobel winner), 188–89
Kasturba Gandhi Balika Vidyalaya, 302
Kennedy, Justice Anthony, 61
Kenya, 90–92, 329
Kerala, 323

labor market demand, 258; MENA structural issues in, 202–4; training targetted to, 315–16; vs. skills acquired, 314
Lalela Project, 263–64
Latin America, 131–32, 221, 259
Lăutari, 286, 289n2
law: and adolescents, 29–30, 59–60; on child labor in India, 294–96; enforcement vs. prevention, 132; humanitarian, breakdown of, 134; prohibiting child marriage, 310; U.S., criminal, and brain science, 60–63, 68–70, 74
least restrictive solution, 32
Lebanon, 155, 156, 187, 195, 260

left-behind Roma children, 280
"left behind" youth, and unemployment, 253–54
legacy, 248; of adolescence, 2, 107–8; of conflict, 14, 150–54
Legal Action for Persons with Disabilities, 331
legal age, 59–60; of majority, strategies for determining, 71–72; of marriage, 298; of marriage for women, 297; to work, in India, 294
Liberia, 153, 160, 162, 330
life course calendars, 39–40, 53
life without parole for juveniles, 60–62, 68–69
limbic system, 63–64
localized supports, 85–87
"long family," 42–43
Los Angeles Unified School District, 96n12
luxury of adolescence, 10, 12

Machel, Graca, 143, 157, 159
Maghreb, 188
mainstreaming, 311–13
mandatory sentence, 68–69
Mandela, Nelson, 266
marginalized people, 3, 14, 41, 275; child soldiers as, 175
marginal workers, children as, 305–6n1
marketable skills: lack of, 11, 314
marriage, 198; arranged, 280–81; definition used, 54n2; in Italy, 43; nonconventional forms of, 209; rising age at, 190; of Roma girl of eleven, 281. *See also* child marriage, early marriage
Mashreq, 188
Maslow's hierarchy of needs, 109, 136
Maslow, Abraham, 136
maternal health, 7, 52, 192–93
maternal mortality, 4, 9, 297; and early marriage, 281; statistics on, for adolescents, 12
mattering, 113, 115
maturity, 9, 24; judgments of, and race, 73; neurobiological, 60–63, 71–72; vs. age, 10, 28–29; vs. vulnerability, 2
Maya, 158
meanings, social, 79–80
medical model of disability, 81; and CRC, 327–28

Mediterranean model, of adolescence, 41–43
Mehta, Pratap Bhanu, 323
MENA (Middle East and North Africa), 187–88; education issues in, 197–200; informal employment in, 203–4f; limits on youth participation in, 206–7; women's employment in, 204–6t; youth unemployment in, 200–206t, 255
menstruation, 105, 281; (menarche) shock at, 196
mental health, 12, 34, 194–95, 227, 230; adolescent, 68, 231; crisis in, for marginalized youth, 229; of former child soldiers, 140; and gender discrimination, 229; and girls' education, 219; postconflict, 154–60
Mental Health Policy (Sierra Leone), 144
Mental Health Policy Group (India), 230
mentoring, 15, 95, 262; postplacement, 315, 321
merit, vs. universalization, 301
Merton, Robert, 254
Michigan, 68–69
microenterprises, 261
microfinance for women, 228
migration, 11, 24, 40–41, 203, 208; of adolescents, 40–41, 278–80; control of, 56n18; control of, vs. best interests, 55n16; UN sessions on youth, 13
Millennium Development Goals, 8, 194, 211n9, 217, 256
Miller v. Alabama, 61
minority groups, 295, 315; best interests in, for adolescents, 44–54; ethnic, 8; and high unemployment, 252–53; school discipline of, 253; and school infrastructure, 277
mitigation, 69–70
models: of adolescence, clash between, 44, 47–48; of adolescence, Mediterranean, 41–43; of adolescence, North European, 41; ecological, with human rights agenda, 116–17f; human accomplishments through supports, 87f; individual-environment interface, 86f; SAFE, of child protection, 135–38f; of transition to adulthood, 49, 52–54
modifications and equality, 81
moral guidance, as parental support, 114

moral pressure, 116, 311–12, 321
moral relativism, 55n12
Morocco, 199
movement, freedom of, 29
Mozambique, 36
MTV's Voices, 90
Mukhyamantri Balika Cycle Yojana, 306n5
municipalities: for implementation, 244–47; investment in youth policies for, 131
murder, 8, 68–69, 279
Muslim Brotherhood, 207
MVF (M. Venkatarangaiya Foundation), 295–96, 311–13, 321, 324; achievements, 313t
myelination, 64, 107–8, 110

Nairobi African Youth with Disabilities Declaration, 97n18
National Child Labour Program (India), 296
National Commission for Protection of Children's Rights (India), 307n8
National Education Association (U.S.), 253
National Forensic Medical Institute of Colombia, 127–28
National Human Rights Ombudsman (Colombia), 128
National Institute of Open Schooling (India), 302
National Policy for Children (India), 309
National Policy for Youth (Brazil), 242
National Program for Youth Inclusion (Brazil), 242
National Secretariat for Youth (Brazil), 242
National Youth Commission (Sierra Leone), 144
National Youth Development Agency (South Africa), 262–63, 265
National Youth Policy (India), 309
nature and nurture, 67–68
Nepal Framework for Child-friendly Local Governance, 164
neural pathways, 107–8, 158
neurobiological maturity, 60–63, 71–72; individualized assessments of, 73
neuroplasticity, 68
neuroscience: legal age and, 60–63; policy and, 65–66, 68, 70–74; "seductive allure of," 62; socioemotional development and, 106–9; as support for behavioral research, 68, 70
New Media Academy, 88–89
New Yorker cartoon, 60
New Zealand, 34
"No Child Left Behind" Act (NCLB, U.S.), 253–54
"nomad camps," 48–51, 56n19
nondiscrimination, 3, 30–31, 87–93; vs. special needs, 17–18, 328
nonnegotiable approach, 311–12
nonstate actors, 134
"normal," 77–78
Norman, Sam Hinga, 161–62
norms: changeable, 53; conflict over, 25; decentering, 78; globalization and, 5–6, 192; legal provisions of, 39; sociocultural and violation of rights, 52–54. *See also* social norms
North Africa, 255
Northeastern University, 252–53
North European model of adolescence, 41
Norway, 329
"nothing about us without us," 18, 83, 330
nurturance, 102, 107

Obama, Senator Barack, 253
octopus of agencies, 80–81f
Office of the Human Rights Ombudsman, 162
Olympic Games (2016), 240
Oman, 193, 211n12
Open Basic Education (India), 302
Optional Protocols (CRC), 33
Organization of American States (OAS), 163
outreach network, self-sustaining, 262
outsourcing, 322
Oversight Councils for Social Policy (Brazil), 243

"pacified" favelas, 247–48; questions about, 240
Palestinian territories, 188
parental support: cross-cultural research on, 114–15; for education, 197–99, 318; mothers as enablers of education, 225. *See also* families
parents, 15; and agency deprivation, 84–85; attributes of support from, 114–15;

authority of, over Arab youth, 192; and disrespect for adolescents, 111; influence of, over girls, 222–28; investments of, in children's future, 286, 322–23; rational disinterest in education of, 276; and street children, 241–42; and trauma of civil war, 153. *See also* families
Paris Principles on Children with Armed Groups, 143
participation: of adolescents, 164–66; and best interests for adolescents, 51–54; child, in decisions, 299; of citizens, 243–47; definition of (CRC), 55n15; Nepal and children's priorities for government, 164; policy of, adolescent, 138; in program design, 131, 181; as respect for individuality, 112; right to, 115, 135–36, 191; right to, of adolescents, 28, 32–33, 46–48, 52; and rule-following, 113. *See also* youth participation
participative status (CRC), 27–28
partnerships, 15, 265; multisector, 314–22; public-private, 16, 256–57, 262–63
patriarchy, 223, 299
peace, 248; building of, 154–67; "peace centers," 165–66; youth and, 166–67
peer pressure, 53–54, 65–66, 70; and popularity, 104
peers: programs to engage, postconflict, 154–55, 159–60; relationships with, 103–4; risk-taking and, 112–13
pelvic organ prolapse, 210n4
personal assistance (PA), 85–87, 89
Peru, 35–36
piggybacking, on existing network, 322
plasticity of brain. *See* brain development
"play therapists," 159–60
policies, 13, 15–16, 246–47; for adolescent mental health, 229; of adolescent participation, 138; and adolescent rights, 28; for adolescents with disabilities, 93–94; as agency enhancing or depriving, 93; and barriers to Arab women's employment, 205–6; based on human rights, 289; and centrality of equality in CRPD, 328; on child labor, gaps in, 294–96; for child protection, 298–300; citizen input into, 243–47; and developmental science, 118; development of holistic, 208; disability, and social model, 82; and discrimination, 53; on early marriage, 118–19; on education, 301–2; and empirical research, 14–15; for encouraging cultural diversity, 275, 287; failure of, 8–9; for gender equity, 196; for girls' education, 219, 228, 285; for improving employment, 203–4, 255–56; lack of, 11; on legal age, and neuroscience, 60–63; MVF's impact on, 324; need for integration among, 145; and neuroscience, 9–10, 68, 70–74; postconflict, and adolescent potential, 166–67; and poverty, 53; recommendations for, for adolescent disability rights, 93–95; for recruitment prevention, 173–75; to redress historic inequalities, 272; for reintegration, 176–82; for reintegration, 141–42, 171; for restorative education, 302–4; rights-based approach and, 3–4; social and economic, deficiencies in, 209; youth, inadequate, 130–31, 206–7; for youth in Brazil, 242–47
policy makers, and best interests, 23, 28–29
polio survivors, 318
politics, 164, 200; and disconnect with general public, 163–64; exclusion of Arab youth from, 208; and government job creation, 211n12; led by older generation, 207; polarization of, 150–51; and political will, 8
popularity, 104
poverty, 14, 53, 174, 229, 275–77, 303; and agency deprivations, 98n22; and children's work, 56n25; and education, 198–99; intergenerational transmission of, 276–77, 284; in urban Brazil, 238–42, 249n6; and violence, 127–33, 249n10; vs. stereotype as rich, 273
power relations, 80–81, 304
preadolescence, 24, 63
prefrontal cortex, 60–61, 63–64, 67–68
prejudices, 16, 289; strategies for, 274
prevention, 14–15; of child soldier recruitment, 142, 143–44, 159–60, 172–75, 181–82; vs. repression, 131, 132–33
primary school, 220, 251; and former child soldiers, 174, 176–78; girls dropout rate from, 232n6; overcrowding of, 300, 306n7; universal enrollment in, 197–98, 218, 231n1, 301

Pritchett, Lant, 323, 324n4
private sector: formal employment limited in, 203–4; and job creation, 256; and job placement, 314–22; and schools, for experiential learning, 252; and solutions to youth unemployment, 259
problem solving, 7, 265, 317, 321
programs: development of, 141–42, 181; innovative, for girls, 306n5; integration among, 145–46; scalability and replicability of, 321–22; for teens to help rehabilitate community, 159–60; for youth unemployment, 256–57
protection, 8–9, 14–15, 27; failures of state, 296; lack of, for basic rights, 135; legal, less, for those with disabilities, 329–30; leverage points for, 144; in local youth groups, 131; postconflict, in education, 155; and recruitment prevention, 172–75; right to, and safety, 115; vs. autonomy, 7; vs. empowerment, 29; for youth in Brazil, 236–38, 245, 247
Proyecto Productivo, 179
pruning. *See* synaptic pruning
psychological functioning, 108, 110, 144. *See also* mental health
psychosocial rehabilitation, 138–45, 154–60, 177
puberty, 2, 7, 40, 105, 196; and brain development, 63–64, 107–8; and gender segregation, 49–50; parenthood at, 281; variations in, 24, 37
public sphere, 188
punishment: "assisted repatriation" as, 45–46, 48; juveniles and, 60–62, 68–70, 129–30; proportionality of, 11

Qatar, 34
quality education, 261, 277; vs. compulsory education, 323–24. *See also* education; educational quality

race: and judgments of maturity, 73; and poverty, 238–39; in U.S. youth unemployment, 252–53
racial divide, crossed on Internet, 282–83
racism, 49, 151, 152, 274, 288
radio station, 288
Randolph, Jennings, 143

rape, 6, 140, 195, 227. *See also* sexual violence; violence
Ravitch, Diane, 253–54
reason orientation, 82, 91–92, 94
reconciliation, 156, 180
recruitment: of child soldiers, 141; of child soldiers as war crime, 161–62; of child soldiers, in Colombia, 154; of child soldiers, prevention of, 131, 142–45, 159–60, 172–75, 181–82; of child soldiers, voluntary, 170, 172–74; into armed groups, 135; youth, and gangs, 128–29. *See also* child soldiers
Rede Rio Criança (Rio Child Network), 244
"Reflection Learning," 259–60
reframing, 6, 17–18, 84; and decentering norms, 77–78; of disability, 87–93, 328
refugees, 4, 187, 195
reintegration, 14–15; of former child soldiers, 140–45, 170–71, 176–82; postconflict, 7, 156
relationship building, 79, 106, 179–80, 286; for change, 321–22; postconflict, 155
rentier states, 187
repression, 129–30, 131
reproductive health, 7, 34; lack of information on, 193–94, 195–96, 280; lack of services for, 208; as maternal health, 210–11n7; programs for, 299, 305; right to, 11–12
research: on abuse and brain patterns, 108; on adolescents with disabilities, 78–79; on child soldier demobilization in Colombia, 171–81; on councils in Brazil, 246; cross-cultural, on adolescent development, 109–16; on education for girls in rural India, 222–27; on Indian girls with disabilities in job program, 317–20; and interventions, 145; lack of, on health of Arab youth, 192–95; policy making and, 14–15; on war-affected youth in Sierra Leone, 138–45
resilience, 6, 14–15, 260–65; of adolescents, 159–60; in war-affected youth, 140, 144–45
resources, 218; adolescents as, 159–60, 166–67; optimization of, through coordination, 145–46; reallocation of, for quality, 222

respect: for individuality, 111–12, 115; for life, lack of, 152; as motivator, 286; and schools, 275; for working, 319
responsibility, sense of, 223, 226
restorative education, 302–4
Rethinking Juvenile Justice (Scott & Steinberg), 72
Return to Happiness, 159–60
Revolutionary Armed Forces of Colombia (FARC), 128, 154, 174
rewards and adolescent brains, 63–67
Right of Children to Free and Compulsory Education Act (RTE, India), 220, 301–2, 306–7n7, 309, 323–24
rights: denial of, 304; for girls at cost to them, 227; progressive exercise of, 23; and recruitment prevention, 172; and responsibilities, 14; before responsibilities, 9–10; before responsibilities, 28–29
rights-based approach: to adolescence, 3–4, 13–14, 29–30, 44; benefits of, 3–4; to child health and well-being, 136–38; to child labor, 295–96; to education, 16–17; to people with disabilities, 326–32; SAFE model as, 145
rights-implementation gap, 236–37, 247
rights-respecting transition, 25, 77–78
rights violations, 154, 161; and sociocultural norms, 52–54; of youth with disabilties, 326–27
rights, women's, 18n5
right to be heard, 32–33
right to development, 32, 46–47, 52
right to education, 10–11, 31, 50, 52–54, 199, 296
right to expression, 29
right to family unity, 44–48, 52
right to freedom of movement, 29
right to health, 52
right to information, 9, 29
right to participation, 46–48, 52
right to privacy, 29
right to protection, 52
Rio de Janeiro, 239–41, 244–46, 249n10; interventions in slums of, 247–48
risk-taking, 60, 65–66; adolescent, 25–26, 29; and peers, 112–13; and survival, 32; of war-affected youth, 141–43
rites of passage, 25, 40

RMSA (Rashtriya Madhyamik Shiksha Abhiyan), 231, 302, 306n5; National Secondary Education Campaign, 218–19; objectives of, 221
Robert's Rules of Order, 92
role models, 170, 288; adolescents as, 159–60; coaches as, 264–65; female, for girls, 224–25; lack of, 153, 273–74, 277
Roma, 30; and case study of teenage couple, 50–51; and gender segregation, 49–50; in Italy, 43–44, 48–54, 56nn19, 20; in Romania, 270–89; teenagers as adults, 276; three stories of hope for Roma youth, 285–86; traumatic history of, 271–72
Romania: as developed country, 275; Roma in, 270–89
"Romani activities," 50–51
Romanian Ministry of Education, 278
Romani CRISS, 277
Roper v. Simmons, 60–62, 65–66, 72–73
Rostas, Marioara, 279
Roudi-Fahimi, Farzaneh, 192
Rudari, 286, 289n4
rural areas, 35, 45, 47, 218; and child labor, 40; and early marriage, 232n10; girls' education in, 222–28; limited access to education in, 55n14, 199, 306–7n7; progams for youth in, in India, 314–22; school attendance, 300
Russia, 221
Rwanda, 9, 158, 162

SABLA (Empowerment of Adolescent Girls, India), 299
Saboshego, Potwalo, 160–61, 163
SAFE model of child protection, 136–37, 137f, 140–46; and CRC, 138 and war-affected youth, 142f
safety, 135, 222; and connectedness, 141; and right to protection, 115; for socio-emotional development, 109–10
safety/freedom from harm (SAFE model), 136–37, 140–42
Said, Fatima Abu, 260
Sakhshar Bharat–National Literacy Mission, 302
Salazar-Xirinachs, Jose Manuel, 259–60
Salem, Rania, 190
Sarafina! (musical and film), 262
Sarva Shiksha Abhiyan, 301, 312

Scalia, Justice Antonin, 65–66
Schioppa, Tommaso Padoa, 41
school dropouts, 293, 302–3; for early marriage, 280, 310; as failures, 300–301; Roma, 49, 274, 276
school expulsion, 253
school infrastructure: in Indian education, 221–22, 231n4, 232n5; investments in, 285; lack of health services in, 196; in minority communities, 253, 277; vs. quality improvement, 323
school to work, 14, 15–16, 26, 40; breakdown of transition from, in MENA, 202; multiple pathways for, 252
School-to-Work Transition Surveys, 202
secondary education, 13, 47, 248, 276; access to, in rural areas, 55n14; challenges in, 218; cost of inaction on, in Rwanda, 9; for girls, barriers to, 222–27; for girls, strategies to support, 226–30; for India's future, 220–21; in Italy, 48–51, 54n5; lack of, 300; and mental health integration, 230; no right to, in India, 301–2; as a right, 10–11; universal enrollment in, 218–19
self-actualization, 136
self-awareness, 103, 106
self-control, 64, 67–68, 70; and consistent limits, 113
self-determination, 82, 90, 91–92, 94
Self Employed Women's Association (SEWA), 222
self-esteem, 320
self-expression, 16
self-management, 103, 106, 111
self-realization, 10, 16
self-regulation, 84
self-worth, 223
Sen, Amartya, 78, 82, 85, 87
sensation seeking, 63–64, 67
September 11, 191
Servicio Nacional de Aprendizaje (SENA), 178
Severs, Coralie (poet), 77–78
sexual development, 8, 106–7; timeline of, 104–6
sexuality, 7, 25, 32, 104–6, 193–94; barriers to education on, 196; exploitation of, 9; and information on safe sex, 299; and sexual identity, 106

sexually transmitted infections (STIs), 35, 193
sexual violence, 170; rape, 6, 140, 195, 227; and slavery, 271; towards people with disabilities, 78–79, 329–31
shame, 226
Shanu Project, 219, 222–27, 229–30
"shock of order," 240
Sierra Leone, 156; civil war in, 138–39, 149; Special Court for, 161–62; study of former child soldiers in, 138–45, 157–58, 167n
Silver Scorpion (comic book and web series), 89–90
Singerman, Diane, 190
skill development, 11, 17, 259–60, 314; and competence, 113–14; complete system of, with placement, 321; gained in armed groups, 179; large-scale, for future, 313–14
Skill Development Initiative (India), 296
slavery, 238, 271, 287
Soacha case, 128
soccer, 240, 264–65
social actors, 79–80, 96n2
social capital, 281, 286
social change, 153, 155–56, 237, 304; through sports, 264–65; thoughtful, 228
social ecologies, 134–35, 218, 226; of communities and child protection, 136–38; for girls' educational success, 230
socialization, 25, 88–89, 107
social justice, 3, 223, 260; and the disability community, 96n7
social mobility, 276, 286
social mobilization, 307n8, 321
social model of disability, 81–82, 328
social networking, 188
social norms, 39–40, 47, 119; and advocacy, 116; and Arab women's work, 204; backlash to challenges of, 227; as disabling, 17–18, 82–84; erosion of, in civil war, 152; vs. legal entitlements, 223. *See also* norms
social relationships, 102–4, 110–11; healthy, lack of experience with, 180
social situations, and ideology formation, 97n19
social structures, 271

social transformation, 289n1
social understandings, new, through engagement, 92
societal dynamics: and girls' education, 219, 228–31
Society for Elimination of Rural Poverty, 314–15
socioeconomic patterns, 35, 254; and models of transition to adulthood, 53; and Roma girls' health, 280; stratification in, 199
socioemotional development, 106–7, 109–16. *See also* development, adolescent
soft skills, 257–58, 316, 319
solutions, 16, 32, 52–53, 118–19, 132–33; from systems thinking, 251–66
South Africa, 115, 153, 160–61, 255; youth agency in, 260–65
South African Department of Arts, 262–63
South African Department of Sport, 264
South African National Gallery, 263–64
Spain, 34
Spear, Linda, 107–8
Special Court for Sierra Leone, 161–62
specialization in employment, 41
special needs, vs. nondiscrimination, 17–18, 328
spoiling, as agency deprivation, 84–85, 96n8
sports and social change, 264–65
St. Andrew's Episcopal School, 263
stakeholders, 15; engagement with all, 311–12, 321
stampede, 261
states, 132, 187; ability of, to protect child rights, 136; incapacity of, 151–53; neglect by, of children with disabilities, 327; obligations of, to adolescents, 15, 33–37; obligations of, to protect rights, 296; as perpetrators, 151
statistics: on adolescent maternal mortality, 12; on adolescents, 11; on Albanian youth in Italy, 45, 47t, 48; on child labor, 42, 54n6, 293–94; on child marriage, 11–12, 297, 306n6; comparative, on homicides, 127–28, 239; on demobilization in Colombia, 175; on education in India, 300, 306; on education in MENA, 197–98f; on people with disabilties, 78, 326; on poverty in Brazil, 238; on Roma children in Italy, 48–49t, 56n20; on school children in Italy, 42; on Sierra Leone's civil war, 138–39; on youth living with family in Italy, 42–43t; on youth unemployment, 11, 42, 200–202, 252–53, 255
Statute on the Rights of the Child (Brazil, 1990), 236–37, 243–44, 247
stereotypes, 156, 273
stigma, 15, 17–18, 139, 167n1; and adolescents with disabilities, 78–79; ethnic identity and, 272–75, 286; postconflict, 140–41
storytelling, 88–89, 262
strain theory, 254
street children, 8, 24, 35–36, 240–42; Albanian youth as, 47; policy for support of, 244–46
structural causes: of inequity, 82; of violence, 130–32; of youth unemployment in MENA, 202–4, 208
structural disadvantage, and adolescents with disabilities, 81–82
stunting, 98n22
sub-Saharan Africa, 12, 255
substance abuse, 34, 35, 194. *See also* alcohol; drugs
Sudan, 193
suicide, 26, 34, 66, 157, 229, 231; among Mayan adolescents, 158
suicide bombers, 128
superhero with disabilities, 89–90
superpower, 90
supports, 94–95; agency-enhancing, 85–87; for socioemotional development, 109–16
survival, 10, 32, 56n25, 136–37
survival strategies, 141–45, 262
Sweden, 35
synaptic pruning, 63, 107–8, 157
Syria, 89–90, 155, 189, 202
System for the Guarantee of Rights (Brazil), 244, 247
systems-thinking approach, 254, 259, 265–66

Tahrir Square, Cairo, Egypt, 207
Take off the Masks (play), 263
Tanzania, 327
Tawila, Sahar El-, 191
Taylor, Charles, 162

technology, 4, 37; assistive (AT), 85–88; communications, 207; information, 11, 314
terrorism, 134
testosterone, 105
test scores, 199
theater, 260, 262
thresholds to adulthood, 40, 42–43
toolkits: CRC as, 37; of human rights, 3, 30
"toxic stress," 140
traditional Roma families, 281, 286; and gender segregation, 49–50
training, 241, 259–60, 315, 319, 324
transformation, 288, 305
transformative learning: agency-enhancing, 87–93; and shifts in consciousness, 95
transition, 35; and adolescence, 2; to adulthood, increased difficulty of, 4; to adulthood, models of, 41, 49; postconflict, 153, 163–64; rights and responsibilities in, 14; rights-respecting, 25
Transnistria, 271
transparency, 178, 181, 245, 247
trauma, 14–15, 171; and agency deprivations, 98; historic, of Roma, 271–72; war-related, 11, 144, 151, 153, 155
treatment philosophies, 80–82
Trendsetter Initiative, 262–63
Trends in International Mathematics Study, 199
truth commissions, 160–61; contents of, and public dialogue, 154
Tunisia, 2, 188, 190, 196
Turin, Italy, 48–49
Tutsis, 158

U.S. Department of Education, 253–54
U.S. National Council on Disability, 94
U.S. Supreme Court, 60–62, 69, 72–73
Uganda, 330–31
Ujjwala (India), 299
unaccompanied migrant youth, 43–48, 55–56n17
UN Committee on the Rights of the Child. *See* Committee on the Rights of the Child (CRC Committee)
UN Convention on the Rights of Persons with Disabilities (CRPD). *See* Convention on the Rights of Persons with Disabilities (CRPD)
UN Convention on the Rights of the Child. *See* Convention on the Rights of the Child (CRC),
unemployment, 4, 26, 49, 255; of former child soldiers, 175–76; and gender, 205t; global, potential responses to, 255–56; and level of education, 200–202, 201t. *See also* youth unemployment
UNESCO, 220–21
UN Human Development Index, 329
UNICEF, 24, 78–79; and children in war, 134, 149; and investing in adolescents, 256, 284; on Roma early marriage, 285; and youth mental health, 195
United Nations, and youth unemployment, 256–57. *See also under* UN
United Nations Children's Fund. *See* UNICEF
United States, 115, 132, 329; criminal law and brain science in, 60–63, 68–70, 74; workforce readiness of, 252–54
Universal Design for Learning (UDL), 88–89
universal human rights, 52, 289
University of Bucharest, 278
University of Sorbonne, Paris, 279
UN Population Fund, 196
UN secretary-general, 256
UN sessions on youth migration, 13
UN Summit "Youth Dialogue," 256
UN Youth Employment Summit, 257
UPP (Unidades de Polícia Pacificadora), 239–40
urbanization, 240

video, 88–89, 91, 273, 289n1
violence, 4, 7, 8, 11, 14–15, 153–54; against people with disabilities, 17, 327, 329; and counterviolence, 239–41; culture of, 151; cycle of, 127, 131–32, 149–50; despair and, 158, 167; gender-based, 5–6, 91; reduction in, 217–18; structural causes of, 130–32
vocational training, 35, 42, 45–46, 178, 258–59; availability and value of, 261; deficiencies of, 314; and life skills, 299; limited access to, in rural areas, 55n14; and Roma in Italy, 48–51; vs. academic careers, 258–59
voice, 188, 189, 263

wages, 202; and gender, 205, 293–94
waiting period, 202, 208
war-affected youth. *See* child soldiers
war crimes, 161–62
War-Torn Societies Project, 150
Waxman, Seth, 62
Wessels, Mike, 173–74
"whenever possible," 328
Winterveld, South Africa, 263
women, 18n5; in Arab popular uprisings, 188–89, 207; and female role models, 225; and work, in MENA, 204–206
women's self-help groups (SHGs), 314–15, 317, 321–22
work, 42, 310; of adolescents, 32; disincentives to seeking, 202; home-based, 295
work readiness, 203, 258–59
World Bank, 150, 160, 174, 218–19, 220; and adolescents, 23–24; on cost of Roma exclusion, 284; on criminal violence costs, 154; study on vocational training by, 314; and Youth Employment Network, 256–57
World Enabled, 87–93
World Health Organization, 78–79; estimates by, of sexual violence, 329; guidelines on preventing early pregnancy, 118–19
World Soccer Cup, 240, 264
Woβmann, Ludger, 323

YearUp, 178
Yemen, 188–89, 190, 198, 211n12
youth, as term, 249 n5
Youth 4 Work, 317–20
Youth Ability Summit, 89–90
Youth Apprenticeship, Program of (Brazil), 242
youth bulge, 190–92
Youth Civic Engagement and Dialogue Program (Roma), 288
youth development: focus on potential of. in MENA, 191; mechanisms and polices for, in MENA, 206–7; through sports, 264–65
Youth Development through Football, 264
youth employment: challenges of, in MENA, 200–206; in Italy, statistics on, 42; through skill development and job placement, 314–22. *See also* employment; under jobs; unemployment; skill development; youth unemployment
Youth Employment Network, 256–57
youth participation, 13, 256–57, 260–65, 288, 303–4; in activism, 62, 242–43, 260–61; in Arab popular uprisings, 188–89, 191; contributions of, 260–61; in the CRPD treaty negotiations, 330; in organizations welcoming to youth, 242–43; in peace, 166–67; in solutions for unemployment, 265; in youth program design, 131. *See also* participation
youth power, 97n19
youth unemployment, 42; consequences of, 195, 254; global trends in, 254–56; intersecting dynamics of, 251–66; in MENA, 200–206; statistics on, 11; in U.S., 252–53. *See also* unemployment
Youth with Physical Disability Development Forum, 330
YouTube, 91, 289n1

ACKNOWLEDGMENTS

This book grows out of a sustained reflection on the coming of age of the 1989 UN Convention on the Rights of the Child. The François-Xavier Bagnoud (FXB) Center for Health and Human Rights at Harvard University, the book's institutional home, used the twenty-first anniversary of this landmark international law to explore the impact of placing the rights of children and young people at the core of the human rights agenda. The FXB Center was particularly concerned to investigate the relationship between human rights and human coming of age. This book evidences our individual and collective reflections, our research, and the commitment of many colleagues to build the neglected field of adolescent studies.

I am grateful to all the contributors who agreed to work within our brief. Many are overworked practitioners, advocates, and activists, who had to burn the candle at both ends of the day to meet our deadlines. I am also grateful to our editor, Peter Agree, whose encouragement and faith in the project never wavered, and to two anonymous reviewers who provided astute suggestions, several of which are reflected in the revised manuscript. A superb copy editor enhanced the final draft substantially. I owe a huge debt of gratitude to many friends and colleagues who suggested references, experts, debates, and ideas that nourished the project—including Heather Adams, Abhijit Banerjee, Elizabeth Bartholet, Susan Bissell, Martha Chen, Beena Choksi, Liz Cohen, Ana Colbert, John and Jean Comaroff, Nancy Cott, Steven Hyman, Siddharth Kara, Michele Lamont, Jennifer Leaning, Nevena Milutinovic, Reema Nanavaty, Emma Rothschild, Amartya Sen, Kay Shelemay, and Lucie White. Without the exquisite teamwork of my FXB colleagues Sarah Dougherty, Arlan Fuller, Angela Murray, and Bonnie Shnayerson, this book would not have seen the light of day. And without my beloved family, I would not value any of the stages of my life half as much as I do.